List of Patterns

ACCESS CONTROL REQUIREMENTS 267
ASSET VALUATION 103
AUDIT REQUIREMENTS 369
AUDIT TRAILS AND LOGGING REQUIREMENTS 378
AUTHENTICATOR 323
AUTHORIZATION 245
AUTOMATED I&A DESIGN ALTERNATIVES 207
BIOMETRICS DESIGN ALTERNATIVES 229
CHECK POINT 287
CONTROLLED EXECUTION ENVIRONMENT 346
CONTROLLED OBJECT FACTORY 331
CONTROLLED OBJECT MONITOR 335
CONTROLLED PROCESS CREATOR 328
CONTROLLED VIRTUAL ADDRESS SPACE 339
DEMILITARIZED ZONE 449
ENTERPRISE PARTNER COMMUNICATION 173
ENTERPRISE SECURITY APPROACHES 148
ENTERPRISE SECURITY SERVICES 161
EXECUTION DOMAIN 343
FILE AUTHORIZATION 350
FRONT DOOR 473
FULL ACCESS WITH ERRORS 305
I&A REQUIREMENTS 192
INFORMATION OBSCURITY 426
INTEGRATION REVERSE PROXY 465
INTRUSION DETECTION REQUIREMENTS 388
KNOWN PARTNERS 442
LIMITED ACCESS 312
MULTILEVEL SECURITY 253
NON-REPUDIATION REQUIREMENTS 396
PACKET FILTER FIREWALL 405
PASSWORD DESIGN AND USE 217
PROTECTION REVERSE PROXY 457
PROXY-BASED FIREWALL 411
REFERENCE MONITOR 256
RISK DETERMINATION 137
ROLE RIGHTS DEFINITION 259
ROLE-BASED ACCESS CONTROL 249
SECURE CHANNELS 434
SECURITY ACCOUNTING REQUIREMENTS 360
SECURITY NEEDS IDENTIFICATION FOR ENTERPRISE ASSETS 89
SECURITY SESSION 297
SINGLE ACCESS POINT 279
STATEFUL FIREWALL 417
THREAT ASSESSMENT 113
VULNERABILITY ASSESSMENT 125

Security Patterns
Integrating Security and Systems Engineering

Markus Schumacher
Eduardo Fernandez-Buglioni
Duane Hybertson
Frank Buschmann
Peter Sommerlad

John Wiley & Sons, Ltd

Other Wiley Editorial Offices

John Wiley & Sons Inc., 111 River Street, Hoboken, NJ 07030, USA

Jossey-Bass, 989 Market Street, San Francisco, CA 94103-1741, USA

Wiley-VCH Verlag GmbH, Boschstr. 12, D-69469 Weinheim, Germany

John Wiley & Sons Australia Ltd, 42 McDougall Street, Milton, Queensland 4064, Australia

John Wiley & Sons (Asia) Pte Ltd, 2 Clementi Loop #02-01, Jin Xing Distripark, Singapore 129809

John Wiley & Sons Canada Ltd, 22 Worcester Road, Etobicoke, Ontario, Canada M9W 1L1

Wiley also publishes its books in a variety of electronic formats. Some content that appears in print may not be
available in electronic books.

Library of Congress Cataloging-in-Publication Data

Security patterns : integrating security and systems engineering / Markus Schumacher ... [et al.].
    p. cm.
  Includes bibliographical references and index.
  ISBN-13: 978-0-470-85884-4 (cloth : alk. paper)
  ISBN-10: 0-470-85884-2 (cloth : alk. paper)
 1. Computer security. 2. Systems engineering. I. Schumacher, Markus.

QA76.9.A25S438 2005
005.8--dc22
                                                                2005026865

British Library Cataloguing in Publication Data

A catalogue record for this book is available from the British Library

ISBN-13 978-0-470-85884-4 (HB)
ISBN-10 0-470-85884-2 (HB)

Typeset in 10/12pt Sabon by Laserwords Private Limited, Chennai, India
Printed and bound in Great Britain by Anthony Rowe Ltd, Chippenham, Wiltshire
This book is printed on acid-free paper responsibly manufactured from sustainable forestry
in which at least two trees are planted for each one used for paper production.

For you, dear reader!
Go and create secure software systems.

Markus

To Minjie, Lian, and Anna.

Eduardo

For my wife, Diane, for making considerable sacrifice to
allow me to work on this book.

Duane

For Martina, Bebé, and Anna.

Frank

For Andrea.

Peter

Contents

Chapter 1   **The Pattern Approach**   **1**

Patterns at a Glance   2

No Pattern is an Island   4

Patterns Everywhere   4

Humans are the Target   5

Patterns Resolve Problems and Shape Environments   6

Towards Pattern Languages   7

Documenting Patterns   9

A Brief Note on The History of Patterns   11

The Pattern Community and its Culture   12

Chapter 2   **Security Foundations**   **15**

Overview   16

Security Taxonomy   17

General Security Resources   26

Chapter 3   **Security Patterns**   **29**

The History of Security Patterns   30

Characteristics of Security Patterns   31

Why Security Patterns?   34

Sources for Security Pattern Mining   37

Chapter 4   **Patterns Scope and Enterprise Security**   **47**

The Scope of Patterns in the Book   48

Organization Factors   49

Resulting Organization   51

	Mapping to the Taxonomy	53
	Organization in the Context of an Enterprise Framework	53
Chapter 5	**The Security Pattern Landscape**	**59**
	Enterprise Security and Risk Management Patterns	59
	Identification & Authentication (I&A) Patterns	62
	Access Control Model Patterns	67
	System Access Control Architecture Patterns	69
	Operating System Access Control Patterns	71
	Accounting Patterns	73
	Firewall Architecture Patterns	77
	Secure Internet Applications Patterns	78
	Cryptographic Key Management Patterns	80
	Related Security Pattern Repositories Patterns	83
Chapter 6	**Enterprise Security and Risk Management**	**85**
	Security Needs Identification for Enterprise Assets	89
	Asset Valuation	103
	Threat Assessment	113
	Vulnerability Assessment	125
	Risk Determination	137
	Enterprise Security Approaches	148
	Enterprise Security Services	161
	Enterprise Partner Communication	173
Chapter 7	**Identification and Authentication (I&A)**	**187**
	I&A Requirements	192
	Automated I&A Design Alternatives	207
	Password Design and Use	217
	Biometrics Design Alternatives	229
Chapter 8	**Access Control Models**	**243**
	Authorization	245
	Role-Based Access Control	249
	Multilevel Security	253
	Reference Monitor	256
	Role Rights Definition	259
Chapter 9	**System Access Control Architecture**	**265**
	Access Control Requirements	267
	Single Access Point	279

Check Point   287
Security Session   297
Full Access with Errors   305
Limited Access   312

Chapter 10   Operating System Access Control   321
Authenticator   323
Controlled Process Creator   328
Controlled Object Factory   331
Controlled Object Monitor   335
Controlled Virtual Address Space   339
Execution Domain   343
Controlled Execution Environment   346
File Authorization   350

Chapter 11   Accounting   355
Security Accounting Requirements   360
Audit Requirements   369
Audit Trails and Logging Requirements   378
Intrusion Detection Requirements   388
Non-Repudiation Requirements   396

Chapter 12   Firewall Architectures   403
Packet Filter Firewall   405
Proxy-Based Firewall   411
Stateful Firewall   417

Chapter 13   Secure Internet Applications   423
Information Obscurity   426
Secure Channels   434
Known Partners   442
Demilitarized Zone   449
Protection Reverse Proxy   457
Integration Reverse Proxy   465
Front Door   473

Chapter 14   Case Study: IP Telephony   481
IP Telephony at a Glance   482
The Fundamentals of IP Telephony   483
Vulnerabilities of IP Telephony Components   488
IP Telephony Use Cases   488

Securing IP telephony with patterns   493
Applying Individual Security Patterns   497
Conclusion   500

Chapter 15 Supplementary Concepts   **503**
Security Principles and Security Patterns   504
Enhancing Security Patterns with Misuse Cases   525

Chapter 16 Closing Remarks   **531**

References   **535**

Index   **555**

Foreword

Security has become an important topic for many software systems. With the growing success of the Internet, computer and software systems have become more and more networked. Researchers are already developing scenarios in which millions of devices are connected and cooperatively running web-based commerce, government, health, and other types of security-sensitive systems. Much of the research effort in these scenarios is devoted to security aspects.

What could happen if, in a pervasive health scenario, cardiology data collected by wireless sensors attached to your body and pre-processed by software on your PDA is intercepted and manipulated by an unauthorized person during its transmission to your doctor? Or think of a scenario in which the software in your car is updated remotely because an attacker has compromised the manufacturer's servers. What if your car, which has just been 'updated,' no longer brakes, but instead activates its drive-by-wire accelerator? What if, in the near future, the control tower that just took over handling of the aircraft in which you are a passenger discovers that the plane no longer does what the pilots or the tower want, but, instead, what some hijackers want it to do? Perhaps worst of all, think about potential for disaster should someone maliciously take over control of a nuclear power plant…

You simply do not want these things to happen! In other words, you require the system to ensure a proper level of confidentiality and integrity before you trust and use it.

Although the importance of security is widely acknowledged, only a few projects address it with the appropriate priority. Security is still an afterthought in many projects. Check the latest security articles in your favorite IT magazine, and you will find reports of successful intrusions into, or denial of service attacks against, all sorts of enterprise-level systems—which, ironically enough, are often not performed by experts, but by high-school kids or students via very simple measures like scripts.

So why is there this discrepancy between the acknowledgement of security and its prioritization in software development? Certainly not because security is still an unexplored field in software. Moreover, security requirements are often expressed vaguely or not at all, and software architectures often expose limited security-related decisions. To survive in today's networked and open computing world, it is crucial to go beyond the realms of authentication.

Project managers, software architects, developers, testers, and other stakeholders of a software system need to ensure that security is an integral part of all software projects.

This is where the book you are holding steps in. Unlike other books on the market that tend to cover the latest research ideas and new security technologies, this new book covers real-world knowledge and experience from international security experts. It uses patterns, a successful and widely adopted technology for describing, communicating, and sharing knowledge. The authors guide you through the field of security, address key questions, and clearly show you how to build secure systems, and present corresponding proven solutions.

For example, how do you identify an organization's or system's security needs, and how do you define an appropriate security approach to meet these needs? Is confidentiality a security property you need in your system, or integrity, availability, or accountability? Or even a mixture of the four? And how do you ensure these properties by appropriate means of prevention, detection, and response? Via identification and authentication (I&A)? Or do you also need a means of access control and authorization in your systems, or even accounting and auditing? And how do all services interact to provide a consistent and coherent security concept for your system? Once you know what security services you need and how they interoperate, what are their different realization options? For example, is a password-based or a PKI-based I&A appropriate to meet your security needs? And what different options are available to you? Smart cards? RFID tags? Or is it sufficient that you provide a log-on service for your system that requests your user ID and password?

You can imagine such a list of questions can be continued and detailed, not only for identification and authentication, but also for all other security services and mechanisms that can be provided: access control and authorization, accounting and auditing, and so on.

So while security is a wide and non-trivial field, it is nevertheless important that you address it appropriately in order to build successful software systems. Ignoring security due to lack of overview and knowledge could be catastrophic. I'm not a security expert, but after working on this book I had a much better understanding of the topic, allowing me to address it more explicitly, more prominently, and more constructively in my daily work as a software architect.

In addition to the technical value and contribution of this book, there is another aspect that makes it special. This book has been written from the heart of the patterns community. All its authors have carefully crafted the scope of their patterns to avoid overlap, and they have integrated all the relationships between the patterns to ensure a common look-and-feel. The result is a network of complementary, mutually-supporting patterns that provide a solid coverage of important security areas. The value of this network is significantly bigger than the sum of the values of all its constituent patterns: you get the whole picture, not just its individual bits and pieces.

Finally, I'd like to invite you to take the opportunity to read and enjoy the patterns presented in this book. I hope that the security issues prove relevant for your systems, enrich your design knowledge, and enhance your overall understanding of security.

I'm sure you'll like this book as much as I do.

Frank Buschmann

Senior Principal Engineer
Siemens AG, Corporate Technology

About this Book

Much attention has recently been devoted to security issues, and it has become apparent that a high security level should be a fundamental prerequisite for all business processes—both in the commercial and public sector. The steadily increasing number of reported security incidents indicates that organizations need additional help in addressing basic security issues, ranging from enterprise plans through software systems to operational practices.

In general, security is not adequately addressed in enterprises and the systems that they build and operate. One reason is that security covers a broad area: it is a big challenge to define secure business processes and to develop and operate the corresponding systems and applications securely. The situation is becoming more challenging because of the increasing openness of systems and enterprises, due largely to the rise of the Internet and e-business technologies. It is very difficult achieve security, especially in distributed environments, as there are many different organizations, individuals, technical components and mechanisms involved. In addition, trust relationships change frequently, which makes a complete analysis of security requirements very hard. As modern business processes become more and more complex, the overall problem space is no longer easily comprehensible for the people involved. Specifically, there are three key issues:

- Security is often an afterthought in system design and implementation. The enterprise context and requirements that drive system security are not addressed explicitly, and are not incorporated into system architectures. What is needed is to begin to address security up-front, rather than the 'repair-service' approach we observe today.

- Many security breaches can be traced back to well-known security problems that still appear over and over again. Default passwords that are documented in the software manual are one example. Storing sensitive information on a public Web server is another example. These are manifestations that security is being given a low priority, or of a lack of understanding of security issues. The dominant goal in these cases is to enhance functionality and performance, not to mitigate risk.

- Enterprise planners, system architects and developers, and operations managers have inadequate knowledge of security. As a consequence, they rely heavily on security specialists to understand their security needs and to provide security solutions. However, there are not enough security specialists to satisfy the need. Furthermore, in many cases, the security specialists find themselves repeating the same solutions for each enterprise or each system development project. This is an unnecessary waste of their time, and keeps them from addressing more complicated problems.

The key to addressing these issues is that—while many security problems are new or complicated—a significant number of basic security problems in an enterprise context are well understood, and well-established solutions exist for them. Over time, the security specialists who have encountered the same basic problems and found themselves repeating the same basic solutions have developed a good understanding of these problems and solutions. To some degree, these have been captured in the security literature and in security-related standards. But the knowledge codified in the literature and standards is not readily accessible to those who do not devote full time to security.

The purpose of this book is to capture some of these basic problems and solutions, and to make them available in a form usable by enterprise planners, system architects and developers, and operations managers. What form would make this knowledge accessible and easy to apply? How can we learn from previous errors and make proven, working solutions to recurring problems available to everyone?

The approach in this book is to apply the idea of *patterns*, which are an established software development technique. The basic idea behind patterns is to capture expert knowledge in the form of documentation with a specific structure containing proven solutions for recurring problems in a given domain. In particular, security patterns can be used when the people responsible for enterprises or systems have little or no security expertise. This allows them to address basic security issues themselves, instead of depending on security specialists to perform this task for them each time. This frees security specialists to help solve new or more complex security problems.

People will probably continue to develop and use second-class security solutions. Even relatively unskilled computer users, if they are intent on hacking, are able to carry out damaging attacks using widely-available scripts. Developing first-class solutions is an enormously difficult problem, exhibiting too many cases of inadequate requirements, ill-formed design concepts, poor architectures, inadequate specifications, immature software development practices, overdependence on system administration, poor operations, and uninformed top management. The earlier we start to treat security as an equivalent requirement with the appropriate priority, the quicker our knowhow and skills about seamless security solutions will evolve. This would considerably reduce the residual risk of using software applications and systems in sensitive environments. More and more we depend on having secure systems, and we need systematic solutions. Our belief is that security patterns are a step in this direction.

The Book's Intended Audiences

This book is intended for anyone who has a little knowledge of security but who needs to incorporate basic security functions into his organization or system, either because they are required to do so, or because they understand the importance of security. The book is also useful for specialists to use as a design guide, to compare systems, and to teach about systems.

In particular, we address the following audiences:

- At the enterprise level, everyone who is or should be interested in enterprise security, such as enterprise planners, enterprise architects, strategists, and policy makers, as well as business process engineers and business process re-engineering specialists. The main issue for these groups is to understand how to define basic enterprise security needs and constraints. Security patterns for this target group are presented in Chapter 6, *Enterprise Security and Risk Management*. We also recommend that they look at the patterns that are described in Chapters 7 to 13, to understand how enterprise security plans are reflected or satisfied in enterprise operations.

- At the IT system level, system architects, software designers and developers, project managers, product vendors, service suppliers and others interested in system security. These groups have to understand how to design basic system security functions and incorporate them into system architectures and designs, and how to select among alternative security solutions. We have compiled a set of corresponding security patterns in Chapters 7 to 13. At this level it is also important to understand the enterprise security constraints described in Chapter 6, *Enterprise Security and Risk Management*, and how they affect system security requirements.

- At an operational level, operations managers, operations staff, and other people interested in operations security. Their interest is to understand how to define and adopt basic security practices in enterprise and system operations. Relevant security patterns are discussed in Chapter 7, *Identification and Authentication (I&A)*, Chapter 10, *Operating System Access Control*, Chapter 11, *Accounting*, Chapter 12, *Firewall Architectures*, and Chapter 13, *Secure Internet Applications*.

It is clear that all these levels interact, and a complete understanding of security requires some degree of understanding of all of them.

There are further groups who may find the book useful, and can read any chapters of interest:

- Security specialists will be interested in comparing our security taxonomy with others. They may also want to see how familiar security solutions are represented in the form of patterns. They can also use or reference the patterns to reduce the number of times they have to repeat the same answers to the same security questions.

- Researchers, teachers, and students can use the book to understand current best practice in security. They may also find potential areas for extensions to our approach. For example, they could examine the security taxonomy to find areas not covered by current patterns. Advantages of security patterns for this target group could include their use in the design of new systems, understanding of complex systems, comparison of systems, and for teaching purposes: security patterns are used in university security courses, for example.

- Security auditors can improve their understanding using this new representation of best security practice. The collection of patterns also include *forces* and liabilities to watch for: in the Patterns community, we use the term 'forces' to describe goals and constraints that reveal the intricacies of a problem and define the kinds of trade-offs that must be considered in the presence of the tension or dissonance they create.

- Government acquisition or procurement specialists might get help in understanding a new representation of best security practice that can be included in an acquisition document such as a Request for Proposal or Statement of Work.

Structure of the Book

The first chapter, *The Pattern Approach*, provides a general introduction to the overall pattern paradigm. In addition to a discussion of the pattern approach, the chapter presents the pattern template we use in the book.

Chapter 2, *Security Foundations*, introduces key security concepts. We provide a general overview of security, followed by a taxonomy of security areas and a set of general security resources.

Applying patterns to the area of security results in a new, domain-specific pattern type: security patterns. In Chapter 3, *Security Patterns*, we outline how security patterns have evolved, and describe their distinguishing characteristics. We also discuss the benefits of using security patterns, and data sources for identifying security patterns.

Chapter 4, *Patterns Scope and Enterprise Security*, describes the scope and context of security patterns and explains how they are organized in the book.

Chapter 5, *The Security Pattern Landscape*, presents thumbnails for all the patterns in this book, as well as related security patterns that we reference, but are not contained in the book. In many cases these are published elsewhere.

Chapters 6 through 13 present the security patterns themselves.

In Chapter 6, *Enterprise Security and Risk Management*, we present security patterns at the enterprise level. These patterns emphasize the security considerations that planners need to incorporate into their development of enterprise-level strategy, planning activities, business models, goals, and policies.

Chapter 7, *Identification and Authentication (I&A)*, introduces service patterns that support aspects of the I&A service and selected individual patterns in this system. Identification and Authentication (I&A) services address the task of recognizing an actor—that is, a user, a process or any other system—that is interacting with a business system.

Chapter 8, *Access Control Models*, presents patterns that specify accepted access-control models as object-oriented, declarative patterns that can be used as guidelines in the construction of secure systems. There is also a pattern that documents the dynamics of evaluating requests according to the constraints defined by the declarative models. Finally, we also show a pattern that helps to find the rights associated with roles in a role-based access control (RBAC) model.

Chapter 9, *System Access Control Architecture*, presents access-control patterns at the architectural level. There is a pattern that shows why and how to gather the underlying requirements for a system under consideration from a generic set of access control requirements. The remainder of this chapter contains patterns that deal with the architecture of software systems to be secured by access control.

Chapter 10, *Operating System Access Control*, presents patterns for access control services and mechanisms targeted at operating systems that describe how the operating system controls access to resources such as memory address spaces and I/O devices.

Chapter 11, *Accounting*, presents patterns for audit and accounting services and mechanisms. Decision makers need to be aware of any security events that occur that involve their assets. This need is addressed by security audit and accounting patterns.

Chapter 12, *Firewall Architectures*, presents a pattern language for describing different types of firewalls. This language can be used as a guide to select a suitable firewall type for a system or to help designers build new firewalls.

Chapter 13, *Secure Internet Applications*, presents patterns for Internet security that specialize patterns from Chapter 8, *Access Control Models*, and Chapter 12, *Firewall Architectures*, within the domain of Internet applications.

Chapter 14, *Case Study: IP Telephony*, presents a case study of an emerging technology that demonstrates how to use security patterns to incorporate security into real-world system engineering scenarios. The most appropriate patterns of this book are applied to selected use cases in IP telephony systems.

Chapter 15, *Supplementary Concepts*, discusses selected complementary concepts that can be used in conjunction with security patterns. In particular, we present the pattern-related notion of security principles and so-called 'misuse cases.'

Chapter 16, *Closing Remarks*, provides our conclusions and an outlook on future work that deals with security patterns and related concepts.

Guidelines for the Reader

In addition to the obvious option of reading the book from cover to cover, you can choose alternative paths though the book.

This book is divided in three parts. The first part, which comprises Chapters 1 through 3, provides relevant background information about security patterns. If you are not familiar with patterns, read Chapter 1, *The Pattern Approach*, which contains a brief introduction to the ideas behind software patterns. If you are not familiar with security, read Chapter 2, *Security Foundations*, which provides basic concepts and pointers to sources of detailed security knowledge. Based on that, Chapter 3, *Security Patterns*, discusses the notion of security patterns.

The second part of the book, Chapters 4 through 13, contains a catalog of selected security patterns that address different topics. You can work through the catalog chapter by chapter to get an impression of typical security problems and proven solutions that occur at the different levels.

To understand how security patterns can be organized, read Chapter 4, *Patterns Scope and Enterprise Security*, which builds on our security taxonomy. If you want to get a quick overview of our security patterns, as well as related security patterns that are not presented in this book, read Chapter 5, *The Security Pattern Landscape*. This chapter can be used as a reference and a navigation tool.

Reading the patterns in Chapters 6 through 13 can be done in any desired sequence, or with any desired subset of the patterns. Within a given pattern, the key topics to read are *Context*, *Problem*, and *Solution*. The other parts of the patterns are optional and provide further information about implementing the pattern. We also identify the relationships between the patterns. You can therefore also start with any pattern and use the references to related patterns to navigate through the book.

If you have read the introductory chapters and security patterns are new to you, we suggest that you start with security patterns that are easy to understand and that are used in many situations. Examples are:

- Password Design and Use (217)
- Single Access Point (279)
- Front Door (473)

In the third part of the book we discuss applications, extensions and future directions of a pattern-based security approach. If you are looking for examples that describe how security patterns can be applied, look at the case study provided in

Chapter 14, *Case Study: IP Telephony*. If you are interested in techniques that can complement or augment the concept of security patterns, have a look at a few examples in Chapter 15, *Supplementary Concepts*. Conclusions and a look at the future of this work are given in Chapter 16, *Closing Remarks*. As these chapters build on the patterns in the book, you should read them last.

About the Authors

Many people contributed to this book. In this section we provide short biographies of all the authors and editors in alphabetical order. We also show briefly who contributed to which part of the book. Finally, we express our thanks to all the other people that helped to bring this book to a successful conclusion.

Short Biographies

Frank Buschmann

Frank Buschmann is Senior Principal Engineer at Siemens Corporate Technology in Munich, Germany. His research interests include object technology, software architecture, frameworks, and patterns. He has published widely in all these areas, most visibly in his co-authorship of the first two POSA volumes, *A System of Patterns* and *Patterns for Concurrent and Networked Objects*. Frank was a member of the ANSI C++ standardization committee X3J16 from 1992 to 1996. He initiated and organized the first conference on patterns held in Europe, EuroPLoP 1996, and is also a co-editor of the third book in the PLoPD series by Addison-Wesley. In his development work Frank has led design and implementation efforts for several large-scale industrial software projects, including business information, industrial automation, and telecommunication systems. In addition, Frank serves as the series editor for Wiley's series in software design patterns.

Susan Chapin

Susan Chapin has worked in research on information system technologies and issues relating to the management of security. She investigated the Windows NT/Windows 2000 operating system from an information security perspective, participated in the development of a multi-level operating system for the Defense Information Systems Agency (DISA), and supported the development of high-level security architectures for the US Treasury Department, which included a focus on issues and uses of enterprise-wide directory services for the Internal Revenue Service (IRS). Some of her recent research has included studies of procedures to support the true integration of security into an enterprise architecture. Susan retired from MITRE in September 2003.

Nelly Delessy-Gassant

Nelly Delessy-Gassant is a Ph.D. student at Florida Atlantic University, working under the direction of Dr. Eduardo B. Fernandez. Her dissertation work is about trust in systems using Web Services. She is the author of several security patterns, for example in the area of firewalls.

Paul Dyson

Paul Dyson has built large-scale internet-based systems for a number of companies that include Philips, Lastminute.com, ThinkNatural.com and Interbrew. On these projects Paul has taken the role of application architect, designing both hardware and software architectures, as well as providing technical leadership to the development teams. He is a conference presenter and has chaired international events such as EuroPLoP and OT.

Ben Elsinga

Ben Elsinga is a specialist in information architecture and information security. He has carried out several assignments in the areas of risk analyses, security architecture, as well as acting as an interim security manager and a lecturer on information security courses. Within Capgemini Benelux, Ben led all research and information security development activities. He created a competence network of security specialists and consultants, and is member of the board of the Dutch information security society (GvIB). The vision Ben has is that information security should be integrated into every change, and that humans are the weakest link in the chain. He feels very comfortable in dynamic environments and from an innovative and result-driven attitude he likes to create new and secure business solutions. In an environment that contains the combination of system development and information security, Ben takes responsibility for a team of specialists to fulfill challenging assignments. He is a Capgemini certified senior IT architect, specialized in system development and information security. Ben successfully passed a B-screening by the Dutch government, and he is also a certified Prince-2 practitioner and is also a certified CISSP in information security.

Eduardo B. Fernandez

Eduardo B. Fernandez (Eduardo Fernandez-Buglioni) is a professor in the Department of Computer Science and Engineering at Florida Atlantic University in Boca Raton, Florida. He has published numerous papers on authorization models, object-oriented analysis and design, and fault-tolerant systems. He has written three books on these subjects. He has lectured all over the world at both academic and industrial meetings, and has created and taught several graduate and undergraduate courses and industrial tutorials. His current interests include security patterns and Web Services security. He holds an M.S. degree in Electrical Engineering from Purdue University and a Ph.D. in Computer Science from UCLA. He is a Senior Member of the IEEE, and a Member of ACM. He is an active consultant for industry, including assignments with IBM, Allied Signal, Motorola, Lucent, and others.

Mei Fullerton

Mei Fullerton recently completed her M.S. in Computer Science at Florida Atlantic University (May 2005). Since then she has worked as a software engineer at Office Depot, Delray Beach, Florida.

Manuel Görtz

Manuel Görtz is a researcher in the field of context-aware communication services. He holds an M.Sc. (Diplom) in Electrical Engineering and Information Technology from the Technischen Universität Darmstadt (TUD). He joined the Multimedia Communication Lab headed by Prof. Ralf Steinmetz at TUD in 2000. He recently received his Ph.D. in Electrical Engineering and Information Technology on the topic of 'Efficient Real-time Communication Services Utilizing Contexts.'

Manuel Görtz has actively working in the area of Voice over IP for many years. He was a member of the task-force that hosted the IP telephony trial for the Darmstadt scientific region, analyzing security threads and operational issues. He has worked for many years in industry projects to design and prototype communication solutions for the future. Manuel is an author of numerous peer-reviewed papers and several invention reports. His key expertise lies in the domain of signaling, advanced communication services and security patterns.

Jody Heaney

Jody Heaney is a Principle InfoSec Engineer in the Information Security Center at the MITRE Corporation in McLean, VA. She has been involved in many different program areas, including work with DARPA, the National Security Agency (NSA), all branches of the military, the Intelink Management Office (IMO), and the Intelligence

Community (IC). She has conducted research into the foundations of information assurance (IA) and has published papers on security modeling and access control. She was one of the original developers of the System Security Engineering Capability Maturity Model (CMM) and NSA's Information Assurance Technology Framework (IATF). In her current IA leadership role for the IC CIO, the focus is on identifying cross-cutting IA technologies suitable for the entire IC, especially for cross-security-domain technologies, and information sharing. She has maintained a strong interest in integrating information systems security into the mainstream of software and systems engineering processes.

Aaldert Hofman

Aaldert Hofman has elaborate knowledge and experience in sophisticated and complex information systems. He graduated in Informatics at Twente University in Enschede, the Netherlands and joined Capgemini in January 1990. During the first years of his career he was involved in the architecture of large administrative systems within social security. Since 1997 he has been assigned to projects in banking and insurance services. His expertise is in both architecture and security. He oversees the complexity in these fields and is able to align business to available IT resources. Aaldert is experienced in bridging the gap between business and IT both in his assignments and his coaching in architecture and security. Aaldert has been interested in the use of patterns since the famous GoF book on *Design Patterns*. Working in knowledge-intensive areas such as identity management and information security, he was convinced that knowledge capture by the use of patterns could be very helpful. He therefore joined the security patterns community during 2001, together with his colleague Ben Elsinga. They submitted security patterns to EuroPLoP 2002 and 2003, where they met the editors of this book and discussed their ideas. In their projects the use of security patterns has lead to better control of access rights, improving quality and time-to-market.

Duane Hybertson

Duane Hybertson is a researcher and member of the technical staff in the Center for Innovative Computing and Informatics at the MITRE Corporation in McLean, VA. He has a broad background in software engineering, both in research and practice. He has conducted research into the foundations of systems architecture, and has published papers on a uniform modeling approach to architecture and software engineering. He has supported architecture development and helped to define evolutionary processes for large information systems at the National Geospatial-Intelligence Agency (NGA), which supports both the US Department of Defense (DoD) and the intelligence community. He has applied architecture and modeling concepts to enterprise engineering, and is extending the model-oriented approach to complex systems.

His recent research has been in capturing security patterns and determining how to integrate these patterns into a usable enterprise engineering context.

Malcolm Kirwan, Jr.

Malcolm Kirwan, Jr. is a Lead Software Systems Engineer and Scientist at the MITRE Corporation in McLean, VA. Malcolm has spent his career performing activities throughout all phases of the systems and software development lifecycles. His experience ranges from designing and developing software for real-time embedded systems and simulation systems, to designing and incorporating security solutions into enterprise and system architectures.

Maria M. Larrondo-Petrie

Dr. Larrondo-Petrie is Associate Dean of Engineering and Professor of Computer Science & Engineering at Florida Atlantic University (FAU), and a member of the Secure Systems Research Group at FAU. She serves on the ASEE Minority Division Board, is Vice President of Research of the Latin American and Caribbean Consortium of Engineering Institutions, was on the ACM SIGGRAPH Education Board and was President of Upsilon Pi Epsilon Honor Society for the Computing Sciences.

Andy Longshaw

Andy Longshaw is an independent consultant, writer and educator specializing in enterprise platforms (both .NET and J2EE), Web-based technologies, Web Services, and components, particularly the design and architectural decisions required to use these technologies successfully. In recent years, Andy has worked on Internet technology projects and architecture for organizations such as Tesco Stores and Barclays Bank.

Andreas L. Opdahl

Andreas L. Opdahl is Professor of Information Systems Development at the Department of Information Science and Media Studies, University of Bergen, Norway. He is the author, co-author or co-editor of more than fifty journal articles, book chapters, refereed archival conference papers and books on multi-perspective enterprise modeling, requirements engineering, information systems architecture, software performance engineering and other areas. He serves regularly as a reviewer for premier international journals and on the program committees of renowned international conferences and workshops, and is a member of IFIP WG8.1 on Design and Evaluation of Information Systems.

Ann Reedy

Ann Reedy is a researcher and member of the technical staff in the Center for Innovative Computing and Informatics at the MITRE Corporation in McLean, VA. She has a broad background in both software engineering and enterprise architecture. She has supported the development of both enterprise architecture frameworks and enterprise architectures for DoD and a broad range of civil agencies. In addition to her recent research work on security patterns at MITRE, she has been working with Syracuse University in integrating security and enterprise engineering concepts in support of the Federal Enterprise Architecture Security and Privacy Profile. She is currently involved in providing enterprise architecture courses through the MITRE Institute and the Federal Enterprise Architecture Certification Institute.

Naeem Seliya

Naeem Seliya completed his Ph.D. in Computer Science at Florida Atlantic University in July 2005. His dissertation work was about the classification of error-prone software modules.

Sasha Romanosky

Sasha Romanosky, CISSP, holds a Bachelor of Science degree in Electrical Engineering from the University of Calgary, Canada and is currently pursuing graduate studies in Information Security at Carnegie Mellon. Sasha has been working with Internet and security technologies for over eight years, predominantly within the financial and e-commerce industries at companies such as Morgan Stanley and eBay. He co-authored the book *J2EE Design Patterns Applied* and has published other works on security patterns. Recently, Sasha collaborated with other leading industry professionals to develop the Common Vulnerability Scoring System (CVSS), an open framework for scoring computer vulnerabilities. His current research interests include vulnerability management and security metrics. His passion is information security. Sasha would like to thank his shepherds Duane Hybertson and Aaldert Hofman, as well as Markus Schumacher, for his vision in this book. Finally, Sasha would like to thank Theresa for her never-ending love and support.

Markus Schumacher

Markus Schumacher studied Electrical Engineering and Information Technology at the Darmstadt University of Technology (TUD). After finishing his studies in 1998, he was the leader of the IT Transfer Office (ITO) team that was—and still is—engaged in numerous national and international research projects in cooperation with well-known companies and public institutions that include SAP AG, T-Systems, Fujitsu

Laboratories, Digital Equipment Corporation, Siemens, Tenovis/Bosch Telecom, and the European Union. He planned and organized the 'Hacker Contest' in which participants alternately play the roles of 'attacker' and system administrator, thereby learning basic modes of attack as well as how to secure applications, operating systems and networks against them. The course is still offered by Markus' former colleagues. Springer Verlag has published the results of this course as a book in the Xpert Press series. In May 2003, Markus finished his dissertation about 'Security Engineering with Patterns', also published by Springer in the LNCS series. In 2003, Markus joined the Product Security team of SAP AG in Walldorf, Germany. There he led a Common Criteria certification project, was responsible for reporting the compliance of SAP NetWeaver to the SAP product standard for security, and was a team member in the SAP Security Response team. In July 2005 he joined SAP's Research and Breakthrough Innovation division, where the new Business Process Platform (BPP), as well as new BPP-based solutions, are being developed.

Guttorm Sindre

Guttorm Sindre is Professor of Information Systems in the Department of Computer and Information Science, Norwegian University of Science and Technology. He is the author and co-author of more than fifty articles in refereed international journals or conferences. His primary research fields are requirements engineering, conceptual modeling, and information systems development. He serves as a reviewer for international journals and on the program committees of renowned international conferences and workshops.

Peter Sommerlad

Peter Sommerlad is a software engineer in heart and soul. He currently teaches as professor for informatics at HSR Hochschule für Technik, Rapperswil, a position he has held since fall of 2004. He heads the Institute for Software (http://www.ifsoftware.ch), which tries to improve software practice in Switzerland under the motto 'better software, simply faster.'

From 1997 on Peter has practiced patterns and Agile software development in Switzerland. In the late 1990s he and his team implemented Internet applications and security infrastructure for the Swiss financial industry.

In addition to teaching and programming, Peter writes patterns and shepherds other pattern authors. He is member of Hillside Group, Hillside Europe, the Swiss Software Engineering Network SWEN, ACM and the IEEE Computer Society.

Peter's major acknowledgement goes to his wife Andrea: 'Without her love and care I would no longer be in this world.' Peter is a leukemia survivor, so he is grateful to Professor Hans-Jochem Kolb and his team at the Jose-Carreras transplantation unit in Munich for their care and support during his treatment. He encourages all readers to become registered stem-cell donors to help other leukemia patients.

Peter's appreciation for this book goes to his co-editors and co-authors, for their feedback and their encouragement over work on security patterns. His special thanks go to Joseph Yoder and Jeffrey Barcalow, for allowing him to put their patterns into shape for this book.

The Birth of this Book

In the very beginning it was Ben Elsinga who sent an e-mail to Markus. Markus had just setup a Web page about security patterns on his site, and Ben liked this idea. Shortly after that, Eduardo shepherded Markus's first paper about security patterns for PLoP 2001 and the idea for the book was born. This was the beginning of a closer discussion about security patterns, and resulted in the first Focus Group 'Thinking about Security Patterns' at EuroPLoP 2001. There, a mini-community came together and started to work: Juha Pärsinnen, Sami Lehtonen, Ben Elsinga, Frank Buschmann, Eduardo Fernandez, Duane Hybertson, Markus Schumacher, Manuel Görtz, and Aaldert Hofman. At this conference Duane and Frank joined the team of editors. A year later, most of the group met again for a second Focus Group at EuroPLoP 2002, which laid the foundations for this book. At this conference there was a dedicated workshop for security patterns and Peter Sommerlad, another co-author of POSA1, joined the editorial team. This was very important, as he is both a pattern enthusiast and a security practitioner. Beside these face-to-face workshops, Sasha Romanosky joined the community by e-mail.

The end of this story is this book. which is the result of three years of work by twenty-one people, and we are very proud that it is in your bookshelf now. It would be even better to put it on your desk.

Who Wrote What?

The editors wrote the introductory chapters as well as the last chapter. Markus Schumacher compiled and integrated all material of the book. Frank contributed Chapter 1, *The Pattern Approach*, offered his rapid shepherding skills and was a good advisor in critical phases. Duane and Eduardo contributed to Chapter 2, *Security Foundations*. Duane, Eduardo, and Markus wrote Chapter 3, *Security Patterns*. Many thanks to Aaldert Hofman and Ben Elsinga who contributed Section 3.3, *Why Security Patterns?*.

Chapter 4, *Patterns Scope and Enterprise Security* was written by the MITRE Team, namely Jody Heaney, Duane Hybertson, Susan Chapin, Malcolm Kirwan Jr. and Ann Reedy. Chapter 5, *The Security Pattern Landscape* was the joint idea of the editors and some of the authors, and was compiled by Duane and Markus. The MITRE team and Sasha Romanosky contributed the introduction and the patterns for Chapter 6, *Enterprise Security and Risk Management*. All the patterns in Chapter 7,

Identification and Authentication (I&A) were written by the MITRE team. All the patterns in Chapter 8, *Access Control Models* were written by Eduardo B. Fernandez: the ROLE-BASED ACCESS CONTROL (249) pattern was co-authored by Mei Fullerton. The author of the ACCESS CONTROL REQUIREMENTS (267) pattern in Chapter 9, *System Access Control Architecture* is the MITRE team. The other patterns in this chapter are based on a pattern language of Joseph Yoder and Jeffrey Barcalow and have been rewritten for this book by Peter Sommerlad. Chapter 10, *Operating System Access Control* was written by Eduardo B. Fernandez and Chapter 11, *Accounting* was contributed by the MITRE team. The patterns in Chapter 12, *Firewall Architectures* have been jointly written by Eduardo B. Fernandez, Maria M. Larrondo-Petrie, Naeem Seliya, Nelly Delessy-Gassant, and Markus Schumacher. The patterns in Chapter 13, *Secure Internet Applications* were contributed by Andy Longshaw, Paul Dyson and Peter Sommerlad.

Chapter 14, *Case Study: IP Telephony* was written by Manuel Görtz. Aaldert Hofman and Ben Elsinga wrote Section 15.1, *Security Principles and Security Patterns* of Chapter 15, *Supplementary Concepts.* Andreas L. Opdahl and Guttorm Sindre wrote Section 15.2, *Enhancing Security Patterns with Misuse Cases.*

Acknowledgements

First of all we would like to thank the Hillside Europe Group for their support and encouragement. When all this started a few years ago, they gave us the opportunity to discuss many of the patterns that are now in this book in writer's workshops that were explicitly dedicated to security. Besides, we could shape the agenda for this book in several Focus Groups. Consequently, very special thanks go to the participants of the workshops and the Focus Groups. In particular, we would like to thank Sami Lehtonen, Juha Pärsinnen, and Kristian Elof Sørensen.

We thank Rick Dewar, Ralph Johnson, Munawar Hafiz, Craig R.P. Heath, Peter G. Neumann, Dan Thomsen, and Joseph Yoder for their insightful comments on earlier versions of our work. The comments of all the reviewers helped us to shape and polish the contents of the book. Acknowledgements to those people who helped with the improvement of specific patterns are also given at the end of each introduction to the pattern chapters.

Special thanks also go to the Wiley team who supported us throughout this project: Gaynor Redvers-Mutton who encouraged us to go ahead and smoothly handed over to Sally Tickner, Sarah Corney, Jonathan Shipley, David Barnard, Drew Kennerley, Fleur Hamilton, and Nick Mannion. We would also like to thank our copy editor, Steve Rickaby.

All those that have been forgotten—please accept our deepest and honest apologies, we owe you (at least) a beer from the Kloster Irsee brewery. Everything that is good is the result of a good idea and a great team that realized it, and a great community that supported it. If you, dear reader, find a 'bug' in this book, blame us, the editors.

The Pattern Approach

It is not necessarily complicated. It is not necessarily simple.

Christopher Alexander, in 'The Timeless Way of Building'

In this chapter we introduce the concepts of patterns and two approaches to organizing and connecting them: pattern systems and pattern languages. In addition, we outline the major application areas and purpose of patterns, as well as their history in the software community. Last, but not least, we discuss how patterns are mined, documented, and prepared for publication and presentation.

1.1 Patterns at a Glance

Developer enthusiasm for patterns has been almost unquenchable since the release of the seminal work by the Gang-of-Four[1] [GoF95] just a decade ago. Software developers from around the world leapt on the 'new idea,' with the hope that patterns would help them untangle tricky problems into a well-knit solution—something with elegance, directness, and versatility. Patterns found their way into many software development projects. A movement had begun. It was, and still is, thriving.

A major reason for the success of patterns is that they constitute a 'grass roots' initiative to build on, and draw from, the collective experience of skilled designers. It is not often that a new development project tackles genuinely new problems that demand truly novel solutions. Developers may sometimes arrive at similar solutions independently or often recall a similar problem they solved successfully in a different situation, reusing its essence and adapting its details to resolve the new problem. Expert developers can draw on a large body of such solution schemes for both common and uncommon design problems. This practical experience guides them when building new applications.

Distilling commonalities from the pairing of application-specific design problems and their solutions leads comfortably to the concept of patterns: they capture these solutions and their relationship to the problem, framing them in a more readily-accessible form. From a very general birds-eye perspective, a pattern can be characterized as:

A solution to a problem that arises within a specific context.

Though this characterization captures every pattern's main structural property well, it does not tell the whole story. The context-problem-solution trichotomy is necessary for a specific concept to qualify as a pattern, but it is not sufficient. In particular, it does not specify how to distinguish a true pattern from an 'ordinary' solution to a problem. In fact, it requires much more for a software concept to be a true pattern:

- A pattern describes both a process and a thing: the 'thing' is created by the 'process' [Ale79]. For most software patterns—thus also for security patterns— 'thing' means a particular high-level design outline or code detail, including both static structure and intended behavior. In other words, a pattern is both a spatial configuration of elements that resolve a particular problem—or in which a particular problem does not arise—and a set of associated instructions to create this configuration of elements most effectively.

---

[1] The authors of this book, Erich Gamma, Ralph Johnson, Richard Helm, and John Vlissides, are named after the 'Gang-of-Four' in Chinese politics.

- A true pattern presents a high-quality, proven solution that resolves the given problem optimally. Patterns do not represent neat ideas that might work, but concepts that have been applied successfully in the past over and over again. Consequently, new ideas must first prove their worth in the line of active duty, often many times, before they can truly be called patterns. Because they capture practice and experience, patterns can help novices to act with greater confidence and insight on modest-sized projects, as well as supporting experts in the development of large-scale and complex software systems.

- Patterns support the understanding of problems and their solutions. Presenting a problem and a solution for it is not enough for a pattern, as this leaves several important questions unanswered. Why is the problem a hard problem? What are the requirements, constraints, and desired properties of its solution? Why is the solution as it is and not something else? A good pattern does not withhold this information. The forces associated with its problem description provide the answer for the first two questions, and the discussion, or consequences, of its solution the latter.

- Patterns are generic—as independent of or dependent on a particular implementation technology as they need to be. A pattern does not describe a particular solution, a specific arrangement of components or classes dependent on a particular programming paradigm or language, but a set of interacting roles that define an entire solution space. Christopher Alexander puts it this way [AIS+77]: 'Each pattern describes a problem which occurs over and over again in our environment, and then describes the core of the solution to that problem, in such a way that you can use this solution a million times over, without ever doing it twice the same.'

- A pattern tells a story and initiates a dialog. As every pattern presents timeless and proven experience, it tells a success story. To be precise for software patterns, a 'successful software engineering story,' to borrow an observation from Erich Gamma. But a pattern is not only a story, it also initiates a dialog with its readers about how to resolve a particular problem well—by addressing the forces that can influence the problem's solution, by describing different feasible solutions, and finally by discussing the trade-offs of each solution option. A pattern thus invites its readers to reflect on the problem being presented: to think first and then to decide and act explicitly and consciously.

- Patterns celebrate human intelligence. Patterns are not automatic derivations from problem ingredients to fully-baked solutions. Patterns often tackle problems in more lateral ways that can be indirect, unusual, and even counter-intuitive. In contrast to the implied handle-turning nature of many rigid development methods, patterns are founded in human ingenuity and experience.

A true pattern exposes all of the above properties—if it is lacking any of them, it is probably just a solution to a problem, and most likely a specific design and implementation decision for a specific system, but not a pattern. Adapting the existing definition from the first volume of the *Pattern-Oriented Software Architecture* series [POSA1], this leads to the following characterization of the notion of patterns:

A pattern for software architecture describes a particular recurring design problem that arises in specific design contexts, and presents a well-proven generic solution for it. The solution consists of a set of interacting roles that can be arranged to form multiple concrete design structures, as well as a process for creating any particular structure.

This general definition serves well for the purpose of this book, although we narrow it to security patterns but also extend it to include enterprise and requirements patterns as well as architecture.

1.2   No Pattern is an Island

Though each pattern focuses on providing a self-contained solution for resolving one specific problem, patterns are not independent of one another. In fact, there are many relationships between patterns [POSA1]. The most important relationship is refinement: the solution proposed by a particular pattern can often be implemented with help of other patterns, which resolve sub-problems of the original problem. To put it in another way, 'each pattern depends on the smaller patterns it contains and on the larger patterns in which it is contained' [Ale79]. Other important relationships among patterns are variation and combination [POSA1].

It is the relationships between the patterns, together with their genericity, that allows them to be combined and integrated with one another to form large software architectures and designs that are coherent and consistent in their whole as well as in their details. Conversely, without these relationships, patterns would only be able to resolve isolated problems, with no, or at best limited, effect on a larger design or even an entire software architecture [POSA4].

1.3   Patterns Everywhere

Software patterns can exist at any scale and for many problem areas. In their early days—the mid 1990s—the focus was on object-oriented design patterns of general applicability. The Gang-of-Four book [GoF95] presents the most widely-known patterns of this kind. The scope of these patterns, however, had only a small impact on entire software or system architectures, because they covered how to structure specific components, or how to organize their relationships and interactions. This gap was first filled by the POSA team [POSA1] who were the first to present patterns at the level of coarse-grained software architecture. Other authors completed the pattern space to the 'bottom,' the level of programming. For example, James O. Coplien—commonly known as 'Cope'—published patterns that deal with C++-specific issues like memory management and string handling [Cop92], and Kent Beck wrote his famous patterns book *Smalltalk Best Practices* [Bec97]. Yet all these patterns, although covering different scopes, were general in nature: general architecture, general design, and general programming.

The first patterns that had a more specific focus were Martin Fowler's analysis patterns [Fow97]. Not only did Martin introduce another level of scope to patterns—patterns that describe the fundamental structure of, and workflow within, an application domain—his patterns focused on two specific areas: health care and corporate finance.

Since then patterns have spread into many other specific areas, ranging from concurrent and networked systems and programming [Lea99] [POSA2], server components [VSW02], human–computer interaction [Bor01], memory constraint systems [NW01], resource management [POSA3], and others [Ris00]. Recently, security was identified as another area of hot interest for patterns, and this book is intended to serve this need.

1.4 Humans are the Target

A valid question to ask is 'What is the target audience for patterns.' There are many answers to this question, depending on who you ask, but all leading pattern experts share a common view: patterns are for, and about, humans. This statement is also consistent with Christopher Alexander's—the architect, in the sense of buildings, not software, who invented patterns—understanding of patterns [Ale79].

The correctness of this position becomes obvious when reflecting on the previous sections of this chapter. All the properties of patterns that we have discussed so far are aimed at presenting problems and their solutions in a way that humans can understand: when such problems arise, what the problems are, what to consider when resolving them, how they can be resolved, how their solutions are implemented, and why these solutions are as they are. Much effort is also expended in presenting patterns in an appealing, dialog-initiating, and story-telling—in other words, human-readable—form.

Humans are also the only audience for patterns. We discovered that it is next to impossible to formalize patterns, a necessary precondition to making patterns machine-readable and automatable. Thus the audience for patterns does not include computers or any other type of machine, nor the many software development tools that run on such computers or machines.

This distinguishes patterns from other design or modeling techniques, for example, the Unified Modeling Language [BRJ98]. Artifacts that are created with such techniques are not only intended to be human-usable and human-readable: they can also be input to tools that then execute formal consistency and correctness checks on them, simulate them, and even generate code fragments from them. At first glance such techniques might seem superior to patterns. However, in real-world practice they are only useful for documenting, implementing, and tuning an already-designed system. They do not support us in the creative act of designing a new system and understanding its challenges—but patterns do!

1.5   Patterns Resolve Problems and Shape Environments

Now that we know that software patterns intend to support humans in understanding and building software systems, we can ask what concrete purpose they serve in that context.

The most obvious—and of course correct—answer is: software patterns help humans to understand and resolve problems. Why else do they contain human-readable descriptions of problems and their solutions? The problem areas that software patterns address are the organizational, analysis, architecture, design, and programming aspects of software development.

However, software patterns do not just specify arbitrary solutions to software development problems. As we discussed in earlier sections of this chapter, a pattern represents proven and practiced experience—timeless solutions to recurring problems that can be implemented in many different ways—presented so that people can understand, and talk about, the problems, the solutions, and their influencing forces and trade-offs.

When analyzing the way in which software patterns resolve the problems they address, we see that they do this by shaping environments: patterns introduce spatial configurations of elements that exhibit specific behavior. From a system development perspective we can also say: when applied, a pattern transforms a given structure in which a particular problem is present into another structure in which this problem is resolved.

Some pattern experts take this observation as an argument to invert the perspective, to better emphasize the focus on humans that patterns have: patterns shape environments in which particular problems do not occur, and in which humans thus feel comfortable.

Which perspective best serves you, or the particular application under development or refactoring, is a matter of your own preference. If you reflect on them long enough, however, you will discover that they are mutually supportive. With patterns, developers are more confident of avoiding problems or resolving them well, while customers and users are more confident that problems are avoided or resolved well. Thus both camps feel more comfortable that they are getting the 'right' thing.

1.6 Towards Pattern Languages

Experience in developing software with patterns reveals that the explicit relationships that can exist between patterns, as outlined in Section 1.2, *No Pattern is an Island*, are not enough to use patterns successfully. The reason for this is the existence of additional implicit relationships between patterns. When developing a real-world system, not only one design and implementation problem must be resolved, but many different and orthogonal ones. If we resolve one problem by applying a pattern and implementing it in a specific way, this creates a concrete design. This design then defines a framework for resolving subsequent problems—which, unfortunately, narrows their potential solution space. Consequently, it can happen that it is impossible to resolve the subsequent problems most optimally—or not even good enough—due to the constraints set by the existing design.

The patterns community tried to address this fact by structuring and organizing the pattern space. The goal of all such activities was to achieve a better overview of the patterns that exist for resolving a particular problem, and to elaborate how patterns can be combined into meaningful larger structures. Pattern catalogs [GoF95] and pattern systems [POSA1], therefore, present more than one pattern for resolving important design problems, for example object creation or location-independent inter-process communication. Pattern systems also discuss how to best combine their constituent patterns to form concrete software architectures and designs. The following is the original definition for pattern systems [POSA1]:

A pattern system for software architecture is a collection of patterns for software architecture, together with guidelines for their implementation, combination and practical use in software development.

Without delving into details, it is obvious from this definition that a pattern system can give a great deal more support for using patterns in practical software development than individual patterns can ever do. Yet pattern systems still do not address all the needs of a professional and holistic software development using patterns. In particular:

- What are the important design and implementation problems that arise during the development of a specific type of software system?
- How do all these problems relate to one another and in what order are they resolved most optimally?
- What (alternative) patterns can help to resolve each problem most effectively in the presence of the other problems?
- What are the criteria for deciding which of the alternative patterns for resolving a particular problem is most suitable in a given situation?

■ How is the selected pattern instantiated most effectively within the existing (partial) software architecture?

Recognizing this leads almost directly to the concept of pattern languages [POSA4]. In a nutshell:

A pattern language is a network of tightly-interwoven patterns that defines a process for resolving a set of related, interdependent software development problems systematically.

For example, there are pattern languages that support

■ Constructing entire applications, for example distributed systems [POSA4], or business information systems [Fow97]

■ Developing major application parts such as components [VSW02]

■ Addressing problem areas of common interest, such as security or human computer interaction [Bor01]

■ Programming in a good style, for example, the Smalltalk best practice patterns [Bec97]

Basically, a pattern language exposes the same properties as an individual pattern, but at a higher, system-oriented level. It defines both a process and a thing, produces designs of high quality, allows the creation—or generation—of many alternative designs, supports the understanding of the challenges associated with a specific problem domain or the development of a specific application type, and tackles problems in an intelligent, often unusual and lateral way.

The following excerpt from [POSA4] summarizes the concrete look-and-feel of a high-quality pattern language.

> One or more patterns define the 'entry point' of the pattern language and address the most fundamental problems that must be resolved when building its 'thing'. The entry point patterns also define the starting point for the language's process: every software development that uses the language begins there. The creation process for the chosen entry point pattern then describes what concrete activities must be performed to resolve the specific problem that this pattern addresses. This process not only specifies how to implement the proposed problem resolution, however. It also suggests other patterns from the language that could be used to address sub-problems of the original problem, as well as the order in which to apply these other patterns. If several alternative patterns are referenced for resolving a particular sub-problem, the trade-offs of each alternative are described and hints are given for how to select the 'right' alternative for a specific application.

> Following any of the pattern suggestions made by the entry point pattern's creation process, the process defined by the pattern language leads to another pattern and its associated creation process—which is then applied to resolve the problem that the other pattern addresses. This process can reference yet more patterns, to resolve sub-problems of the sub-problem of the initial problem. Using either a breadth-first or a depth-first approach, or even a mixture of both approaches, this iterative process of following a pattern reference and applying the referenced pattern's creation process continues until there are no more pattern references to follow. The particular path taken through the pattern language then defines a sequence—or 'sentence'—of patterns that guides the design and implementation of the 'thing' that is this language's subject.

A pattern language is the highest organizational form for patterns currently known. It also the most successful organizational form with respect to the original goal of software patterns: to support the construction of real-world, productive software most professionally. For this reason, the patterns in this book are organized whenever possible into a pattern language, instead of just cataloguing them separately.

1.7 Documenting Patterns

Patterns, whether they are stand-alone or integrated into a pattern system or pattern language, must be presented in an appropriate form if we are to understand and discuss them. A good description helps us grasp the essence of a pattern immediately—what is the problem the pattern addresses, and what is the proposed solution? A good description also provides us with all the details necessary to implement a pattern, and to consider the consequences of its application.

Many pattern forms are known and used [POSA4], but for this book we decided to follow the format developed for the *Pattern-Oriented Software Architecture* series [POSA1], as it best fits our goals and audience:

Name

The name and a short summary of the pattern.

Also Known As

Other names for the pattern, if any are known.

Example

A real-world example demonstrating the existence of the problem and the need for the pattern. Throughout the description we refer to examples to illustrate solutions and implementation aspects, where this is necessary or useful.

Context

The situations in which the pattern may apply.

Problem

The problem the pattern addresses, including a discussion of its associated forces.

Solution

The fundamental solution principle underlying the pattern.

Structure

A detailed specification of the structural aspects of the pattern, using appropriate notations.

Dynamics

Typical scenarios describing the run-time behavior of the pattern.

Implementation

Guidelines for implementing the pattern. These are only a suggestion, not an immutable rule. You should adapt the implementation to meet your needs, by adding different, extra, or more detailed steps, or by re-ordering the steps. Whenever applicable we give UML fragments to illustrate a possible implementation, often describing details of the example problem.

Example Resolved

Discussion of any important aspects for resolving the example that are not yet covered in the *Solution*, *Structure*, *Dynamics*, and *Implementation* sections.

Variants

A brief description of variants or specializations of a pattern.

Known Uses

Examples of the use of the pattern, taken from existing systems.

Consequences

The benefits the pattern provides, and any potential liabilities.

See Also

References to patterns that solve similar problems, and to patterns that help us refine the pattern we are describing.

It is important to note that not all fields of this pattern form are mandatory. For example, not all patterns have alternative names or variants. Alternatively, for some patterns it is hard, or unnecessary, to provide detailed descriptions of its structure, behavior, and implementation, because all information can be integrated well into the core solution description. Likewise, if an example is embedded within every section of the form, there may not be a need for separate example sections.

Writing patterns is hard. Achieving a crisp pattern description takes several review and revision cycles. Many experts from all over the world have helped us with this activity, and we owe them our special thanks. Thus, we give credit to all who helped to shape a particular pattern in the introduction to each chapter.

1.8 A Brief Note on The History of Patterns

The architect Christopher Alexander laid the foundations on which many of today's pattern approaches are built. He, and members of the Center for Environmental Structure in Berkeley, California, spent more than twenty years developing an approach to architecture that used patterns. This 'entirely new attitude in architecture and planning' is published in a series of books [ANA+87] [AIS+77] [Ale79] [ASA+75]. Alexander describes over two hundred and fifty patterns that span a wide range of scale and abstraction, from structuring towns and regions down to paving paths and decorating individual rooms. He also defined the fundamental Context-Problem-Solution structure for describing patterns, the 'Alexander form.' Recently, some software pattern writers have started to distance themselves a little from Alexander, since they feel that his views on patterns do not translate directly into software patterns. They acknowledge the importance of Alexander's work, but would like to go their own way. Despite this discussion, however, Alexander's work is well worth reading by everybody who is interested in patterns.

The pioneers of patterns in software development are Ward Cunningham Kent Beck. They read Alexander's books and were inspired to adapt his ideas for software development. Ward and Kent's first five patterns deal with the design of user interfaces—their patterns WINDOW PER TASK, FEW PANES, STANDARD PANES, NOUNS AND VERBS, and SHORT MENUS mark the birth of patterns in software engineering.

Four software design experts—known as the 'Gang-of-Four' in the pattern community—paved the way for the wide acceptance of patterns in software engineering. Erich Gamma, Richard Helm, Ralph Johnson, and John Vlissides are the authors of the seminal work *Design Patterns – Elements of Reusable Object-Oriented Software* [GoF95]. Many other software experts followed the path paved by the Gang-of-Four, as we briefly summarized in Section 1.3, *Patterns Everywhere*, producing an almost endless list of publications on patterns. At the current end of this path is this book. Its goal is to fill a still-blank spot on the world map of patterns: security.

1.9   The Pattern Community and its Culture

Software engineers all over the world are currently documenting their experience using patterns. This community is very active, interactive and supportive, with the goal of sharing and integrating knowledge, and spreading the word about successful software development practice.

The major forum of the pattern community is the PLoP (Pattern Languages of Programming) conference series, which is held in the US (the original PLoP and Chili-PLoP), Germany (EuroPLoP), Scandinavia (Viking PLoP), Brazil (Sugar Loaf PLoP), Japan (Mensore PLoP), and Australia (Koala PLoP). Its proceedings are published as a series of books [PLoPD1] [PLoPD2] [PLoPD3] [PLoPD4].

The culture celebrated by the pattern community—and consequently the culture of its PLoP conferences—differs significantly from other, more traditional cultures for presenting and discussing scientific work. It exhibits the following characteristics:

- A focus on practicability. The community looks for pattern descriptions of proven solutions to problems, rather than on presenting the latest scientific results.

- An aggressive disregard of originality. Pattern authors do not need to be the original developers of the solutions they describe.

- Non-anonymous review. Patterns are 'shepherded' rather than reviewed. The 'shepherd' contacts the authors of pattern papers and discusses the patterns with them. The goal is to improve the pattern such that it can be accepted for review at a PLoP conference and suffer as little rejection as possible.

- Writer's workshops instead of presentations. At PLoP conferences, patterns are discussed in writer's workshops made up of conference attendees, rather than being presented by their authors in open forum.

- Careful editing. Authors get the chance to include the feedback from the writer's workshops, and all patterns are copy-edited before they appear in the final conference proceedings or other book publications.

Most patterns presented in this book were discussed at the PLoP and EuroPLoP conferences, and thus went through its quality assurance process. In fact, the idea for this book was born at a security pattern workshop at EuroPLoP 2002. This guarantees that the book covers the collective experience of world-leading security experts, rather than the ideas and experiences of a sole and possibly novice individual.

To discuss patterns and pattern-related issues, the pattern community also offers several mailing lists and a World Wide Web page. The URL of the pattern home page is:

`http://www.hillside.net/patterns/`

This page provides useful information about forthcoming pattern events and available books on patterns, and offers references to other Web pages about patterns. There are also several Internet mailing lists on patterns. You can find their details and information on how to subscribe to them on the patterns home page shown above.

The unofficial steering committee of the pattern community is Hillside Incorporated, also known as the 'Hillside Group,' and its European arm Hillside Europe e.V. The Hillside Group is a non-profit organization made up of leading software experts: its main goal is to propagate the use of patterns in software development, to lead the pattern community, and to give support to newcomers in this new discipline of software engineering. The 'spiritual father' of the Hillside Group is Kent Beck. The Hillside Group also organizes and sponsors the PLoP conference series.

By joining the pattern community you can take advantage of all this experience, captured in many well-documented patterns that are ready for practical use. You will also be able to share your own experience in software development with other experts by writing your own patterns. We thus invite you to join the pattern community if you are not already part of it. Visit the pattern home page, subscribe to the pattern mailing lists, look at the various pattern books, attend the PLoP conferences, capture your own experience as patterns and share them with experts from all over the world. You will certainly be rewarded by many positive 'Aha!' effects, just as we were when we first discovered patterns.

CHAPTER

2

Security Foundations

My mother used to say that there are no strangers, only friends you haven't met yet. She's now in a maximum security twilight home in Australia.

Dame Edna Everage

In this chapter we present an introduction to the field of security. This introduction includes a general overview of security, followed by a taxonomy of security areas. A list of security resources is also provided. The scope of this introduction is intended to be the unabridged field of security at both enterprise and system levels, although there is more emphasis on information technology (IT) related security. The patterns we present later in the book cover many, but not all, of the areas of security introduced in this chapter.

2.1 Overview

In the broadest sense, security is the totality of all services and mechanisms that protect an enterprise. Several terms have been used over time for this, but generally with more limited meanings:

- *Data confidentiality* refers only to protection against unauthorized disclosure of data

- *Data integrity* involves maintaining data accuracy and completeness and protecting system components

A basic aim of security is to isolate or restrict actors—the humans or automated processes—that are the active entities in systems from having unrestricted access to the resources, such as data and all other forms of information, of the system. Such isolation or restriction is typically provided via a myriad of services and mechanisms that include physical controls such as door locks, and technical controls such as access controls. The security field is extremely diverse, with one end of its spectrum involving protection of a system and the building that houses it from fire and other disasters, and the other involving decision-making processes that determine who may access system resources, where and when. Security may be thought of as constituting three logical areas: *procedural, environmental or physical,* and *technical.* While there is some overlap between the areas and all need to be integrated, one can usually identify a particular mechanism as one of these types.

- Procedural security measures include administrative security or management constraints. They encompass operational, administrative, and accountability procedures.

- Environmental or physical security measures include all elements of personnel and physical security.

- Personnel security involves the policies and procedures required to establish authorization.

- Physical security protects all enterprise resources and assets from physical hazards.

- Technical security measures include all communications, data, and automated information systems security. The latter includes protecting the authenticity and integrity of message traffic, protection of all hardware, software, and firmware, and protection of the data handled by the systems.

While every enterprise will have its own reasons for desiring appropriate security measures, it is easy to see at least three fundamental ones that might apply. First, the enterprise resources need to be protected because of their value to the enterprise—company secrets must remain company secrets and the buildings should not fall down. Second, many resources may require protection due to public law and/or regulations—employee data must be kept private and employees should not be subjected to unhealthy environments. Third, safety and integrity are often requirements for the processes run on automated information systems. For example, planes flown on autopilot could crash if their processes were corrupted.

The degree of security necessary for every enterprise will reflect the environments in which the enterprises operate. For automated information systems, the environment will include the authorizations and roles of people with access to the systems, physical security measures of the environment (such as secure rooms), sensitivity of the resources controlled by the systems, and the system's inherent protection mechanisms.

2.2 Security Taxonomy

Over the years security experts have worked to establish security properties, approaches, and necessary services, and have identified commercial products for securing important enterprise assets by applying security engineering. To understand the relationships between these diverse security elements, they need to be organized into a usable taxonomy.

The security area has long lacked a single unified taxonomy, but numerous specialized security taxonomies have been developed for specific purposes. The security taxonomy that will be used in this book is shown in the figure on page 18. This taxonomy is based on information from existing security taxonomies. It is not seen as the final word on security taxonomies—it is defined merely for the purposes of this book.

The taxonomy is arranged to support development of an enterprise security architecture. The three major divisions of the taxonomy, *Security Strategy and Policy*, *Services*, and *Mechanisms and Implementations*, are layered architectural divisions. Mechanisms and Implementations instantiate Services, and Services instantiate Security Strategy and Policy, which is driven by business strategies and needs.

The remainder of this section describes the various areas of this taxonomy.

Enterprise Business Strategies

The starting point for a security architecture is high-level information about the enterprise business strategy: plans, requirements, factors, external constraints, existing enterprise policies, and other information that distinguishes this enterprise from others. This information is essential, but it is outside the security taxonomy proper.

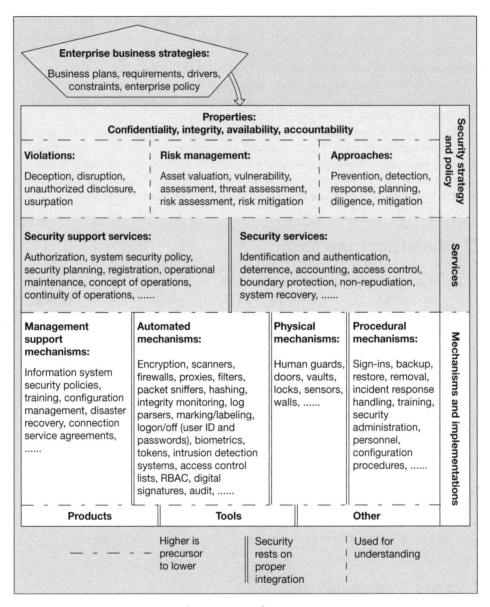

The taxonomy of security

Security Strategy and Policy

Enterprise decision-makers would like all activities that affect their enterprise to be consistent with accomplishing the enterprise's goals, reflected here in Enterprise Business Strategies. One of the important elements that gives rise to later requirements is the establishment of enterprise policies for security. The development of such policies has derivative elements, such as interpretation of superior regulations—such as strategic goals or legal requirements—and standards. Specific policies are evolved for information systems later in the process.

Whether the enterprise activities involve the introduction of an additional business opportunity, or maturing a business from an initial concept, the enterprise decision-maker identifies the items that are important to the enterprise and the business events that are essential to the realization of business goals.

The decision-maker's hope is to have the items of importance, business events and people all working synergistically to accomplish enterprise goals. This state of synergy, free of any problems, is what decision-makers tend to consider normal operation.

However, reality dictates that the enterprise must be prepared for things to go wrong within the enterprise. Security measures address events that hamper normal operations, where the events result from malicious or inadvertent actions. These events may prevent these items of importance from being used to benefit the enterprise, or may even damage the enterprise. The role of security is to provide a degree of confidence that the enterprise can remain in a state of normal operation, or recover to a state of normal operation, when something does go wrong.

Business events that contribute to the productivity of an enterprise usually involve *assets*, including both *information assets* and *tangible assets* such as money, items of value, classified documents, vehicles, and facilities, which constitute the items of importance to the organization. There are also *actor assets*[1], such as people and software processes, that initiate business-relevant events to get the day-to-day business of the enterprise done. External actors, such as weather systems or hackers, although not necessarily business assets, but may also impact the business.

While actors and assets are often thought of as the only objects important to security, *actions*—for example *execute procedure*, *pay invoice*, *collect time reports*—are another critical ingredient. We use the term *action* to include business processes and workflows that can affect policies and procedures. In some cases the actor is very important; in others the actor is not important but the actions must occur in a particular sequence. Sometimes the action may by itself be innocuous, but because of when, where, or with/by/to whom it occurs, it causes damage. Security addresses all three components of potentially-damaging business events: the actors who initiate them, the actions that can be performed, and the assets the actors and actions may affect.

---

[1] We recognize that sometimes actors are treated as assets, depending on the particular enterprise view.

Another common misapprehension is that security should prevent harmful events from occurring. In fact it is almost impossible to prevent 100% of harmful events. Another very important component of security, therefore, is detecting harmful events and responding to them when they occur. Sometimes it is more cost-effective to invest enterprise resources in detection and response than to attempt to prevent harmful occurrences. In the end, the overall goal of enterprise security is not preventing harmful events, but mitigating the damage that could be caused by potential or actual harmful events.

Properties

When considering assets, actions, and actors, security is concerned with the protection of assets, ensuring that actions are appropriate, and holding actors responsible for their actions. Every asset has some set of associated properties that describes its needs for security.

The major security properties are *confidentiality*, *integrity*, *accountability*, and *availability*, defined for our purposes as follows:

- *Confidentiality* is the property that data is disclosed only as intended by the enterprise
- *Integrity* is the property that enterprise assets are not altered contrary to the enterprise's wishes
- *Accountability* is the property that actions affecting enterprise assets can be traced to the actor responsible for the action
- *Availability* is the property that enterprise assets, including business processes, will be accessible when needed for authorized use

Note that security properties often have subsidiary or related elements. For example, survivability is considered part of availability. Privacy, which is related to confidentiality, has roots in constitutional law and social justice requirements, and defines individuals' rights to control the collection, storage, and dissemination of information about themselves. Depending on the issues and problems to be resolved, an enterprise may consider a related element or property more significant than the primary properties we have defined.

Security properties are sometimes characterized in other ways, such as security objectives or states. Selecting one of these terms is to some extent a matter of context or preference. The term *property* refers to the fact that an asset has certain characteristics: if a data item has confidentiality, then it has the characteristic or property that it is disclosed only as intended. The term *objective* refers to the fact that an enterprise has certain goals for certain assets: an enterprise may desire that its strategic planning data have confidentiality. The term *state* refers to the fact that security properties may change over time or context: a data item may have confidentiality now, but may not tomorrow, or it may have confidentiality in a controlled database but not on a public Web site.

We chose *property*, in part because most security glossaries define confidentiality and related concepts in terms of properties.

Violations

Violations are malicious or inadvertent actions that have the potential to impair the security properties of assets. *Unauthorized disclosure*, *deception*, *disruption*, and *usurpation* are the major classes of violations. Each class of violation is related to a major class of *vulnerability*, or path by which an active enterprise can be attacked. The difference is that while a violation is an unwanted result, a vulnerability is a potential mechanism for achieving the result.

To understand the categories of violation, think of an enterprise as a living entity with a working interior and a protective opaque perimeter, defined not just by physical limits, but also by behaviors of people and systems associated with the enterprise. The living enterprise also has the ability to perform goal-driven actions, an ability to view or sense the world around it, and the ability to interact with the external world.

Each of the top-level violation areas addresses a number of smaller elements, as identified in [ISG00]:

- *Unauthorized disclosure* encompasses all violations in which the opaqueness of the protective perimeter is violated—that is, when information about an asset of the enterprise is inappropriately released to, or obtained by, any entity, whether hostile, friendly, or indifferent. An example of direct *exposure* might be an enterprise employee leaving a sensitive document on a table at Starbucks. Other types of disclosure include *interception*, unauthorized access to data traveling between authorized sources and destinations, *inference*, indirect access by reasoning from characteristics or by-products of communications, and *intrusion*, obtaining access by circumventing security protections, such as by trespass or cryptanalysis.

- *Deception* includes all cases in which the external 'senses' of the enterprise are deluded by presentation of false information, leading potentially to inappropriate actions by the enterprise. An example would be causing the enterprises's senior management to acquire and deploy software containing hidden backdoors. Types of deception include *masquerade* or spoof, in which an unauthorized entity poses as an authorized entity, *falsification*, in which false data deceives an authorized entity, and *repudiation*, in which an entity deceives another by falsely denying responsibility for an act.

- *Disruption* is injury to the working interior of the enterprise. Types of disruption include *incapacitation*, the prevention or interruption of system operation by disabling a system component, *corruption*, an undesirable alteration of operation by unauthorized modifications to system functions, data, or physical assets, and *obstruction*, interruption to the delivery of services by hindering operations. Examples include willful physical destruction of enterprise property, injury to human members of the enterprise, unauthorized changes to data, incapacitating a computer system by flooding it with input, or natural disaster such as fire or flood.

■ *Usurpation* is subversion of the command structure that directs the working interior of the enterprise. Types of usurpation include *misappropriation* or theft, obtaining unauthorized logical or physical control of a resource, and *misuse*, causing a system component to perform a function or service that is detrimental to system security. Examples include theft of physical or information resources, using backdoor software to redirect, suppress, and replace internal e-mail communications, or placing covert human agents in an organization to accomplish the same goals through written or verbal communications.

Because the four categories of violations deal with fundamental components that must exist for an enterprise to function, they cover a very broad range of situations. They do not include capture of products that have already left the enterprise, such as theft of a computer after it has been purchased and installed in someone's home. However, they do include capture of products still within the enterprise boundaries, such as the hijacking of an enterprise transportation truck carrying computers to retail merchants, since that is equivalent to disruption when it occurs within the enterprise boundary.

Risk Management

Risk management is identified in the taxonomy to demonstrate that it is necessary, both to aid in identifying the kinds of violations that might occur and to aid in development of the security solution. Risk management is necessary because it produces a sense of the real enterprise risks. Understanding real enterprise risk is an essential precursor to identifying the potential violations against which protection is actually needed. Understanding which forms of protection are actually needed is in turn an essential precursor to determining where and how to apply resources in a way that will yield positive results.

Risk management encompasses all forms of risk assessment and mitigation planning for the enterprise. The major risk management activities are asset valuation, assessments of threats, vulnerabilities, and risks, and mitigation strategies:

■ *Asset valuation* is an activity that is necessary to understand the enterprise's assets. Asset valuation applies to both tangible and intangible assets. As described in [Pet01], evaluating tangible assets involves the stated value along with any depreciation, while evaluating intangible assets involves judging the quantitative or qualitative value of the asset.

- *Threat* and *vulnerability assessments* are activities necessary to understand the protection approaches that will be needed.

- *Risk assessment* and *mitigation* are repetitive processes necessary to understand the approaches or services that are needed to provide the required asset protection.

Approaches

Security approaches define groups of related ways to address potential security violations. Once enterprise staff know the protections that are actually needed, they can determine the most resource-effective approaches to providing the required protection.

The security approaches identified in this book are *Planning, Prevention, Detection, Response* and *Diligence* [DCD+02]:

- *Planning* procedures define enterprise-wide standard operating procedures for prevention, detection, and response. Planning is normally expressed in the form of documentation.

- *Prevention* protects the security attributes of enterprise business assets by actively impeding undesirable activities that would compromise those assets.

- *Detection* identifies or detects undesirable activities that may compromise enterprise business assets.

- *Diligence* procedures are ongoing proactive measures that update security plans to improve the overall security posture of the enterprise.

- *Response* procedures address violations after they have been detected.

The purpose of these approaches is to lay the groundwork for the prevention of undesirable actions and for dealing with them effectively when they do occur. The approaches usually are not used alone, but in various combinations, with different relative effort expended on each. Specifically, prevention of undesirable actions cannot stand alone. Prevention usually must be associated with other measures:

- Detecting activities that evade prevention or that were not previously detected.

- Planning for actions allowed by actors and for allowed sequences of actions.

- Establishing procedures for performing allowed actions.

- Planning improvements.

- Managing security.

- Responding to undesirable actions that do occur.

Note that there is no predefined sequence for using these approaches. For example, a violation response may activate further prevention capabilities.

Services

Security services are general safeguards that help achieve both enterprise and system security needs. They are divided into security services and security support services. Security services instantiate one or more approaches to controlling potential or actual violations of desired security properties. Several examples are:

- *Access control* services limit access to the resources of a system to authorized entities—people, programs, and processes—only, and for authorized actions, such as how you access information.

- *Accounting* services track events that occur, that is, they observe events and record and make available information about those events. One use is to enable actions on a system to be traced to individuals, through the use of mechanisms like auditing and logging.

- *Boundary protection* services help protect a security perimeter or boundary from unauthorized penetration through the use of automated mechanisms such as firewalls, guards, and intrusion detection systems, or physical mechanisms such as walls, human guards, or even deterrents such as 'No Trespassing' signs.

- *Non-repudiation* capability or services provide protection against false denial of involvement in a communication.

- *System recovery* services provide the ability to restore a system's computational capability and data files after a system failure.

Some security services support others rather than directly supporting the approaches. For example, an *Identification and authentication* service enables the recognition of an entity and validates the identity of the entity, but also supports other services including access control and accounting.

Security support services address the underlying infrastructure that supports security services. For example:

- *Registration* support services capture the information necessary to support the identification and authorization service.

- *Authorization* support services grant access rights to an entity, while this information supports the access control service.

- *System security policy* support services define a set of laws, rules, and practices that establish how a system manages, protects, and distributes sensitive information.

The security literature sometimes defines security services to include all levels of safeguards. In this taxonomy, we distinguish between higher-level or more general safeguards, which we call *services*, and lower-level or more specific safeguards, which we call *mechanisms*. One reason is that in many cases, the higher-level services can be implemented by multiple mechanisms, as discussed in the next section.

Mechanisms

Security services are dependent on the physical, procedural, or automated mechanisms available to implement those services. Mechanisms are dependent in turn on commercial products and other tools that implement those mechanisms.

The terms in the Mechanisms and Implementations section of the taxonomy are not in a one-to-one relationship with the terms in the Services section. One mechanism may support multiple services, and some services may need support from multiple mechanisms. Therefore all the required services must be taken into account when considering mechanisms and implementations.

A broad assortment of security mechanisms is available to implement the various security and security support services. Four groupings are provided in our taxonomy to attempt to gain a better perspective on the mechanisms: management support mechanisms, automated mechanisms, physical mechanisms, and procedural mechanisms. In an architecture, selections from all four groups of mechanisms are likely to be integrated to support one or more services.

Management support mechanisms are mechanisms that control the other groups of mechanisms. Several examples are:

- *Information system security policies* address specific characteristics of information systems. They expand and particularize for specific mechanisms the requirements captured in higher-level policies. They will usually establish the kinds of controls that are needed.

- *Security training* may be provided at many levels, including security officers, maintenance staff, and end users.

- *Configuration management* mechanisms play an important role in ensuring that enterprise systems are configured correctly to establish and maintain a secure state.

- *Disaster recovery* mechanisms establish the ability for an enterprise to restore/ replace information, information systems, and other systems and continue to operate in the face of natural or other disasters such as fire, flood, power failure, loss of key personnel, or massive data corruption.

- *Connection service agreements*, sometimes called *interface agreements*, delineate the requirements for both sides of automated connections and define assumptions, expectations, and exclusions.[2]

---

[2] Connection service agreements are well-covered in the IBM e-business patterns [IBM].

Automated mechanisms are mechanisms that rely on information technology. It is common for the term 'security' to be used to mean automated mechanisms that support security services. Automated mechanisms may support only one service directly, for example access control lists directly supporting only access control, or they may support multiple services, for example encryption supporting identification and authentication (I&A), access control, and many others. A brief list of automated mechanisms is provided in the taxonomy. Obviously, there are many other automated mechanisms.

Physical mechanisms include human guards, their locations and protective weapons; physical boundaries established using vaults, locks, and walls, and physical sensors that detect physical movement, changes in temperatures, moisture, smoke, or other problems.

Procedural mechanisms address the development, dissemination, and enforcement of security procedures for the enterprise. Typical security procedures for an enterprise include back-up procedures, restoration procedures, facility sign-in procedures, procedures for configuring systems, procedures to remove systems, procedures addressing personnel security, and procedures for incident response handling.

Physical and procedural mechanisms are essential components of enterprise security. They can support single or multiple services, and can affect the need for other mechanisms in any group. For example, access control might be established using either an automated decision based on I&A and access control lists at each system, by a guard at a vault entry point, or both. Equally, a human guard may support the I&A service and the access control service at the same time.

Procedural mechanisms are often necessary to support management support mechanisms. For example, the configuration management process requires procedures for change request approval. In other cases, procedural mechanisms support automated mechanisms. For example, the response to a security incident affecting an automated mechanism may involve procedures for documenting the incident or restoring the system.

2.3 General Security Resources

To find a structured and systematic introduction to security, the simplest approach is to find a good book. Many books and other resources about security are available. Our goal here is to identify what we consider some of the best resources.

Most books fall into one of the following two categories:

- *General security textbooks*, intended for general introduction to the subject. They try to cover most of the relevant topics. Some of the best are [And01], [Bis03] [Gol99], [Pfl03], [Sum97]. [Bis03] is a detailed book with lots of theory, while [Gol99] is concise and conceptual. [And01] has a descriptive, practical approach.

- *Books on specialized topics*. These may cover cryptography, network security, Web Services security, or similar topics.

Another classification of security books is:

- *Practitioner-oriented*, with no theory and usually containing collections of examples. These do not provide a conceptual foundation, but may be acceptable for the study of specific systems and for implementation details.
- *Books oriented towards university courses*. Their technical level is generally higher and they require more Computer Science background. The books mentioned above fall in this category.

Another way to acquire a general introduction to security is to take a course. Many universities offer graduate or undergraduate courses. SANS [SANSb] and the Computer Security Institute [CSI03] offer a variety of short courses.

Web resources are useful because of their easy availability, but their level of quality is very variable. Some are sites with news about incidents or new technical developments, for example Security Advisor [ADV], CERT Coordination Center [CERTa], Devx [DEVX], Google Security Directory [Google], IEEE Security [ITS], Microsoft Developer Network [MSDN], National Institute of Standards and Technology [NIST03], the SANS Institute [SANSb], and the Yahoo! Security and Encryption directory [Yahoo]. Others present vendor material, which is useful if you are looking for descriptions of specific systems, but it is unwise to trust their evaluations or comparisons.

A number of security journals are published, such as ACM Transactions on Security [ACM], Computers and Security [CAS], and InfoSecurity Magazine [ISM]. Some general technical journals publish articles about security, for example Communications of the ACM [ACM] and IEEE Transactions on Dependable and Secure Computing [ITD]. A few of these are available on the Web.

Conferences are a useful way to gain access to tutorials on latest developments, to see new products, or to see the current research on security. There are several research conferences about security:

- IFIP WG 11.3 Working Conference on Data and Application Security,
  `http://seclab.dti.unimi.it/~ifip113`
- IEEE Conference on Security and Privacy,
  `http://www.ieee-security.org/`
- ACM Computers and Communications Conference,
  `http://www.acm.org/sigsac/ccs.html`
- European Symposium on Research in Computer Security (ESORICS),
  `http://www.laas.fr/~esorics/esorics.html`

Other conferences are industry oriented and emphasize current products and practical aspects:

- RSA Data Security Conference,
  `http://www.rsaconference.com`
- Computer Security Institute Annual Computer Security Conference,
  `http://www.gocsi.com/#annual`
- SANS Annual Conference,
  `http://www.sans.org/SANS2003`
- Annual Computer Security Applications Conference (ACSAC),
  `http://www.acsac.org`

3

Security Patterns

Most interesting of all, however, is the lesson that the bulk of computer security research and development activity is expended on activities which are of marginal relevance to real needs. A paradigm shift is underway, and a number of recent threads point towards a fusion of security with software engineering, or at the very least to an influx of software engineering ideas.

Ross Anderson, in 'Why Cryptosystems Fail'

In this chapter we explain the concept of security patterns and our approach to them in the book. The security patterns discussion builds on the security introduction in this chapter and on our general patterns introduction. We discuss foundations of security patterns in terms of history, pattern structure, and motivation. We also discuss sources of knowledge for security patterns in terms of mining for security patterns. Finally, we present running examples that appeared to be useful in some patterns in the book.

3.1 The History of Security Patterns

Yoder and Barcalow wrote the first paper on security patterns [YB97]. They included a variety of patterns useful in different aspects of security. Yoder and Barcalow used the GoF template to describe security aspects and to structure their patterns as a pattern language. Before them, at least three papers [FP01] [FWF94] [Ess97] had shown object-oriented models of secure systems without calling them 'patterns' or using one of the standard pattern templates. In the following year, 1998, two more pattern contributions were published: a pattern language for cryptography [BRD98], and a pattern for access control [NG98]. Several others have appeared subsequently, and we have now a substantial collection, a good number of which appear in this book.

It is more convenient to show these patterns according to the architectural levels to which they belong than to classify them chronologically:

- At the abstract level we have patterns that describe security models, including [FP01], patterns for access matrix authorization, ROLE-BASED ACCESS CONTROL (249) (RBAC), and multi-level models, and [Wel99], a pattern for the Clark-Wilson model. A simpler pattern for RBAC appears in [YB97].

- Some patterns deal with abstract models of enforcement and include SINGLE ACCESS POINT (279) [YB97], CHECK POINT (287), a type of REFERENCE MONITOR (256), [YB97], and REFERENCE MONITOR (256) [Fer02]. One possible implementation of REFERENCE MONITOR (256) is the INTERCEPTOR pattern in [POSA2].

- An implementation model of RBAC in the form of a set of patterns is shown in [KBZ01].

- Capabilities are a good way to implement access matrix rights at the hardware and operating system level. Their application to control access to classes is described in [Fra99]. The use of metaclasses and reflection is another interesting way to implement these models at such levels [Wel99].

- Several security patterns for Java appear in [Jaw00]. An implementation of RBAC using Java is described in [Giu99].

- Patterns for operating systems were developed in [Fer02] and [FS03]. These include CONTROLLED OBJECT FACTORY (331), CONTROLLED OBJECT MONITOR (335), AUTHENTICATOR (323), VIRTUAL ADDRESS SPACE, CONTROLLED EXECUTION ENVIRONMENT (346), and REFERENCE MONITOR (256). These contributions have been merged for this book.

- Patterns for firewalls are discussed in [FLS+03c] and [Sch03]. These include packet filter and proxy-based firewalls. These two papers have been updated, extended, and merged in this book.

- Pattern languages for cryptography are described in [BRD98] and [LP01].

- Patterns for distributed systems include BODYGUARD [NG98], a framework for access control and filtering of distributed objects, which combines several patterns [HLF00]. The GoF book [GoF95] mentions the possible use of proxies for distributed systems security. A pattern for a remote secure proxy is given in [Amo01]. Authentication in distributed systems is considered in [Bro99] and [FW03].

- Agent systems is a new area in which security patterns have been applied recently [MGS03].

- Layers, one of the fundamental patterns in [POSA1], was re-interpreted as a security pattern in [FP01].

- All these patterns are about systems aspects. Enterprise-oriented patterns appeared for the first time at EuroPLoP 2002, including patterns for task-based rights management [EH02] and for a variety of management aspects [Rom02].

Some paper discuss general aspects of security patterns:

- A general discussion of security patterns including some network security patterns is presented in [SR01].

- Araujo and Weiss link patterns to non-functional requirements in [AW02].

- The correspondence of patterns to levels is discussed in [FF99].

The PLoP 2002 and EuroPLoP 2002 and 2003 conferences had Focus Groups on security patterns and a special Web site, http://www.securitypatterns.org, has been created to keep track of existing patterns and to establish a non-profit forum for security pattern enthusiasts [Sch]. This book is the result of the EuroPLoP meetings. Beside this mini-community, other groups have started to work on security patterns. A selection of these patterns is outlined in Chapter 5.

3.2 Characteristics of Security Patterns

Referring to the pattern template we introduced in Section 1.7, *Documenting Patterns*, we identify the key pattern elements that reveal the characteristics of a security pattern. Not all elements are listed here, as there is no difference between security patterns and regular patterns (for example, regarding structure and dynamics). In short, we define a security pattern as follows:

A security pattern describes a particular recurring security problem that arises in specific contexts, and presents a well-proven generic solution for it. The solution consists of a set of interacting roles that can be arranged into multiple concrete design structures, as well as a process to create one particular such structure.

Example

In order to illustrate the context of a security pattern, references to concrete examples could be provided. Analogies to real-world scenarios are also suitable, such as the evolution of a medieval village that is used in Chapter 9, *System Access Control Architecture*, which helps to introduce the context and problem. In some situations a quite straightforward example is useful, while in other situations a more elaborate example fits better. For example, protecting the addresses of a monastery—a tribute to the monastery of the Kloster Irsee, which hosts the EuroPLoP conferences—addresses security in a small organization with hardly any experience or awareness of security. In contrast, protecting gemstones in a museum addresses security in quite a large organization with experience and awareness on security.

Context

The context of the security pattern describes the situation—the general environment and conditions—under which the problem occurs. It can also be useful to list patterns that set the context, that is, patterns that have been applied before. Such patterns might be required to ensure that certain requirements or assumptions hold.

Problem

In the field of security a problem occurs whenever an asset, such as an enterprise, a system, or an application, is protected in an insufficient way against abuse, or a situation arises that can allow security violations. Such security violations can occur at different levels, such as organization, architecture, and operations, and this determines the type of the solution. In addition, every application—for example, financial management—has both functional requirements and non-functional requirements: the associated forces. Non-functional requirements include non-security requirements such as performance, as well as security requirements such as the confidentiality of business financial data.

In the process of applying countermeasures in the form of security components or systems, such as biometric authentication, to satisfy the security non-functional requirements of the mission system, an analogous set of requirements applies to the security system: functional, non-security non-functional (for example, performance), and security non-functional (for example, confidentiality of biometric information).

Security usually has an impact on many other requirements, such as performance and usability. For example, a specific solution can be easier to learn, slower, or more difficult to use. The figure illustrates how various forces can support or hinder one another. Based on the preferences of the user—for example, performance is an important issue—the most suitable solution needs to be identified. The solution must balance such conflicting requirements.

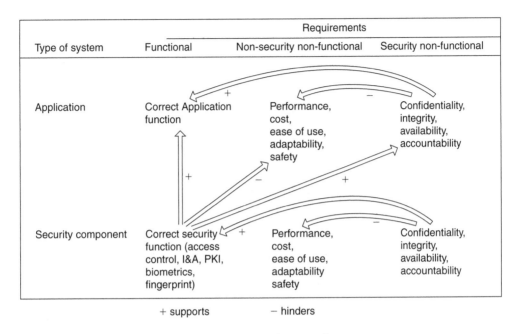

	Requirements		
Type of system	Functional	Non-security non-functional	Security non-functional
Application	Correct Application function	Performance, cost, ease of use, adaptability, safety	Confidentiality, integrity, availability, accountability
Security component	Correct security function (access control, I&A, PKI, biometrics, fingerprint)	Performance, cost, ease of use, adaptability safety	Confidentiality, integrity, availability, accountability

+ supports   − hinders

The impact of security forces

Solution

Appropriate solutions are determined by the context, the problem and the forces of the pattern. Note that security patterns are not limited to architectural or design patterns. Depending of the type of the problem, the fundamental solution principle can be at one or more different levels—organization, architecture, operations, processes, and so on. Countermeasures are applied to reduce the effect of an attack or threat. Such countermeasures—prevention, detection, reaction—have different effects on the overall security level.

Consequences

A discussion of the benefits and drawbacks of a solution helps us understand the consequences of applying a security pattern, and to understand how the forces have been resolved. As we have already noted, security is always hard to prove. In fact it is much easier to show how something goes wrong. It can be useful to show how the security pattern can be applied in an incorrect way, that is, it helps to warn about pitfalls and refer to variants of the pattern.

See Also

As some solutions may introduce new security problems, additional patterns usually have to be considered. The same holds true for problems that are only partly solved, or related problem areas that could not be considered within the given security pattern at all.

We have not mentioned the Structure, Dynamics, Implementation, Example Resolved, Variants, or Known Uses parts of the pattern form here, as they are not specific to security patterns.

3.3   Why Security Patterns?

Patterns have proven successful in many areas of software development, and they appear to be particularly valuable for secure systems development. Specifically, we see the following advantages of a pattern approach to security:

- Patterns codify basic security knowledge in a structured and understandable way.

- The pattern representation is familiar to software developers and system engineers, a key portion of their audience.

- Because patterns are already used to capture organization and system engineering knowledge, using patterns to capture security knowledge helps to improve the integration of security into systems and enterprises, where it is clearly needed.

- Much of current security focus is on low-level implementation and products. One of the goals of this book is to focus on higher-level architecture and enterprise issues. Using the pattern approach at all levels extends the security focus in a single common structure and terminology, which helps to integrate the higher and lower levels.

In general, the explicit pattern discussion of context, problem, and forces provides guidance in using the patterns. We will discuss this in the following from different points of view.

Does Only the Solution Matter?

There are many misunderstandings about security, in particular about its terminology and about the way to address and establish an adequate level of security. In general, people tend to think only about solutions. This applies not only to those working in security, but also to those who do not work in this area. Risks are involved in this behavior, since the consequence might be that we do not know the problem solved, the consequences of the chosen solution or the forces that influence the correct working of the solution. We will also not learn from the pitfalls others have experienced. We also do not question whether the best solution for another organization is also the best solutions in our situation. Hence, by implementing the solution, we might in fact provide the organization and ourselves with a false sense of security.

Patterns can be extremely valuable for security because they emphasize not only the solution, but also the problem. The pattern template forces us to document the problem explicitly, enumerate the forces, explain the context of the problem and the solution, as well as its pitfalls and consequences.

A Solution, But What is the Problem?

To reiterate, security is an area in which people focus heavily on the solution and hardly ever think about the problem. Often it is very helpful to ask people about the problem they have solved (or think they have solved). For example, if PKI[1] is the answer (the solution), well, what was the question (the problem)?

Security solutions usually affect multiple security aspects. Take the example of a VPN (virtual private network): it provides confidentiality, which is why it is called a *private* network, but it also provides integrity, since most VPNs use cryptography to ensure integrity by hashing. In certain implementations, a VPN might also provide authentication.

At first sight we only see the benefits. But in practice, a solution without a well-defined problem has disadvantages as well. Because things change over time: people responsible for security, both in design and operation, come and go, threats come and go, solutions come and go. In the end everybody still knows the solution, but they tend to forget about the original problem that was solved by this solution. So how should people react when a new product, a new feature or a new threat comes along? Also, if the problem is not well defined, we might be solving the wrong problem.

In Which Situations Can the Solution Be Applied?

Once you have determined that you do have the same problem, you might consider to apply the same solution. Another interesting aspect now arises for consideration: the context of the problem.

Imagine you are a sheep farmer and you consider building a four-foot high fence. That might be the solution to the problem of your animals getting out of your farm. But will this solution fit for any farmer with the problem of his animals getting out of the farm? Will this solution work for a chicken farmer with the problem of his chicken getting out of the farm? That is the importance of the context of the problem.

---

[1] Public key infrastructure (PKI) is a system that allows third-party vetting of user identity and binding of public keys to users. The public keys are typically in certificates.

There are multiple aspects to consider in the context of the problem:

- *Type of organization*: the size of the organization, the style of management, local or international, and so on
- *Line of business*: governmental, financial, industrial, and so on
- *Culture of the organization or its users*: formal or informal, hierarchically structured, and so on
- *Traditional or e-business*: purely traditional, business-to-business, business to consumer, e-government, and so on
- *High reputation, in the spotlight*: low-profile, the level of media attention, public reputation, attractiveness to hackers, and so on

What Forces Determine the Solution?

By now you have established that you not only consider the same solution, but that in fact you do have the same problem in the same context. Alas, this still does not guarantee the correct working of the solution. There are specific forces that influence the correct working of the solution, and it's wise to learn these forces and take them into consideration when building the solution.

These forces may include, but are not limited to:

- The number of users
- The use to which the system is put
- The type of users
- Whether the system exists in a homogenous or a heterogeneous environment
- The awareness of security in the organization

The benefit of a pattern is that relevant forces are documented and explained in the pattern, which helps you to recognize and deal with the forces when you choose the solution.

What are the Consequences of the Solution?

Do you always know the consequences of your choices? Well, of course there are certain situations in life in which you certainly do not even want to know the consequences of your choices. In providing security however, it is better to think about the consequences beforehand in order to avoid mistakes, incomplete or even wrong solutions.

A pattern describes the consequences of the solution it provides, which can include:

- Maintenance: regular or irregular, amount or frequency, and so on
- Costs: not only in buying, but also licenses, long-term costs, and so on

- Decrease of usability
- Suitability of the solution in the future
- Knowledge: required education, knowledge maintenance, ease of understanding, and so on
- Whether it is a point solution or part of a framework

Lessons Learned (By Others)

One of the best parts of a pattern, which you get for free, is the experience of others. Practical experience, not theory—that is what this is about. What did others learn about implementing the solution? How do they describe the things to do or not to do. In fact, things not to do might even be more valuable. Benefits and pitfalls are also included. One of the most interesting aspects to consider is the situation in which the solution is *not* applicable, despite the problem and the context. These are things you will not find in textbooks.

There is More Than the Solution

Of course, the solution is the most important and interesting part of a pattern. However, there is definitely more to consider. Rethink the problem, pay attention to the context and think about forces, consequences and lessons learned. Furthermore, references point to more detailed treatment of specific subjects, and a system of patterns shows how different but related security areas are interconnected, which further promotes security integration. These aspects together are part of a pattern—and that is the added value of a pattern.

It is critical to implement the right solution, especially in security, taking into account all necessary aspects, because just implementing the solution might lead to a false sense of security. Using security patterns helps you to address this.

3.4 Sources for Security Pattern Mining

In Chapter 2 we discussed some general resources for acquiring an introduction to security. However, such resources can also serve the purpose of documenting security patterns. There are several ways to 'mine' patterns from these and other knowledge resources. For example, Norm Kerth and Ward Cunningham identified three general approaches to pattern mining [KC97]. Following an *introspective approach*, people analyze systems that they have already built and try to identify solutions that worked well. By its very nature, this approach leads to patterns that are limited to individual experiences. An author must therefore take care that other experts also agree that his insights are indeed patterns, and that they apply the same solutions to a given problem, too.

Applying an *artifactual approach*, the pattern's author examines software arti-facts for systems in whose design and development they were not involved. Here the author investigates systems that have been built by different people who were trying to solve a similar problem. They try to find the commonalities and to write them down in a more abstract, unified form. The chances are high that this will result in a pattern, but as the author is not necessarily an expert, had the experts the oppor-tunity to look at the resulting pattern, additional refinements to the pattern might be necessary.

Finally, the *sociological approach* involves several experts in the problem domain. Different people who have built similar systems are asked how they solved particular problems and why the solutions were good. Through interviews the problems in the system and the interactions between developers can be determined. Here it is possible to acquire direct feedback on the pattern from the experts themselves. In this way, a sound pattern can be expected as a result.

Note that this list might not be complete, while combinations of these approaches are often applied to achieve useful results.

Enterprise Security Standards

Many security standards and guidelines are available as a source for mining security patterns. This has several advantages, such as:

- Using standards can be a source of inspiration. Experts usually know the solu-tions to given problems. However, if you ask them to write down their know-how, they may run into trouble, because they rely on knowledge that is a result of long-lasting experience. In other words, their knowledge is not explicitly available in their minds. Security standards helps to express the more difficult aspects of security patterns, allowing the authors to concentrate fully on the solution.

- You can expect security experts to have written the standards. Public feedback helped to improve such standards over time, so they should be sound in both form and content. One can also expect that following security standards will contribute to the completeness of a security pattern system, as its gaps can be identified more easily.

- Security standards help to achieve a more standardized terminology for security patterns. They can also help to ensure that standard security requirements are met.

In the remainder of this section we introduce selected security standards and discuss how they can be useful for mining security patterns.

ISO 17799

The focus of the ISO 17799 standard is the management of security [ISO17799]. The British Standards Institute (BSI) developed the standard as British Standard 7799. As it was widely used beyond the national level, however, it finally became an international standard and was adopted by the ISO. Today it is used all over the world, and several tests and audits that are compliant with ISO 17799 are available.

The standard is organized in a chapter and section hierarchy that represents topics and subtopics of security management. For example, the topic 'Physical and Environmental Security' is subdivided into 'Secure Areas,' 'Equipment Security,' and 'General Control.' Pattern authors can refer to this as an analogous context hierarchy.

Each subtopic is introduced with a brief discussion of its objectives: what should be achieved by the application of the subsequent controls. This can be seen more as a description of forces than the actual problem, as the objectives describe requirements in a given context. The actual problem is outlined in the description of each control. However, this is only a rudimentary support for pattern authors, as the level of detail doesn't go beyond very short—and sometimes vague—statements of what the problem actually is. For example, 'Equipment should be sited or protected to reduce the risks from environmental threats and hazards, and opportunities for unauthorized access.'

The controls describe best practices in the various areas of security management. By their nature, these controls are at a rather high level and should be supplemented with additional and more detailed documentation.

If available, relationships to other controls are mentioned as references to the corresponding section.

ISO 13335

Similar to ISO 17799, this standard addresses the management of IT security [ISO13335-1]. The standard is divided into three parts. Part 1 presents an introduction at a high management level. Parts 2 and 3 provide more detailed information for those in charge of developing and implementing security.

The management approach starts with a hierarchical determination of policies. The process begins with the definition of IT security objectives, strategies, and policies at the enterprise level. These are derived from more general enterprise objectives, strategies, and policies. In turn, policies at the system level are derived from the IT security policies.

Within this process, several key security concepts are addressed. For example, the standard identifies different kinds of assets, threats, vulnerabilities, and so on. It is also discusses how these elements are related to each other: for example, threats *exploit* vulnerabilities. This helps to address all relevant aspects of security. Setting up such a terminology can help pattern authors to classify problems and solutions appropriately.

Based on this, a couple of generic security management processes are discussed. These have to be in place to ensure that the security policies are met. Examples are configuration management, change management, risk management, and risk analysis. These processes can be seen as categories in which security activities take place. They can be used, for example, to narrow the context of security patterns, or to find groups of related security patterns.

It is important to note that the standard provides 'guidance, not solutions, on management aspects of IT security.' It can be seen as an aid for structuring security patterns properly.

Common Criteria

The Common Criteria define another international security standard [ISO15408]. National security organizations from the governments of the Netherlands, Canada, France, Germany, Great Britain, and the USA developed the Common Criteria to merge their own security standards. Here we show how the context, problem and solution elements of a security pattern could be standardized and formalized according to the Common Criteria. Note that the Common Criteria do not provide possible solutions or hints for relations between patterns.

- The Common Criteria's environmental assumptions describe security aspects of the environment in which the IT system is intended to be used. There are several assumption categories, which cover assumptions about administrators, users, data protection, communications, physical protection, and procedural protection. The user assumptions, for example, help to determine what kinds of users there are, what their motives are, their attitudes, and their access privileges. Such assumptions have to be assured by other security patterns on which the given security pattern relies. Often the IT system must comply with security policy statements. Thus an optional description of them helps to specify the context more precisely. A general policy statement could be, for example, that all information must be marked and labeled.

- The Common Criteria's security objectives address all of the identified security aspects. They reflect the stated intent and shall be suitable to counter all identified threats and cover all identified organizational security policies and assumptions.

- The Common Criteria's threats are directly related to the security objectives. One only perceives a threat if a security objective applies to the environment or the IT system, and vice versa. The security objectives are something one wants to achieve (that is, a goal) whereas the threats are something one wants protection against (that is, non-goals). The Common Criteria provide certain categories of threats and lists of detailed attacks. As such the security objectives, threats and attacks can be assigned to the problem section of a security pattern.

Specifying the forces helps to define clearly what functional security requirements have to be met by the IT system and its environment to counter the identified threats in a reasonable way. We will discuss these in more detail later.

IT Baseline Protection Manual

The German IT Baseline Protection Manual offers the default security countermeasures that should be considered for any IT system [BSI02]. Overall threat scenarios are assumed, and a process for the establishment and preservation of an appropriate security level is described. A straightforward procedure for determination of the current security level by conducting a plan or actual comparison is provided. As such this standard is not necessarily limited to national use, and is another valuable source for mining security patterns.

The IT Baseline Protection Manual provides countermeasures against threats that can occur in different layers. This seems to fit naturally with the pattern terminology. However, there are several important differences. With respect to the context, a 5-tier IT baseline protection model is provided. This covers universally applicable aspects, the infrastructure, IT systems, networks, and IT applications. Within these layers several modules can be identified. For example, the module 'Unix system' belongs to the layer of IT systems. Each module is assigned to a layer and a description of the module specifies the context in more detail. Within this description, assumptions concerning the module and its environment are made.

Threats are organized into five 'catalogs' in which each represents a class of threats that characterize them by their origin: force majeure, organizational shortcomings, human failures, technical failures, and deliberate acts. There are several hundred individual threats, about a third of them belonging to the class of deliberate acts. Beside a description of each threat, references to related threats are provided. Examples of recent occurrences of corresponding attacks are also sometimes given. Each module contains a threat scenario, a list of typical threats that are assumed to IT baseline protection of the given module.

The safeguard catalogs that contain sets of countermeasures are also organized into classes. The characteristic of each class is the point at which a countermeasure is going to be applied: infrastructure, organization, personnel, hard- and software, communications and contingency planning. For each safeguard, a responsibility for initiation and implementation is assigned. A description of how to implement the safeguard is provided. If available, relationships to complementary countermeasures are listed. Furthermore, additional controls are mentioned, such as check-lists of questions.

The IT Baseline Protection Manual also features several types of relationships. First of all, there are explicit relationships between the modules. This can be seen as a sort of precondition, allowing a sense of a hierarchy to be implemented: the countermeasures of a more general module hold also for a lower-level module. There are also relationships between threats, as well as between countermeasures. However, each module covers more than one problem and more than one solution in a given layer-based context. This is not consistent with the pattern paradigm of one context, one problem, one solution, and blurs the relationships between threats and counter-measures. As a consequence each module contains more than one pattern, and the relationships and dependencies between them are not obvious to pattern authors. Although a matrix that shows the assignment of threats and countermeasures is available, this additional knowledge cannot be used in a straightforward way, because one would always have to check explicitly which countermeasures protect against which threats.

Enterprise and System Architecture Resources

Beside national and international security standards, there are several companies and organizations that offer security information at a broad architectural enterprise and system level. In the following we discuss selected examples briefly.

NIST

Founded in 1901, the National Institute for Standards and Technology (NIST) is an agency within the U.S. Commerce Department's Technology Administration. One of NIST's eight divisions is the Computer Security Division (CSD), which publishes much information about security [NIST03]. They offer and promote awareness programs and research programs, as well as programs for developing security standards, metrics, and tests and validation programs. They also guide people in planning, implementing, managing and operating secure IT environments.

The home page of the Computer Security Resource Center (CSRC) Web site offers much information that can help in writing security patterns. For example, a set of best practices, check-lists and implementation guidelines is provided. There is also is a set of relevant federal requirements for writing security policies, together with an example. Beside such information organized by topic, NIST also offers a variety of security-related documents in their digital library.

SANS Institute

The SANS (Sys-Admin, Audit, Network, Security) Institute was established as a research and education organization in 1989 [SANSb]. The idea is that people involved in system and network security can share their knowledge—'the lessons they are learning'—and identify solutions for recent problems. As a recognized forum for security professionals, the SANS Institute provides several programs and products that are valuable and usually free of charge sources for mining security patterns.

For example, the security policy project gives guidance for everyone that needs to develop and implement a security policy [SANSc]. The resources provided include a primer to policy development, together with example policies and templates. Such information is very useful when you are looking for patterns at the enterprise level.

Another important resource is the SANS Information Security Reading Room [SANSd]. This contains more than 1,100 contributions that are categorized in seventy different security categories. For example, you can find white papers on case studies, best practices, firewalls and perimeter protection, encryption and VPNs, and many more. Note that SANS tries to ensure the accuracy of its information, but the papers are offered 'as is.'

Burton Group

The Burton Group is an example of a company that has offered analysis of infrastructure technologies since 1990. One of the areas it covers is the provision of guidance in enabling secure access to business services over standard infrastructures.

A research and consulting service of the Burton Group deals, for example, with directory and security strategies. This includes topics such as identity management—authentication, access management, provisioning, as well as single or reduced sign-on, the security of directory services and Web security—intrusion, detection, prevention and response, as well as managed security services.

The Burton Group claims to offer unbiased insights at the enterprise level. It is possible to access their library as a guest, although access is only possible if you register as a client.

Operational and Run-time Resources

Searching for security patterns leads to another viewpoint. To an engineer, it makes sense to examine situations in which systems have failed. Learning from typical errors and trying to find out how they could have been prevented can also provide input for security patterns: the author can look for common pitfalls in specific systems. Because of this, we also introduce selected sources, that provide information on system and run-time problems that need immediate fixes. There are also resources of this kind that provide information at the architectural level.

Computer Incident Response Teams

Engaged in security improvement since the Morris Internet worm incident in the late eighties, the Computer Emergency Response Teams (CERT) are counted among the most respected security information providers. CERTs are often non-profit organizations that evolve from larger security projects or organizations. The ancestor of all CERTs is the CERT Coordination Center (CERT/CC) at Carnegie Mellon University [CERTa]. In Germany there are, for example, the DFN-CERT [DC], which evolved from the German Research Network (Deutsches Forschungsnetz, DFN) and the

RUS-CERT [RC] established at the University of Stuttgart. Another well-known example is the Australian CERT-AU [CA].

A primary goal of any CERT organization is to assemble, process and provide information about vulnerabilities. By means of advisories, they warn regularly about severe vulnerabilities that could have major impact. They also observe areas such as viruses and Trojan horses. As CERTs attach great importance to the completeness of the information included in the advisories, these are not always up-to-date, as it requires time to collect and verify all the information about a specific vulnerability and how it can be fixed. Furthermore, CERTs follow a non-disclosure publication policy—they only publish an advisory when a fix or workaround is guaranteed. Often this also delays the publication of an advisory.

Beyond advisories, CERT/CC offers two other types of notifications:

■ Vulnerability notes contain information about recently-discovered vulnerabilities. These notes can evolve into advisories at a later time.

■ Incident notes, which contain information about the occurrence of exploitations of potential vulnerabilities.

Hacker Groups

Hacker groups constitute another important group of security information providers. Motivated in various ways and typically with high expertise, these groups of people are engaged in uncovering vulnerabilities. Some of them also publish their insights. In contrast to CERT-like organizations, they often don't care whether a too-early disclosure of a vulnerability and its exploitation could lead to severe damage. Exchanging information, hacker groups often operate Web sites and sometimes public USENET newsgroups or instant messaging channels. The Chaos Computer Club (CCC) and Phrack are examples of hacker groups that offer their own Web content.

Security Companies

Many consulting companies for security, as well as manufacturers of security software, publish security-related information on a regular basis. By nature this is not an unselfish act, but rather a proof of competence. In the case of a software manufacturer, it can also be seen as advertising for their product portfolio.

For example, the Australian company INFILSEC Systems Security called its vulnerability database a 'vulnerability engine' that can serve as a tool for manufacturers, system administrators, security consultants and analysts. The idea was to develop and operate a central repository for vulnerabilities of operating systems, applications, and protocols. Besides, it was planned to store information about solutions and to use mailing lists such as Bugtraq as input.

Another example is Internet Security Systems (ISS), which sells security software and offers consulting services. They also operate the vulnerability database X-Force.

Software and IT Companies

Software and IT companies represent another source of security information on their own. They publish information about security problems and corresponding solutions that employ their products. We can safely assume that almost no company publishes such information on a voluntary basis. Typically, information is only released if a vulnerability is publicly discovered by a third party such as a CERT or a hacker groups. Such information is therefore usually available before an official announcement by the company affected. Microsoft's security mailing list is one example of such a vendor-driven publication about product-related security information.

Newsgroups and Mailing Lists

Presuming that wily hackers always have up-to-date information about security holes, newsgroups on USENET and dedicated security mailing lists represent the most recent information sources that are publicly available. Contributions come from hackers, employees of IT companies and other IT professionals. As representatives for such newsgroups, we use the following examples:

- `comp.security.unix`
- `comp.security.ssh`
- `comp.security.misc`
- `de.comp.security`
- `comp.lang.java.security`
- `comp.os.ms-windows.nt.admin.security`
- `comp.os.netware.security`
- `comp.security.firewalls`

There are also several security mailing lists—[Bugtraq03] and [Alert03] being among the most useful. A more complete list of both security-related newsgroups and mailing lists is provided by Hurler [Hur00].

4

Patterns Scope and Enterprise Security

First comes thought; then organization of that thought, into ideas and plans; then transformation of those plans into reality. The beginning, as you will observe, is in your imagination.

Napolean Hill

This chapter describes the scope and context of the security systems and patterns and how they are organized in the book. Chapter 5 presents a catalog that briefly identifies and describes known security patterns. Almost all of them are contained in this book: some are published elsewhere, and a few are identified as potential patterns (that is, they are not yet written). The actual patterns are documented in Chapters 6 through 13.

This organization scheme is motivated by two aims. The first is to present the pattern material in a clear way to our primary audiences, and to facilitate their use of the patterns. The second is to structure the pattern material in a way that is consistent with the security domain. The two aims imply a need for an organization that enterprise engineers and planners, systems and software engineers, and operations managers will find useful, and that simultaneously maps to the security taxonomy described in Chapter 2. This chapter describes the organization we defined to achieve those aims.

This chapter is structured as follows:

- First, a discussion of the scope of the various parts of the book is presented in Section 4.1 to help explain the organization.

- This is followed by a discussion of organization factors in Section 4.2. The factors represent more specific requirements for the organization scheme.

- Section 4.3 then describes the resulting organization of the pattern landscape catalog (Chapter 5) and the patterns (Chapters 6 through 13).

- Section 4.4 describes the mapping of the security taxonomy to the patterns chapters.

- Section 4.5 presents an example of how the pattern organization can support both security integration and separation as part of a larger engineering and organizational context, using an enterprise architecture framework.

4.1   The Scope of Patterns in the Book

What is the relative scope of the proposed security taxonomy in Chapter 2, the survey catalog in Chapter 5, and the described patterns, pattern systems, and pattern languages in Chapters 6 through 13? The answer is shown in the figure below. The areas in this figure are defined this way:

- S—Security problems for which no patterns are documented

- K—Known or potential security patterns listed in the catalog (Chapter 5) but not described in the book

- B—Security patterns described in the book Chapters 6 through 13

- N—Known non-security patterns (that is, patterns written for another purpose) that can support security properties, listed in the catalog but not described in the book

A complete security taxonomy is given in Chapter 2—its scope is represented by the box in the figure, which includes spaces S + K + B. The catalog in Chapter 5 has the same scope as the large circle in the figure, which includes spaces K + B + N and represents all known security-related patterns. The patterns in Chapters 6 through 13 are represented by the small circle in the figure, which are a subset of the catalog.

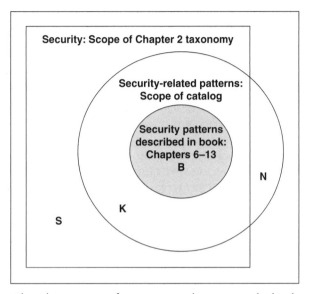

The relative scope of taxonomy and patterns in the book

4.2 Organization Factors

Two primary factors influenced our pattern organization scheme and are discussed in this section. The first factor is the structure of the audience of the book, in terms of the primary audience groups and the perspective of each group. The second factor is the need to understand security in two seemingly contradictory ways: separation and integration. Separation is the consideration of security apart from other enterprise and engineering concerns. Integration is the consideration of security as an integrated part of the larger enterprise and engineering picture.

Audience Perspectives

This section describes the perspectives of the primary audiences of the patterns in the book that were introduced in About this Book on page xvii.

Enterprise engineers and strategic planners. This audience is concerned with enterprise-wide security issues. Although security is applicable to each information system, an enterprise that builds, owns, or operates information systems does not and should not define a new security approach for each individual system. Enterprise planners must define security policies, risks, constraints, and requirements that apply across the enterprise and that place constraints on system development and the operational environment. They are also concerned with the external view of the enterprise and security issues related to interactions with suppliers, partners, customers, and regulators. They must balance conflicting business factors, such as producing maximum service and security with minimum cost. They view security as an enterprise strategic property: is the enterprise secure and does it follow good security practice?

System developers—architects, designers, implementers. This audience is concerned with incorporating security into systems and software engineering. They must design and build systems that satisfy both functional and security requirements, and that conform to the overall enterprise's security policies and constraints. They also have a system life cycle perspective that ranges from system requirements, through implementation and evolution. They view security as a system (nonfunctional) property: is the system secure?

Operations managers. This audience is concerned with running secure operations. They must define procedures to be followed at run-time to maintain security of both the enterprise and the systems, and that conform to the overall enterprise's security policies and constraints. They view security as an operational property: are the operations secure?

The Need for Separation and Integration

In the audience perspectives above, security is portrayed as a property or '-ility' of an enterprise or system, in the class of properties such as reliability, safety, performance, usability, and maintainability. In another sense, however, security is more than that. Security is a multidimensional domain of knowledge and expertise that includes a variety of areas or categories of known problems and solutions, such as identification and authentication (I&A), authorization, accountability, availability, integrity, and confidentiality. A degree of maturity of understanding has been achieved in many of these security areas, both in terms of known problems and known solutions, enabling the definition of patterns.

Both of these perceptions of security—as a property and as a separate domain of knowledge—are important. Security, as a domain of knowledge, lends itself to the development of a stand-alone security pattern language, or a system of security patterns, analogous to the pattern language for building and planning that Christopher Alexander and his colleagues defined [AIS+77] or to Doug Lea's system of design patterns for avionics control systems [Lea94]. A further reason for isolating security as a standalone issue is that the security of a system or enterprise often needs to be analyzed separately, not only for troubleshooting, but also for test and certification to operate.

However, there is an important difference between the treatment of patterns in the security domain and those in building construction or avionics. That difference stems from the fact that security is a property of a system that is built for some purpose other than security. Lea's avionics patterns can be used to build avionics software, and Alexander's building patterns can be used to build a neighborhood or an office building. On the other hand, while security patterns can be used to address the security aspects of a system, these patterns must be integrated and used in the trade-off process with other aspects of the system, including not only other properties, but also the operational functionality of the system itself.

An important example is the concept of resolving forces. Alexander seems to suggest ([AIS+77] and [Ale79]) that a pattern solution resolves conflicting forces or constraints so that all are satisfied. This claim, despite the poetic and appealing way in which it is presented, is problematic in the realm of engineering, because compromises among conflicting goals—for example, fast, cheap, good—have to be made. In security, perhaps the most dominant conflict is between the degree of security of the system and the functionality or usability of the system. That is why the discussion of forces in Chapter 3 talks about *balancing* forces, because they cannot all be resolved in one solution. It is easy to produce a wide-open non-secure system, or a secure closed system (that is, a 'secure rock' that interacts with nothing). Clearly, the necessary trade-off analysis cannot be done within the separate security patterns system. Such an analysis requires consideration of security in the larger engineering and regulatory context of a system or enterprise and the constraints levied by this context.

The bottom line is that security and security patterns need to be considered in both ways: as separated from other aspects of a system or enterprise, and as integrated with other aspects. Any organization scheme must support the dualism of separation and integration of security patterns.

4.3 Resulting Organization

This section explains the pattern organization that results from the perspectives we describe in Section 4.2. We describe the concept of *security view*, which underlies much of the organization in this book. We also describe how patterns are organized.

The Concept of Security View

A natural mechanism for addressing the need for the separation and integration of an area of concern in a system or enterprise is to define a view that addresses that concern. Our organizational approach assumes that security issues are most conveniently addressed in the form of a security view. This view is the basis for defining the scope and contents of a complete system of security patterns.

Separation is achieved by the fact that the security view is considered separately from other enterprise and system views. The patterns material in this book represents a security view, and its organization is driven by the security taxonomy, as explained in the subsequent parts of this section.

Integration is more difficult to achieve than separation. A general approach is to map the security view to other enterprise and system views. Since these other views vary by enterprise and system methodology, no single mapping is possible. A multi-pronged approach is used in this book to facilitate the integration of security patterns into all aspects of engineering and operations. The organization approach to integration includes these elements:

- Address security at both enterprise and system levels, and at both engineering and operations activities
- Capture common approaches and policies in enterprise security patterns that can be used for all systems in the enterprise
- Tie system and operations security to business needs in an enterprise context
- Address security throughout the life cycle, including planning, requirements, and architecture, not just during implementation or operation
- Address security at all levels of composition, including overall system level, not just component level—having secure components does not mean the system is secure
- Address trade-offs between enterprise and system forces versus security forces, to show the links from security into the larger engineering and organizational context

An example of integration using an enterprise framework is given in Section 4.5.

Patterns Organization

The security view organizes the patterns into eight chapters. Chapter 6 presents enterprise level patterns. Enterprise engineers and strategic planners constitute the primary audience for Chapter 6's patterns. These patterns emphasize security considerations that planners need to incorporate into their development of enterprise level strategy, planning activities, business models, risk assessment, goals, and policies.

Chapters 7 through 13 present system-level patterns. System analysts and developers, and to a limited extent operations managers, constitute the primary audience of these patterns. The patterns are intended to facilitate the goal of building security into systems, and achieving the security goals and policies defined at the enterprise level. The application of the patterns is intended to yield a collective security view of the system.

4.4 Mapping to the Taxonomy

The figure below maps the eight patterns chapters (6 through 13) to the security taxonomy in Chapter 2. Security strategy, driven by overall business strategy, corresponds to Chapter 6 patterns. These patterns address security issues at the strategic enterprise-wide level. The patterns are targeted to the organization as a whole, and they define solutions that constrain every system in the enterprise, as well as security management and operations. See figure on page 54.

The access-control models in Chapter 8, and the architectural-level access-control patterns in Chapter 9, map to the services level of the taxonomy. The firewall patterns in Chapter 12 map to Automated Mechanisms in the taxonomy. The remainder of the patterns chapters—7, 10, 11, and 13—map to both Security Services and Automated Mechanisms in the taxonomy. The are no patterns in the book that address Management Support, Physical, or Procedural Mechanisms in the taxonomy.

4.5 Organization in the Context of an Enterprise Framework

We present a brief example here to illustrate how an enterprise can promote separation and integration of security as part of a larger engineering and enterprise-planning context. The reason for including such an example is that security in general, and the use of the patterns in this book in particular, does not occur in isolation. Security is an important element of a larger purpose, which is to conduct the business of an organization and to engineer and operate systems in support of the business.

There are many ways an engineer or enterprise planner can use the patterns in engineering and management. We use the Zachman Framework for Enterprise Architecture [Zac87], [SZ92], [ZIFA] as an example, because it covers the scope of both enterprise and system, and it is a widely-used framework for enterprise engineering.

The Zachman Framework provides architectural views as vertical columns, and levels of information models as horizontal rows. The models cover enterprise levels— the top two rows—and system levels—the bottom three rows. The Zachman views are represented in the six columns in the matrix: Data, Function, Network, People, Time, and Motivation. See figure on page 55.

The Zachman Framework is used as the basis for adding a security view [HHR02], [HHR+02]), as shown in the figure below. The security view is treated as an additional column added to the Zachman Framework, shown on the right. Thus, one can consider an enterprise security view in the same way that one can consider a data view or functional view. The security view addresses all model levels, from the enterprise scope to the technology model and detailed representations. Integration within the security view is achieved via a system of patterns that captures the relationships between patterns across all these levels. See figure on page 56.

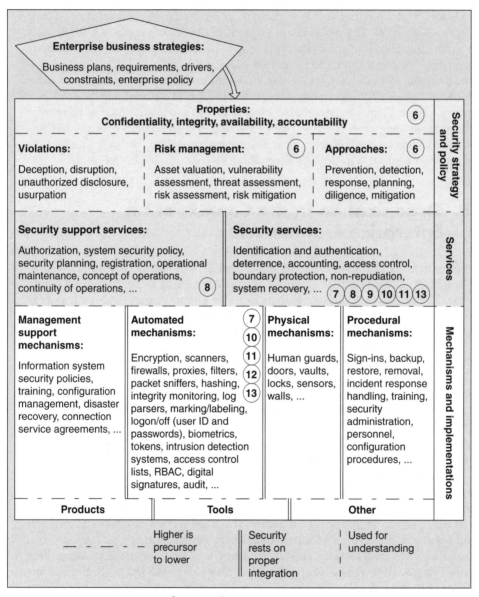

Mapping of pattern chapters to security taxonomy

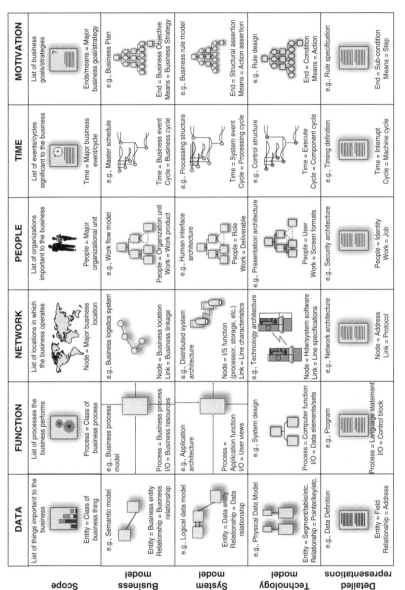

	DATA	FUNCTION	NETWORK	PEOPLE	TIME	MOTIVATION
Scope	List of things important to the business Entity = Class of business thing	List of processes the business performs Process = Class of business process	List of locations in which the business operates Node = Major business location	List of organizations important to the business People = Major organizational unit	List of events/cycles significant to the business Time = Major business event/cycle	List of business goals/strategies Ends/means = Major business goal/strategy
Business model	e.g., Semantic model Entity = Business entity Relationship = Business relationship	e.g., Business process model Process = Business process I/O = Business resources	e.g., Business logistics system Node = Business location Link = Business linkage	e.g., Work flow model People = Organization unit Work = Work product	e.g., Master schedule Time = Business event Cycle = Business cycle	e.g., Business Plan End = Business Objective Means = Business Strategy
System model	e.g., Logical data model Entity = Data entity Relationship = Data relationship	e.g., Application architecture Process = Application function I/O = User views	e.g., Distributed system architecture Node = I/S function (processor, storage, etc.) Link = Line characteristics	e.g., Human interface architecture People = Role Work = Deliverable	e.g., Processing structure Time = System event Cycle = Processing cycle	e.g., Business rule model End = Structural assertion Means = Action assertion
Technology model	e.g., Physical Data Model Entity = Segment/table/etc. Relationship = Pointer/key/etc.	e.g., System design Process = Computer function I/O = Data elements/sets	e.g., Technology architecture Node = Hdw/system software Link = Line specifications	e.g., Presentation architecture People = User Work = Screen formats	e.g., Control structure Time = Execute Cycle = Component cycle	e.g., Rule design End = Condition Means = Action
Detailed representations	e.g., Data Definition Entity = Field Relationship = Address	e.g., Program Process = Language statement I/O = Control block	e.g., Network architecture Node = Address Link = Protocol	e.g., Security architecture People = Identity Work = Job	e.g., Timing definition Time = Interrupt Cycle = Machine cycle	e.g., Rule specification End = Sub-condition Means = Step

The Zachman framework (C) 1982–2005 John A. Zachman, www.zachmaninternational.com

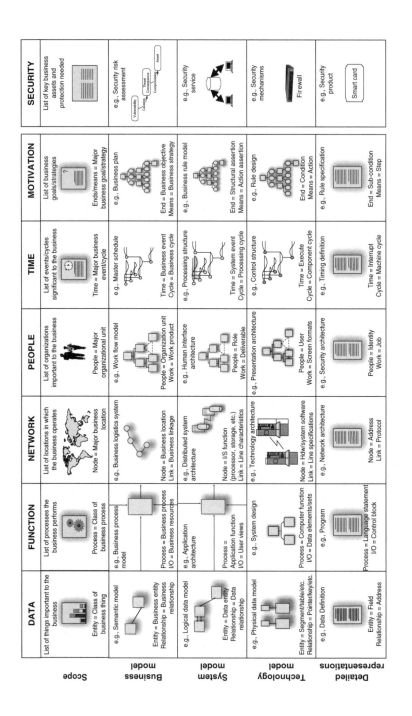

	DATA	FUNCTION	NETWORK	PEOPLE	TIME	MOTIVATION	SECURITY
Scope	List of things important to the business	List of processes the business performs	List of locations in which the business operates	List of organizations important to the business	List of events/cycles significant to the business	List of business goals/strategies	List of key business assets and protection needed
	Entity = Class of business thing	Process = Class of business process	Node = Major business location	People = Major organizational unit	Time = Major business event/cycle	Ends/means = Major business goal/strategy	
Business model	e.g., Semantic model	e.g., Business process model	e.g., Business logistics system	e.g., Work flow model	e.g., Master schedule	e.g., Business plan	e.g., Security risk assessment
	Entity = Business entity Relationship = Business relationship	Process = Business process I/O = Business resources	Node = Business location Link = Business linkage	People = Organization unit Work = Work product	Time = Business event Cycle = Business cycle	End = Business objective Means = Business strategy	
System model	e.g., Logical data model	e.g., Application architecture	e.g., Distributed system architecture	e.g., Human interface architecture	e.g., Processing structure	e.g., Business rule model	e.g., Security service
	Entity = Data entity Relationship = Data relationship	Process = Application function I/O = User views	Node = I/S function (processor, storage, etc.) Link = Line characteristics	People = Role Work = Deliverable	Time = System event Cycle = Processing cycle	End = Structural assertion Means = Action assertion	
Technology model	e.g., Physical data model	e.g., System design	e.g., Technology architecture	e.g., Presentation architecture	e.g., Control structure	e.g., Rule design	e.g., Security mechanisms
	Entity = Segment/table/etc. Relationship = Pointer/key/etc.	Process = Computer function I/O = Data elements/sets	Node = Hdw/system software Link = Line specifications	People = User Work = Screen formats	Time = Execute Cycle = Component cycle	End = Condition Means = Action	Firewall
Detailed representations	e.g., Data Definition	e.g., Program	e.g., Network architecture	e.g., Security architecture	e.g., Timing definition	e.g., Rule specification	e.g., Security product
	Entity = Field Relationship = Address	Process = Language statement I/O = Control block	Node = Address Link = Protocol	People = Identity Work = Job	Time = Interrupt Cycle = Machine cycle	End = Sub-condition Means = Step	Smart card

Adding a security view to the Zachman Framework (C) 1982–2005 John A. Zachman, www.zachmaninternational.com

Zachman's six column views are characterized respectively as 'what,' 'how,' 'where,' 'who,' 'when,' and 'why.' In this vein, the additional security view could perhaps be characterized as 'what security' or 'what protection'. The Zachman columns are useful because each addresses a common area of concern. Security is an important area of concern that can be added to this set. The concept of views is certainly flexible enough to accommodate this.

The figure on page 58 shows the Zachman rows overlaid on the mapping of taxonomy to patterns chapters shown in the figure on page 54. Zachman rows 1 and 2 (the Scope and Business Model) map to the Enterprise level of the taxonomy, which is the scope of the patterns described in Chapter 6. Zachman row 3 (the System Model) maps to the Services part of the taxonomy. Zachman row 4 (the Technology Model) maps to the Mechanisms part of the taxonomy. Together, rows 3 and 4 cover the scope of patterns in Chapters 7 through 13. Zachman row 5 (Detailed Representations) maps to the Products part of the taxonomy, which is not addressed by the patterns in this book.

Further integration of security patterns into the engineering context is facilitated by the fact that the elements of any cell in the Zachman Framework (that is, an intersection of row and column) have relationships to other cells, rows, and columns. Because of this, the elements of the security view and their relationships to the rest of the Zachman Framework can be thought of as forming a 'security plane.' The plane overlays the entire framework, both columns and rows, with security concerns, in a way that promotes integration of security with other engineering models throughout the framework. The modularity of the plane enables integration, in the sense that the security concerns in a given cell can be designed in an integrated way with the non-security concerns in that cell.

The combination of security view and security plane therefore allows us to achieve both separation and integration of security in an enterprise engineering context. The security view supports separate analyzability—for example, to certify that a system has adequate security—and separate security patterns. The security plane, on the other hand, shows the integration of security with the other engineering concerns. The plane also helps to achieve completeness of security concerns across the entire framework.

The result will be a security view recognizable as a separate yet integrated aspect of the whole enterprise architecture. The planning rigor imposed by using an enterprise framework provides the opportunity to incorporate security into all levels of IT planning, decision-making, and engineering effectively.

Enterprise business strategies:

Business plans, requirements, drivers, constraints, enterprise policy

Properties: Confidentiality, integrity, availability, accountability (6)			Security strategy and policy
Violations: Deception, disruption, unauthorized disclosure, usurpation	**Risk management:** (6) Asset valuation, vulnerability, assessment, threat assessment, risk assessment, risk mitigation	**Approaches:** (6) Prevention, detection, response, planning, diligence, mitigation	

Z1–2

Security support services: Authorization, system security policy, security planning, registration, operational maintenance, concept of operations, continuity of operations, ... (8)	**Security services:** Identification and authentication, deterrence, accounting, access control, boundary protection, non-repudiation, system recovery, ... (7)(8)(9)(10)(11)(13)

Services — **Z3**

Management support mechanisms:

Information system security policies, training, configuration management, disaster recovery, connection service agreements, ...

Automated mechanisms: (7)(10)(11)(12)(13)

Encryption, scanners, firewalls, proxies, filters, packet sniffers, hashing, integrity monitoring, log parsers, marking/labeling, logon/off (user ID and passwords), biometrics, tokens, intrusion detection systems, access control lists, RBAC, digital signatures, audit, ...

Physical mechanisms:

Human guards, doors, vaults, locks, sensors, walls, ...

Procedural mechanisms:

Sign-ins, backup, restore, removal, incident response, handling, training, security administration, personnel, configuration procedures, ...

Mechanisms and implementations — **Z4**

Products	Tools	Other	**Z5**

– – – – Higher is precursor to lower

‖ Security rests on proper integration

│ Used for understanding

Zn = Zachman Framework row n

Security patterns mapped to Zachman framework

CHAPTER

5

The Security Pattern Landscape

The real voyage of discovery consists not in seeking new landscapes but in having new eyes.

Marcel Proust

This chapter provides thumbnails of all patterns contained in the book, as well as related and referenced security patterns that are not contained in the book, but which are in many cases published elsewhere. You can use this chapter as a quick overview, as a desktop reference, or as a navigation tool through the pattern catalog.

5.1 Enterprise Security and Risk Management Patterns

Enterprise security and risk management patterns address enterprise-wide security issues. The assumed context for an enterprise that uses these patterns is that the enterprise has some function or mission and wants to address security issues as they relate to that mission. The scope of patterns includes policies, directives, or constraints that apply to all systems and all operations across the enterprise. The sequence of these patterns is shown in the figure below.

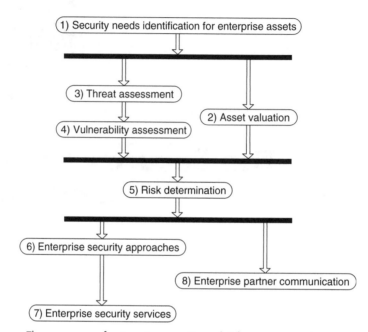

The sequence of enterprise security and risk management patterns

Security Needs Identification for Enterprise Assets

This is the root pattern for all enterprise security concerns. It helps resolve the issue of whether security is really needed and, if it is, what properties of security should be applied for a particular enterprise. Security properties considered include confidentiality, integrity, availability, and accountability.

Asset Valuation

Asset valuation helps you to determine the overall importance an enterprise places on the assets it owns and controls. Loss or compromise of such assets may result in anything from hard costs, such as fines and fees, to soft costs due to loss of market share and consumer confidence.

Threat Assessment

Threats are the likelihood of, or potential for, hazardous events occurring. They can affect any asset or object on which an enterprise places value. An enterprise threat assessment identifies the threats posed to the enterprise's assets, and determines the likelihood or frequency of their occurrence.

Vulnerability Assessment

A vulnerability is a weakness that could be exploited by a threat, causing the violation of an asset's security property. Conducting an enterprise vulnerability assessment helps to identify the weaknesses of the enterprise's assets and the systems that enable access to them, and evaluates the severity if a vulnerability were to be exploited.

Risk Determination

Risk determination is the final stage of a risk-assessment process, and incorporates the results from an asset valuation, a threat assessment and a vulnerability assessment. Using the input of these patterns, the enterprise is able to evaluate and prioritize the risks to its assets.

Enterprise Security Approaches

This pattern guides an enterprise in selecting security approaches, that is, prevention, detection, and response. Security approaches are driven by the security properties its assets require, such as confidentiality, integrity, and availability, and by assessed security risks. Security approaches also provide a basis for deciding what security services should be established by the enterprise.

Enterprise Security Services

This pattern guides an enterprise in selecting security services for protecting its assets, after the required security approaches—prevention, detection, response—have been identified. It helps to establish the level of strength or confidence each security service should offer, based on priorities. Primary examples of such services are identification and authentication, accounting/auditing, access control/authorization, and security management.

Enterprise Partner Communication

Enterprises often partner with third parties to support their business model. These third parties may include application and managed service providers, consulting firms, vendors, outsourcing development teams, and satellite offices. As part of this relationship, access must be granted to allow data to travel between the organizations. Without attention to the protection of that data and the methods by which they are transferred, one or both organizations may be at risk.

Other Related Patterns

IBM provides a series of e-business patterns that address enterprise interaction [IBM]. These patterns relate to the ENTERPRISE PARTNER COMMUNICATION (173) pattern. The IBM patterns focus on variations in topology, while ENTERPRISE PARTNER COMMUNICATION (173) focuses on process and exchange methods. More details are provided in the discussion of ENTERPRISE PARTNER COMMUNICATION (173) at the end of this collection.

The Appropriate Process Movement has identified a set of risks and produced corresponding risk-mitigation patterns [APM] that have some relation to the set of risk assessment patterns. While both sets of patterns address risk management, the Appropriate Process Movement patterns are oriented more towards general engineering and project risks, while the risk-assessment patterns in this collection are focused on security risks.

5.2 Identification & Authentication (I&A) Patterns

The relationships between the patterns for I&A is shown in the figure below. The figure also shows which patterns are introduced in this chapter. Additional potential patterns are also shown to present a more complete I&A picture. See figure on page 63.

I&A REQUIREMENTS (192) is the root pattern of all I&A patterns, as it helps to determine which of the subsequent patterns should be used. This pattern helps you to capture your specific requirements for the I&A service as a black box. AUTOMATED I&A DESIGN ALTERNATIVES (207) assumes that you will use some form of automated I&A, as opposed to physical or procedural I&A. Multiple types of automated I&A are available, and AUTOMATED I&A DESIGN ALTERNATIVES (207) helps to you select one or more types.

- Patterns for two of the automated I&A types are presented in this chapter: first, PASSWORD DESIGN AND USE (217) provides best practice guidance on password I&A. This guidance applies both to designers, who enforce constraints on passwords, and users, who select passwords.
- Second, the BIOMETRICS DESIGN ALTERNATIVES (229) pattern helps you to select among multiple biometrics I&A alternatives that are available.

Several potential patterns are related to the I&A patterns.

- SESSION MANAGEMENT SERVICE: a service that establishes linkages between an external entity, a set of actions, and the identity that is output from I&A.

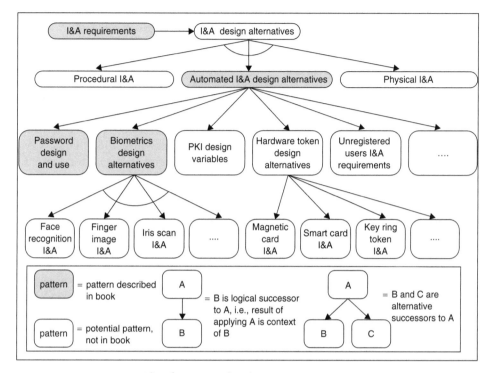

Identification and authentication patterns

- ACTOR REGISTRATION OR ENROLLMENT SERVICE: a security support service that establishes links between an external entity and an internal identity record.
- ACCESS CONTROL SERVICE: this service uses the identity output from I&A.
- ACCOUNTING SERVICE: this service uses the identity output from I&A.

The Access Control service is described by the patterns in Chapters 8, 9, and 10 of this book. The Accounting service is described by the patterns in Chapter 11 of this book.

I&A Requirements

An identification and authentication (I&A) service must satisfy a set of requirements for both the service and the quality of service. The function of I&A is to recognize an individual and validate the individual's identity. While each situation that calls for I&A is unique, there are common generic requirements that apply to all I&A situations. This pattern provides a common generic set of I&A requirements. The pattern also helps you to apply the general requirements to your specific situation, and helps you to determine the relative importance of conflicting requirements.

I&A Design Alternatives

Three general strategies exist to satisfy I&A requirements: automated I&A, physical I&A and procedural I&A. Physical and procedural I&A includes measures such as a human guard reviewing ID badges, or a sign-in procedure. Automated I&A encompasses computer-based measures such as user IDs and passwords. I&A DESIGN ALTERNATIVES helps you to select one or more of these general strategies for a specific domain or situation.

Automated I&A Design Alternatives

This pattern describes alternative techniques for automated I&A, as opposed to procedural or physical I&A. It helps you to select an appropriate I&A strategy that consists of a single technique, or a combination of techniques, to satisfy I&A requirements. Techniques considered include password, biometrics, hardware token, PKI, and I&A of unregistered users.

Physical and Procedural I&A

Physical and procedural I&A includes measures such as a human guard reviewing ID badges, or a sign-in procedure. This pattern helps you to design an appropriate mechanism, or set of mechanisms, for achieving physical and procedural I&A for a specific domain or situation.

Password Design and Use

This pattern describes security best practice for designing, creating, managing, and using password components in support of I&A REQUIREMENTS (192). This pattern can aid three audiences: engineers, in selecting or designing commercial products that provide password mechanisms, administrators, in the operation and management of password mechanisms, and users, in improving their selection and handling of passwords.

Biometrics Design Alternatives

This pattern aids the selection of appropriate biometric mechanisms to satisfy I&A requirements. Biometric mechanisms considered are face recognition, finger image, hand geometry, iris recognition, retinal scanning, signature verification, and speaker verification. Additional mechanisms, including DNA, are identified for completeness.

Face Recognition

Face recognition is a physical biometric technique that analyzes distinguishing facial features. This pattern helps you to design an appropriate face-recognition mechanism to satisfy I&A requirements for a specific domain or situation.

Finger Image

Finger image is a physical biometric technique that looks at the patterns found in the tip of the finger. Finger images may be captured by placing a finger on a scanner, or by electronically scanning inked impressions on paper. This pattern helps you to design an appropriate finger image mechanism to satisfy I&A requirements for a specific domain or situation.

Hand Geometry

Hand geometry is a physical biometric technique that involves analyzing and measuring the shape of the hand from a 3-D perspective. This pattern helps you to design an appropriate hand geometry mechanism to satisfy I&A requirements for a specific domain or situation.

Iris Recognition

Iris recognition is a physical biometric technique that analyses the unique features that are found in the colored ring of tissue that surrounds the pupil of the eye. This pattern helps you to design an appropriate iris recognition mechanism to satisfy I&A requirements for a specific domain or situation.

Retinal Scanning

Retinal scanning is a physical biometric technique that analyses the pattern of the blood vessels at the back of the eye. This pattern helps you to design an appropriate retinal scanning mechanism to satisfy I&A requirements for a specific domain or situation.

Signature Verification

Signature verification is a behavioral biometric technique that analyses the way an end user signs their name. The signing features such as speed, velocity and pressure exerted by the pen are as important as the static shape of the finished signature. This pattern helps you to design an appropriate signature verification mechanism to satisfy I&A requirements for a specific domain or situation.

Speaker Verification

Speaker verification is a part-physical, part-behavioral biometric that analyses patterns in speech. It compares live speech with a previously-created speech model of a person's voice. This pattern helps you to design an appropriate speaker verification mechanism to satisfy I&A requirements for a specific domain or situation.

PKI Design Variables

The use of Public Key Infrastructure (PKI) for I&A involves a number of significant variables and constraints that require design decisions. These include mechanisms for private key storage and protection, public-key cryptographic mechanisms, generation of certificates and keys, distribution of certificates and keys, the cost of creating the infrastructure, whether to use a proprietary or non-proprietary solution, legal constraints and considerations, and other variables. This pattern identifies the variables, the options and trade-offs for each, and provides guidance to help you achieve an integrated design.

Hardware Token Design Alternatives

Several categories and types of hardware token mechanism are available to support I&A. Examples include magnetic stripe cards, such as ATM cards or employee badges, contactless or RFID (radio-frequency identification) cards, one-time password tokens such as ActivCard or SecurID, and 'smart' cards. This pattern defines the alternatives available and their characteristics and trade-offs, to help you to define a token-based design that satisfies I&A requirements for a specific domain.

Magnetic Card

Types of magnetic cards used for I&A include ATM cards, debit cards, and employee badges. Most use PINs (personal identification numbers) to counter the problem of card theft. This pattern helps you to address the design issues involved in magnetic card I&A and to define a mechanism that will satisfy I&A requirements.

One-Time Password Token

One-time password (OTP) tokens are designed to counter the problem of password theft by producing passwords dynamically that are then used only once. Often they are used in conjunction with a user ID and PIN. Examples include counter-based or event-based tokens in which a user prompts for the next OTP, and time-based tokens in which the token generates a new OTP periodically, such as every minute—which must be time synchronized with a server/authenticator. Other variations are asynchronous, such as challenge-response password tokens. This pattern helps you to address the design issues involved in OTP token I&A and to define a mechanism that will satisfy I&A requirements.

Smart Card

The 'smart' card token is typically a plastic card in which an integrated circuit chip is embedded, which gives it both data storage and computational capability. It has many potential uses, one of which is to authenticate the identity of the card holder. This pattern helps you to address the design issues involved in smart card I&A and to design a smart card that will satisfy I&A requirements.

Unregistered Users I&A Requirements

In some cases a modest level of I&A is needed when a preceding registration step is not possible or not cost-effective. A common approach in these cases is to use 'functional' information about the person, that is, information that was acquired in the normal course of business. Such information usually includes both public items, such as name or e-mail address, and private items or secrets, such as the individual's mother's maiden name. This pattern helps you to define the requirements for I&A when pre-registration is not used.

Actor Registration

Most I&A approaches involve identifying and authenticating an actor against a previously-established known record. Determining how the known record is established is the function of actor registration. This pattern helps you to design a registration mechanism for an actor or user. The type of information recorded depends on the I&A mechanism used. For example, if you are using an ID and password mechanism, then you need to define a user account ID and establish a password. If you are using signature verification, you need to capture user signature samples. This pattern covers the more common types of I&A mechanisms, such as those identified in this book.

5.3 Access Control Model Patterns

High-level models represent the security policies of the enterprise. These models define security constraints at an architectural level, the application level, and are enforced by the lower levels. None of the patterns that describe the models have dynamics sections, because they are purely declarative. REFERENCE MONITOR (256) brings dynamics for evaluating requests according to the constraints defined by the declarative models. We also provide ROLE RIGHTS DEFINITION (259), to help in finding the rights associated with roles in an RBAC model.

The figure shows how the access control patterns are related to each other.

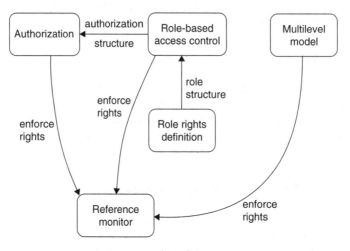

Access control model patterns

Authorization

This pattern describes who is authorized to access specific resources in a system, in an environment in which we have resources whose access needs to be controlled. It indicates, for each active entity that can access resources, which resources it can access, and how it can access them.

Role-Based Access Control

This pattern describes how to assign rights based on the functions or tasks of people in an environment in which control of access to computing resources is required and where there is a large number of users, information types, or a large variety of resources. It describes how users can acquire rights based on their job functions or their assigned tasks.

Multilevel Security

In some environments data and documents may have critical value and their disclosure could bring serious problems. This pattern describes how to categorize sensitive information and prevent its disclosure. It discusses how to assign classifications (clearances) to users, and classifications (sensitivity levels) to data, and to separate different organizational units into categories. Access of users to data is based on policies, while changes to the classifications are performed by trusted processes that are allowed to violate the policies.

Reference Monitor

In a computational environment in which users or processes make requests for data or resources, this pattern enforces declared access restrictions when an active entity requests resources. It describes how to define an abstract process that intercepts all requests for resources and checks them for compliance with authorizations.

Role Rights Definition

'Least privilege' is a fundamental principle for secure systems. Roles can directly support the least privilege principle, but a systematic approach to assigning only the required rights to each role is required. This pattern provides a precise way, based on use cases, of assigning rights to roles to implement a least-privilege policy.

5.4 System Access Control Architecture Patterns

An access control security service is essential for systems that permit or deny their use explicitly. A set of patterns that deal with the architecture of software systems to be secured by access control are provided, based on a generic set of access-control requirements. The relationships between these patterns is shown in the figure below.

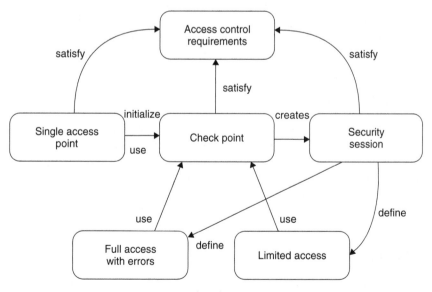

Access control architecture patterns

Access Control Requirements

The function of the access control security service is to permit or deny someone the right to perform an action on an asset, such as create, read, modify, or delete a data file. While each situation that calls for access control is unique, there are common generic requirements that apply to all access-control situations. This pattern provides a common generic set of access control requirements. The requirements address both the access control function and the properties of the access control service, such as ease of use and flexibility. The pattern also helps you to apply the general requirements to your specific situation, and helps you to determine the relative importance of conflicting requirements.

Single Access Point

If you need to provide external access to a system, but want to protect it from misuse or damage, define a single access point that grants or denies entry to the system after checking the client requiring access. The single access point is easy to apply, defines a clear entry point to the system, and can be assessed when implementing the desired security policy.

Check Point

Once you have secured a system using SINGLE ACCESS POINT (279), a means of identification and authentication (I&A) and response to unauthorized break-in attempts is required for securing the system. CHECK POINT (287) makes such an effective I&A and access control mechanism easy to deploy and evolve.

Security Session

Verifying a user's identity and access rights for every system function can be tedious. To keep track of who is using the functions and their corresponding access rights, systems establish a security session after a user has logged in successfully. A unique reference to the session object is made available, instead of passing all access rights or re-authenticating a user repeatedly. Queries regarding a user's security properties are delegated to the attached session object via the session reference.

Full Access with Errors

Designing the user interface for a system in which different users are granted different access rights can be challenging. At one end of the spectrum is the approach taken by this pattern, which provides a view of the maximum functionality of the system, but issues the user with an error when they attempt to use a function for which they are not authorized.

Limited Access

Designing the user interface for a system in which different users are granted different access rights can be challenging. This pattern guides a developer in presenting only the currently-available functions to a user, while hiding everything for which they lack permission.

5.5 Operating System Access Control Patterns

We present architectural patterns for access control in operating systems. We assume here that resources are represented as objects, as is common in modern operating systems.

The figure on page 72 shows how these patterns relate to each other. For example, authentication is needed for file access and for controlled object access, a subject must be authorized to access an object in a specific way, and we need to make sure that the requestor is not an impostor.

The other three patterns, CONTROLLED OBJECT FACTORY (331), CONTROLLED OBJECT MONITOR (335), and CONTROLLED PROCESS CREATOR (328), complete the definition of the CONTROLLED EXECUTION ENVIRONMENT (346) pattern, where the creation of and access to objects are controlled. The diagram also shows that the CONTROLLED OBJECT MONITOR (335), the CONTROLLED EXECUTION ENVIRONMENT (346), and the FILE AUTHORIZATION (350) patterns are concrete examples of the REFERENCE MONITOR (256) of Chapter 8.

Requirements for the AUTHENTICATOR (323) pattern can be found in Chapter 7.

Authenticator

This pattern addresses the problem of how to verify that a subject is who it says it is. Use a SINGLE ACCESS POINT (279) to receive the interactions of a subject with the system and apply a protocol to verify the identity of the subject.

Controlled Process Creator

This pattern addresses how to define and grant appropriate access rights for a new process.

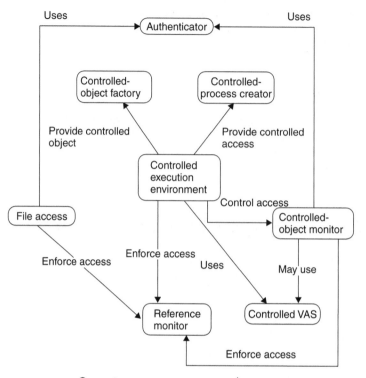

Operating system access control patterns

Controlled Object Factory

This pattern addresses how to specify the rights of processes with respect to a new object. When a process creates a new object through a factory (see FACTORY METHOD and ABSTRACT FACTORY [GoF95]), the request includes the features of the new object. These features include a list of rights to access the object.

Controlled Object Monitor

This pattern addresses how to control access by a process to an object. Use a reference monitor to intercept access requests from processes. The reference monitor checks whether the process has the requested type of access to the object.

Controlled Virtual Address Space

This pattern addresses how to control access by processes to specific areas of their virtual address space (VAS) according to a set of predefined access types. Divide the VAS into segments that correspond to logical units in the programs. Use special words (descriptors) to represent access rights for these segments.

Execution Domain

Unauthorized processes could destroy or modify information in files or databases, with obvious results, or could interfere with the execution of other processes. Therefore, define an execution environment for processes, indicating explicitly all the resources that a process can use during its execution, as well as the type of access to the resources.

Controlled Execution Environment

If a process execution environment is uncontrolled, processes can scavenge information by searching memory and accessing the disk drives where files reside. They might also take control of the operating system itself, in which case they have access to everything. Use AUTHORIZATION (245) to define the rights of a subject. From these rights we can set up the rights of processes running on behalf of the subject. Process requests are validated by CONTROLLED OBJECT MONITOR (335) or REFERENCE MONITOR (256) respectively.

File Authorization

This pattern describes how to control access to files in an operating system. Authorized users are the only ones that can use a file in specific ways. Apply AUTHORIZATION (245) to describe access to files by subjects. The protection object is now a file component that may be a directory or a file.

5.6 Accounting Patterns

Security events are violations that occur during operational activities. Decision makers need to be aware of security events that occur involving their assets. This need is addressed by security audit and accounting. The figure shows how all the requirements and potential design patterns are related, and indicates which ones are presented in this book. See figure on page 74.

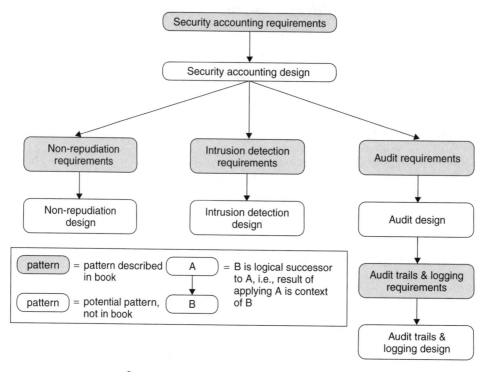

Security accounting patterns and relationships

Security Accounting Requirements

A security accounting service must satisfy a set of requirements for both the service and the quality of service. The function of security accounting is to track security-related actions or events, such as damage to property, attempts at unauthorized database access, or transmission of a computer virus, and provide information about those actions. While each situation that calls for security accounting is unique, there are common generic requirements that apply to all security accounting situations. This pattern provides a common generic set of security accounting requirements. The pattern also helps you apply the general requirements to your specific situation, and helps you to determine the relative importance of conflicting requirements.

Security Accounting Design

General security accounting functions are capture, store, review, and report. Several services are available to support accountability and the security accounting functions.

These services include audit, intrusion detection, and non-repudiation. This pattern helps you design an approach for satisfying your accounting requirements by employing an appropriate combination of these services.

Audit Requirements

The audit function is to analyze logs, audit trails or other captured information about an event, such as entering a building or accessing resources on a network, to find and report any indication of security violations. This pattern provides a common generic set of audit requirements, and helps you prioritize them.

Audit Design

Audit is a security service that scrutinizes logs, audit trails or other captured information and attempts to discern more detailed information about an event. It analyzes the event information for any indication of security violations. This pattern provides guidance to help you design an audit mechanism that satisfies your audit requirements and identifies your logging requirements.

Audit Trails and Logging Requirements

The audit trails and logging function is to capture audit logs and audit trails about events and activities that occur within an organization or system, to enable reconstruction and analysis of those events and activities. This pattern provides a common generic set of audit trails and logging requirements, and helps you prioritize them.

Audit Trails & Logging Design

Audit Trails & Logging is a security service that automates the capture of activities and events that occur within an enterprise, system, or defined domain. Audit trails are a series of records about system events or user activities. Audit trails can be used to reconstruct events, determine who is responsible for events, what malicious or unwanted activities have occurred, and analyze any problems. Logs are individual trails of information that may be combined into an audit trail. This pattern provides guidance to help you design an audit trail and logging mechanism that satisfies your requirements.

Intrusion Detection Requirements

Intrusion detection is a security service that automates the monitoring of events occurring in a computer system or network, and analyzes these events for any indication of security violations. This pattern provides a common generic set of intrusion detection requirements, and helps you prioritize them.

Intrusion Detection Design

There are times when accounting results are used to support detection and response security approaches. That is, accounting results need to be obtained and provided with the explicit purpose of allowing a quick response to an event. Intrusion detection systems (IDS) are an example of this case. The Intrusion Detection service is used to monitor and analyze unauthorized or unwanted attempts to access a perimeter or a controlled area that is of importance to an enterprise. This pattern provides guidance to help you to design an intrusion detection mechanism that satisfies your requirements.

Non-Repudiation Requirements

The function of non-repudiation is to capture and maintain evidence so that the participants of a transaction or interaction cannot deny having participated in that activity. This pattern provides a common generic set of non-repudiation requirements, and helps you prioritize them.

Non-Repudiation Design

Non-repudiation is focused on the capture of events and the creation of links between actors and events. Non-repudiation provides a degree of confidence that parties who engaged in an event cannot later deny that engagement. Non-repudiation corresponds to a prevention approach to security, in that it attempts to prevent violation of accountability. This pattern provides guidance to help you design a non-repudiation mechanism that satisfies your requirements.

Other Related Patterns

The Web application security patterns repository (see Section 5.10) has a LOG FOR AUDIT pattern that is a variation of AUDIT TRAILS AND LOGGING REQUIREMENTS (378) in this chapter. The NAI security patterns repository also has a SECURE ASSERTION pattern that maps conventional assertions to a system-wide intrusion detection system. IBM provides a series of e-business patterns that address enterprise interaction, which is available at:

```
http://www-106.ibm.com/developerworks/patterns/
```

IBM's CREDENTIAL PROPAGATION pattern enables non-repudiation of transactions initiated by the user at the back-end.

5.7 Firewall Architecture Patterns

Several types of firewall exist that represent trade-offs between complexity, speed, and security, and which are tailored to control attacks on specific layers of the network. We present a set of patterns to describe different types of firewalls. These patterns can be used as a guide to select a suitable firewall type for a system, or to help designers build new firewalls.

The figure shows the patterns, their relationships and dependencies.

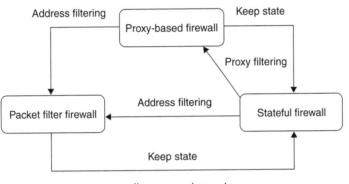

Firewall pattern relationships

Packet Filter Firewall

Some of the hosts in other networks may try to attack the local network through their IP-level payloads. These payloads may include viruses or application-specific attacks. We need to identify and block those hosts. A packet filter firewall filters incoming and outgoing network traffic in a computer system based on packet inspection at the IP level.

Proxy-Based Firewall

A proxy-based firewall inspects and filters incoming and outgoing network traffic based on the type of application service to be accessed, or performing the access. This pattern interposes a proxy between the request and the access, and applies controls through this proxy. This is usually done in addition to the normal filtering based on addresses.

Stateful Firewall

A stateful firewall filters incoming and outgoing network traffic in a computer system based on state information derived from past communications. State information generally describes whether the incoming packet is part of a new connection, or a continuing communication whose connection was approved previously. In other words, states describe a context for each packet.

5.8   Secure Internet Applications Patterns

This set of patterns focuses on secure Internet applications. They specialize the patterns in Chapter 9, *System Access Control Architecture* and the firewall patterns in Chapter 12, *Firewall Architectures*. Dealing with Internet applications, they can give more concrete implementation guidance than those more generic patterns.

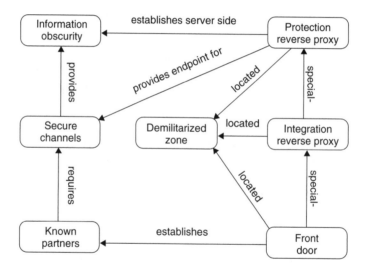

Secure Internet applications patterns

Information Obscurity

All systems are potentially liable to attack, whether from internal or external sources. If the information held by a system is sensitive, it should be protected. Part of this protection can take the form of obscuring the data itself, probably through some form of encryption, and obscuring information about the environment surrounding the data.

Secure Channels

Messages passing across any public network—particularly the Internet—can be intercepted. The information contained in such messages is thus potentially available to an eavesdropper. For sensitive communication across a public network, create encrypted SECURE CHANNELS (434) to ensure that data remains confidential in transit.

Known Partners

An organization conducting e-commerce, offering services, or publishing information using Web technologies must make their service easily accessible to their users. However, if these interactions are commercially sensitive or of a high value, we want to ensure that the users with whom we are interacting are who we think they are, and the users themselves want to be sure that our system is what they think it is. By introducing a system of KNOWN PARTNERS (442), identified uniquely in a way that can be authenticated, we can be sure of who is interacting with our system. We can also prove to users that we are who they think we are.

Demilitarized Zone

Any organization conducting e-commerce or publishing information over Web technologies must make their service easily accessible to their users. However, any form of Web site or e-commerce system is a potential target for attack, especially those on the Internet. A Demilitarized Zone (DMZ) separates the business functionality and information from the Web servers that deliver it, and places the Web servers in a secure area. This reduces the 'surface area' of the system that is open to attack.

Protection Reverse Proxy

Putting a Web server or an application server directly on the Internet gives attackers direct access to any vulnerabilities of the underlying platform (application, Web server, libraries, operating system). However, to provide a useful service to Internet users, access to your server is required. A packet filter firewall shields your server from attacks at the network level. In addition, a PROTECTION REVERSE PROXY (457) protects the server software at the level of the application protocol.

Integration Reverse Proxy

A Web site constructed from applications from different sources might require several different servers because of the heterogeneous operating requirement of the different applications. Because of the Internet addressing scheme, this distribution across several hosts is visible to the end user. Any change of the distribution or switch of parts of the site to a different host can invalidate URLs used so far, either cross-links to the Web site or bookmarks set up by users. An INTEGRATION REVERSE PROXY (465) alleviates this situation by providing a homogenous view of a collection of servers, without leaking the physical distribution of the individual machines to end users.

Front Door

Web applications and services often need to identify a user and keep track of a user's session. Integrating several such services allows a single log-in and session context to be provided. A reverse proxy is an ideal point to implement authentication and authorization, by implementing a Web entry server for your back-ends. A sophisticated reverse proxy can even access external back-ends, providing the user's id and password automatically from a 'password wallet.'

5.9   Cryptographic Key Management Patterns

Many services in a distributed public network such as the Internet require secure communications. Security in communications consists of confidentiality, integrity, authenticity, and non-repudiability. These aims can be achieved with cryptography.

Key management plays a fundamental role in secure communications, as it is the basis of all cryptographic functions. Sami Lehtonen and Juha Pärssinen have compiled a set of ten patterns for key management [Leh02]. They are designed to answer basic key management requirements in respect of secure communications. As such they build a foundation for subsequent security services such as I&A and SECURE CHANNELS (434) that provide confidentiality of sensitive information. Note that these patterns are not described in this book.

Secure Communication

Alice wants to communicate with Bob but there might be somebody eavesdropping. They want to keep their secrets and not reveal them to Eve the eavesdropper. How to prevent data from being intercepted? Alice and Bob use a public symmetric algorithm for encrypting data.

Cryptographic Key Generation

Secure communications between Alice and Bob are possible with encryption. Alice and Bob have decided to use symmetric encryption. How should they generate good symmetric encryption keys securely? Alice follows three steps:

1. Alice gathers enough seeding material from a reliable source.
2. She generates a 128-bit key with a one-way hash function from that seeding material.

3. She compares the generated key against a list of known weak keys of the encryption algorithm to be used. If the key is known to be weak, she goes to step 1.

This session key is used only in one communication session.

Session Key Exchange with Public Keys

Alice and Bob are going to encrypt data to be transferred between them. Alice has created a session key. They don't have certificates, because certificates are expensive. How can they deliver the session key securely? Authentication requires digital signatures, as well as certificates or public keys. Alice encrypts the session key with Bob's public key, adds a digital signature with her private key and sends it to Bob. Bob can then verify the digital signature with Alice's public key and decrypt the session key with his private key.

Public Key Exchange

Alice and Bob are going to encrypt data to be transferred between them. They have decided to use public key encryption for session key transfer. Alice and Bob have created asymmetric key pairs. Either:

a. They live in the same city.
b. They live on different continents.

How should they exchange public keys?

a. Both Alice and Bob write their public keys on a digital media, such as a floppy disk. They meet each other face-to-face and hand over their public keys. Alice talks with Bob and may even see his driving license. Alice can be sure about Bob's identity.
b. Alice sends her public key to Bob via e-mail. Alice calls Bob, they talk to each other, and after she has verified Bob's identity, she gives Bob a hash generated from her public key. Bob is able to check if the public key arrived unmodified by regenerating the same hash.

Public Key Database

Alice and Bob have created asymmetric key pairs and swapped their public keys. They may have several other public keys from other people. How can they assure integrity and authenticity of public keys without losing accessibility? Alice saves her private key on digital media and puts it in a secure place. She distributes her public key. However, its integrity must be assured. Alice adds a digital signature and stores a backup copy of the key database in a secure place. If someone modifies Alice's key database, the digital signature won't match any more, revealing the attempt to attack. If this happens, Alice can always fetch the back-up copy.

Session Key Exchange with Server-side Certificate

Alice and Bob are going to encrypt data to be transferred between them. Alice has created a session key. Either Alice wants to remain anonymous, or she doesn't have a certificate. Bob also doesn't know who Alice is. Both Alice and Bob know Trent and trust him. How should Alice deliver the session key? Bob sends his certificate (public key is certified) to Alice. Alice verifies from Trent that the certificate is valid, then encrypts the session key with Bob's public key and sends it to Bob. Bob decrypts the session key with his private key.

Session Key Exchange With Certificates

Alice and Bob are going to encrypt data to be transferred between them. Alice has created a session key. Both Alice and Bob require authentication. They know and trust Trent. How should deliver the session key? Alice and Bob exchange their certificates (public keys are certified). They both verify each others certificates from Trent. Alice encrypts the session key with Bob's public key, adds a digital signature with her private key and sends it to Bob. Bob can verify the digital signature with Alice's public key, and decrypt the session key with his private key.

Certificate Authority

Alice wants to exchange keys with certificates. Alice knows a trusted person, Trent. Alice needs a certificate. Alice calculates an asymmetric key pair and sends the public key to Trent. Trent creates a certificate for the public key. He adds a digital signature to the certificate. Trent delivers the certificate to Alice.

Cryptographic Smart Card

Alice has her certified public key and a private key. Alice needs storage for her keys. Alice's key pair and certificate are stored on a smart card, which also handles their use. Even Alice herself cannot read the private key.

Certificate Revocation

It is possible for a certificate to become insecure, for example by compromise of the private key is compromised. However, when exchanging the session key with certificate(s), Alice needs to know whether or not Bob's certificate is valid. How Alice can be sure about the validity of Bob's certificate? If Alice notices that her private key has been compromised, she informs Trent about it. Trent maintains a list of invalid certificates that have not expired. This list is called a Certificate Revocation List (CRL). Alice gets the CRL from Trent and stores it. When the CRL expires, she gets a new CRL. When Alice gets a certificate from Bob, she looks at the CRL to see if the certificate has been revoked. If Alice and Bob communicate with each other again, and Alice has not obtained a new CRL, there is no need to look at the CRL again.

5.10 Related Security Pattern Repositories Patterns

As of today, the following repositories of security patterns are known. This list is not exhaustive.

Web Application Security

Darrel M. Kienzle and Matthew C. Elder compiled a security patterns repository consisting of twenty-six patterns and three mini-patterns. The focus of these patterns is on Web application security. The patterns are available at http://www.modsecurity.org/archive/securitypatterns/. The final report of this project contains thumbnails for all patterns [KE02].

Available and Protected Systems

The Open Group published a technical guide that contains security design patterns. The catalog contains available system patterns and protected system patterns. [BH04]. It can be downloaded from the Open Group Web site at http://www.opengroup.org.

J2EE Security, Web Services and Identity Management

A group at SUN (Chris Steel, Ramesh Nagappan, Ray Lai) offers a set of architectural security patterns for J2EE-based applications, Web Services and identity management. An outline of their patterns is available [SNL05].

CHAPTER

6

Enterprise Security and Risk Management

Take calculated risks. That is quite different from being rash.

George S. Patton

This chapter contains patterns that address enterprise-wide security issues. The assumed context for an enterprise that uses these patterns is that the enterprise has some function or mission, and wants to address security issues as they relate to the larger enterprise mission. Some of the important information that is input to these enterprise security patterns is provided by this larger context. For example, the enterprise has some knowledge of its assets and how important they are to the enterprise: this information is important input for the security patterns.

The focus of the patterns in this chapter is not on security issues that relate to specific systems or operations within the enterprise. That focus is the province of later chapters. However, the scope of patterns in this chapter does include policies, directives, or constraints that apply to all systems and all operations across the enterprise.

Enterprise level security concerns, as addressed in this chapter, are organized in four topic areas: identifying basic needs, assessing risks, moving toward mitigation and safeguarding, and external enterprise considerations. The topics and their associated security concerns are summarized in Table 6.1.

This section elaborates on the concerns identified in Table 6.1, introduces the patterns presented in this chapter, and describes how each pattern addresses the concerns.

Before an organization can protect its assets, it needs to know what assets it has and what types of protection they need. SECURITY NEEDS IDENTIFICATION FOR ENTERPRISE ASSETS (89) is intended to help you obtain this knowledge. It is the root pattern for all enterprise security concerns. It helps determine which properties of security should be applied to the assets of a particular enterprise. Security properties considered include confidentiality, integrity, availability, and accountability.

After applying this pattern, the next step typically is to apply a set of risk assessment patterns to further calibrate the security needs of each asset type and so determine more specific security requirements. The set of risk patterns in this chapter help to evaluate assets, analyze threats, vulnerabilities, and risks, and assists in deciding how much protection is needed for each business asset type.

Table 6.1   Enterprise topics and security concerns

TOPIC	SECURITY CONCERNS
Identifying basic needs	• What assets are important to the enterprise (for example data, systems, physical property, employees)? • What asset properties need to be protected (for example confidentiality, integrity, availability, accountability)?
Assessing risks	• What is the value of enterprise assets? • What threats exist, that is, what potentially harmful circumstances might lead to violations of asset security? • What vulnerabilities exist, that is, what asset weaknesses can be exploited by a threat? • What are the relative risks to enterprise assets based on asset valuation, threat and vulnerability assessments?
Moving toward mitigation and safeguarding	• What security approaches (for example planning, prevention, detection, operational diligence, and response) are needed to protect assets and mitigate risks? • What security services (for example identification and authentication, accounting, access control) are needed to protect assets and mitigate risks?
External enterprise considerations	• How can an enterprise protect its assets when communicating with external partners?

Risk is the possibility of loss or injury. Risk management in general comprises two major activities: assessing what the risks are, and eliminating or mitigating the risks. The former is called *risk assessment*, and the latter is called *risk mitigation*. In security, risk management involves assessing and mitigating risk of loss due to security violations. From a security pattern perspective, risk assessment is a bounded problem that can be described in a few patterns. Security risk mitigation, on the other hand, is a very large area that involves most of the security disciplines, including policies, services, mechanisms, management, and operations. Therefore, risk assessment patterns are presented in this chapter, while risk mitigation is implicitly addressed in the subsequent patterns in this chapter and succeeding chapters.

Risk assessment in general can be performed in a quantitative or qualitative manner. A quantitative approach attempts to measure factors with precise metrics. A qualitative approach uses more relative or subjective measures such as rankings. The risk patterns provided in this chapter do not require that precise metrics be used, and the guidance uses qualitative scoring. However, the authors realize that quantitative risk assessments can also prove useful for some enterprises. If you are using the patterns and have quantitative metrics available for the factors, you can apply the patterns in a quantitative manner.

We need to make a clarifying point about risk management as addressed in this book. Most of the security risk literature refers to systems instead of enterprises, that is, most risk-related activity has traditionally been done at a system level, while we are presenting risk assessment at the enterprise-wide level. Our risk assessment pattern system and the patterns that it contains are general enough that they can be applied at the strategic enterprise level, and can also be applied to each system. Some risk mitigation occurs at the enterprise level, but most mitigation and safeguarding occurs at the system or operational level.

Assume that you have determined your security needs and risks at the enterprise level, and you want to put in place the safeguards to protect organizational assets and mitigate risks. The safeguards include security services and mechanisms. They typically exist at the system or operational level, and are covered in the chapters that follow. It is difficult to make a direct connection between the organizational needs and risks, on one hand, and the design and implementation of system services, on the other hand. The two patterns in this section are designed to bridge the gap. First, ENTERPRISE SECURITY APPROACHES (148) helps to map basic the security approaches of prevention, detection, and response to the organizational needs and risks. Second, ENTERPRISE SECURITY SERVICES (161) identifies services, such as identification and authentication or access control, that correspond to a selected approach to protect assets and mitigate risks.

For example, suppose that you have identified enterprise financial data as an asset that needs to be kept confidential from competitors. It would be better to prevent unauthorized disclosure from occurring than to detect when such disclosure occurs and try to recover from it. A typical security service to achieve prevention is access control. In this example, ENTERPRISE SECURITY APPROACHES (148) helps to select prevention as the appropriate approach, and ENTERPRISE SECURITY SERVICES (161) helps to identify access control as an appropriate service. Note in the latter case that ENTERPRISE SECURITY SERVICES (161) does not specify how access control will be achieved—that is the purpose of access control patterns in later chapters.

How can an enterprise protect its assets in its interaction with external partners? ENTERPRISE PARTNER COMMUNICATION (173) is intended to help achieve this goal. It is the final pattern presented in this chapter.

The risk patterns in this chapter, and the ENTERPRISE PARTNER COMMUNICATION (173) pattern, were written by Sasha Romanosky. The remaining patterns were written by a team at the MITRE Corporation consisting of Jody Heaney, Duane Hybertson, Susan Chapin, Malcolm Kirwan Jr. and Ann Reedy. Hybertson and Romanosky wrote the introductory material for the chapter, and Duane integrated the material into the chapter.

Frank Buschmann and Peter Sommerlad provided helpful shepherding comments for the MITRE patterns. Aaldert Hofman and Duane Hybertson provided shepherding comments for Sasha's patterns. Markus Schumacher provided helpful comments on integrating the material into the chapter.

6.1 Security Needs Identification for Enterprise Assets

This is the root pattern for all enterprise security concerns. It helps resolve the issue of whether security is really needed and, if it is, what properties of security should be applied for a particular enterprise. Security properties considered include confidentiality, integrity, availability, and accountability.

Example

A new wing of a museum of gemstones is to be opened. The museum has significant previous experience handling gems, and theft is a large enough risk for the museum to want protection from the unauthorized removal of any gems. The museum also has information about the collections, and employee information, that should be protected from damage or deletion, and in some cases should be kept confidential. How can the museum determine the assets that need security protection, and which types of protection?

Context

An enterprise considers security as a significant non-functional requirement. Key business factors and assets of the enterprise are understood.

Problem

An enterprise that considers security to be important must plan for appropriate security in accordance with the overall enterprise business plans. An enterprise may need to address legacy security plans and policies for the enterprise, or develop completely new ones. The same will apply to any information technology (IT) systems that are major assets of the enterprise. For the IT systems, the enterprise may need to adopt an existing security architecture or specify a new target architecture. To determine the most appropriate security to select and implement, the enterprise must establish its validated security needs.

How can realistic enterprise security needs be explicitly identified?

The resolution of this problem is strongly intertwined with the environment of the enterprise, which consists of the following *forces*:

- The enterprise needs to comply with laws and regulations, such as privacy laws
- It needs to handle sensitive information in a way that protects confidentiality
- It must comply with its own existing policy, especially any security policies
- It needs to provide sufficient protection for mission-critical business assets
- It must ensure that the security employed has minimum potential impact on business efficiency and efficacy—that is, it does not protect more than is necessary
- It must know when undesired events occur
- It must be able to recover from undesired events
- Overall costs need to be minimized

Solution

Systematically and explicitly identify the types of business assets that need protection and determine the types of protection they need. This activity is typically performed by an enterprise architect or strategic planner, and includes five steps:

1. *Identify the business assets* of the enterprise:

    - Information or data assets such as personnel and financial data
    - Physical assets such as personnel and buildings

2. *Identify business factors* that influence the security protection needs of assets, both external and internal to the enterprise:

    - Laws and regulations, such as privacy laws: see [DoJ02], [EU95], [EU02], and [FOIA96]
    - Enterprise partner relationships
    - Enterprise mission, goals, and objectives
    - Desire for strong enterprise financial health

- Business processes, such as accounting and ordering processes
- Sensitive business events, such as the monthly payroll processing
- Locations at which business processes and events occur

3. *Determine which assets relate to which business factors.* Examples include:

- A privacy law may apply to employee data
- Certain physical asset types may exist only at certain business locations
- Selected financial data may need to be shared with an enterprise partner

4. *Identify what types of security may be needed*: see [ISO15408], [CMU03], [DCD+02], and [NSA02]. Our recommended set is:

- Protection against inadvertent or unauthorized disclosure: confidentiality
- Protection against inadvertent or unauthorized modification: integrity
- Making business assets available for authorized use: availability
- Attribution of responsibility for actions: accountability

Confidentiality, integrity and availability are the core properties of security literature. Accountability is also important, but it has a different context. Confidentiality, integrity and availability are attributes of an asset, while accountability is not. When someone is specifying security properties of enterprise assets, it is important to identify who is responsible for security related activities, and that is where accountability comes in.

5. Based on the business factors, *determine for each asset type which types of security are needed*. The desire for security must be balanced against the resources required to achieve security in making this determination. More details about the association of common types of assets, types of security needed, and business factors are provided in the Implementation section below.

These steps can be applied in a linear fashion, as listed, but other alternatives are also possible. The Dynamics section discusses allowable sequences.

Structure

Using the UML class diagram notation, the general relationships among assets, business factors, and security properties are illustrated in the figure below. A *security need* is an association between an *asset type* and a *security property*: each asset type needs a security property. A given asset type may need any number of security properties (0, 1, or multiple), while a given security property may be needed by any number of asset types. *Business factors* influence security needs. The security properties are listed in the figure, as well as common asset types and business factors:

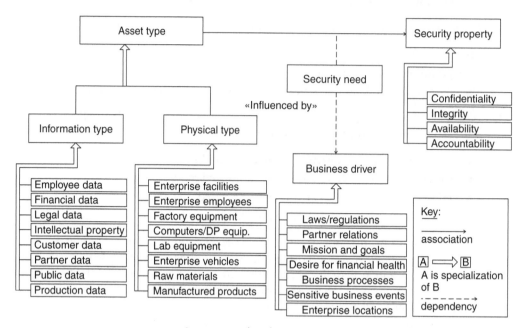

Security needs solution structure

Dynamics

Allowable sequences for performing the solution steps are shown in the figure on page 93. Identifying assets and identifying business factors are essentially independent activities, and can therefore be performed in parallel. However, both activities must be performed prior to determining relationships between assets and business factors. There is often some iteration among these three steps. Defining the set of security properties is also independent, and can be performed in parallel with the first three steps.

Defining properties can also be trivial, providing that the enterprise planner agrees with our suggested set of properties: confidentiality, integrity, availability, and accountability. Some enterprises may want to focus on a subset of these, or add related properties such as privacy, safety, or reliability. Several references discuss this issue further: see [ISO15408], [CMU03], [DCD+02], and [NSA02]. In any case, both defining properties and defining relationships must be performed prior to the last step, determining asset security needs.

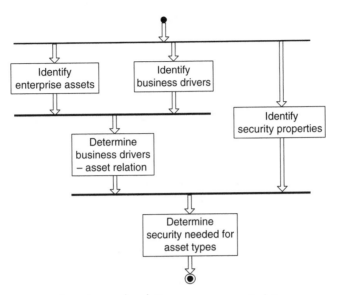

Security needs solution sequence constraints

Implementation

Business factors tend to present conflicting forces regarding security. Some, such as laws and regulations, the sensitivity of certain assets, and the desire to be viewed as a secure enterprise, encourage a high level of security. Others, such as cost constraints, the need for financial health, and the desire to be viewed as open and accessible, encourage a minimum degree of security. The result of this trade-off is that assets need to be differentiated according to their importance to the enterprise.

An investment in security is needed for critical assets, while a greater degree of risk may be accepted for non-critical assets. Critical assets typically are those whose loss or damage would cause significant harm to the enterprise, such as assets whose protection is required by law, strategic plans and other assets related to competitive advantage, irreplaceable items, the reputation of the enterprise, or assets whose loss would entail significant cost impact. Non-critical assets are those whose loss or damage would cause little or no harm to the enterprise, such as easily replaceable items, or information that could be divulged with little or no effect.

In addition to criticality of asset, the types of security needed can also vary by type of asset. Confidentiality and integrity typically apply to data. Integrity and availability apply to physical assets as well. Availability applies to services and may also apply to data. Accountability applies to actions taken on assets. To some degree confidentiality conflicts with availability—the more available an asset is, the less confidential it tends to be.

In some cases, one asset or type of asset may require all types of security protection. A software program is an example:

- It may be proprietary, in which case it requires confidentiality
- It needs to be protected against unauthorized change, and it thus requires integrity
- It must be accessible for authorized users, and it thus requires availability
- Any changes made to it must be known and attributed, and it thus requires accountability.

The following tables identify typical asset categories that need protection, the type of security needed to protect the assets, the business factors that influence the need, and some explanatory discussion. The tables provide common examples from an enterprise perspective, but they should not be construed as addressing all possible asset types. Table 6.2 lists and discusses protection of information assets, while Table 6.3 lists and discusses protection of physical assets.

In using the above tables, it is important to understand, first, that the information is generated from an overall enterprise perspective, and second, that specific combinations may vary from those in the tables for a given enterprise.

An example will illustrate both of these points. Table 6.2 indicates that personnel data needs availability, while financial data does not. The reasoning is that, in a typical enterprise, availability of finance information is not needed outside the finance department and the senior officers, while availability of personnel data is needed by multiple parts of the enterprise, such as human resources, finance, training, and

Table 6.2 Common information asset categories and protections

ASSET TYPE	PROTECTION NEEDED	BUSINESS FACTORS	DISCUSSION
Personnel data (including payroll)	Confidentiality, integrity, availability, and accountability	• Privacy laws • Competition issues	Privacy law will require that personnel private information be treated confidentially. Enterprise staff will need assurance that only human resource staff can modify their information. The data will need to be available to human resource staff as needed, and to financial staff to support payroll. Changes to personnel data must be accountable within the enterprise.

Table 6.2   Common information asset categories and protections (*continued*)

ASSET TYPE	PROTECTION NEEDED	BUSINESS FACTORS	DISCUSSION
Financial data (enterprise financial data)	Confidentiality, integrity, accountability	• Reporting requirements of tax collection agency • Competition issues • Nature of the enterprise (public, private, or stock-held)	Financial laws and the regulations of government agencies must be upheld in the enterprise or legal repercussions will ensue. Such laws and regulations will require that the financial data be protected from unauthorized modifications and that when modifications occur, there is a clear record of accountability in the enterprise. No enterprise willingly provides its financial data to its competition; the confidentiality of this information must be protected.
Legal data (for example, contracts and information on legal proceedings)	Confidentiality, integrity, accountability	• Law • Competition issues	An enterprise will need to provide confidentiality under contract law that may also require confidentiality of information related to participants in the contract. The modification of such contracts should be restricted to authorized and knowledgeable personnel and there should be a clear record of accountability in the enterprise.

Table 6.2   Common information asset categories and protections (*continued*)

ASSET TYPE	PROTECTION NEEDED	BUSINESS FACTORS	DISCUSSION
Intellectual property (data and processes)	Confidentiality, integrity, availability	• Partially dependent on the nature of the enterprise (public, private, stock-held) • Some competition issues	While some intellectual information (for example, advertisements) will be for the public, others, such as sensitive business processes, will not. Sensitive intellectual property may need restricted access. At the same time, if the business process contains design specifications, it may also need to be highly available within the enterprise.
Customer and business partner data (including personal and financial data and intellectual property)	Confidentiality, integrity, accountability	• Competitive issues • Service issues if a public company	Enterprise privacy information may be contained in this data. If competitors are aware of the relationships with customers and business partners, they can cause an enterprise to lose its competitive edge. Access to all customer and partner data should be accounted for to ensure that it is not altered in unauthorized ways, and that access to the data is restricted.
Public data (product/service information, advertisements, public enterprise information)	Integrity, availability	• Service issues	Unauthorized modification of the data could result in loss of enterprise reputation and/or business share. When such public information is made unavailable, a denial of service situation arises.

Table 6.3 Common physical asset categories and protections

ASSET TYPE	PROTECTION NEEDED	BUSINESS FACTORS	DISCUSSION
Buildings	Integrity, availability	• Critical business processes	An enterprise needs to protect the buildings that provide a work environment for the enterprise from unauthorized modifications or destruction. By doing so, they also promote the availability of the buildings for the enterprise.
Employees	Availability, accountability	• Critical business employees and processes	An enterprise needs to provide environments that are safe for personnel to ensure the availability of critical personnel. In part they accomplish protecting personnel by establishing accountability for employees.
Raw materials/ durable goods/ manufactured products	Integrity, availability	• Need to minimize the cost of doing business	Raw materials and durable goods need to be available for use in business processes as required. The enterprise needs to be able to assure its client base that manufactured products will be available as required. Damage, theft, or destruction of raw materials/durable goods will make them unavailable to support business processes. Likewise, damage, theft, or destruction of products will make them unsalable to clients.

security. Clearly the finance department needs availability of financial data, but this pattern is an enterprise-level pattern, and across the typical enterprise availability of financial data is not a significant issue. In addition, this table is only representative of common associations. There may be variations for specific enterprises—each will have its own business processes that may differ.

Example Resolved

This example solves the problem identified as the problem example described earlier. The museum enterprise identifies the following asset types and business factors:

Information asset types

- Museum employee data
- Museum financial/insurance data, partner financial data
- Museum contractual data and business planning
- Museum research and associated data
- Museum advertisements and other public data
- Museum database of collection information

Physical assets

- Museum building
- Museum staff
- Museum collections and exhibits
- Museum transport vehicles

External business factors

- Insurance policy constraints
- International laws and agreements relative to on-loan materials
- Privacy laws
- Museum charter
- Goals and strategies relative to exhibits
- Loan of materials and accessions (acquisitions)
- Requirements or constraints of organizations that loan materials

Internal business factors

- Tracking of exhibit items/cataloguing
- Item data, including location and value (both a factor and an asset)
- Exhibit planning, including loan agreements, transport and installation plans and schedules, legal contracting with exhibitors

- Accession (acquisition) planning, via purchase or loan or gift
- Legal data (acquisition)
- Cost constraints, including funds available for acquisition, personnel and patron data (including donation amounts), financial data (how much depends on charter: public, private, semi-public, and so on), and cost of security
- Intellectual property, such as studies and research data, statistics and papers
- Public information, including hours and current exhibit schedules (near term) as well as brochure and exhibit publications
- Building plans
- Importance of enterprise reputation for security
- Importance of enterprise reputation for accessibility
- Sensitive business events, including accession of new items, asset transport to alternate locations, cleaning/caretaking of assets, and special temporary accession for on-loan exhibits

The planner generates a scope statement listing all the above information. The scope statement will be presented to and refined with the museum director. Together they will work to generate an asset protection list such as that shown in Table 6.4.

Known Uses

Identification of enterprise assets and their security needs is best practice, but is often done informally or as part of security risk analysis. A few examples that illustrate concepts in this pattern—and in some cases were sources for the guidance in the pattern—are briefly discussed here.

The Systems Security Engineering Capability Maturity Model (SSE CMM) [CMU03] defines capability levels of a security engineering process, associated with risk assessment. It has elements in common with this pattern:

- It addresses security across the scope of the enterprise
- It addresses coordination of security needs driven from external entities, including laws, policies, standards
- The assess impact process includes identifying and characterizing enterprise assets and the need for confidentiality, integrity, availability, accountability, authenticity or reliability.

PriceWaterhouseCoopers has a process for designing an enterprise security framework that incorporates many of the elements of this pattern [PWC01]. It tailors a security process based on the business requirements and factors of an enterprise. It includes asset inventory collection and information classification.

Mint Business Solutions has defined an approach to security in the context of best practice in enterprise information management [MBS03]. Within this broad

Table 6.4 Establishing security properties for the museum:

ASSET TYPE	REQUIRED SECURITY PROPERTIES	BUSINESS FACTOR
Museum employee data	Confidentiality (HR, management, individual) Integrity (HR, individual only) Availability (HR and management) Accountability (changes in HR)	• Privacy law • Enterprise/employee relations
Museum financial/ insurance data, partner financial data	Confidentiality Integrity Basic accounting	• Contractual obligations • Financial reporting laws
Museum contractual data and business planning	Confidentiality Integrity Basic accounting	• Museum/partner relationships • Protect acquisition and transport plans and strategies • Protect scheduling data • Insurance policy constraints
Museum research and associated data	Confidentiality (restricted to narrow group)	• Museum charter requirements • Intellectual property • Enterprise/employee relations • Enterprise/public reputation
Museum advertisements and other public data	Integrity	• Enterprise/public reputation • Museum charter requirements • Partner reputations for loan exhibits
Museum building	Integrity Accountability (for any change)	• Insurance policy constraints • Enterprise/employee relations • Enterprise/public relations
Museum staff	Availability (safety)	• Enterprise/employee relations • Laws • Enterprise/public reputation
Museum collections and exhibits	Integrity Availability Accounting	• Insurance policy constraints • Enterprise/partner relations • Costs

framework, they base their security approach on the ISO standard 17799. This standard identifies a set of controls that include:

- Organization of assets and resources, with relation to managing information security
- Asset classification and control, so that they may be identified and protected
- Information security policy
- Compliance with any criminal and civil law, statutory, regulatory or contractual obligations, and any other security requirement

These controls correspond to the identification of assets and business factors for security addressed in this pattern.

Other standards and practices, including ISO 13335 Part 3 [ISO13335-3], SANS Institute [SANSa], and Operationally Critical Threat, Asset, and Vulnerability Evaluation (OCTAVE) [AD01], discuss asset identification as part of the overall risk analysis process. OCTAVE is an asset-driven evaluation approach that requires an analysis team to identify information-related assets such as information and systems that are important to the organization.

Consequences

SECURITY NEEDS IDENTIFICATION FOR ENTERPRISE ASSETS (89) has the following **benefits**:

- It facilitates making balanced and informed decisions about enterprise security needs, by making the competing forces and business factors explicit. The trade-offs in these factors cause a clear distinction to be made between critical and non-critical assets. The result is increased likelihood that security properties will be applied where needed. That is, protection needs will be explicitly designated for the most critical assets.
- An additional beneficial result of applying this pattern is that traceability of business asset protection needs back to the relevant business factors is produced and is available for additional use. This information offers a useful rationale to support the evolution of security needs over time. It can also be used, as indicated above, as a basis for more detailed protection requirements in ENTERPRISE SECURITY SERVICES (161).

SECURITY NEEDS IDENTIFICATION FOR ENTERPRISE ASSETS (89) also suffers from the following **liabilities**:

- Applying this pattern does not come free of charge. It requires an investment of resources, including the time of people who have intimate knowledge of enterprise assets and business factors. While the benefits of applying the pattern are expected to exceed these costs, it is possible for an enterprise to assign people to this task who have less than adequate knowledge of enterprise assets and business factors, and thus to obtain results that are inaccurate or not useful.

■ It is also possible for an enterprise to produce good results from this pattern, but then fail to make use of the results in succeeding patterns.

In both cases, the cost of applying this pattern can exceed the benefits.

See Also

After applying this pattern, the next step typically is to apply a set of risk-assessment patterns to further calibrate the security needs of each asset type to determine more specific security requirements. The set of risk patterns in this chapter help with asset valuation, threat assessment, vulnerability assessment, and risk determination, and assists in deciding how much protection is needed for each business asset type. While SECURITY NEEDS IDENTIFICATION FOR ENTERPRISE ASSETS (89) is somewhat internally focused, the risk assessment patterns include both internal and external considerations.

Following risk assessment, the next step is to assess enterprise security approaches that meet the combined security needs and requirements from this pattern and from the risk assessment.

6.2 Asset Valuation

Asset valuation helps you to determine the overall importance an enterprise places on the assets it owns and controls. Loss or compromise of such assets may result in anything from hard costs, such as fines and fees, to soft costs due to loss of market share and consumer confidence.

Also Known As

Impact Assessment, Business Impact Analysis

Example

The museum has begun a risk assessment and identified the following assets to be in scope:

Information Assets

- Museum employee data
- Museum financial/insurance data, partner financial data
- Museum contractual data and business planning
- Museum research and associated data
- Museum advertisements and other public data
- Museum database of collections information

Physical Assets

- Museum building
- Museum staff
- Museum collections and exhibits
- Museum transport vehicles

They must now determine the overall importance of these assets.

Context

An enterprise has determined which assets are to be included in the overall risk-assessment process, and must now ascertain the value it places on those assets.

Problem

The ability to define an asset's value is a key component of any risk assessment. Threats and vulnerabilities that target and expose an asset are only significant within the context of the asset's value. Without this determination, an enterprise is unable to properly assess the risks posed to its assets.

How can an enterprise determine the overall value of its assets?

An enterprise must resolve the following forces:

- It must develop a standardized way of assessing and describing an asset's worth
- It must provide consistent results despite the subjectivity inherent in this process
- It must be able to assess, as much as possible, the soft costs due to loss or compromise of an asset
- It may not be able fully to evaluate the safety impact due to the loss of an asset without having previously experienced a harmful event
- When evaluating hard costs, an enterprise may waste time on incidental costs, or those of much lesser value relative to the asset

Solution

Systematically determine the overall value of the assets identified in the scope of the risk assessment. This process means to perform the following four steps:

1. Determine the security value.

   Determine the security value of the asset based on the importance the enterprise places on guaranteeing the asset's information security properties: confidentiality, integrity, availability and accountability.

2. Determine the financial value.

   Determine the financial value of the enterprise asset based on the cost of repair or replacement as well as the cost to maintain and operate the asset. Remember that costs such as electricity and storage are probably distributed across many assets.

3. Determine the impact to business.

   Determine the value of the asset in relation to the impact a compromise of the asset would have on the enterprise's business processes.

4. Determine the overall value and build an asset valuation table.

   Combine the results of the security, financial and business valuations and determine the overall value the enterprise places on the asset. Enter these results into the asset valuation table.

Dynamics

The allowable sequence for performing the asset valuation process is shown in the next figure. The three factors, security value, financial value, and business impact, can be assessed in any order. The results are collected and entered into the asset valuation table.

Implementation

For each section, create a value rating scale by defining a range, then providing an accompanying description. Examples for security value, financial value and business impact have been provided in Tables 6.5, 6.6, and 6.7 respectively. To maintain consistency with THREAT ASSESSMENT (113) and VULNERABILITY ASSESSMENT (125), six ratings are defined. Note that the ratings may be modified according to the preference of the enterprise, although they should remain consistent throughout the risk assessment.

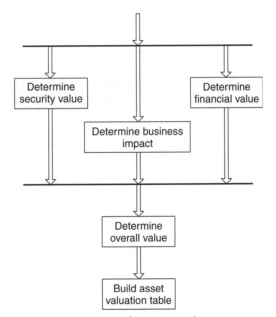

Sequence constraints of the asset valuation process

1. Determine the security value.

   Determine the security value of an asset by considering the following:

   ■ Demand for multiple security properties of a single asset. An asset that requires all four properties would have a significantly higher value than an asset that has a single requirement.

■ The extent of the consequence due to a compromise of an asset's security property. For example, the consequence of the unauthorized modification to a payment transaction could be far more severe than modification to a research and development document, though they both require integrity protection.

■ Health and safety implications resulting from the loss or damage of physical assets, for example ladders, bridges, security guards, or informational assets, such as evacuation procedures, fire containment and first aid instructions.

The information security requirements are normally provided by the asset owner. Otherwise, the security needs of the asset can be identified by applying SECURITY NEEDS IDENTIFICATION FOR ENTERPRISE ASSETS (89).

Use Table 6.5 to qualify the security value placed on the asset.

2. Determine the financial value.

Determine the financial value of an asset by considering the following:

■ Cost to replace or repair asset due to a damaging event

■ Regulatory or legal penalties, fines or fees incurred due to a security violation

Table 6.5 Security requirements rating

RATING	QUALITATIVE	DESCRIPTION
6	Extreme	The asset requires an extreme degree of confidentiality, integrity, and availability. Compromise of these security properties would expose massive amounts of confidential information and endanger public safety.
5	Very high	The asset requires a very high degree of confidentiality, integrity, availability or accountability. Compromise of one or more of these properties would expose sensitive information and possibly endanger public safety
4	High	The asset requires a high degree of confidentiality, integrity, availability or accountability. Compromise of these properties would expose sensitive information, violating local or federal legislation.
3	Medium	The asset has a moderate requirement for information security controls. Compromise of the security properties would violate corporate policy and possibly local or federal legislation.
2	Low	The asset has a low requirement for security. Compromise of the asset would expose only non-critical information or data.
1	Negligible	The information is publicly available or the asset has no information security value for the enterprise.

- Transaction value for which the asset is responsible
- Time incurred by an employee or contractor to receive, configure, or maintain an asset
- Loss of productive employee time, or work backlog incurred

Replacement and repair costs can be obtained from an enterprise's procurement department, which in turn obtains them either from a VAR (value-added reseller) or directly from the vendor. Regulatory fines and penalties are usually publicly and readily available from the entity that enforces the fines, such as a local or federal government. Hard costs associated with assets that serve a health and safety purpose include hospital and insurance fees, as well as the cost of a cleanup from a fire or flood.

Use Table 6.6 to qualify the financial value placed on the asset.

3. Determine the impact to business.

   Determine the impact to business processes by considering the following:

   - Loss of customer or investor confidence as a result in the compromise of the asset
   - Loss of competitive advantage due to compromise of security properties
   - Impact to enterprise partner relationships. or other contractual repercussions
   - Lack (or presence) of alternate service: that is, if an alternate service exists that can fulfill customer needs, than the loss of one service (or asset) may have reduced implications

Table 6.6 Financial value rating

RATING	QUALITATIVE	DESCRIPTION
6	Extreme	The asset has an extreme monetary value for the enterprise. Loss or damage of the asset would probably bankrupt the enterprise.
5	Very high	The asset has a major monetary value. Loss or damage of the asset would impose a substantial financial burden on the enterprise.
4	High	The asset has a significant monetary value. Repair or replacement would require significant funds.
3	Medium	The asset has moderate financial value. Loss or damage of the asset would require financial repurposing.
2	Low	The asset has low financial value to the company.
1	Negligible	The asset has no monetary value.

- Extent of disruption to other enterprise services due to asset dependencies
- Percentage of customer base affected by outage or degradation of service

Disaster recovery and business continuity plans found in many enterprises may already sort assets by value to the organization. This can provide a starting point for defining the relative business value an enterprise places on the asset.

Business impact is inherently more subjective and difficult to assess than hard costs. Quite often one may not be able to completely predict the loss of customer confidence, or the extent of loss of competitive advantage. One may, however, draw on events that have occurred to other enterprises of similar size in similar markets.

Use Table 6.7 to qualify the business value placed on the asset.

4. Determine the overall value.

   Determine the overall value the enterprise places on the asset from the results of the security, financial and business impact valuations. Use Table 6.8 to qualify the overall value of the asset to the enterprise and collect them in Table 6.9.

   There will not be direct translation from these three ratings to the single overall value. It is more likely that the overall value will be the highest of the three ratings. That is, if an asset has a very high security value, but a low financial value, its overall value should still be appropriately high.

Table 6.7   Business impact rating

RATING	QUALITATIVE	DESCRIPTION
6	Extreme	The enterprise cannot function without this asset. Its compromise or loss would result in immediate termination of critical business services.
5	Very high	This asset represents a major service of the enterprise. Its loss would result in termination of a critical service or severe degradation of many services.
4	High	This asset supports many enterprise services. Its loss would results in termination of a major service or degradation of services.
3	Medium	This asset supports a fair number of customers, or supports a major service of the enterprise. Its loss would result in degradation of more important services.
2	Low	This asset supports an ancillary enterprise service. Its compromise would have a slight impact on business services.
1	Negligible	The loss of asset would have no impact to the business.

Table 6.8 Overall asset value scale

RATING	QUALITATIVE	DESCRIPTION
6	Extreme	The enterprise places the highest possible value on this asset. Its compromise results in human deaths, immediate and total loss of business services or financial bankruptcy.
5	Very high	The asset represents or supports a critical business function for the enterprise. Loss or damage of it results in severe financial, security or health repercussions.
4	High	The asset is highly valued because of its security requirements or customer focus. Its loss would result in considerable harm to customer services and reputation.
3	Medium	The asset is of moderate value. It has some security needs and financial value. Compromise of it would impede the enterprise's mission.
2	Low	This asset is of minor financial value. Compromise of it results in little business impact.
1	Negligible	The asset has insignificant importance for the enterprise. It is easily replaced or repaired. It has little to no security requirements and represents no health impact.

Table 6.9 Asset valuation table template

ASSET	SECURITY VALUE	FINANCIAL VALUE	BUSINESS IMPACT	OVERALL VALUE

Example Resolved

After applying ASSET VALUATION (103), the museum has determined the value for its information and physical assets. These are shown in Tables 6.10 and 6.11 respectively.

Table 6.10 Information asset valuation table

ASSET	SECURITY VALUE	FINANCIAL VALUE	BUSINESS IMPACT	OVERALL
Museum employee data	5	3	5	5
Museum financial/insurance data, partner financial data	4	3	4	4
Museum contractual data and business planning	4	3	4	4
Museum research and associated data	3	2	3	3
Museum advertisements and other public data	1	2	2	2
Museum database of collections information	3	3	4	4

Table 6.11 Physical asset valuation table

ASSET	SECURITY VALUE	FINANCIAL VALUE	BUSINESS IMPACT	OVERALL
Museum building	5	5	6	6
Museum staff	6	5	6	6
Museum collections and exhibits	5	6	5	6
Museum transport vehicles	3	2	2	3

Variants

An enterprise may choose a different scale, or demand a more complete qualitative description. This is certainly acceptable: the important consideration is that the scale be consistent throughout the use of the pattern and for all assets. For example, [Pel01] uses the following qualitative values for information sensitivity:

■ High: extreme sensitivity—restricted to specific individual need to know. Its loss or compromise may cause severe financial, legal, or reputation damage to the enterprise.

■ Medium: used only by specific authorized groups with legitimate business need. May have significant adverse impact, possible negative financial impact.

■ Low: information for internal business use within the company. May have adverse impact, negligible financial impact.

[Pel01] also uses the following quantitative table to describe financial loss:

Table 6.12 Financial loss scale

FINANCIAL LOSS	VALUATION SCORE
Less than $2,000	1
Between $2k and $15k	2
Between $15k and $40k	3
Between $40k and $100k	4
Between $100k and $300k	5
Between $300k and $1M	6
Between $1M and $3M	7
Between $3M and $10M	8
Between $10M and $30M	9
Over $30M	10

Known Uses

An asset valuation is a key component of all widely-accepted risk assessments, including those from [NIST800-30], [ISO13335-3], [ISO17799], [Pel01], and others. While they differ slightly in their approach, their purposes and overall goals are consistent.

Consequences

This pattern has the following benefits:

- An enterprise obtains a realistic and complete view of which assets are most critical to its business.
- The results of the asset valuation can be used to develop or update an enterprise's disaster recovery and business continuity plan documents.
- A qualitative value can be easier to obtain than hard costs required by a quantitative asset valuation, thus expediting the overall risk assessment process.

As well as the following liabilities:

- An enterprise may be forced to change its practices if it determines that an asset is worth a great deal more than it thought—a change which may be difficult and expensive. This will undoubtedly become a benefit in the long-term.
- The individuals implementing the pattern may find difficulty in translating results from other parties—for example, hard costs or subjective results—into values consistent with the rating system used here.

6.3 Threat Assessment

Threats are the likelihood of, or potential for, hazardous events occurring. They can affect any asset or object on which an enterprise places value. An enterprise threat assessment identifies the threats posed to the enterprise's assets, and determines the likelihood or frequency of their occurrence.

Example

The museum has begun a risk assessment and identified the following assets to be in scope:

Information asset types

- Museum employee data
- Museum financial/insurance data, partner financial data
- Museum contractual data and business planning
- Museum research and associated data
- Museum advertisements and other public data
- Museum database of collections information

Physical Assets

- Museum building
- Museum staff
- Museum collections and exhibits
- Museum transport vehicles

The museum has also identified the major security needs for these assets using SECURITY NEEDS IDENTIFICATION FOR ENTERPRISE ASSETS (89), and must now determine the threats to those assets.

Context

An enterprise has defined the assets to be included in a risk assessment and must now identify the events that could cause harm to those assets.

Problem

Enterprise assets face a barrage of attacks and hazardous events from all directions. Without effectively acknowledging the origins and frequency of these threats, an enterprise may never recognize the extent to which their assets are at risk.

How can an enterprise identify harmful events and determine the likelihood of their occurrence?

An enterprise must resolve the following forces:

- It must identify only those threats that have the potential for causing damage
- The type of business in which an enterprise is engaged will strongly affect the potential threat sources it will face
- The enterprise would like to develop a standardized way of identifying threats and assessing their likelihood, to be consistent with subsequent threat assessments
- The solution should address all assets included in the scope of a risk assessment, including informational and physical assets and, ideally, should be able to address vulnerabilities in non-IT systems

Solution

Systematically and explicitly identify and assess the threats against an enterprise and determine the types of protection they need. This activity is typically performed by an enterprise architect or strategic planner, and includes the following steps:

1. Identifying threats.

   Identify major threat sources that could potentially impact the assets defined by the scope of the risk assessment and trace their threat actions and consequences.

2. Building a threat table.

   Build a threat table by grouping threats first by asset type, then threat source.

3. Creating a likelihood scale.

   Create a scale for rating the frequency of attempted events, or likelihood for events occurring. This scale will represent the expected rate of occurrence of a given hazardous (natural or accidental) event, or an attack attempt.

4. Rating each threat.

   Rate each threat according to the likelihood scale, and update the threat table to reflect this rating.

Dynamics

First, identify threats to the assets define by the scope of the risk assessment and build a threat table. A threat likelihood scale can also be developed in parallel. Finally, using the severity scale, rate each threat and update the threat table. The allowable sequence for performing a threat assessment is shown in the figure below.

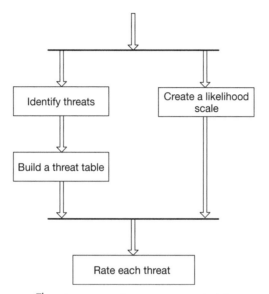

Threat assessment sequence constraints

Implementation

The implementation of the process for assessing threats is described below.

1. Identifying threats.

    A threat consists of three parts: the threat source, action and consequence.

    ■ The threat source is that which initiates an attack or causes an event: a youth, an employee, or a fire, for example.

    ■ The threat action is the specific method by which an attack or event is carried out. An e-mail worm, a careless command entry, or water short-circuiting a motherboard are examples of threat actions.

    ■ The threat consequence is the security violation that results from the successful realization of the harmful event. Disruption of service, exposure of data, or destruction of hardware are some examples of the consequences that may occur.

Commonly, the threat source and threat action are grouped together and referred to as simply a 'threat.'

When determining threats it is only necessary to consider those that are relevant to the assets, as defined by the scope of the risk assessment. Similarly, when an infrastructure is modified, such as when new applications are installed or new communication paths created, this threat landscape will change. Guidelines for defining the threat landscape include the following:

- Specific environmental threats can quickly be removed given geographical or geological situations. For example, earthquakes cannot occur where there is no tectonic collision, tsunamis can only reach so far inland—although a flood can certainly occur in a building with a water supply.

- Threats that have no measurable chance of occurring within the life expectancy of an asset can be eliminated. Forms of material decay or deterioration, or astronomical hazards—while all being possible—have such a low frequency of occurrence that they can realistically be ignored.

- Threats can only target vulnerabilities. If a system isn't vulnerable to an exploit, then there is no threat, and consequently no risk. Consider a network environment consisting solely of Unix machines. Attacks launched against that network exploiting a buffer overflow on a Microsoft IIS Web server will obviously be ineffective, and thus the threat landscape should not include these threats.

- Alterations to the management of data or other enterprise assets will alter the threat landscape. An attack that was previously not possible may now exist. For example, providing remote VPN access to employees now exposes an enterprise to residential-based threats.

Threat sources

Sources of threats can be natural or human in origin. Natural threat sources are environmental forces frequently referred to as 'Acts of God.' Examples of natural threat sources include the following: tsunami, earthquakes, wind, snow, or rain storms.

Human threat sources can be deliberate (attacks) or accidental (errors). Deliberate human threat sources are attackers and are differentiated by their motives, capabilities, and the assets they target. Those who seek to deliberately cause harm include the following:

- Hackers. They are generally motivated by mischief or grandstanding and may only seek publicity or notoriety among their peers. They employ simple tools, often precompiled using point-and-click interfaces created by others. While the tools may not be sophisticated, the results can range from the minor annoyance of a defaced Web page to major damage caused by the mass dissemination of malware such as worms or viruses.

■ Professional criminals. They are motivated by financial reward and thus may steal credit card numbers, personal health information (PHI) or specialized documents such as corporate trade secrets, blueprints or recipes, and offer them for sale to competitors, the corporation from which they were stolen, or the individuals themselves. Their techniques are more advanced than the youth hacker, both in organizational structure, technological skills and attack execution.

■ Terrorists. They care little for Web page defacement, but more for infrastructure disruption and destruction. Their methods can be crude but highly effective. The targets can be civilian, diplomatic, or military personnel in addition to public infrastructure systems such as power generation and distribution, water processing, telecommunications, financial/banking, emergency services, or transportation systems. Terrorist groups are often well funded and highly organized.

■ Internal threat. Current or past employees who are angry or disgruntled are motivated by revenge or anger. They know the assets and the defences of an organization, and can destroy data or interrupt services, posing a serious threat to any enterprise.

Accidental threat sources are actors who inadvertently cause damage or compromise the security posture of an asset. They may be employees or customers who are careless, inattentive or poorly-trained. This form of threat source might also be an application that is simply performing as programmed and mistakenly compromises a system.

Threat actions

Threat actions are the actual events that exploit the weakness of a system. They are the methods used by attackers to gain control of assets, they are the naturally-occurring events that cause damage to systems, and they are the mistakes made by negligent users. They fall into the following categories:

■ Natural. This includes extremes or fluctuations in temperature, causing metal fatigue or structural distress, electrical failures, surges, spikes or brownouts, fires, as well as natural disasters such as lightning strikes, earthquakes, uncontrolled flow of water into buildings or rooms through. rain, floods, inundation, storms or hurricanes.

■ Human deliberate. An example might be an attacker masquerading as a system administrator, using social engineering techniques to gather personal information about users, or an employee planting a logic bomb in a system, scheduled to erase critical system files.

■ Human accidental. For example, a data center employee who inadvertently stumbles and jerks the power cord from a production server, or an employee transferring a file from a personal laptop to a corporate desktop, unaware that the file is infected with a virus.

Threat consequences

The realization of a threat can result in the violation of one or more of the security properties defined throughout this book: confidentiality, integrity, availability, or accountability. Regardless of the source or action of the threat, the consequences will be one of disclosure, deception, disruption, or usurpation, as discussed by the security violations in Chapter 2.

2. Building a threat table.

   Grouping by asset type becomes useful when the final risk to each asset is determined. Further grouping by threat source ensures that one does not overlook the fact that the same threat action can be initiated by different sources, each with a corresponding, and possibly different, frequency. For example, theft can occur from both a professional criminal and an employee. However, the frequency of theft from employees may be significantly higher than that of a criminal.

   The threat consequence is included for each threat action, and provides supporting clarification of the possible outcome of an incident.

   It is possible that the threat table will be updated after the completion of the vulnerability assessment. Given the tight relationship between threats and vulnerabilities, identification of vulnerabilities can lead to the discovery of new threats that were previously not considered.

3. Creating a likelihood scale.

   While difficult to determine in precise quantitative terms, qualitative values can be used and numeric estimates can be correlated. As an example, Table 6.13 shows a modified version of the probability levels given by [Herr02].

Table 6.13 Event likelihood

RATING	LIKELIHOOD	DESCRIPTION
6	Extreme	The threat action is continually occurring
5	Very high	The threat action occurs very often
4	High	The threat action regularly happens
3	Medium	The threat action occurs infrequently
2	Low	This threat action rarely takes place
1	Negligible	The occurrence of this threat action is extremely unlikely within a human lifetime

Note that this table does not represent the only way to categorize event frequencies. Other threat assessments methodologies exist that define their own scale and they are equally valid. The important point is that an enterprise use the same scale year after year, to provide consistent results between assessments.

4. Rating each threat.

Each threat will have a certain likelihood or frequency of occurrence, and as expected, some will transpire more often than others, based on specific factors. Note that this is not the frequency of successful violations in which damage has occurred, but an event or attack that could cause damage.

To estimate or predict the frequency of a threat, it is necessary to consider many issues. Factors that affect the likelihood of a natural threat include the following:

■ Proximity to dangerous chemical or petroleum factories. A few additional miles from an industrial incident may make the difference between a precautionary evacuation of a facility and human fatalities.

■ The possibility of extreme weather patterns and fluctuations such as heat, wind, rain. While internal temperatures can be controlled to a certain degree, external temperatures can overload the control systems, affecting both human and mechanical systems. Specific geographical locations will naturally be more prone to such fluctuations and extremes.

■ The state of the operating facilities with regard to structural integrity, fire suppression, and other emergency response systems. Older, less sturdy buildings may require constant refurbishment, resulting in disruption of service.

Factors that affect the likelihood of a deliberate human threat include:

■ The time since a vulnerability has been publicly known. The longer since the vulnerability has been discovered, the greater the number of attackers that will be aware of it, and the more opportunity there will be to catalog, research and develop tools to exploit it.

■ Whether or not a working exploit is available for the vulnerability. Graphical user and command-line interface exploits certainly have a much greater chance of being used than ones that require custom development such as coding. Having precompiled or point-and-click code reduces the knowledge level required to launch an attack: suddenly, one does not need detailed knowledge of the vulnerability in order to exploit it.

■ The frequency of attack attempts. The more frequent the number of attack attempts, the greater the chance of a successful attack.

■ The potential reward offered to an attacker. Hacker challenges and monetary reward increase the chances of an attack.

- The asset value. High-wealth businesses and assets attract more attention than those of lesser value, and therefore offer more incentive for compromise. Attackers will therefore not generally target systems that contain no value, or provide no reward. There are two exceptions to this, however: either an attacker targets the system out of curiosity or simply to prove that it can be done, or an attacker breaches a useless system only to provide a launching point to another system of value (for example, compromising a home computer in order to penetrate a corporate network).

- The perceived difficulty of realizing a successful attack. If the asset is known to be heavily protected and the chances of reward low, the fewer will be the number of attempts.

- Public visibility and sentiment towards the business. Organizations that are viewed as having an unpopular affiliation, or that act inappropriately, may incur more attacks as a result.

- Employee morale. Low employee morale frustrates employees and can cause malicious or vengeful retaliation. It can also simply cause indifference to quality and service. Either way, low morale increases the potential for accidental or deliberate threat actions.

- Past prosecutions. If an organization is known for seeking retribution and prosecution of crimes, attackers will seek easier or less risky targets.

Factors that affect the likelihood of an accidental human threat include:

- The availability of skilled employees. If unqualified personnel are required to manage sensitive or complex systems, the opportunity for errors due to ignorance or mistakes increases greatly.

- Security measures. Administrative controls, such as user awareness and emergency training, educates users on policies and procedures, making them less susceptible to social engineering attacks and more aware of information security requirements.

- The frequency of changes to systems, including patches, upgrades, and other modifications. The more frequently changes are made, the more potential there will be for mistakes or corruption due to new configurations.

Arguably the most reliable method for determining the frequency of future events is historical data. Naturally-occurring events are often recorded by educational and governmental organizations for study. Commercial and governmental references exist that record information security attacks. Relevant data can also be collected from the enterprise's own systems. Some examples of useful sources include the following:

- Historical almanacs (in the cases of natural disasters).

- News archives including federal services. For example
  `http://www.fema.gov/`

- Information security newsletters and Web sites. For example, `http://www.securityfocus.com`, CERT, Symantec, FedCIRC and SANS.
- Current and archived intrusion detection, incident response and application system log files.
- Previous threat assessment documents, if available, may also contain particularly relevant information.

Example Resolved

From SECURITY NEEDS IDENTIFICATION FOR ENTERPRISE ASSETS (89), the museum has identified its informational and physical assets:

Information Asset Types

- Museum employee data
- Museum financial/insurance data, partner financial data
- Museum contractual data and business planning
- Museum research and associated data
- Museum advertisements and other public data
- Museum database of collections information

Physical Assets

- Museum building
- Museum staff
- Museum collections and exhibits
- Museum transport vehicles

After use of THREAT ASSESSMENT (113), the museum has identified a brief list of threats to information and physical assets, as shown in the threat Tables 6.14 and 6.15, respectively.

Known Uses

Threat assessment is, for example, defined in the ISO Technical Report 13335-3 [ISO13335-3]. This definition of the process focuses on three tasks: identification of threat sources, the threat target, and the threat likelihood. It identifies that determining the likelihood should take into account the threat frequency, the threat motive and geographical factors such as proximity to industrial factories. This technical report differentiates the threat likelihood simply as high, medium and low. The actual determination and definition is left to the implementer of the threat-assessment process.

Table 6.14 Threats to information assets

THREAT ACTION (FREQUENCY)	THREAT CONSEQUENCE
Natural	
Electrical spike in computer room (3)	Incapacitation, corruption of informational assets
Loss of electronic documents (3)	Incapacitation of informational assets
Professional criminals	
Theft of information assets (3)	Misappropriation, incapacitation, misuse, exposure, corruption of informational assets
Employees	
Unauthorized access to informational assets (5)	Exposure, falsification, incapacitation, misappropriation of informational assets
Data entry errors (5)	Corruption of information assets
Leaking confidential information (3)	Exposure of information assets

Table 6.15 Threats to physical assets

THREAT ACTION (FREQUENCY)	THREAT CONSEQUENCE
Natural	
Museum fire (3)	Incapacitation of physical assets
Fatigue of support fixtures, building structural failure (3)	Incapacitation of physical assets
Failure of monitoring and alarming systems (4)	Intrusion, misappropriation of physical assets
Professional criminals	
Theft of museum collections and exhibits (2)	Misappropriation of museum collections and exhibits
Physical attack against employees (3)	Incapacitation of employees

Table 6.15 Threats to physical assets (*continued*)

THREAT ACTION (FREQUENCY)	THREAT CONSEQUENCE
Employees	
Accidental damage to museum collections and exhibits (4)	Incapacitation of museum collections and exhibits
Accidental damage to vehicles (4)	Incapacitation of museum collections and exhibits
Theft of museum collections and exhibits (2)	Misappropriation of museum collections and exhibits
Misconfiguration of monitoring and alarm systems (4)	Incapacitation, obstruction of monitoring and alarm systems
Museum patrons	
Accidental damage to museum collections and exhibits (3)	Incapacitation of museum collections and exhibits

NIST also describes a complete risk management process whose first step is a risk assessment [NIST800-30]. Steps 3.2 and 3.5 in this process are dedicated to the identification of threats and determination of their likelihood. This publication also uses a likelihood scale of high, medium and low. In making the determination of the likelihood of a threat, this scale also incorporates the existing controls and their capability to neutralize the threat. NIST also separates the identification of threats and the likelihood of their realization into two separate processes.

In her publication *Security Engineering and Information Assurance*, Debra Herrmann describes the need for a complete information security process to identify threats, their type, source, and likelihood [Herr02].

Microsoft describes a threat and countermeasures pattern that offers alternative methods for identifying and assessing threats through 'Threat Modeling' [Mei03]. The authors use a method called STRIDE that categorizes threats based on the 'goals and purposes of the attacks.' The categories that make up the acronym are: spoofing, tampering, repudiation, information disclosure, denial of service and elevation of privileges.

Consequences

This pattern has the following benefits:

- The solution provides the enterprise with an understanding of the factors that increase both the existence and the frequency of harmful events.
- It identifies the consequences incurred should a given threat be realized.
- The threat assessment is a major component of the risk assessment pattern set that will prioritize and ultimately result in a more secure organization.

It also has the following liabilities:

- Accurate historical data may not be available, preventing the enterprise from acquiring useful threat frequency data.
- The effort required to conceive of all possible threats can be too time consuming for an enterprise. Constraints may therefore have to be placed on the completeness of the threat landscape.

6.4 Vulnerability Assessment

A vulnerability is a weakness that could be exploited by a threat, causing the violation of an asset's security property. Conducting an enterprise vulnerability assessment helps to identify the weaknesses of the enterprise's assets and the systems that enable access to them, and evaluates the severity if a vulnerability were to be exploited.

Also Known As

Vulnerability Analysis

Example

The museum has begun a risk assessment and identified the following assets to be in scope:

Information asset types

- Museum employee data
- Museum financial/insurance data, partner financial data
- Museum contractual data and business planning
- Museum research and associated data
- Museum advertisements and other public data
- Museum database of collections information

Physical assets

- Museum building
- Museum staff
- Museum collections and exhibits
- Museum transport vehicles

The museum has also identified the potential threats to those assets and must now determine vulnerabilities that can compromise those needs.

Context

An enterprise has defined the assets to be included in a risk assessment, and has identified potential threats, for example through applying THREAT ASSESSMENT (113). It must now identify the vulnerabilities that can be exploited by those threats.

Problem

Enterprise assets and the controls protecting them may be fully secure, or may have numerous weaknesses, some of which may never be exploited, and some of which may be exploited every day. Without proper cataloguing of these vulnerabilities, an enterprise might never recognize the extent of the weaknesses of their assets.

How can an enterprise identify vulnerabilities to its assets and determine the severity of those vulnerabilities?

An enterprise must resolve the following forces:

- It might have experience with a single tool or method for discovering weaknesses, but may not be aware of other techniques that can reveal other, potentially critical, vulnerabilities.

- It need only identify vulnerabilities for which threats exist, and therefore the enterprise must be able to determine if a given vulnerability has an associated threat.

- It would like to develop a standardized way of identifying vulnerabilities and assessing their severity, in order to be consistent with subsequent vulnerability assessments.

- The solution should address all assets included in the scope of a risk assessment, including informational and physical assets, and, ideally, should be able to address vulnerabilities in non-IT systems.

Solution

Systematically identify and rate probable vulnerabilities of the enterprise assets. This process involves the following five steps:

1. Collect threat information.

    Collect information on threats. For example, if THREAT ASSESSMENT (113) has been used, appropriate threat information is available from the resulting threat table.

2. Identify vulnerabilities.

    Using the threat table, identify the vulnerabilities of the assets and the systems protecting them defined in the scope of the risk assessment.

3. Build a threat-vulnerability table.

    Extend the threat table by associating each vulnerability with a threat action.

4. Create a severity scale.

    Create a scale for rating the severity of vulnerabilities. This scale will represent the degree to which an asset is susceptible to a vulnerability, and the potential impact should the vulnerability be exploited.

5. Rate each vulnerability.

   Rate each vulnerability according to the severity scale and update the threat-vulnerability table to reflect this rating.

Dynamics

The allowable sequence for performing the vulnerability assessment process is shown in the figure.

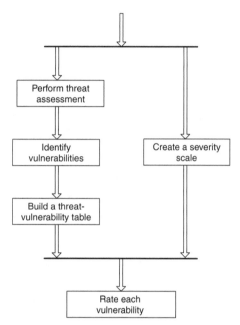

Vulnerability assessment sequence constraints

First collect appropriate threat information. Then, using the methods outlined, identify all vulnerabilities and associate them with threats in the threat table, creating the threat-vulnerability table. A vulnerability severity scale can be developed at any time. Finally, using this scale, rate each vulnerability.

Implementation

The implementation of the process for assessing vulnerabilities is described below.

1. Collect threat information.

   Threat information should include a list of events that could cause harm to assets and provide context for the vulnerabilities.

2. Identify vulnerabilities.

    Use any of the following methods to identify vulnerabilities exploitable by the threats in the threat table.

    2.1. System characteristics.

    [WT03] describes four main causes of system vulnerabilities, and while it focuses on software applications, the causes can be generalized to help identify weaknesses in non-IT systems.

    - Those that can be caused by dependency failure. Rarely, if ever, does an application not interact with other applications or systems to perform its function. These interactions may be with database tables, shared system libraries, network services or devices, or operating system resources. The behavior of the application in the event of a failure or unavailability of these dependencies is a prime target for attack. For example, how would an application respond when a security library could not be loaded? Does it bypass all security calls, log an error and continue, or halt all operation and alert operators? How does an application respond to low system resources such as low disk or memory conditions?

    - Those that can be caused by unanticipated data input. The absence of data input validation is a very common mistake. It can also be the most damaging, because the results can range from denial of service to complete subversion of the system through full administrator access. Buffer overflows and SQL injection are two of the most prevalent examples of this class of attack.

    - Those that can be caused by design vulnerabilities. As the size and complexity of an application grows, it becomes more difficult to identify and validate the flow and integrity of data. The potential for exploiting design flaws therefore increases. Such design flaws may include use of cleartext protocols where encrypted ones are necessary, acquiring escalated privileges by circumventing access or authorization controls, assumptions made by designers or developers regarding the use of or operation of the application, and jumping outside the bounds (and constraints) of the system to perform unauthorized tasks or operations.

    - Those that can be caused by implementation vulnerabilities. A most secure design can still lead to a substantial vulnerability if the implementation is faulty. This provides another reason why scale and complexity are impediments to secure systems. The larger and more intricate a design, the more opportunities there will be for implementation errors.

An example is software that deals with sensitive information. It must ensure that while processing the information, it is not temporarily copied to either disk or memory unprotected. Replay attacks, 'bait and switch,' and 'man in the middle' are all examples of implementation vulnerabilities: a replay attack is a form of network attack in which a valid data transmission is maliciously or fraudulently repeated or delayed, while a bait and switch is a form of fraud in which the fraudster lures in customers by advertising goods at an unprofitably low price, then reveals to potential customers that the advertised goods are not available, but that a substitute is. A 'man in the middle attack' (MITM) is an attack in which an attacker is able to read, insert and modify messages between two parties without either party knowing that the link between them has been compromised.

2.2. Development life cycle.

[NIST800-30] recognizes that vulnerability identification is dependent on the nature of an IT system and its phase in a development life cycle. Differentiation is made between systems being designed, systems being implemented, and systems in production.

For systems or applications that have not yet been designed, 'the search for vulnerabilities should focus on the organization's security policies, planned security procedures, system requirement definitions, and the vendors' or developers' security product analyses.' At this stage, these design documents and product specifications are all that are available for security review.

For systems that are in the process of being implemented, vulnerability identification 'should be expanded to include more specific information, such as the planned security features described in the security design documentation and the results of system certification test and evaluation.' This is where security auditing tools can first be used to test applications before they are released into production. These tools generally perform signature-based checks to test for known weaknesses.

Finally, for systems that are already in production, vulnerability identification 'should include an analysis of the IT system security features and the security controls, technical and procedural, used to protect the system.' For these systems, security auditing tools as well as penetration tests will identify weaknesses most effectively, although not necessarily safely. They function by directly testing for the presence of known exposures, as opposed to theorizing their existence based on documentation, policy or a countermeasure that is supposed to block an attack. Penetration tests can be a complex effort requiring the cooperation of many departments, including information security, operations, and application development. As mentioned, these tests can be most effective because they test the weakness of the IT system as well as the countermeasures that are (or should be) in place.

2.3.   Other.

Specialized techniques for identifying vulnerabilities in IT systems include the following:

- *Vulnerability scanning.* Vulnerability scanning is the act of running automated tools or procedural tests on networks and applications in order to detect or confirm the presence of vulnerabilities [WTS03].
- *Penetration tests.* Penetration testing is a procedure that attempts to circumvent, disable or otherwise defeat the security controls of a system using any available tool or technique.
- *Vulnerability catalogs.* These catalogs provide a list of vulnerabilities for specific applications and configurations. Examples include:

  - CERT Knowledgebase: `http://www.cert.org/kb`
  - CVE database: `http://www.cve.mitre.org`
  - NIST ICAT: `http://icat.nist.gov`

- Open Source Vulnerability Database: `http://www.osvdb.org/`
- *Vendor advisories and patch lists.* Commercial vendors and Open Source developers will often provide vulnerability advisories for their products.
- *Information security forums and mailing lists.* These lists provide a popular discussion and distribution forum for security vulnerabilities. For example:

  - Bugtraq: `http://www.securityfocus.com/`
  - SANS: `http://www.sans.org`
  - RISKS: `http://catless.ncl.ac.uk/Risks/`
  - Dartmouth College Institute for Security Technology Studies: `http://news.ists.dartmouth.edu/`

3. Build a threat-vulnerability table.

    Extend the threat table by pairing vulnerabilities with threats, creating a threat-vulnerability table. Recall that threats are grouped by threat source (natural, hacker, criminal, and so on), accommodating situations in which the same threat action (for example theft) originates from multiple sources (for example employees and criminals).

    This table format enforces the restriction that it is only necessary to consider vulnerabilities for which threats exist. If a vulnerability is found to have no associated threat, either remove the vulnerability from consideration, or update the threat table to include the threat.

    To determine whether a vulnerability has an associated threat, ask yourself if there is any way that the security properties (confidentiality, integrity, availability, and accountability) of an asset could be compromised as a result of the

Table 6.16 Vulnerability severity scale

RATING	SEVERITY	DESCRIPTION
6	Extreme	1. The vulnerability is trivially exploitable and commonly found, or 2. Major loss of life and destruction of systems would occur
5	Very high	1. The vulnerability is easily exploitable and found in most systems, or 2. Some loss of life and major destruction of systems would occur
4	High	1. Exploiting the vulnerability would be a challenge but it exposes many systems, or 2. Human physical injury, some destruction of systems would occur
3	Medium	1. The vulnerability is difficult to exploit, and exposes some systems, or 2. Significant disruption of service and compromise of confidentiality, availability, or integrity of assets would occur
2	Low	1. The vulnerability would be very difficult to exploit, with no real gain, or 2. Slight disruption of service or mild compromise of security properties would occur
1	Negligible	1. This is a theoretical vulnerability only exploitable with massive infrastructure or computing power, or 2. Minor distraction to business processes and no compromise of security properties would occur

weakness. Importantly, this does not answer the question of who caused the compromise, or how it occurred, but simply whether it could occur.

4. Create a severity scale.

   Create a severity rating scale by first defining a rank, then assign a meaning and description to each rank. An example is shown in Table 6.16. The rating represents the degree to which the asset is susceptible to the vulnerability, and the potential impact should the vulnerability be exploited. Note that the range and description are at the discretion of the enterprise—it can change the range, severity term, and description as appropriate. The important consideration is that the table remain constant throughout the risk assessment and across the enterprise.

5. Rate each vulnerability.

   Rate the severity of each vulnerability according to the considerations listed below.

5.1. General factors:

- The number of threats that can be realized as a result of a given vulnerability being exploited. Also, the number of systems affected by the vulnerability. If a single vulnerability provides the opportunity for many threats to be realized (and perhaps many subsequent vulnerabilities to be exploited), then the severity should be reflective of this.

- The prevalence of the systems affected by the vulnerability. Some vulnerabilities may impact uncommon or infrequently-used applications or enterprise resources, while others may impact a ubiquitous Internet service or physical infrastructure.

- Whether or not the weakness exists in default configurations or installations.

- Whether there are any preconditions that need to exist before the vulnerability can be exploited, such as the compromise of other systems or security controls.

- Whether the affected asset is responsible for monitoring or protecting other assets.

- Whether the attacker needs to lure victims to a hostile server in order to exploit a vulnerability.

5.1. Existing security controls.

Security measures that are already in place significantly affect both an enterprise's susceptibility (resistance) to a vulnerability, and the severity of damage it causes.

- *Preventative controls.* These controls are employed to inhibit attacks and prevent harmful events from reaching their destination. Firewalls, anti-virus scanners, code reviews, encryption techniques, fences, door locks, and so on are all forms of preventative controls.

- *Detective controls.* Detective controls are employed to discover attacks. By the time these controls are used, an attack or event has already occurred. These controls must be capable of reacting very quickly to prevent loss or damage. Technical examples are intrusion detection systems (IDS)—either host-based or network-based, audit trails, and so on. Physical detective controls would include tripwires, and IR or motion sensors. An administrative control would be a policy dictating mandatory job rotation and job vacation.

- *Corrective controls.* A potentially harmful event has occurred, and the detective controls have recognized it. Now the corrective controls are employed to mitigate the impact or loss due to the event. Intrusion prevention systems (IPS), and auto-restore features (as found in Windows XP, for example) are some examples of technical corrective controls. Physical controls would include doors or gates that lock automatically, trapping any intruders, fire suppressant systems, and security alarms.

■ *Recovery controls*. These controls are designed to recover from the loss or damage incurred by the event. Backups, disaster recovery (DR) and business continuity plans (BCP) are examples of recovery controls.

Note that deterrent controls are not included, as they assist in reducing the threat or probability of an incident.

Example Resolved

After applying a sequence of THREAT ASSESSMENT (113) (providing the threat action frequencies) and VULNERABILITY ASSESSMENT (125) patterns, the museum has identified the vulnerabilities to information and physical assets shown in Tables 6.17 and 6.18 respectively. The threat action frequency values of both tables are taken from THREAT ASSESSMENT (113).

Table 6.17 Threat-Vulnerabilities table for information assets

THREAT ACTION (FREQUENCY)	VULNERABILITY (SEVERITY)
Natural	
Electrical spike in computer room (3)	Lack of surge protection, uninterruptible power system (UPS) (4)
Loss of electronic documents (3)	Incomplete or corrupt data backups (4)
Professional criminals	
Theft of information assets (3)	Susceptibility of employees to bribery (3)
	Lack of proper physical controls for document storage (locks, safe) (4)
Employees	
Unauthorized access of informational assets (5)	Weak information security controls enabling unauthorized access (3)
Data entry errors (5)	Lack of data validation during form input (2)
Leaking confidential information (3)	Exposure of information assets (3)

Table 6.18   Threat-vulnerability table for physical assets

THREAT ACTION (FREQUENCY)	VULNERABILITY (SEVERITY)
Natural	
Museum fire (3)	Failure of fire alarm system (6)
	Failure of fire suppression system (5)
Fatigue of support fixtures, building structural failure (3)	Lack of regularly scheduled inspections (4)
Failure of monitoring and alarm systems (4)	Lack of regularly scheduled inspections (4)
Professional criminals	
Theft of museum collections and exhibits (2)	Lack of regular alarm testing procedures (3)
	Lack of adequate storage and protection of physical assets (3)
Physical attack against employees (3)	Lack of security training for employees (4)
Employees	
Accidental damage to museum collections and exhibits (4)	Carelessness of employees when handling/cleaning exhibits (2)
Accidental damage to vehicles (4)	Carelessness of employees while driving vehicles(2)
	Lack of regularly scheduled maintenance checks (4)
	Lack of adequate employee background checks (4)
Theft of museum collections and exhibits (2)	Lack of regular alarm testing procedures (3)
	Lack of adequate storage and protection of physical assets (3)
	Susceptibility of employees to bribery (4)
Misconfiguration of monitoring and alarm systems (4)	Lack of regular alarm testing procedures (3)
Museum patrons	
Accidental damage to museum collections and exhibits (3)	Carelessness of museum patrons when viewing exhibits (2)

Variants

The SANS Institute and the CERT Coordination Center at Carnegie Mellon are two renowned information security centers. They provide vulnerability lists and databases of common vulnerabilities. [CERTb] uses a purely quantitative scale of 0 to 180 to rank the severity of a vulnerability., whereas [SANSe] uses the following qualitative scheme:

- *Critical* vulnerabilities are those where essentially all planets align in favor of the attacker. These vulnerabilities typically affect default installations of very widely-deployed software, result in root compromise of servers or infrastructure devices, and the information required for exploitation (such as example exploit code) is widely available to attackers.
- *High* vulnerabilities are usually issues that have the potential to become critical, but have one or a few mitigating factors that make exploitation less attractive to attackers.
- *Moderate* vulnerabilities are those where the scales are slightly tipped in favor of the potential victim. Exploits that require an attacker to reside on the same local network as their victim, or only affect non-standard configurations or obscure applications, are likely to be rated moderate.
- *Low* vulnerabilities usually do not affect most administrators, and exploitation is largely unattractive to attackers. Often these issues require the attacker to have some level of access to a target already, require elaborate specialized attack scenarios, and only result in limited damage to a target.

[NIST800-30] uses the following definitions for vulnerability severity:

- *High*. Exercise of the vulnerability (1) may result in the highly-costly loss of major tangible assets or resources, (2) may significantly violate, harm, or impede an organization's mission, reputation, or interest, or (3) may result in human death or serious injury.
- *Medium*. Exercise of the vulnerability, (1) may result in the costly loss of tangible assets or resources, (2) may violate, harm, or impede an organization's mission, reputation, or interest, or (3) may result in human injury.
- *Low*. Exercise of the vulnerability (1) may result in the loss of some tangible assets or resources, (2) may noticeably affect an organization's mission, reputation, or interests.

The Common Vulnerability Scoring System [CVSS] is an open framework that can be used by any security or application vendor to determine the overall severity posed by a vulnerability. Three categories of metrics are scored and combine to produce a final score.

- The base metric represents the properties of a vulnerability that do not change over time, such as access complexity, access vector, degree to which the vulnerability compromises the confidentiality, integrity and availability of the system, and requirement for authentication to the system.

- The temporal metric measures the properties that do change over time, such as the existence of an official patch or functional exploit code, and the level of effort to remedy the vulnerability.

- The environmental metric measures the properties of a vulnerability that are representative of users' IT environment, such as prevalence of the affected system and overall potential loss.

Known Uses

A vulnerability assessment is a key component of all widely accepted risk assessments, including those from [NIST800-30], [ISO13335-3], [Pel01], and others. While they differ slightly in their approach, the purposes and overall goals are consistent.

Consequences

This pattern has the following benefits:

- An enterprise obtains a list of all vulnerabilities that could impact their systems, some which may have been previously unknown.

- The enterprise is able to rank the vulnerabilities according to severity and potential impact.

- An enterprise is able to recognize which vulnerabilities can be discounted where there are no accompanying threats.

It also has the following liabilities:

- A thorough vulnerability scan involves the coordination of many departments and may be difficult to initiate if these departments are not in cooperation.

- This pattern cannot be used in isolation to patch or eliminate vulnerabilities. The results of VULNERABILITY ASSESSMENT (125) should be returned to the RISK DETERMINATION (137) pattern, where the final risk can be determined and an appropriate control implemented.

6.5 Risk Determination

Risk determination is the final stage of a risk-assessment process, and incorporates the results from an asset valuation, a threat assessment and a vulnerability assessment. Using the input of these patterns, the enterprise is able to evaluate and prioritize the risks to its assets.

Also Known As

Risk Evaluation

Example

The museum has identified the following assets as part of the its risk assessment:

Information asset types

- Museum employee data
- Museum financial/insurance data, partner financial data
- Museum contractual data and business planning
- Museum research and associated data
- Museum advertisements and other public data
- Museum database of collections information

Physical assets

- Museum building
- Museum staff
- Museum collections and exhibits
- Museum transport vehicles

It has also completed the three major steps in a risk assessment, as defined by ASSET VALUATION (103), THREAT ASSESSMENT (113), and VULNERABILITY ASSESSMENT (125). It must now assimilate this information, evaluate the overall risk, and present the results.

Context

An enterprise has defined the assets to be included in a risk assessment and has evaluated the importance of those assets in an asset valuation table. As well, it has performed a threat assessment and vulnerability assessment and collected unique combinations of threats and vulnerabilities in a threat-vulnerability table.

Problem

Once the work has been done to determine an asset's worth and assess the threats and vulnerabilities that affect it, its overall risk needs to be determined. Without a formal method for determining risk, how can one be assured that effort expended in protecting an asset is too high or too low?

How does an enterprise evaluate the risks posed to its assets?

An enterprise must resolve the following forces:

- The results of the risk assessment must be understood by the executive team if they are to address risk in the enterprise effectively.

- Determination of risk is directly related to asset value, threat likelihood, and vulnerability severity.

- Conducting a risk assessment requires resources such as time, people and project funding, as well as a commitment to follow up the results.

- Quantitative risk measures imply greater precision and are therefore preferred over qualitative indicators, but only if the quantitative scores are based on adequate measurements: false precision in risk levels is misleading.

Solution

Systematically determine the risk that is posed to each enterprise asset. This process involves the following four steps:

1. Collect results from ASSET VALUATION (103), THREAT ASSESSMENT (113) and VULNERABILITY ASSESSMENT (125).

   Recall that the previous stages of the risk assessment are the asset valuation, threat assessment and vulnerability assessment. Apply those patterns and collect the following:

   - The asset valuation table: this table shows the overall value of enterprise assets.
   - The threat-vulnerability table: this table is a catalog of threats and their associated vulnerabilities. Each threat includes a likelihood rating, and each vulnerability includes a severity rating.

2. Associate threat-vulnerability pairs with assets.

   Using the threat-vulnerability table, identify all threat-vulnerability pairs that pose a direct risk to each asset separately.

3. Evaluate risk.

   Evaluate a risk equation using the numerical values for asset valuation, threat likelihood and vulnerability severity. The result will represent the final risk posed to each asset.

4. Present the results.

   Sort the results in order of decreasing risk. Use qualitative terms, a color scale or other scale system (as appropriate) to display the results.

Dynamics

The allowable sequence for performing RISK DETERMINATION (137) is shown in the figure:

- First, collect the asset valuation and threat-vulnerability tables from ASSET VALUATION (103) and VULNERABILITY ASSESSMENT (125), respectively.
- Use a risk equation to calculate the risk posed to each asset.
- Finally, sort and present the results in descending order.

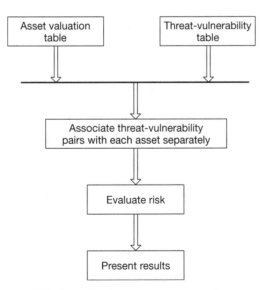

Risk determination sequence constraints

Implementation

The implementation of the process for risk determination is described below.

1. Collect results from ASSET VALUATION (103), THREAT ASSESSMENT (113) and VULNERABILITY ASSESSMENT (125). Apply these three patterns and collect the asset valuation and threat-vulnerability tables.
2. Associate threat-vulnerability pairs with assets.

    In both THREAT ASSESSMENT (113) and VULNERABILITY ASSESSMENT (125), we grouped assets by either physical or information type, rather than individually. At this stage of RISK DETERMINATION (137), we now need to consider the threat-vulnerability pairs for each asset separately.

    The threat-vulnerability table lists all threat actions and their corresponding vulnerabilities. Each of these pairs may pose a risk to one or more informational or physical assets. Therefore, identify all the threat-vulnerability pairs that affect each asset directly. The condition of 'affecting directly' is important, because to associate all threat-vulnerability pairs for every asset would lead to identical and, ultimately, meaningless results. However, a single threat-vulnerability pair may certainly affect multiple assets directly.

3. Evaluate risk.

    Regardless of the actual equation or method used to evaluate risk, it must consider the following properties:

    - The more vulnerabilities that exist in an asset and the systems that enable access to it, the greater the risk.
    - The more severe the vulnerabilities, the greater the risk.
    - The greater number of threats that could exploit a vulnerability, the greater the risk.
    - The more likely the threats, the greater the risk.
    - The more valuable an asset, the greater the risk.
    - The risk to an asset is zero if no threats or vulnerabilities exist for that asset.

    Any number of equations could be used to calculate a risk value, including those presented in the Variants and Known Uses sections. For the purposes of this pattern, we will use the following equation for each asset included in the scope of the risk assessment:

    $$\text{Risk}(A) = \text{SUM}[\text{Threat} * \text{Vulnerability}](A) * \text{Asset Value}(A)$$

This can be read as, 'the risk to asset 'A' is the sum of all unique combinations of threat likelihood, multiplied by the vulnerability severity, multiplied by the asset value.'

4. Present the results.

Present the results in order of descending risk. The greatest risk will have the highest numerical value, whereas the lowest risk will have the lowest numerical value. All values will be greater than zero, and the numbers will most certainly vary from one risk assessment to another.

If necessary, the raw numerical values can be presented in a table. However, a more intuitive effect can be achieved by using qualitative terms, consistent with those used throughout the risk assessment pattern set. First, on a scale of 1 (representing the lowest possible risk value) to the highest risk value, create 6 equal ranges, labeled as: Negligible, Low, Medium, High, Very high and Extreme. Then group each asset according to its qualitative value.

4.1. Understanding and presenting the results.

The importance of sorting and clearly presenting the results to a senior management team cannot be overemphasized. It is their task to interpret the results and develop plans to mitigate, transfer or accept the risk, often as part of an overall risk management strategy. Generally, this senior management team will only be interested in the risk values relative to other assets, so the actual value itself is not important. An exception to this is when the results from one assessment are compared with those from another assessment, perhaps from previous years. A declining value, for example, would demonstrate a reduction in risk, either due to fewer or less likely threats, more effective security controls, or declining asset value.

4.2. Qualitative versus quantitative risk determination.

Although the final results can be given in numerical terms, RISK DETERMINATION (137) (as with ASSET VALUATION (103), THREAT ASSESSMENT (113) and VULNERABILITY ASSESSMENT (125)) is very much a qualitative process. The values used in these patterns reflect the relative numerical values, rather than objective, quantifiable numbers.

Example Resolved

Using the asset valuation table and threat-vulnerability table as input to RISK DETERMINATION (137), the museum has evaluated and prioritized the risks to its assets. The complete results of the risk equation for three museum assets are presented below, and the remaining results are summarized in Table 6.22.

Evaluation of Risk Equation

1. Risk evaluation for museum building.

    From the threat-vulnerability table of VULNERABILITY ASSESSMENT (125), the museum has identified three threat-vulnerability pairs that affect the museum building, as shown in Table 6.19.

    ASSET VALUATION (103) identified the museum building as having a value of 6. The risk equation can therefore be written as follows:

    $$\text{Risk} = (3*6 + 3*5 + 3*4) * 6$$
    $$\text{Risk} = (18 + 15 + 12) * 6$$
    $$\text{Risk} = (45) * 6$$
    $$\text{Risk (museum building)} = 270$$

Table 6.19 Threat-vulnerability pairs for museum building

THREAT ACTION (FREQUENCY)	VULNERABILITY (SEVERITY)
Natural	
Museum fire (3)	Failure of fire alarm system (6)
	Failure of fire suppression system (5)
Fatigue of support fixtures, building structural failure (3)	Lack of regularly scheduled inspections (4)

2. Risk evaluation for museum collections and exhibits.

    The museum collections and exhibits asset has an asset value of 6, with the threat-vulnerability pairs as shown in Table 6.20.

    $$\text{Risk} = (33 + 12 + 16 + 12 + 12 + 8 + 20 + 12 + 6) * 6$$
    $$\text{Risk} = (131) * 6$$
    $$\text{Risk (museum collections and exhibits)} = 786$$

3. Risk evaluation for museum employee data.

    $$\text{Risk} = (12 + 12 + 21 + 15 + 10 + 9) * 5$$
    $$\text{Risk} = 79 * 5$$
    $$\text{Risk (museum employee data)} = 395$$

Table 6.20 Threat-vulnerability pairs for museum collections and exhibits

THREAT ACTION (FREQUENCY)	VULNERABILITY (SEVERITY)
Natural	
Museum fire (3)	Failure of fire alarm system (6)
	Failure of fire suppression system (5)
Fatigue of support fixtures, building structural failure (3)	Lack of regularly scheduled inspections (4)
Failure of monitoring and alarm systems (4)	Lack of regularly scheduled inspections (4)
Professional criminals	
Theft of museum collections and exhibits (2)	Lack of regular alarm testing procedures (3)
	Lack of adequate storage and protection of physical assets (3)
Physical attack against employees (3)	Lack of security training for employees (4)
Employees	
Accidental damage to museum collections and exhibits (4)	Carelessness of employees when handling/cleaning exhibits (2)
Theft of museum collections and exhibits (2)	Lack of regular alarm testing procedures (3)
	Lack of adequate storage and protection of physical assets (3)
	Susceptibility of employees to bribery (4)
Misconfiguration of monitoring and alarm systems (4)	Lack of regular alarm testing procedures (3)
Museum patrons	
Accidental damage to museum collections and exhibits (3)	Carelessness of museum patrons when viewing exhibits (2)

Table 6.21 Threat-vulnerability pairs for museum employee data

Natural

Electrical spike in computer room (3)	Lack of surge protection, uninterruptible power system (UPS) (4)
Loss of electronic documents (3)	Incomplete or corrupt data backups (4)

Professional criminals

Theft of information assets (3)	Susceptibility of employees to bribery (3)
	Lack of proper physical controls for document storage (locks, safe) (4)

Employees

Unauthorized access of informational assets (5)	Weak information security controls enabling unauthorized access (3)
Data entry errors (5)	Lack of data validation during form input (2)
Leaking confidential information (3)	Exposure of information assets (3)

4. Complete results.

   Risk values have been calculated for the remaining assets and are presented in Table 6.22.

   Table 6.22 Prioritized risks for museum assets

ASSET	RISK VALUE
Museum collections and exhibits	786
Museum employee data	395
Museum staff	342
Museum financial/insurance data, partner financial data	316
Museum building	270
Museum contractual data and business planning	232
Museum database of collections information	232
Museum research and associated data	147
Museum transport vehicles	120
Museum advertisements and other public data	98

Presentation of results

6 equal ranges (from 1 to 786) have been created, as shown in Table 6.23, and the final qualitative results are presented in Table 6.24.

Table 6.23 Qualitative risk translation

RATING	RANGE
Extreme	656–786
Very high	525–655
High	394–524
Medium	263–393
Low	132–262
Negligible	1–131

Table 6.24 Qualitative risks for museum assets

ASSET	RISK
Museum collections and exhibits	Extreme
Museum employee data	High
Museum staff	Medium
Museum financial/insurance data, partner financial data	Medium
Museum building	Medium
Museum contractual data and business planning	Low
Museum database of collections information	Low
Museum research and associated data	Low
Museum transport vehicles	Negligible
Museum advertisements and other public data	Negligible

Variants

An alternative formula for risk determination is provided by [Mei03]:

$$Risk = Probability * Damage\ Potential$$

in which both the probability and damage potential variables are represented numerically as values from 1 to 10, giving a minimum and maximum risk value of 1 and 100 respectively. To achieve qualitative results, 'low' represents any risk from 1 to 33, 'medium' represents risks from 34 to 66, and 'high' represents risks from 67 to 100. Note that because this method is threat- based, it gives the risk of a particular threat, as opposed to the risk posed to an asset.

Appendix E of [ISO13335-3] provides a number of examples of the use of matrices to evaluate risk, in which each example places emphasis differently. One example offers an asset-based evaluation, whereas another assesses the risk of given threats. While these examples recognize the inherent relationship between threats and vulnerabilities, they do not provide a formal way of accounting for them.

Known Uses

[NIST800-30] uses a 3x3 matrix made up of threat likelihood and threat impact. Qualitative values of threat likelihood (high, medium, low) are converted numerically to ratings of 1.0, 0.5, and 0.1 respectively. Qualitative values of threat impact (high, medium, low) are converted numerically to ratings of 100, 50, and 10 respectively. Risk is then computed by multiplying the threat likelihood by threat impact for each identified threat-vulnerability. The resulting value represents the 'degree or level to which an IT system, facility or procedure might be exposed if a given vulnerability were exercised.' Note that while this method is clear and straightforward, it does not provide an overall risk rating to a given asset, but simply the risk of a single threat-vulnerability pair.

[Pel01] describes an Annual Loss Exposure (ALE)—an equation that provides a quantitative method for calculating loss. The ALE is calculated from the value of an asset (A) multiplied by the likelihood of a threat occurrence (L) as follows: $ALE = A * L$. The likelihood value used is calculated from a multiplier table in which an occurrence of once a day is 365, once a month is 12, once a year is 1, once every 5 years is 1/5, and so on.

Consequences

This pattern has the following benefits:

■ The enterprise is now able to identify and address the risks posed to its assets, as part of a risk mitigation effort.

■ The qualitative results provided are much easier to calculate, prioritize and interpret.

■ The results can be archived and used to track the progress of asset risk among consecutive risk assessments.

As well as the following liabilities:

■ The risk equation may not account for all the properties of the relationship between threat, vulnerability, and asset value.

■ The results are based on the completeness and subjectivity of ASSET VALUATION (103), THREAT ASSESSMENT (113) and VULNERABILITY ASSESSMENT (125), and therefore cannot be objectively verified or guaranteed.

■ Because of the various methods for calculating an actual risk value, an enterprise may find it difficult to identify the particular equation that meets their risk assessment needs.

6.6 Enterprise Security Approaches

This pattern guides an enterprise in selecting security approaches, that is, prevention, detection, and response. Security approaches are driven by the security properties its assets require, such as confidentiality, integrity, and availability, and by assessed security risks. Security approaches also provide a basis for deciding what security services should be established by the enterprise.

Example

A new wing of an existing museum of gemstones is to be opened. Business planning activities have provided an enterprise scope in terms of needs, concerns, and assets. Application of SECURITY NEEDS IDENTIFICATION FOR ENTERPRISE ASSETS (89) has identified security properties applicable to each asset type. The dominant asset type for the museum is gemstones. Gems are valuable and should not be stolen or manipulated, so their required properties are availability and integrity. Another important asset type is documentation and records of gem properties, which require confidentiality, integrity, and availability. The museum needs to determine the security approaches most appropriate for achieving these required security properties, and how those approaches should be coordinated for the museum.

Context

Business assets that require protection and their required security properties (confidentiality, integrity, and availability) are understood, for example from applying SECURITY NEEDS IDENTIFICATION FOR ENTERPRISE ASSETS (89). Enterprise or business unit security risks (not system risks) are sufficiently understood, for example, from applying RISK DETERMINATION (137) and its closely-related patterns.

Problem

To integrate security into a business model, an enterprise or organization needs to determine preferred security approaches for achieving the security properties of its assets. Planning and operational diligence are security approaches that are always necessary to ensure effective security. In contrast, prevention, detection, and response are security approaches that may be applied in different proportions to each asset type and security property combination. Some business asset/property combinations will have one preferred approach. For example, critical assets that require the integrity property and that cannot be repaired or replaced will have a focus on prevention, since detection and response do not offer a solution to business impairment. On the other hand, assets that require the integrity property but are not critical, or that can be easily and cheaply repaired or replaced, will have a focus on detection of integrity problems and response (usually replacement).

How can security approaches be selected and integrated across an enterprise?

The forces applicable at the business model level of organization concerns are still abstract and are strongly intertwined with the business processes of the organization. The enterprise needs to resolve the following forces:

- The security properties identified for enterprise assets must be achieved.

- Security risks cannot be eliminated, but can be significantly reduced by a combination of prevention, detection, and response approaches.

- For critical assets, prevention is preferable to recovery, that is, it is better to prevent a violation of security than to have the violation occur and then try to recover from it.

- Prevention is sometimes impossible to guarantee, or is prohibitively expensive. A prevention mechanism can fail in the face of an unforeseen attack, but it can still be effective for the regular case.

- Some detection mechanisms can also facilitate prevention, especially when made obvious, such as a prominently-displayed security camera, or a motion sensor that sets off a loud alarm.

- The costs of providing security must be kept to a minimum.

- Security should have minimal negative impact on business process performance and on users (for example, vendors, clients, staff).

- Continuity of operations must be maintained even in the face of security incidents, and you want to recover in a timely and satisfactory way from security incidents that cannot be prevented (for example disaster recovery).

- It should be possible to analyze security incidents to improve your approach.

Solution

Specify an integrated set of approaches that achieve the required security protection for each asset type. The process emphasizes two perspectives, namely, the individual perspective of each asset type, and a holistic perspective of the overall organization. For each asset type, systematically and explicitly examine a set of risk criteria to determine appropriate security approaches and their suggested business priorities. Risk criteria involve the security properties for an asset type, business risk analysis results regarding criticality of the asset, and other high-level business operations information.

From a holistic perspective, ensure that the various approaches for asset types complement and reinforce each other, rather than work against each other.

The process of defining approaches is typically performed by an enterprise architect or strategic planner. The first step is to collect all the necessary information, including asset types and their security needs. Next, information on risk criteria that influence approaches is either collected or generated. Finally, approaches are selected and integrated.

Structure

Table 6.25 shows elements of the structure of this solution. Participating elements include humans involved in defining the solution for a specific situation. Participants also include primary elements of the process of defining a solution: security needs, security approaches, and selection criteria. More details of these three primary elements are also given in the table. The Implementation section gives additional common examples of selection criteria. Multiple criteria apply to each security approach. More than one approach can be selected for each need.

Dynamics

The process introduced in the Solution section is illustrated in the next figure. The process comprises three basic steps: collect information, identify security risk criteria, and determine security approaches for each asset type. The second step varies depending on whether sufficient risk information is available to understand the risk

Table 6.25   Table: elements of selecting enterprise security approaches

PARTICIPATING ELEMENT	SECURITY NEED	SECURITY APPROACH	SELECTION CRITERION
• Business planner/ controller • Enterprise architect • Enterprise security officer • Asset • Security need • Security approach • Selection criterion	• Confidentiality • Integrity • Availability • Accountability	• Prevention • Detection • Response	• Assets are irreplaceable • Asset loss prevents operations of critical business processes • Accountability is needed in case of legal ramifications • Assets must be repaired/ restored as soon as detection occurs • ... (see implementation section)

criteria that affect the security approach. If it is not available, some qualitative level of criteria must be developed.

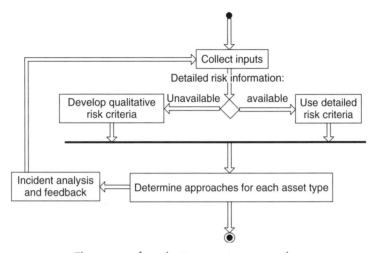

The process for selecting security approaches

The figure also shows an analysis and feedback process. Decisions must be revisited, because the world changes continuously. The figure shows feedback to the 'collect inputs' step, but feedback can go to any of the steps. In addition, if circumstances change sufficiently, feedback can extend beyond the scope of this pattern, to re-apply previous patterns such as RISK DETERMINATION (137).

Implementation

This section first provides further detail on the process, then presents criteria for selecting security approaches.

Process guidelines

1. Collect necessary input information:

    ■ Critical enterprise asset types
    ■ Basic security needs or properties for each asset type
    ■ Specific security risks for each asset type

    Note that asset types and basic security needs might be obtained as a result of applying SECURITY NEEDS IDENTIFICATION FOR ENTERPRISE ASSETS (89). Similarly, specific security risk information obtained as a result of applying RISK DETERMINATION (137).

2. Identify security risk criteria that influence approaches:

   ■ If detailed risk information is available (for example, by applying RISK DE-
   TERMINATION (137)), those criteria can be used here to determine which
   approaches to use: prevention, detection, response (also planning, operational diligence).
   ■ If such detailed risk information is not available, qualitative risk criteria
   such as criticality, ease of replacement, cost of replacement, and harm to
   reputation can be defined and used here.

3. Determine which approaches to use for each asset type.

   More details about the association of types of security needed, risk criteria, and
   approaches are provided below.

4. Revisit approaches for each asset type as circumstances change.

   ■ Decisions to revisit may be time-driven, for example annually.
   ■ Decisions to revisit may be event-driven. Examples are: (1) an organization
   makes a significant change to its business process, (2) a major law is passed
   that requires specific security measures, (3) an organization experiences a
   major security incident that calls into question its security approaches.

Approach criteria

For each asset type, appropriate security approaches and their suggested business
priorities are determined based on desired security properties and risks. If detailed
risks are available, for example, from applying the risk management pattern system
in this chapter, they can be used to determine approaches. If such risks are not known
or available, the qualitative selection criteria shown in Tables 6.26–6.29 can be used.

For example, Table 6.26 would be used to help determine approaches. If accountability is needed for an asset type due to legal ramifications, then detection is an indicated security approach with a high priority.

In using the above tables, it is important to understand that the information is generated from an overall organization perspective. In addition, the tables are not intended to cover all situations for a given organization. The example resolved in the
next section will illustrate both of these points.

The focus on security approaches is typically documented as part of a security concept of operations. A security concept of operations presents approaches for addressing security properties and how the approaches work together to address security
across the organization. The result should balance prevention, detection, and response into an appropriately layered set of defences. Balance is needed among layered asset protections, such as entrances to museum spaces and gem display cases.
Balance is also needed for the focus on approaches, such as prevention versus detection and response.

Table 6.26   Criteria for approaches to achieve accountability

SECURITY APPROACH	BUSINESS PRIORITY	CRITERIA INDICATING SELECTION OF APPROACH AND PRIORITY
Detection	High	Accountability is needed in the case of legal ramifications
	Medium	Validity of business communications and their signatures/sources must be ensured
		Validity of business process flow/ work flow (for example, chain of responsibility or signature) must be ensured
		Assets are in a single or limited number of controllable/ observable locations
Response	High	Means of unauthorized asset access must be closed immediately
		Intrusion claims must be substantiated in order to pursue administrative or legal actions against unauthorized access to assets
	Low	Information asset is non-critical and does not require accountability

Table 6.27   Criteria for approaches to achieve availability

SECURITY APPROACH	BUSINESS PRIORITY	CRITERIA INDICATING SELECTION OF APPROACH AND PRIORITY
Prevention	High	Asset loss prevents operations of critical business processes
	High	Asset loss could result in irreparable harm to enterprise reputation
	Medium	Asset loss severely impacts operations of critical business processes
		Asset loss could result in serious damage to enterprise reputation
	Low	Asset loss will impact business processes
		Asset loss could result in ill will in client and/or customer base
Detection	High	Total prevention of loss or alteration of assets is not possible
		Detection is cost-effective and prevention is not
		Asset can be replaced though very costly

Table 6.27   Criteria for approaches to achieve availability (*continued*)

SECURITY APPROACH	BUSINESS PRIORITY	CRITERIA INDICATING SELECTION OF APPROACH AND PRIORITY
	Medium	Assets are in a single or limited number of controllable/ observable locations
Response	High	Assets must be repaired/restored as soon as detection occurs
		Alterations to assets or other asset characteristics (for example functionality for software assets) must be completely identifiable for repair/replacement
		Means of unauthorized asset access must be closed immediately
		Intrusion claims must be substantiated in order to pursue administrative or legal actions against unauthorized access to assets
	Medium	Assets are of moderate importance to enterprise functions and do not require confidentiality
	Low	Particular enterprise assets interact only with non-critical functions

Table 6.28   Criteria for approaches to achieving confidentiality

SECURITY APPROACH	BUSINESS PRIORITY	CRITERIA INDICATING SELECTION OF APPROACH AND PRIORITY
Prevention	High	Asset reveals highly-confidential or sensitive information.
	Medium	Asset reveals valuable information.
	Low	Asset reveals information.
Detection	Medium	Information assets can be made available in forms in which no damage can be done (for example, read-only forms, or 'sanitized' versions). Since tools to provide such forms are subject to risk, some protection is still needed.
	Low	Intrusions (that is, unauthorized attempts to read or write protected assets) denied, but awareness of them is needed.

Table 6.29 Criteria for approaches to achieve integrity

SECURITY APPROACH	BUSINESS PRIORITY	CRITERIA INDICATING SELECTION OF APPROACH AND PRIORITY
Prevention	High	Asset critical and non-replaceable if corrupted or otherwise damaged.
		Asset extremely costly to replace or repair.
		Asset loss could result in irreparable harm to enterprise reputation.
	Medium	Asset very significant and requires long-lead time to replace or repair.
		Asset cost to replace very high.
		Asset loss could result in serious damage to enterprise reputation.
	Low	Asset significant but replaceable.
		Asset cost to replace or repair moderate.
		Asset loss could result in ill will in client and/or customer base.
Detection	High	Permanent asset alteration will significantly impair enterprise or operation of critical business processes.
		Total prevention of loss or alteration of assets is not possible.
		Detection is cost-effective and prevention is not.
		Asset can be replaced although very costly.
	Medium	Validity of business communications and their signatures/sources must be ensured.
		Validity of business process flow/ work flow (for example, chain of responsibility or signature) must be ensured.
		Assets are in a single or limited number of controllable/ observable locations.
		Information assets can be made available in forms in which no damage can be done (for example, read only forms or 'sanitized' versions). Since tools to provide such forms are subject to risk, some protection is still needed.
	Low	Enterprise information assets need to be accurate and support any/ all legal needs.

Table 6.29   Criteria for approaches to achieve integrity (*continued*)

SECURITY APPROACH	BUSINESS PRIORITY	CRITERIA INDICATING SELECTION OF APPROACH AND PRIORITY
		Intrusions (that is, unauthorized attempts to read or write protected assets) denied, but awareness of them is needed.
Response	High	Assets must be repaired/restored as soon as detection occurs.
		Alterations to assets or other asset characteristics (for example, functionality for software assets) must be completely identifiable for repair/replacement.
		Means of unauthorized asset access must be closed immediately.
		Intrusion claims must be substantiated in order to pursue administrative or legal actions against unauthorized access to assets.
	Medium	Assets are repaired/replaced normally within three days of problem detection.
		Assets are of moderate importance to business functions and do not require integrity.
	Low	Assets should be restored within a week, but longer periods will not impair enterprise operations.
		Information asset is non-critical and does not require integrity.
		Particular enterprise assets interact only with non-critical functions.

Business factors tend to present conflicting forces regarding appropriate balance. Some, such as laws and regulations, sensitivity of certain assets, and the desire to be viewed as a secure enterprise, encourage a high level of prevention. Others, such as cost constraints, the need for financial health, and a desire to be viewed as open and accessible, encourage a minimum degree of prevention with reliance on detection/response. In cases in which the risk is sufficiently low, a 'no action' approach may be selected, that is, the approach is to take no measures of prevention, detection, or response. For example, theft of expensive clothes from a shop can be detected by security tags that sound an alarm when the goods are taken outside. But for very inexpensive clothes, the cost of security tags may exceed the cost of a few stolen items. The shop owner therefore may decide to make no response and just write off the loss.

The process of balancing these forces requires assets to be differentiated according to their importance to the organization. An investment in prevention is needed for critical assets, while a greater degree of risk may be accepted for non-critical assets.

- Critical assets typically are those whose loss or damage would cause significant harm to the organization, such as assets whose protection is required by law or strategic plans. Other critical assets are those that offer competitive advantage, are irreplaceable items, can impact the reputation of an organization, or whose loss would entail significant cost impact.

- Non-critical assets are those whose loss or damage would cause little or no harm to the organization, such as easily-replaceable items, or information that could be divulged with little or no effect.

Obviously, there are many possible asset value gradations between non-critical and critical assets. Balancing forces and approaches can also exploit a fact that was mentioned in the discussion of forces: some detection mechanisms can also provide a measure of prevention. These are typically cases in which potential violators are made aware of detection mechanisms and possible accountability, such as prominently-displayed surveillance cameras or loud alarms.

It is well known that many considerations are brought to bear at this level in determining an appropriate enterprise security strategy. Management may sometimes levy a requirement to address something specific for security that is realistically beyond what can be accounted for in this pattern. It is strongly recommended that such items be captured, so that when appropriate, they can be tracked through to implementation. In cases in which they are inappropriate, developers of the system model will be forewarned that these requirements will need to be revisited with management.

Example Resolved

This section outlines portions of the result of applying the solution to a museum of gemstones. Identification of museum assets and their security properties is available from the Example Resolved section of SECURITY NEEDS IDENTIFICATION FOR ENTERPRISE ASSETS (89). Museum enterprise architects and planners have completed a business unit risk assessment for the new wing of the museum. The architects and planners must now work to identify security approaches for which the museum will be willing to allocate the resources necessary to achieve the security properties identified.

An example outcome is summarized in Table 6.30 on page 159. The column for 'Special notes' has been included to show examples of special considerations and decisions that might be made by management while considering general security approaches.

Note that in the integration perspective, approaches are coordinated. For example, when prevention fails (thief grabs gem), detection and response act as a fallback (laser beam was interrupted, causing automatic doors to close before thief can leave the building).

Known Uses

The prevention-detection-response approaches identified in this pattern, and the process of associating them with risk criteria, are well-established functions in the security community. [Chu02] refers to 'the commonly mentioned prevention-detection-response philosophy...' In a security course description, [SANSf] states that 'general security practitioners, system administrators, and security architects will benefit by understanding how to design, build, and operate their systems to prevent, detect, and respond to attacks.' Sometimes these approaches are included in a broader list of security functions or safeguards. [DCD+02] identifies these categories: planning, prevention, detection, diligence, and response. [ISO13335-4] states (page 44) 'In general, safeguards may provide one or more of the following types of protection: prevention, deterrence, detection, reduction, recovery, correction, monitoring, and awareness.' Criteria details in the Implementation section of this pattern are based on extensive MITRE Corporation experience with our customers.

Consequences

The following benefits may be expected from applying this pattern:

- The pattern fosters management level awareness: all enterprise security patterns help management better understand security as an overall issue, and gives them terminology and simple understanding of the underlying concepts without relying on details of the technology used to implement them.

- It facilitates conscious and informed decision-making about security approaches to satisfy identified security needs.

- It promotes sensible resource allocation to protect assets.

- It allows feedback in the decision process, to better adjust security approaches to the situation at hand by traceability back to business factors and security needs.

- It encourages better balance among the security, cost, and usability of an asset.

- It shows that you can combine approaches to better and more cheaply protect an asset.

The following potential liabilities may result from applying this pattern:

- It requires an investment of resources to apply the pattern. In some cases the cost of applying the pattern may exceed its benefits.

Table 6.30 . Security approaches established for desired security properties

PROPERTIES AND APPLICABILITY	SECURITY APPROACH	BUSINESS PRIORITY FOR APPROACH	SPECIAL NOTES
Protect*Integrity* of museum data: ■ Employee ■ Contractual ■ Financial ■ Partner financial	Prevent	High	Employee data should only be available to HR, staff, & management
	Detect	High	
	Respond	High	
Protect*Integrity* of all other museum data: ■ Insurance ■ Business planning ■ Public data	Prevent	Moderate	While this information is very important, modifications can be detected and emended without high consequences
	Detect	High	
	Respond	Low	
Protect*Integrity* of physical assets: ■ Buildings ■ Collections/exhibits	Prevent	High	This is a critical cost driver
	Detect	High	
	Respond	High	
Protect*Confidentiality* of museum data: ■ Financial/insurance ■ Partner financial ■ Contractual ■ Exhibit plans ■ Research and its data	Prevent	High	These are critical to business operations. Management wants a focus on prevention and detection with high quality encryption.
	Detect	High	
	Respond	Moderate	
Protect*Confidentiality* of employee data:	Prevent	Moderate	Not as critical to business operations. Restrict access to HR, staff & management
	Detect	Moderate	
	Respond	Moderate	
Protect*Availability* of museum employee data:	Prevent	Moderate	HR is only user with critical availability concerns
	Detect	Moderate	

- It requires the involvement of people who have intimate knowledge of assets, and basic knowledge of asset security needs and security approaches. These people typically have high positions in the enterprise and their time is valuable.

- It is possible for an organization to assign people to this task who have a less than adequate knowledge of assets, security needs, or approaches, because they may have more available time or are less expensive. If the people applying the pattern do not have a good knowledge of enterprise assets and their value, the pattern results may be inaccurate or not useful.

- Perception of security needs can differ throughout an organization. This may make it difficult to reach agreement on priorities of approaches. On the other hand, bringing such disagreements to the surface may be a benefit, because they can then be properly discussed and resolved.

See Also

After applying this solution, the next step typically is to apply ENTERPRISE SECURITY SERVICES (161) to select security services that support the approaches selected in this pattern.

6.7 Enterprise Security Services

This pattern guides an enterprise in selecting security services for protecting its assets, after the required security approaches—prevention, detection, response—have been identified. It helps to establish the level of strength or confidence each security service should offer, based on priorities. Primary examples of such services are identification and authentication, accounting/auditing, access control/authorization, and security management.

Example

A new wing of an existing museum of gemstones is to be opened. The museum's management has already identified security as an enterprise concern and determined appropriate security properties and approaches to be supported. Now the management needs to identify what security services will be used. A specific asset group is used in this simple example problem.

The museum has identified three specific gems as irreplaceable due to their financial value. They can only be insured for approximately two-thirds of their actual monetary value. The museum wants to provide integrity and availability for physical protection of the gems, but also confidentiality for the real value of the assets. The museum has determined that prevention will be the primary approach to providing integrity and availability of the gems. Prevention will also provide confidentiality for information that stipulates real monetary values. Detection and response will provide secondary approaches to protecting these gems and resources will be allocated to prevention first. The museum now needs to determine what abstract security services will support the desired properties and approaches.

Context

Business strategies, plans, and operations are understood. These include disaster recovery and continuity of operations strategies, a semantic data model, high-level business process and workflows, business locations, organizational units, and business cycle models. Security approaches (prevention, detection, response) and their priorities have been selected to satisfy the identified security needs of enterprise assets. The approaches might have been selected by applying ENTERPRISE SECURITY APPROACHES (148). The pattern user has a basic awareness of potential security services.

Problem

To fully integrate security into the business model, business planners need to identify the security services needed to protect each category of enterprise asset. Selection of security services will need to balance the resources the museum is willing to allocate in order to address security approaches appropriately. At the business level, planners provide direction about how much emphasis to focus on preventing security incidents, detecting incidents after the fact, and the level of focus for responding to security incidents. Some services, such as access control, emphasize a prevention approach. Other services, such as accounting, emphasize detection and response. Still others, such as identification and authentication, support both prevention and detection.

How do you select and integrate security services across the organization to support security properties using preferred security approaches?

The forces applicable at the business model level of concerns are still abstract and are strongly intertwined with business processes. The enterprise needs to resolve the following forces:

- Customers and clients expect suitable protection of their assets
- Unauthorized access to critical assets that require prevention as the primary protection must be prevented
- A strong ability to discover security incidents provides protection for assets that require detection as a primary approach
- It is necessary to be able to recover from, or actively respond to, incidents for assets where prevention is not suitable or where prevention fails
- Accurate actor identification provides more protection when actors access critical assets
- Strong security services provide greater asset protection, but tend to be harder to use
- Weak security services tend to be easier to use, but provide less asset protection

Solution

Specify an integrated set of security services to address identified security approaches and security properties for each asset type. This process emphasizes two perspectives, namely, the individual perspective of each asset type, and a holistic perspective of the overall organization. Assets can vary greatly. This pattern therefore focuses on associations of security approaches and security services to assist the user in understanding relationships that can then be applied to asset categories. The Implementation section below provides examples. The examples are to help the pattern user to establish a particular set of security services to address all asset security needs for a given organization. From a holistic perspective, it ensures that the various approaches for asset types complement and reinforce each other, rather than work against each other.

The process of defining security services is typically performed by an enterprise architect and systems engineer. The first step is to collect all necessary information, including the asset types and security approaches that have been defined—for example, by applying ENTERPRISE SECURITY APPROACHES (148). Next, services are selected for each asset type and integrated. Finally, a 'human touch' is involved in applying an enterprise level pattern such as ENTERPRISE SECURITY SERVICES (161). Its application helps to shape thoughts about security, but it never can be a one-shot solution. You need feedback and conscious re-visiting of your decisions, because the world and organization change continually. Any of the earlier steps in this process might be revisited. In addition, if circumstances change sufficiently, feedback can extend to the beginning of the reasoning chain, to re-apply previous patterns such as ENTERPRISE SECURITY APPROACHES (148). More details on the process are provided in the Implementation section below.

After applying this solution, the next step typically is to specify requirements for the selected security services—for example, by applying one of these patterns: I&A REQUIREMENTS (192), ACCESS CONTROL REQUIREMENTS (267), or SECURITY ACCOUNTING REQUIREMENTS (360). It is important to note that ENTERPRISE SECURITY SERVICES (161) is organization-wide, while the scope of each service requirements pattern is a system or security domain within the organization.

Structure

Table 6.31 shows elements of the structure of this solution. Participating elements include humans involved in defining the solution for a specific situation. Participants also include primary elements of the process of defining a solution: security approaches, selection criteria, and security services. More details of these three primary elements are also given in the table. The implementation section below gives additional common examples of selection criteria. Multiple criteria apply to each security approach and to each security service. More than one service can be selected for each approach.

Table 6.31 Elements of enterprise services solution

PARTICIPATING ELEMENT	SECURITY APPROACH	SELECTION CRITERION	SECURITY SERVICE
• Business planners/ controllers • Enterprise architect • Enterprise security officer • Asset • Security approach • Selection criteria • Security service	• Prevention • Detection • Response	• Assets are irreplaceable • Continuous record of asset protection is required • Need for daily asset access accounting • System cannot be down more than 8 hours • Financial data could harm partnerships • ... (see implementation section)	• I&A • Access control • Accounting • Security management • ...

Implementation

This section first provides further detail on the process that was summarized in the Solution section, then presents criteria for selecting security services.

Process Guidelines

1. Collect necessary input information:

    ■ Critical enterprise asset types.

    ■ Basic security needs or properties for each asset type. Asset types and basic security needs might be obtained as a result of applying SECURITY NEEDS IDENTIFICATION FOR ENTERPRISE ASSETS (89).

    ■ Specific security approaches for each asset type, including prevention, detection, and response, and the business priority for the approach in each case. Specific approaches and priorities might be obtained as a result of applying ENTERPRISE SECURITY APPROACHES (148).

2. Determine which security services to use for each asset type and approach:

    ■ Determine the factors that apply to your organization

    ■ Identify services that support the approaches, based on applicable factors

    Note that one possible response is to take no action, that is, to accept the risk or ignore the incident, in which case no security service is designated.

More details on relating security approaches to security services are provided below.

3. Revisit security services for each asset type as circumstances change:

■ Decisions to revisit may be time-driven, for example annually.

■ Decisions to revisit may be event-driven. Examples are: (1) an organization makes a significant change to its business process, (2) a major law is passed that requires specific security measures, (3) an organization experiences a major security incident that calls into question its security services.

Approach criteria

Tables 6.32–6.34 correlate security approaches with security services and a business priority. The criteria indicating selection provide typical examples of instances when

Table 6.32 Correlating prevention with security services and business priorities

SECURITY SERVICE	BUSINESS PRIORITY	CRITERIA INDICATING SELECTION	EXAMPLE SECURITY MECHANISMS
Access control	High	Enterprise has irreplaceable assets	Categorize access to assets according to roles and responsibilities, and restrict access to individuals via their roles/ responsibilities
	Moderate	Assets can be damaged deliberately or inadvertently	Encapsulate assets (for example, envelope, encrypt, vacuum)
	Low	Assets require basic level of protection for insurance purposes	Provide physical protection controls
Accounting	High	Continuous record of asset protection is required (for example by a contract)	Real-time audit trail for information assets or sensors for physical assets
	Moderate	Asset access limited and must be accounted for	Pre-defined job functions in organization associated with user roles
	Low	Asset access physically limited but videotapes of area-access required	Videotape of assets, predefined job locations

Table 6.32 Correlating prevention with security services and business priorities (*continued*)

SECURITY SERVICE	BUSINESS PRIORITY	CRITERIA INDICATING SELECTION	EXAMPLE SECURITY MECHANISMS
I&A	High	Enterprise has irreplaceable assets (for example, extremely costly, value lost if modified, not insurable, one of a kind)	Use multiple authentication layers (for example biometrics and passwords) Store identities on smart card with biometric authenticator
	Moderate	Assets replaceable at significant cost	Use token generator for identity authenticator Restrict access to I&A information
	Low	Assets can be replaced as long as problems are detected	Use unguessable authenticator (for example randomly-generated passwords)
Security management	High	User I&A information alterable by single identified person	Only security officer can alter I&A information All I&A information is encrypted in storage and transfer
	Moderate	Only select roles may alter I&A information	SSO and System Administrator can alter I&A information All I&A information is encrypted in transfer
	Low	I&A information should not be easily modified	Access to server where I&A information can be altered is restricted

Table 6.33 Correlating detection with security services and business priorities

SECURITY SERVICE	BUSINESS PRIORITY	CRITERIA INDICATING SELECTION	EXAMPLE SECURITY MECHANISMS
Access control	High	All events needing immediate attention can be specifically identified	Accounting service mechanisms will need extreme granularity Access controls will relay to real-time audit trail
	Moderate	Normal/abnormal functionality is identified and controlled	Accounting service mechanisms provide daily audit trails for all information system functionality

Table 6.33   Correlating detection with security services and business priorities (*continued*)

SECURITY SERVICE	BUSINESS PRIORITY	CRITERIA INDICATING SELECTION	EXAMPLE SECURITY MECHANISMS
	Low	Prevention is highest priority for organization	Select access control activities are reported to accounting service mechanisms for documenting
Accounting	High	Business records need to be accurate and support any/all legal needs	Document all initial business records, any changes to them, and actor involved, in non-repudiable manner
	Moderate	Inability to recover from incident could weaken reputation	Ensure audit trails are reviewed for early detection of incidents
	Low	Need to recover from environmental disruptions	Maintain a history of all business records so that emergencies can be recovered from
I&A	High	Critical interactions are only authorized for specific staff	Use intrusion detection to detect any unauthorized interactions
	Moderate	Sensitive information restricted	Keep complete audit trails for all access to sensitive information
	Low	Need for daily asset access accounting	Assets need identifiers for differentiation
Security management	High	All security management information is company sensitive	Access control is enforced continuously for all this information This information for accounting cannot be altered
	Moderate	All security management information is selectively accessible	Access control with roles ensures the information is current and valid
	Low	Security management information must be periodically reviewed and changes documented	Audit trails must include changes by security officer and system administrators

Table 6.34 Correlating response with security services and business priorities

SECURITY SERVICE	BUSINESS PRIORITY	CRITERIA INDICATING SELECTION	EXAMPLE SECURITY MECHANISMS
Access control	High	Assets are nationally sensitive (for example nuclear plants)	Access requires specific permissions and is restricted by time of day, location, and so on
	Moderate	Financial data could harm partnerships	Access is restricted to a specific community of interest
	Low	Only HR employees should access corporate personnel data	Access authorizations are established by department functions
Accounting	High	Location/condition of specific assets must not be altered	Accounting records must provide continuous monitoring (for example videotape) with immediate alert locking asset location on any change
	Moderate	Any unauthorized changes to asset must initiate notification	If detection indicates unauthorized asset change, accounting service mechanism must send notification to system administrator
	Low	Only physical disasters need immediate responses	Accounting service mechanism only notifies select staff if physical catastrophe occurs
I&A	High	Unknown users must be immediately locked out permanently	Identification used with biometrics secured on a token I&A service mechanism does not have high false positive or negative ratios I&A part of layered defence
	Moderate	When user I&A provides warning, additional means are used to reduce possibility of false positive	Front door human guard, badging system with photo, and identifier and password on automated system
	Low	Users are not allowed to repeatedly provide invalid log-in information	Computer system locks down after preset number of invalid attempts

Table 6.34 Correlating response with security services and business priorities (*continued*)

SECURITY SERVICE	BUSINESS PRIORITY	CRITERIA INDICATING SELECTION	EXAMPLE SECURITY MECHANISMS
Security management	High	System cannot be down more than eight hours	Security management plans and procedures for contingency operation are in place and assure response in 8 hours
	Moderate	System cannot be down more than twenty-four hours	Security management plans and procedures for backup and recovery will restore a functioning system in twenty-four hours
	Low	System information must be accessible on line in two weeks	System backups with all security management information must be run every two days and recovery plans are in place

the organization has set a business priority at a certain level. Example mechanisms that may be employed to offer the service are also provided. Note that these tables could not possibly address all possible security services—instead they focus on fundamental services that will provide a basis for security.

Rows of the tables may be interpreted as follows, using as an example Table 6.32, which addresses prevention as the approach. An organization has identified a need for prevention. I&A is a security service selected as a means of supporting prevention of unauthorized operations on assets. The organization has established prevention as a high business priority for a given asset category, such as irreplaceable assets. In this circumstance a strong I&A service is needed. It may be implemented through the use of both biometrics and passwords structured as multiple authentication layers. Suppose another asset category has a moderate need for prevention, such as assets replaceable but at significant cost. In this case a moderately strong I&A service is needed. It may be implemented through use of biometrics by itself, or use of a token generator. Finally, if the prevention priority for an asset category is low, then a weaker I&A service is needed. This may be implemented through randomly-generated passwords.

The example implementations are not decided in this pattern. The first three columns—service, priority, and criteria—represent organization-wide decisions made in the scope of this pattern. The fourth column, example mechanisms, represents system decisions made in the scope of each system security architecture.

Example Resolved

This example expounds on the problem example provided earlier. As noted, the museum has gems that are irreplaceable and only partially insurable. They have a business priority for ensuring their integrity and availability by preventing their theft or any damage. The museum will therefore need to have strong I&A, access control, accounting, and security management services to protect the gems. Detection and response security approaches will also be provided as backups for the prevention approach. To provide integrity and availability for the detection approach, both I&A and accounting security services will be needed. For the response approach the security management service will also need to be dependable.

The museum also indicated a real need to protect confidentiality of the real value of these gems by preventing that information from being easily obtained. In addition, the museum will need to ensure integrity of that information. This additional consideration for integrity of gem values to have a high business priority will need to be fed back into the earlier work to ensure it is captured. There is a high business priority for prevention of any lapses of confidentiality and integrity of gem data on insurance contracts, attributes (carats), purchase amounts, and appraisal values. To achieve the required prevention approach, stringent I&A, access control, and security management services will be needed. To achieve the required prevention as well as detection and response for preventing integrity violations of gem data, strong mechanisms for all four identified services will be needed.

The museum has now reached a point at which they can begin to determine refinements for security services appropriate to support abstract selected services. Table 6.35 captures the museum's resolution of abstract security services to be used.

Known Uses

The prevention-detection-response approaches identified in this pattern are well established functions in the security community. Likewise, security services identified in this pattern are well-established, although there is lack of consensus on names for some of them, notably accounting. The security services in this pattern are aligned with services in the taxonomy in Chapter 2. To a significant degree, criteria details in the Implementation section of this pattern are based on extensive MITRE Corporation experience with our customers. There are also some standards that include related information. For example, [ISO13335-4] discusses services and mechanisms—under the name 'safeguards'—such as I&A, access control, audit, and security management, and associates these with security properties such as confidentiality and integrity. [NIST800-33] describes a security services model that includes identification, authentication, access control, audit, non-repudiation, and security administration services. The latter also maps services to a set of primary purposes or approaches: prevent, recover, and support.

Table 6.35 Protecting museum assets

MUSEUM ASSET	SECURITY PROPERTY	SECURITY APPROACH	BUSINESS PRIORITY	SELECTED SERVICE
High value gems	Integrity availability	Prevention	High	▪ I&A ▪ Access control, e.g., locked glass display ▪ Accounting ▪ Security management
	Integrity availability	Detection	Medium	▪ I&A ▪ Accounting, e.g., surveillance camera
	Integrity availability	Response	Medium	▪ I&A ▪ Accounting ▪ Security management
Gem insurance contracts, attribute data (i.e., carats), purchase data, and appraisal data	Confidentiality	Prevention	High	▪ I&A ▪ Access control, e.g., a safe ▪ Security management
	Integrity	Prevention Detection Response	High	▪ I&A ▪ Access control ▪ Accounting ▪ Security management

A specific example of how a prevention approach leads to use of the access control service is the Cisco use of Access Control Lists to protect networks, described in [ACL]. Examples of how accounting in the form of audit software supports detection of fraud are described in [CPA].

Consequences

The following benefits may be expected from applying this pattern:

▪ The pattern fosters management level awareness: all enterprise security patterns help management to better understand security as an overall issue, and gives them terminology and simple understanding of the underlying concepts without relying on details of the technology used to implement them.

▪ It facilitates conscious and informed decision making about security services to support identified security approaches.

- It promotes sensible resource allocation to protect assets.
- It allows feedback in the decision process to better adjust security services to the situation at hand by traceability back to business factors and security needs.
- It encourages better balance among security, cost, and usability of an asset.
- It shows that you can combine services to better and more cheaply protect an asset.

The following potential liabilities may result from applying this pattern:

- It requires an investment of resources to apply the pattern, including time to analyze enterprise assets and security approaches. In some cases the cost of applying the pattern may exceed its benefits.
- It requires the involvement of people who have intimate knowledge of assets, and basic knowledge of asset security needs and security approaches. These people typically have high positions in the enterprise and their time is valuable. On the other hand, the pattern allows more people to be aware of the issues, so that after the initial investment of time, other people can be in a position to maintain and evolve the service selection.
- It is possible for an organization to assign people to this task who have less than adequate knowledge of assets, approaches, or services, because they may have more available time or are less expensive. If the people applying the pattern do not have good knowledge of enterprise assets and their value, the pattern results may be inaccurate or not useful.
- Perception of security needs can differ throughout an organization. This may make it difficult to reach agreement on priorities of services. On the other hand, bringing such disagreements to the surface may be a benefit, because then they can be properly discussed and resolved.

6.8 Enterprise Partner Communication

Enterprises often partner with third parties to support their business model. These third parties may include application and managed service providers, consulting firms, vendors, outsourcing development teams, and satellite offices. As part of this relationship, access must be granted to allow data to travel between the organizations. Without attention to the protection of that data and the methods by which they are transferred, one or both organizations may be at risk.

Example

The museum has received a sum of money and is expanding! It wants to expand its services in the following ways:

1. Publish an RSS news feed advertising all upcoming museum events and information.

2. Sell goods online from its Web site. The museum has created a merchant account with a popular payment processor and financial organization. The Web site application will use a programmatic API provided by the payment processor.

3. Outsource the development of a Web site to a third party. One component of the Web site will be a public, e-commerce site selling goods and promoting museum events and exhibits. The second component will be a private, intranet Web site containing an employee directory as well as confidential corporate funding and research and development data. The museum realizes that the third party will require some confidential database tables and documents in order to design and test the application.

4. Subscribe to the International Museum Consortium (IMC) service. This service will publish current and rolling exhibit information to other subscribers. Membership of this service will allow the museum to search and bid for rolling exhibits from any other subscribing museum around the world. They feel it would give them a competitive advantage over other regional and local museums, and will substantially increase their patron attendance. The IMC will provide the software application, centrally manage user accounts and facilitate a bidding and messaging process. The museum already has an infrastructure capable of operating and managing the software application, and simply needs to configure it to access the museum's inventory database.

Each of these projects involves exchanging information with other parties, but vary in the degree of security requirements and in the method of data exchange. The museum clearly recognizes the value of these projects, but is concerned that its personnel, customer, and confidential exhibit information will be at risk of unauthorized access, modification, or denial of service. It would like to implement these projects but needs to protect its data, systems, and reputation.

Context

An enterprise has an existing business process, or is proposing a new business process, that requires information to be exchanged with another entity across a computer network. The business factors that initiated the partnership have already been determined and a high-level service level agreement, complete with disaster recovery and business continuity planning, has been established.

Problem

When an enterprise engages in a business relationship, it typically exchanges information and allows users and/or applications to access privileged resources. Not only can there be risk of theft or manipulation of data, but also risk of unauthorized access to resources by another organization. Furthermore, you may trust the partner with whom you entered into a relationship, but can you trust their contractors, application vendors, networks, or firewall configuration? A breach in their network may lead to a breach in your own.

How can an enterprise protect its systems and data while communicating with external partners?

An enterprise must resolve the following forces:

- It needs to be reasonably assured that sensitive information is protected when traveling beyond its control.

- Security procedures become difficult to manage when one entity does not share the same security requirement and considerations as the other.

- It must conform to legislation when storing and transferring financial or personal health information.

- Applications that communicate with business partners become vulnerable, not only to attack from that partner, but also from attacks from users who defeat the partner's security.

- The services that the partner may access might require special or custom network paths that are not used by regular customers or internal users.

- An enterprise may not have the time or ability to properly evaluate the security controls of the partner, and the partner may not be able to conform to the security requirements imposed by the enterprise (in time).

- Outsourcing software development efforts creates additional challenges, as the data and people may reside across the planet and beyond the immediate reach of the enterprise.

- Both parties must commit to the agreement but be flexible enough to modify the policy should the risk or business requirements change. For example, if transaction volumes dramatically increase, or if vulnerabilities are suddenly discovered in an application.

- The enterprise may require the business partners to conform to a particular interoperability scheme that the partner is not able to match.

Solution

Specify enterprise partner communication in five areas: define the scope and security requirements of the information to be exchanged, audit the business partner, identify and protect communication channels, define exchange methods and procedures, and identify service termination activities.

1. Define scope and security requirements.

   First, define which data or application services are to be exchanged between organizations. Then identify the security requirements for this information.

2. Audit business partner.

   Perform a security audit of the partner organization commensurate with the security requirements of the information and the policies of your enterprise.

3. Identify and protect communication channels.

   Identify and protect communication channels in the following ways:

   - Communication channels: identify the preferred channels of communication.
   - Traffic separation: separate business partner traffic from regular enterprise traffic, and from other partners, wherever possible.
   - Ports and portals: determine the required SINGLE ACCESS POINT (279) connecting the two organizations and secure them.
   - Access controls: apply administrative, physical and technical access controls, as appropriate, to protect the data throughout its life cycle. These controls serve to protect the data while stored either at the enterprise or business partner and as it passes from one system to another.

4. Define exchange methods and procedures.

   First, identify the pre- and post-processing procedures that are to be applied to the data and communication channels. Then maintain and monitor usage logs and reports. This will provide an early warning of performance and stability issues, as well as indication of malicious activity.

5. Perform service termination activities.

    At the completion of the partner agreement, perform the following service termination activities:

    ■ Access revocation: user accounts, authorization privileges and system access should be promptly removed.
    ■ Data sanitization: purge all sensitive information from disk drives, databases and other files
    ■ Repurpose assets: network devices, servers, application resources can now be re-used for other partner communications or internal functions

Structure

The structural components of this pattern are displayed in the figure on page 177.

SINGLE ACCESS POINT (279)s provide a central, auditable entry point into the enterprise. Access controls at these access points enforce restrictions on inbound and outbound traffic. Dedicated communication channels and encryption controls protect the data throughout its transmission and storage. Partitioned storage facilities provide dedicated separation of information between enterprise and partner data.

Implementation

The following steps should be considered during the pattern implementation:

1. Define scope and security requirements.

    Determine the minimum set of data that should be exchanged by sanitizing it as much as possible. That is, strip it of any confidential or unnecessary information. Personally identifiable financial or medical numbers, for example, can be substituted for another unique identification number. There is no need to send more information than necessary. Indeed, extra data may inflate security requirements, incurring additional infrastructure, costs and delays.

    If application services are used, provide interfaces (APIs, URLs) for only those functions that are necessary to fulfill the business requirement. This improves security by limiting the access to the enterprise and its systems.

    The data owner will be able to provide the security requirements of the data. If not, SECURITY NEEDS IDENTIFICATION FOR ENTERPRISE ASSETS (89) can be used. This enterprise pattern provides a process whereby a data owner (or other) can

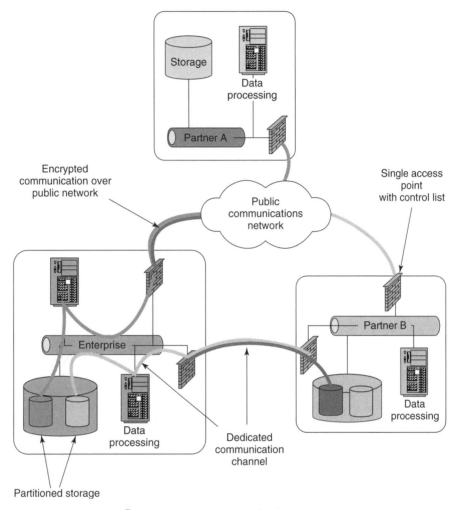

Enterprise partner communication structure

determine the security properties necessary for the exchange of data between organizations. The properties are expressed as follows:

- Protection against inadvertent or unauthorized disclosure: confidentiality
- Protection against inadvertent or unauthorized modification: integrity
- Making business assets available for authorized use: availability
- Attribution of responsibility for actions: accountability

2. Audit business partner.

   An enterprise may require a security audit of the partner before exchanging any information or entering into any business agreement. The purposes of the audit are twofold:

   ■ To evaluate the security policies, practices and controls of the partner. Policies and practices can be evaluated by the enterprise, or it may prefer to acquire independent results from an external consulting firm. Security controls can be tested with a vulnerability scan and/or penetration test.

   ■ To compare and reconcile these results against 'prescribed standards of performance' [Swan00]. Such standards may be enforced by a number of sources: federal or local legislation may define a basic (minimal) level of protection for information exchange, use and storage. The enterprise, itself, may impose much stricter restrictions.

3. Identify and protect communication channels.

   Communication channels include all protocols, hardware devices, communication lines (dedicated and public) and computer network segments over which data will be traveling should be identified. Both the type of data as well as its security requirements will determine (or, at least, strongly effect) the type of communication channel necessary or available. For example, many payment transactions are still sent over value added networks (VANs) using X.400 messaging. Conversely, many modern applications communicate across a public TCP/IP network using a combination of HTTP, HTTPS protocols and HTML, XML or a proprietary message format. Other influencing factors of the type of communication channel include the available technology of the partner organization, industry conventions and budget.

   For traffic separation, dedicated communication channels are preferred, because they reduce the risk of harmful (malicious or inadvertent) events originating from one partner and affecting others, as well as eliminating single points of failure across multiple users. When possible, isolate partner traffic either physically or logically. Physical separation is achieved by using dedicated hardware (servers, firewalls, communication lines) and software. Logical separation is achieved through segmented IP addressing, virtual environments such as multiple operating systems on a mainframe, virtual Web hosts, and multiple databases on a shared installation.

   For each of these communication channels, identify and protect the SINGLE ACCESS POINT (279)s into the enterprise and its systems. Relevant questions to ask are: do additional ports need to be opened up at the firewall or edge routing device, and how will this affect the overall security posture of the environment? Does the network or application need to be modified to allow access for a particular set of users or hosts and will this result in additional threats or vulnerabilities? Will physical access be required by the partner to the enterprise office (or its affiliates)? Will any special arrangements be necessary to support the partner, such as segregated network connectivity (VPN), analogue phone lines, and so on. How will enterprise systems be protected while external partners are on the premises?

Access controls must be applied at any point at which data is passing from one system (user, hardware device, application) to another. Types of access controls include the following:

- Technical access controls used at the network (transmission) layer in routers, firewalls and servers to prevent access from unauthorized hosts. These can be used at the application layer as well, to grant and deny access to specific users.
- Administrative access controls used to define policies and procedures that govern the acceptable circumstances and conditions under which the data can be accessed.
- Physical access controls used to ensure physical protection of the data. For example mechanical door locks to offices, server rooms, and cabinets.

For all implementations of access control, employ a 'failed closed' policy by preventing all access, then granting access for specific entities. This is most commonly used on network perimeter devices such as firewalls, routers and internet servers.

User authorization should be enabled according to the principles of Least Privileges and Separation of Duties [Sal75] and by applying ROLE-BASED ACCESS CONTROL (249). Least Privileges is also known as Need to Know, and is discussed in Security Principles and Security Patterns on page 504). Least Privileges ensures that a particular subject (human or application user) only has the necessary privileges required to perform a given task. An example would be to grant access to write or modify files in a repository, but not delete files. ROLE BASED ACCESS CONTROL is used to assign a subject (user) to one or many roles, with each role allotted a unique collection of privileges. This abstracts the subject from their privileges, providing a business-centric approach and improving the management of access control. The roles of system administrator, sales advisor and purchaser, for example, would all have unique collections of privileges in a corporate directory. Finally, Separation of Duties distributes responsibility (trust) across multiple subjects and is often used in conjunction with ROLE-BASED ACCESS CONTROL (249). For example, partitioning roles (and therefore privileges) of a bank customer with teller and auditor.

4. Define exchange methods and procedures.

   Any form of data exchange will require special pre- or post-processing, depending both on the method of exchange and on any requirements to comply with internal policies or legal regulations. Examples of four common exchange methods and procedures are listed below.

Method 1: On-demand Transfer

This refers to the ad-hoc exchange of information of raw data from one site to another. For example, weather data, news feeds, stock ticker data, and batch file transfer.
  Security related procedures:

1. By what mechanism will data be transferred? FTP, HTTP, private line?
2. How will the data be transferred: pushed or pulled? Automated, batch, manual?
3. What will be the naming convention of the files? For example dated, static, other?
4. Must a file always exist? Will null files be accepted?

Method 2: Real-time Information Exchange

For example, payment processing, EDI. This is payment transaction information, either between financial organizations, or a merchant and a payment processor. The information is sent real-time and contains account (credit card) data and a monetary value. These can be both high or low volume and high or low value transactions. Generally, when a transaction is sent, an authorization or confirmation number is returned for logging.
  Security-related procedures:

1. Will a custom programming API be necessary? If supplied by another entity, will it require review, modification to operate within the enterprise's infrastructure?
2. What are the possible response codes? What do they represent?
3. Can batching (near real-time) be used, or are all transactions individual?
4. Is a notification to other business processes necessary to continue a workflow?

Method 3: Large Volume Information Transfer

For example, managed security outsourcing, and application development outsourcing relationships. This is the large volume shuffling of corporate data. Managed service providers are sent large log files for processing. Development outsourcing companies are provided corporate, and sometimes confidential customer, information used for developing or repairing an application on behalf of the enterprise. Information transfer can occur at any time although not real-time. It requires large bandwidth transmission as well as privacy and integrity controls.

Security-related procedures:

1. Is electronic transfer of the data prohibited? Instead, should the data be transferred physically?
2. What scheduling requirements are required: can the exchange wait until a predetermined time, or does it need to be transferred and processed immediately?
3. What sort of notification, if any, must be made to either humans or applications before or after the data transfer?
4. Will the outsourcing company require direct access to the enterprise's internal networks or servers? Will they require extra privileges to data or user stores?

Method 4: Interactive Application Services

These applications can be accessed by a human or another application in order for one enterprise to provide services to another enterprise. That is, one enterprise is extending its business model to incorporate the services of another enterprise. For example, a Web-based airline reservation site that incorporates the services of a car rental and hotel reservation company, or a third party with network access into the enterprise.

Security-related procedures:

1. What communication and messaging protocols are used?
2. What authentication procedures will exist between applications or networks extensions and what auditing will be performed?
3. What sort of notification, if any, must be made to either humans or applications before or after the data transfer?
4. Who will access the services? Just employees of business partners, contractors or third or fourth parties?

Logging and monitoring

Log files from application servers, firewalls and other application and networking devices will provide important use and access audit trails. They will identify where the access originated, potentially what was being accessed, and for how long. They can be used to monitor use for performance and quality assurance reasons, as well as to provide information for forensic investigations. Such processes may already be employed at the enterprise, but they should also be enabled by the business partner.

Implementation steps (continued):

5. Perform service termination activities.

Access revocation

Temporary and expired user accounts are often a convenient way of gaining access to a system. Therefore, remove all user accounts and entries from access control lists from any network device (firewalls, routers, VPN concentrators), server (hosts files), applications and user stores (database, LDAP, and so on).

Data sanitization

Proper cleaning of disk drives is a critical but often-overlooked task. Specialty tools are available to completely erase entire hard drives or particular files. Also, one or both parties posses data belonging to the other: this data should be completely erased or returned to the business partner in a secure manner.

Asset Repurposing

Only when access controls have been reset and data sanitization has occurred is the asset ready to be reused for another business partner or internal function.

Example Resolved

The museum has chosen to address its four projects as follows:

On-demand News Feed

The museum will make its news data available to other museums or organizations through a free RSS subscription service: the museum just wants to know who's accessing their feeds. The information will be updated as necessary and can be retrieved ad hoc by the other entities. Using SECURITY NEEDS IDENTIFICATION FOR ENTERPRISE ASSETS (89), the museum recognizes that prior to release, the information will require medium confidentiality and integrity, while after release only a low degree of integrity is required. The application server will site behind a firewall in a DEMILITARIZED ZONE (449) and both devices will undergo moderate host hardening and patching. The read-only information will be accessible via FTP or XML over HTTP, and all connections will be logged. To prevent abuse of the feed, request attempts will be limited to ten per hour.

Real-Time Transaction Processing

Payment transactions are initiated from the museum's application and sent real-time from the museum to the payment processor. Each transaction travels across the public internet over TCP/IP and is encrypted end-to-end using the API's encryption algorithm. This ensures confidentiality and integrity of the transaction. The authorization number is stored by the museum.

The payment processor provides this service to hundreds of other merchants and is quite proficient at high availability of all of its systems. The museum is not dual-homed and therefore accepts the risks due to an outage of its Internet service provider. In the event of a failure, however, the museum has obtained contact information for both the payment processor and its ISP.

Outsourcing Web Site Development

Clearly, the transmission of confidential information to the development company, as well as their use of that data, requires protection, specifically, confidentiality and integrity. The museum has performed a security audit of the development company. From this audit, it agrees that the application will be developed and tested on servers protected behind both a corporate perimeter firewall and separate firewall, isolating their development environment from other projects. The development party is the only group with system access to the museum database: data will be incrementally backed up on a nightly basis, fully on a weekly basis, and stored in a locked cabinet to which only the immediate team members and managers have access. Finally, the development company will not share any of the enterprise's information with a third party without prior consent of the museum.

IMC service

The museum recognizes that the exposure of its entire database containing all corporate and personnel information would pose too great a risk. Therefore, the museum chooses to install the IMC software and a new database on a separate network segment from the internal corporate systems in a DEMILITARIZED ZONE (449), isolating it from the corporate network. On a daily basis, only necessary portions of museum and exhibit information will be exported from the authoritative corporate source and imported into the local IMC database. Specifically, donators and funding sources are not exported, nor is financial or human resource information. The museum is provided with an administrative interface that can be used to retrieve messages or update museum information as necessary. The IMC server will marshal all messages between museums over HTTPS only and all user-level requests will be logged.

Variants

[IBM2] describes several patterns for enterprise partner communication. Each pattern builds on the previous pattern's flexibility and ability to meet the increasingly sophisticated demands of the enterprise:

- B2B Topology 1: Document Exchange
- B2B Topology 2: Exposed Application
- B2B Topology 3: Exposed Business Services

- B2B Topology 4: Managed Public Processes
- B2B Topology 5: Managed Public and Private Processes

IBM has also introduced the Trading Partner Agreement [IBM3], an XML-based standard for defining 'how trading partners will interact at the transport, document exchange and business protocol layers. A TPA contains the general contract terms and conditions, participant roles (buyers, sellers), communication and security protocols and business processes, (valid actions, sequencing rules, etc.).' [OASIS00]

[ISO17799] describes security requirements that should be considered when allowing physical or logical access for on-site contractors, trading partners or support staff to enterprise data systems. Examples include the following:

- Description of each service to be made available
- Target level of service and unacceptable levels of service
- Right to monitor and revoke user activity
- Controls to ensure protection against malicious software
- Involvements of third parties with subcontractors
- Clear and specified process of change management

Known Uses

These secure communication procedures are part of many enterprise policies for managing business relationships. For example, many enterprises require a provision in business contracts allowing them to perform a security audit of any third party. Since federal legislations are often the driving force behind this, audits are becoming more and more a priority for senior executives as they become personally responsible for the overall security of their organizations.

Consequences

Use of this pattern provides the following benefits:

- Expectations with respect to security controls and procedures are properly managed.
- Activity and transaction logs are maintained for auditing and compliance for both parties.
- Trustworthy communications enable new business opportunities.
- Sensitive corporate data and systems are not exposed to unnecessary threats or vulnerabilities.
- The exchange procedures can be documented to create a repeatable guideline for subsequent partner agreements.

It also incurs the following liabilities:

- Complex negotiations with business partners may delay the implementation of a new project.
- The cost of a security audit or required controls may be beyond the financial capabilities of the partner entity—but necessary if they wish to do business with the enterprise.
- This pattern does not address integration issues (programmatic interfaces, process flow, messaging) between organizations or applications.

7

Identification and Authentication (I&A)

The Identification and Authentication (I&A) service addresses the need to recognize an actor that is interacting with a business system. This chapter introduces patterns that support aspects of the I&A service, and then presents selected individual patterns in this system. In the context of this book, the I&A pattern system is a service that responds to needs identified in the Enterprise Security and Risk Management pattern system in Chapter 6. In a more general context, the I&A pattern system may respond to needs identified in an enterprise strategy or any service that has a need to identify actors.

An actor that interacts with a business system may be a human being, a process, or other entity. The business system may be the enterprise as a whole or any system within the enterprise. Examples include verifying the identity of users at log-on, identifying a software object at connect time, and verifying individuals at a guarded door. I&A is a basic service. We use I&A results in support of other services. For example, the access control service depends on I&A results to ensure that only legitimate users access the system. The accounting service depends on I&A results to achieve accountability of actions. We describe further uses below.

Key I&A concepts are graphically illustrated in the figure below. In a typical I&A service, an actor approaching a system is placed in contact with the I&A service. The I&A service obtains an identity from the actor, translates the identity to an ID, and authenticates the ID using an authenticator. The term 'system,' as used in the figure, has a broad generic meaning that corresponds to a security domain. For example, in single sign-on, the 'system' associated with the I&A includes all individual systems to which access is granted using the sign-on I&A results.

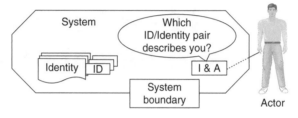

Identification and authentication concepts

There are two primary categories of I&A:

■ Individual I&A determines the individual actor interacting with a process. An example is a person logging on to a computer, as shown in the next figure. Individual I&A applies not only to humans, but also to all processes and other non-human entities.

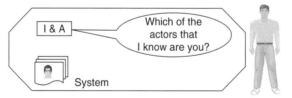

Individual identification and authentication representation

■ Group I&A determines whether an actor interacting with a process is a member of a particular group. Group I&A almost always applies to human I&A activities, as shown in the next figure. An example is a guard checking a badge to be sure that the holder is an employee, but not checking the name on the badge.

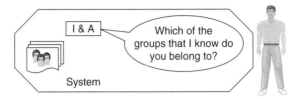

Group identification and authentication representation

Individual I&A is the primary focus of this pattern system, because it is the most common form. However, a significant portion of the pattern material in this chapter is applicable to both group I&A and individual I&A.

The I&A service has many uses. I&A is the most common log-on scenario for computer systems. Another common use is to support other security services. Support for access control, security accounting, non-repudiation, and other security services usually requires knowing either the individual actor or knowing that the individual actor is a member of a specific group. Other business functions outside the security arena also use I&A. For example, I&A is important to the financial accounting functions of a business, because when an actor makes a purchase, the business must allocate the cost to the correct individual or organization so that the bill is sent to the purchaser.

I&A by itself is only one component of a solution that allows a process to know information about an actor. I&A does no more than produce a point-in-time identification. We need other functions to link an actor identified by I&A with a set of actions.

A key point is that a system usually already has an independent record containing attributes for an actor. The function of I&A is to locate that record. Several other components participate in the background activities for identification of an actor. These associated components may or may not be patterns. They include:

- Actor registration: establishes the independent record that will represent the actor within the system.

- Session management: links the identification returned by the I&A function with future actions by the actor—see SECURITY SESSION (297) on page 297.

- Contact establishment: establishes reliable contact with the actor.

- Using function: triggers the I&A process, passes it its required inputs, and receives its outputs. For an example of using functions, see the patterns for Access Control in Chapter 8, 9 and 10 as well as the Accounting patterns in Chapter 11.

The figure below shows an I&A service view from the perspective of other components of an architecture. The I&A service is requested by a using function, which has the responsibility of passing information to the I&A service sufficient to allow the I&A service to determine an identifier and one or more authenticators. The using function may be a software function, or may be some other trigger, such as a person approaching a desk and requesting entry to a restricted area.

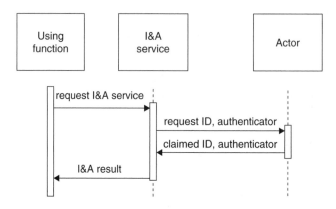

Generic interaction model of I&A service

In many cases the information passed to an I&A service from a using function is contact information that allows the I&A service to obtain the claimed identity and authenticators directly from the actor. For example, in an operating system, a user may request a trusted path to the log-in function, for example by pressing Control–Alt–Delete, while in a reception area a visitor at a desk may be in face-to-face communication with a receptionist. In other cases the information may already pre-exist for the calling function and can be passed to the I&A service. An example is a software entity accessing the system in which the connection request accesses and provides the software entity's identification and authenticator.

In either case, the I&A service returns the result to the using function. The result includes an indicator of success or failure. If the identification and authentication service completes successfully for an information system, it typically also returns an authenticated ID. Whether success or failure, an I&A service offers some degree of certainty associated with its activity. Typically, the degree of certainty is assumed based on knowledge of the I&A service's reputation. However, in some cases an explicit indicator of certainty may also be returned.

The next figure presents the internal components and logic for a typical I&A service for an information system. When a request is made, the service obtains identity and authenticator information, either from the input or by interaction with the actor. The service validates the identity by locating an internal record ID associated with it, and verifies that the authenticator is valid for that ID.

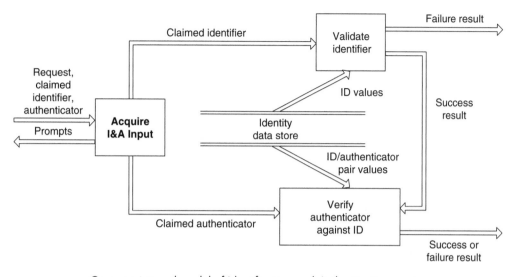

Common internal model of Identification and Authentication service

All the patterns in this chapter were written by a team at the MITRE Corporation, consisting of Jody Heaney, Duane Hybertson, Susan Chapin, Ann Reedy, and Malcolm Kirwan Jr. Susan Chapin and Duane Hybertson wrote the introductory material for the chapter, and Duane Hybertson integrated the material into the chapter. Peter Sommerlad, Markus Schumacher, and Eduardo Fernandez provided shepherding comments for the MITRE patterns. Markus Schumacher provided comments on integrating the material into the chapter.

7.1 I&A Requirements

An identification and authentication (I&A) service must satisfy a set of requirements for both the service and the quality of service. The function of I&A is to recognize an individual and validate the individual's identity. While each situation that calls for I&A is unique, there are common generic requirements that apply to all I&A situations. This pattern provides a common generic set of I&A requirements. The pattern also helps you to apply the general requirements to your specific situation, and helps you to determine the relative importance of conflicting requirements.

Example

The museum gemstones wing will build on the parent museum's intranet, with workstations distributed throughout multiple departments. Based on applying ENTERPRISE SECURITY SERVICES (161), the museum recognizes the need for specific security functions. Among these are access control and security accounting. Both of these functions rely on an I&A service to establish identity. What kind of I&A service does the museum need to support these functions? What other situations call for an I&A service in the museum? After some analysis, Samuel, the museum's system engineer, and Edward, the enterprise architect, come up with these possible situations that require I&A services:

■ Establishing physical access to the museum during business hours

■ Establishing physical access to the museum by staff during outside business hours

■ On-line access to the intranet from within the local area network of the museum wing

■ Remote on-line access to the museum's intranet

■ Access to highly sensitive museum physical assets, especially gemstones

■ On-line access to highly sensitive museum information assets

■ Tracking who is downloading information from the publicly-available museum Web site

■ Support non-repudiation of business transactions on the part of customers or partners

■ Employee accountability of computer and network resource use within the museum

■ Accountability to support identification of the source of computer viruses or a network denial of service attack

The engineers feel that these situations differ in their I&A requirements, but are not sure how to capture the differences. For example, a single mechanism for Web site I&A doesn't work, because Vic the visitor, downloading publicly-available information, has I&A requirements that differ from Manuela the museum manager, who is working from home and retrieving sensitive accounting data. Furthermore, for each of these situations, the museum wants to properly balance conflicting objectives, such as a service that detects would-be hackers versus a service that is easy for employees to use. Typically a strong I&A mechanism that detects most imposters, that is, people who falsely claim to be legitimate, are hard to use, while I&A mechanisms that are easy to use tend to give weaker protection, in too many cases concluding that an imposter is legitimate.

Samuel's initial thinking had been that he could simply select some I&A mechanism such as a password-based log-on or an employee badge. This has given way to the realization that more thought and consideration is needed to ensure that multiple I&A needs are properly addressed. Samuel and Edward recognize that they need to specify a clear and balanced set of requirements for each situation the requires I&A. How can they accomplish this?

Context

An organization or project understands its planned uses of I&A, for example, from applying ENTERPRISE SECURITY SERVICES (161), or from applying one or more of the pattern systems that use I&A, such as the patterns for access control in Chapter 8, 9 and 10 and the accounting patterns in Chapter 11.

The scope is known to be situations in which both identification and authentication are needed. Other situations exist in which only identification is needed without authentication, but those situations are not addressed in this pattern.

Problem

Requirements for I&A often conflict with each other, and trade-offs among them are often necessary. The conflict stated in the Example section is that strength of protection with I&A tends to conflict with ease of use.

I&A comprises both associating an identifier with an actor (identification) and verifying that the association is correct (authentication). I&A is a security service whose results are often used by other security services, including access control and accounting. A basic set of generic I&A requirements exists for all types of use and circumstances. However, these generic requirements need to be specialized for a given I&A domain. In addition, the relative importance of the requirements will vary based on the circumstances. What is needed is (1) to capture the specific set of requirements, and (2) to understand how to differentiate the relative importance of the requirements in specific circumstances to balance or resolve the conflicts.

How can you determine specific requirements for an I&A service, and their relative importance?

Determination of I&A requirements needs to resolve the following forces:

- Owners of I&A services want the services to perform their expected function, that is, correctly to determine whether an actor is associated with an identifier

- Incorrectly confirming the false claim of an imposter can lead to extensive disclosure of or damage to assets

- Incorrectly denying the true claim of a legitimate actor can lead to loss of productivity through denial of service or denial of access to authorized assets

- Users want I&A services to offer good quality of service: rapid response, proper functioning, easy to understand, safe, appropriate for category of user, and supportive of handicapped users

- The enterprise wants its I&A services to be cost effective and provide a good return on investment

- There are often reasons for making identifiers public—for example, e-mail identifiers need to be known so that others can send e-mail

- The I&A service will need to protect against the potential for stolen identities and the impacts of stolen identities and authenticators

Solution

Specify a set of I&A requirements for a specific I&A domain, and determine the relative importance of each requirement. The solution has two aspects: a requirements process and a common set of generic requirements.

Requirements Specification and Prioritization Process

A system requirements engineer, in conjunction with an enterprise architect, typically perform the requirements process. An important first step is explicitly to define the domain for which you are specifying I&A requirements, such as a specific system or facility. Factors such as enterprise constraints that affect specialization and importance of requirements also need to be defined. The I&A requirements for the target I&A domain are then specified, using the generic requirements provided below. The final activity is to define the relative importance of the specified requirements.

Generic Requirements Description

The following set of generic requirements responds to the problem and forces described above. The first two represent I&A functional requirements. The remaining requirements represent I&A non-functional requirements, including requirements for security of the I&A service.

The following analysis is presented to help you understand and apply the first two generic requirements. For the I&A service properly to execute its function, it must be able to deny the identity claims of imposters, and confirm the claims of legitimate actors. In any given I&A episode, any of four outcomes is possible, illustrated in Table 7.1.

Table 7.1 Outcome of I&A situations

ACTUAL SITUATION	I&A SERVICE CONCLUSION	
	Confirmation of actor claim (You are Actor A)	Denial of actor claim (You are not Actor A)
Actor A claims to be Actor A	True positive	False negative
Actor B claims to be Actor A	False positive	True negative

The table shows that the four outcomes result from two variables, namely, the actual situation and the I&A service conclusion. One function of the I&A service is to confirm the identity of legitimate actors, that is, actors who are who they claim to be. This result is a true positive or true acceptance. The second function of the I&A service is to deny the identity of imposters, that is, actors who are not who they claim to be. This result is a true negative or true rejection. A perfect I&A service would result in 100% true positives in situations where the actor is legitimate, and 100% true negatives in situations where the actor is an impostor. But no I&A service is perfect, and two types of errors are possible. One type of error, called a 'false positive' or 'false acceptance,' is confirmation that an imposter is who he claims to be. In Table 7.1, the false positive is erroneous confirmation that Actor B is Actor A. The second type of error, called a false negative or false rejection, is denial that an actor is who he claims to be. In Table 7.1, the false negative is erroneous denial that Actor A is Actor A. If an error occurs, it is then propagated to the function that relies on the I&A service. For example, an access-control service may use a false positive from the I&A service to permit an imposter access to sensitive assets, which can then be damaged or destroyed.

The generic requirements are as follows.

Accurately Detect Imposters

In the context of Table 7.1, this requirement addresses the imposter situation, that is, Actor B claims to be Actor A. The requirement says that the I&A service must recognize that this actor is not Actor A, and deny the claim. The service must result in a true negative and not make the false positive error. Note that this requirement does not ask the I&A service to recognize Actor B as Actor B, but only to recognize that this actor is not the claimed Actor A.

Accurately Recognize Legitimate Actors

In the context of Table 7.1, this requirement addresses the legitimate actor situation, that is, Actor A claims to be Actor A. The requirement says that the I&A service must recognize that this actor is Actor A, and confirm the claim. The service must result in a true positive and not make the false negative error.

A trade-off exists between this requirement and the previous one. A stringent I&A service that provides a very high probability of detecting imposters also tends to have a higher probability of denying the claims of legitimate actors. Conversely, a more accommodating I&A service that provides a very high probability of confirming legitimate actors also tends to have a higher probability of confirming the claims of impostors. When you apply this pattern to your specific system or organization, you need to determine which type of error is more important to avoid.

Minimize Mismatch with user Characteristics

An I&A service is typically used by different categories of users, such as level of experience. Both inexperienced users or novices, and experienced or sophisticated users, want the I&A services to interact with them at their own level. Some I&A techniques require more sophistication than others. Additional characteristics to be considered include fixed versus mobile location of users, and remote versus local users.

Minimize Time and Effort to Use

Performing I&A almost always costs users some time and effort in the process of acquiring access to an enterprise asset. For example, remembering and typing a password, or standing in line to be approved by a security guard, or assigning and maintaining certificates associated with a software module, is not as easy as not typing the password, not needing to wait for the guard, or not assigning the certificate. User effort and time delays associated with I&A adds to the bottom-line cost of enterprise operations, so that in general it is desirable to minimize the effort and time involved in performing I&A. Single sign-on (SSO) is one common approach to minimizing time and effort in the context of an enterprise network, by means of a single authentication that is performed when users initially access the network. This requirement is often in conflict with accuracy requirements, however.

Minimize Risks to User Safety

Issues of safety, such as requiring use of iris-scanning if users could be wearing gas masks, or damage done by retinal scanning, can preclude use of an authentication technique. This requirement is sometimes in conflict with accuracy requirements.

Minimize Costs of Per-user Setup

Establishing a new user or actor in an I&A domain involves generating an identifier for the actor, establishing grounds for authenticating the actor, delivering to the actor any data, tokens, or hardware the actor needs, and training users or software maintainers in the use of the selected technique. Each of these procedures has associated costs that add to the bottom-line costs of establishing or maintaining supported functions. Cost should in general be minimized. This requirement is often in conflict with enterprise accuracy requirements.

Minimize Changes Needed to Existing System Infrastructure

System infrastructure includes equipment, facilities, people, and procedures. System infrastructure support for I&A includes both system-wide support and support at each connection point where actors interact with I&A services.

Changes to existing infrastructure or addition of new infrastructure have associated costs. For example, new equipment costs money to acquire, absorbs employee time to install, and carries maintenance costs. All these costs add to the bottom-line costs of establishing or maintaining supported functions, and in general should be minimized. This requirement is often in conflict with minimizing enterprise accuracy requirements.

Minimize Costs of Maintenance, Management, and Overhead

I&A is a business procedure that can require very substantial time and effort to maintain and manage. All these costs add to the bottom-line costs of running the business and in general should be minimized. This requirement is often in conflict with accuracy requirements.

Protect I&A Service and Assets

I&A assets, especially authenticators and related data, are vulnerable to theft or disclosure. The I&A service itself needs protection, including confidentiality and integrity of I&A data, availability of the I&A process, and accountability for I&A service-related actions. This requirement is supportive of accuracy requirements but is often in conflict with ease of use.

Variations Across Sets of Requirements

The specific values of requirements, and the relative importance of each requirement, vary in different use situations. The use situations given in the Problem section illustrate some of these differences. For example:

- I&A results used in granting on-line access to highly-sensitive enterprise information assets would be likely to place high importance on avoiding false rejections and protecting I&A assets, and lesser importance on minimizing cost and effort to use.

■ I&A results used in tracking who is downloading information or products from publicly-available enterprise Web site would be likely to place high importance on minimizing cost and effort to use, and lesser importance on avoiding false rejections.

Implementation

This section first provides further detail on the process that was summarized in the Solution section, then discusses factors for determining the relative importance of requirements.

Process Guidelines

The requirements process typically includes these steps:

1. Establish the domain for which the I&A service is needed.

   Ensure that the domain has been identified and scoped. Typical I&A domains include an information system, physical facility, network, portal, or entire enterprise. Other constraints may bound the domain—for example, the I&A requirements for entering a designated facility during normal work hours may differ from the requirements outside business hours, such as night-time and weekends: these would represent two domains.

2. Specify a set of factors that affect specialization and importance of requirements.

   The factors include uses of I&A, I&A needs, enterprise constraints, and priorities. You can find a general candidate set of factors in Table 7.2.

3. Specify I&A requirements for the target I&A domain.

   To do this, specialize the set of generic requirements given in the Solution section.

4. Define the relative importance of specific requirements.

   The association of factors and requirements is discussed below.

Factors in Determining Relative Importance

Table 7.2 presents factors for judging the relative importance to the enterprise of the generic I&A requirements that were identified in the Solution section. For each requirement, the table describes how the factors affect the relative priority of the requirement.

Table 7.2 Factors affecting relative importance of I&A requirements

GENERIC REQUIREMENT	FACTOR	IMPACT ON PRIORITY
Accurately detect imposters	Potential cost to the enterprise if a link is made with an identifier to which the actor is not entitled (for example, could be used to give access to assets)	This requirement should have increased priority if inability to detect imposters could cause significant damage to the enterprise or system.
Accurately recognize legitimate actors	Existence of time-critical functions where access is controlled based on actor identifier, potential cost to the enterprise if controlled critical functions are not performed in a timely manner.	This requirement should have increased priority if rejection of legitimate actors for time-critical functions could cause significant damage to the enterprise or system.
	User base sensitivity to temporary denial of service. potential cost in dollars or good-will to the enterprise if users become annoyed	This requirement should have increased priority if rejection of legitimate actors could occur to the point of significant denial of service and user annoyance.
Minimize mismatch with user characteristics	User experience	This requirement should have increased priority if the I&A service could cause significant user frustration by not accommodating user experience level, whether novice or sophisticated.
	User base membership (employees, partners, public, software)	This requirement should have increased priority if the I&A service could cause security risks or significant user frustration by not supporting all user categories, such as employees versus partners.
	User location (local, remote)	This requirement should have increased priority if the I&A service could cause security risks or significant user frustration by not supporting all user locations, such as local versus remote.
	User mobility (fixed or mobile locations, fixed or variable devices)	This requirement should have increased priority if the I&A service could cause security risks or significant user frustration by not supporting user mobility, such as fixed versus mobile locations.
Minimize time and effort to use	Frequency of use	This requirement should have increased priority if the I&A service has heavy use.

Table 7.2   Factors affecting relative importance of I&A requirements (*continued*)

GENERIC REQUIREMENT	FACTOR	IMPACT ON PRIORITY
	User base characteristics	Inability of some users, such as handicapped users, to perform I&A may require changes to the business model. An I&A service that is difficult to use and requires more time may increase the potential costs in money or good-will if users become annoyed. Both should increase the priority of this requirement.
Minimize risks to user safety	Relevant statutes and enterprise policy	Statutes or policy may mandate this requirement, in which case it would in effect have top priority.
	Potential liability of enterprise for injury (for example damage to eye in retinal scan)	This requirement should have increased priority if the I&A service poses significant risk of incurred costs, and negative publicity, from users injured performing I&A.
Minimize costs of per-user setup	Number of users in general terms (hundreds, thousands, millions)	The existence or projection of a large number of users should increase the priority of this requirement.
	Volatility of user base	The existence or projection of a large turnover rate among users should increase the priority of this requirement.
	Existing user knowledge and skills	The existence or projection of a large proportion of novice users should increase the priority of this requirement, while a large proportion of experienced users should decrease its priority. However, for I&A, this factor is usually a minor one in either case.
Minimize changes needed to existing infrastructure	Number of connection points	A large number of connection points for the I&A service should increase the priority of this requirement, because each connection point may need an associated change.
	Predicted restructuring of existing infrastructure	If the infrastructure is already scheduled to be changed for other reasons, this requirement will have reduced priority.

Table 7.2   Factors affecting relative importance of I&A requirements (*continued*)

GENERIC REQUIREMENT	FACTOR	IMPACT ON PRIORITY
Minimize costs of maintenance, management, and overhead	Ability to rely on users properly to protect data or hardware entrusted to them	This requirement should have decreased priority if the users are knowledgeable and trustworthy. However, this assumption has some risk.
	Volatility of user base	The existence or projection of a large turnover rate among users should increase the priority of this requirement.
Protect I&A assets	Cost and risk of authenticator theft	This requirement should have increased priority if the cost and risk of theft of an authenticator, such as a password, is relatively high.
	Cost and risk of I&A service being unavailable	This requirement should have increased priority if the cost and risk of I&A being unavailable is relatively high.

Example Resolved

Samuel the systems engineer and Edward the enterprise architect identify each situation from the museum example above as a separate domain, with a separate set of requirements. The first domain for which they specify I&A requirements is that of the museum employees who access the museum information systems. Table 7.3 shows the requirements they specified for this domain. The first column contains two sets of information: the generic requirement, followed by the specific requirement for the museum. The second column presents the relevant factor for the requirement in this domain, and the third column discusses the resulting importance of each requirement.

Table 7.3   Resolving requirements for museum information system I&A

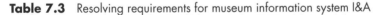

GENERIC/SPECIFIC REQUIREMENT	FACTOR	IMPORTANCE FOR MUSEUM
Accurately detect imposters. The I&A service shall have a minimum certainty of 0.9999 (shall have no more than 1 false acceptance out of 10000 I&A claims of imposters).	Potential costs of not detecting an imposter	All I&A services for workstations in physical asset display and research work areas must satisfy this requirement. The museum considers this to be extremely important.

Table 7.3 Resolving requirements for museum information system I&A (*continued*)

GENERIC/SPECIFIC REQUIREMENT	FACTOR	IMPORTANCE FOR MUSEUM
Accurately recognize legitimate actors. The I&A service shall have a maximum false rejection rate of 0.02 (shall deny no more than 1 actor out of 50 I&A claims of entitled actors).	Existence of time-critical functions	This is a moderate level of concern for the museum wing, as they prefer to incur the costs of hampered staff than to falsely assert the identity of an actor.
	User base sensitivity to temporary denial of service	N/A
Minimize mismatch with users. The I&A service shall support information system users with these characteristics: users are employees interacting with museum information systems, there are local and remote user locations, and the user locations are fixed.	User base membership (employees, partners, public, software)	The museum considers this a moderate concern. Only identified and authenticated actors will be able to log on to the information system. No anonymous users.
	User location	All user locations are known.
	User mobility	All I&A services will have fixed locations.
Minimize time and effort to use. The I&A service shall be easy to use.	Frequency of use	Museum users will not be required to perform multiple log-ons. Training will be provided to ensure workstations are logged off. The museum does not consider this a significant requirement.
	User base characteristics	The museum considers this a moderate concern related to staffing.
Minimize risks to user safety. The I&A service shall provide adequate safety.	Relevant statutes and enterprise policy	Statutes and policy do mandate this requirement for the museum.
	Vulnerability of enterprise to negative publicity	N/A

Table 7.3 Resolving requirements for museum information system I&A (*continued*)

GENERIC/SPECIFIC REQUIREMENT	FACTOR	IMPORTANCE FOR MUSEUM
Minimize costs of per-user setup. The I&A service set-up cost per person shall be as small as possible, and in any case shall be less than $50 per person.	Number of users in general terms	The museum's user base will be restricted to identified and authenticated users. Costs for I&A will be per workstation.
	Volatility of user base	The museum considers this a moderate concern as the rate of staff turnover is not high.
	Existing user knowledge and skills	As noted, the museum intends to provide user training to reduce costs.
Minimize changes needed to existing infrastructure. The I&A service shall be able to interface with existing components from the parent enterprise.	Existing support contracts	The museum considers this requirement extremely important. The I&A for this museum wing must be able to interface with existing components from the parent enterprise.
	Number of connection points	As above, museum costs will be per workstation, the same as the parent enterprise.
	Predicted restructuring of existing infrastructure	Any future infrastructure changes will occur under the parent enterprise funding profile.
Minimize costs of maintenance, management, and overhead. The I&A service shall be cost effective with respect to maintenance, management, and overhead.	Ability to rely on users	User training will be provided.
	Volatility of user base	The museum considers this a moderate concern, as the rate of staff turnover is not high.

Table 7.3   Resolving requirements for museum information system I&A (*continued*)

GENERIC/SPECIFIC REQUIREMENT	FACTOR	IMPORTANCE FOR MUSEUM
Protect I&A assets The I&A service shall protect its security assets, such as passwords.	Cost of authenticator theft	The museum considers this a very important requirement, since it could put physical assets at risk.
	Cost of I&A service being unavailable	The museum will need to address multiple back-up plans for loss of I&A service.

Samuel and Edward determine that the most important I&A requirements for the museum are:

1. Accurately detect imposters
2. Minimize risks to user safety
3. Minimize changes needed to existing infrastructure
4. Protect I&A assets

Known Uses

The general I&A requirements and the process of specifying I&A requirements described in this pattern represent a consolidation of MITRE Corporation's experience in working with multiple customers over several decades. The approach is generally used informally by those customers, as opposed to being codified or published. However, some discussions of I&A requirements exist. Examples include:

- [OMB2003] is a US government policy for electronic authentication of individuals participating in on-line transactions. It discusses some of the non-functional requirements identified in this pattern, such as cost and user burden. [NIST2004] provides technical guidance for this policy.

- [ISO15408] is an international standard that defines evaluation criteria for information technology security. It includes a class or family of criteria that address the requirements for functions to establish and verify a claimed user identity.

- [SEI2004] is a risk-based technique to elicit authentication requirements for electronic transactions. It includes the process of defining context, scope, and nonfunctional I&A requirements.

- [Firesmith2003] describes functional I&A requirements (false positives and false negatives), and discusses I&A domains in terms of requirements scope.

Consequences

You may expect the following benefits from applying this pattern.

■ The pattern fosters explicit definition of I&A domains and a clear connection of requirements to I&A domains. This increases understanding of the full set of domains that are involved in I&A and understanding of the scope of each set of requirements.

■ It facilitates conscious selection of I&A requirements, so that decisions about selecting I&A mechanisms have a clear basis, rather than occurring in a vacuum.

■ It promotes explicit analysis of trade-offs that encourages balancing and prioritizing of conflicting requirements. It helps avoid stronger than necessary I&A, which makes it difficult for valid users, and at the same time it helps to avoid weaker than necessary I&A, which makes it easy for imposters to defeat and therefore provide inadequate protection.

■ It results in documentation of I&A requirements that communicates to all interested parties, and also provides information for security audits.

The potential liabilities of applying this pattern are:

■ It requires an investment of resources to apply the pattern, including time to analyze domains and I&A needs. In some cases the cost of applying the pattern may exceed its benefits.

■ It poses a danger of over-engineering and complexity creep, if stakeholders are offered too many options. You can mitigate this by using the requirements only as guidelines for analysis, or by selecting parts of the pattern that give the most help.

■ The formal selection process may be too long and costly and produce too much overhead. You can mitigate this in the same way as noted above.

■ Specific circumstances might not be covered by generic I&A requirements. You can mitigate this by adding specific requirements and including them in the trade-offs.

■ Documentation of requirements implies that they must be maintained as they change over time. You can mitigate this by keeping the requirements in a form that is easy to update, integrated with other system documentation.

■ Perception of I&A requirements can differ throughout an organization. This may make it difficult to reach agreement on priorities between requirements. On the other hand, bringing such disagreements to the surface may be a benefit of the pattern, because then they can be properly discussed and resolved.

See Also

After applying this solution, the next step is typically to decide what type of I&A to use. If you have made a decision to use only automated I&A, you can apply AUTOMATED I&A DESIGN ALTERNATIVES (207).

7.2 Automated I&A Design Alternatives

This pattern describes alternative techniques for automated I&A, as opposed to procedural or physical I&A. It helps you to select an appropriate I&A strategy that consists of a single technique, or a combination of techniques, to satisfy I&A requirements. Techniques considered include password, biometrics, hardware token, PKI, and I&A of unregistered users.

Also Known As

Decision Tradeoffs for Automated I&A [HHR+02].

Example

Indiana Jones, a museum employee, needs to gain access to the museum intranet while collecting artifacts for the museum from around the world. He wants to check his e-mail abroad and also access the museum's database to evaluate a found artifact. From Jones' perspective, the most important requirements for this I&A service are to support I&A from remote locations and to be easy to use. From the perspective of Samuel the museum systems engineer, the most important requirements for this I&A service are to have high accuracy, especially to reject attempts by non-employees to gain access to the intranet, and to limit I&A overhead. Samuel and his systems engineering group have used I&A REQUIREMENTS (192) to define all four of these intranet I&A requirements as high priority. Now Ivan the intranet architect needs to select an I&A service to satisfy these requirements. The choices available to Ivan are many. They include identifier and password, PKI certificates, multiple biometrics options, and a hardware token with a one-time password. How can Ivan choose among the alternatives?

Context

The person applying this pattern understands the requirements for I&A, along with their relative importance—for example, from the results of applying I&A REQUIREMENTS (192).

A decision has been made to use automated I&A[1].

---

[1] In the remainder of this pattern, the term 'I&A' is intended to mean automated I&A, as opposed to physical or procedural I&A, such as showing a badge to a guard at the front door.

Problem

I&A is a common need for systems and enterprises. Multiple techniques exist for achieving I&A. Different techniques emphasize different types of authenticators. No one technique is the best in all situations. Trade-offs and weighting are typically necessary, because in general the techniques have differing and often complementary strengths and weaknesses. For example, PKI provides high accuracy, but has relatively high infrastructure and cost impact, while passwords provide less accuracy, but have low infrastructure and cost impact.

In addition, certain combinations of techniques can produce an I&A strategy that in some circumstances satisfies requirements better than any of the individual techniques. For example, a combination of password and hardware token is typically stronger than either individual technique, because each compensates for a weakness of the other.

A common perspective for comparing and combining techniques is the following categorization:

- Something you know, for example a password.
- Something you have, for example a hardware token.
- Something you are, for example a biometric characteristic such as an iris image.
- Recently a fourth category has emerged: where you are, for example, derived from either your IP address or through the use of GPS, which is now included in some cell phones and PDAs. This is an additional kind of information available for authentication.

An I&A strategy may be influenced by the selection of strategies for other I&A domains within an enterprise. The enterprise may find it more efficient—in terms of cost, training, and maintenance—if all I&A domains that have similar requirements use the same strategy. For example, the enterprise may decide that the I&A used in granting out-of-hours physical access to all enterprise facilities throughout the country should use the same technique, such as biometrics.

Using a single technique for I&A in an organization is attractive, for example for achieving single sign-on (SSO). On the other hand, using a single technique is also dangerous, because it is a single point of failure, thus violating the 'defence in depth' principle (see Chapter 15). For example, if you are an imposter and your identity claim is accepted, you may be given access to multiple critical resources.

How can a strategy for I&A be selected that satisfies I&A requirements?

Based on the foregoing discussion, we can summarize the forces that influence selection of a strategy that balances techniques to satisfy I&A requirements:

- Some techniques satisfy some I&A requirements better than others.
- In many cases certain combinations of I&A techniques can satisfy requirements better than any individual technique. A common strategy is to combine

techniques from two or more of these categories: something you know, something you have, something you are, and where you are.

- An I&A strategy may be influenced by the selection of strategies for other I&A domains within an enterprise.

- Using a single technique for I&A across an organization may be efficient, but it is also dangerous, because it is a single point of failure.

Solution

Systematically review the characteristics of the available I&A techniques, and select a strategy that consists of one or more techniques. Proven techniques include user ID/password, hardware token, biometrics, PKI, and I&A of unregistered users. These are not the only techniques that exist, or that will exist in the future, but they are the techniques described in this pattern.

   The selection process is typically performed by a person or team serving in the role of system architect, security architect, or enterprise architect, depending on the nature and scope of the domain. The process includes several activities: explicitly assembling the necessary inputs for decision making is an important first step. Inputs include a definition of the I&A domain or scope of the strategy, I&A requirements, and the general values of factors for each I&A technique. The inputs are then used to define specific technique profiles for the chosen domain. With this information, you can compare the I&A requirements with techniques to determine the best matches. Finally, if no individual technique adequately matches the requirements, you can look at combinations of techniques.

Implementation

This section first provides further detail on the process that was summarized in the Solution section, then presents information on technique profiles. Finally, considerations are given for combining techniques and selecting a strategy.

Process Guidelines

The selection process includes the following steps:

1. Assemble the necessary inputs for decision making.

    Two of the inputs are a definition of the I&A domain or scope and the I&A requirements. If you have applied the pattern, both of these inputs should be available. The requirements should include enterprise constraints, and an indication of the importance of each requirement—for example via ranking, weighting, or criticality indicators. The third input is a technique factor profile summary, that is, general values of factors for each technique. Table 7.4 on page 213 provides a summary that you can use for certain I&A techniques.

2. Define the specific technique profiles for this domain.

    The next step is to specialize the general technique factor profile for your specific I&A domain. You can use the technique profiles discussion below to tailor the value of each technique in your domain. For example, if your domain excludes software actors, then satisfaction of the requirement to support a variety of user types (that is, the entry for User Types) is high for all techniques with respect to your domain.

3. Compare the I&A requirements with individual technique profiles.

    If one technique satisfies the requirements, select that technique as the I&A strategy: if not, perform step 4.

4. If no single technique is adequate, look at combinations of techniques.

    Combine techniques that have complementary strengths and weaknesses. You might benefit from the discussion of combinations and the overall organizational perspective that follows Table 7.4.

Technique Profiles

I&A techniques differ in what they use for IDs, identifiers, and authenticators, as well as other characteristics that affect their selection. A description of each technique is given. The purpose of this section is to define their comparative characteristics. Each I&A technique has a characteristic profile with respect to factors affecting the ability of the technique to satisfy the requirements. The profile for each technique is discussed here and summarized in Table 7.4.

User ID/Password

This technique generally scores high on cost effectiveness and usage requirements, but lower on reliability and protection of passwords. Password's ability to avoid confirming imposters is medium at best, because passwords can be obtained through theft or other means. This ability depends on good password practice—for example, the use of hard-to-guess passwords, and not recording passwords in easy-to-find locations. Password's ability to avoid denying legitimate users depends on the likelihood of remembering passwords: good passwords can be somewhat difficult to remember.

Regarding user types, passwords as they are typically defined may not be suitable for software actors. A common belief is that passwords are easy to use. It is true that poor password practice is easy. Good password practice is harder to achieve, but it can be made easier through schemes such as one-time passwords, which is described below.

Biometrics

The biometrics technique profile varies more than other techniques. This is due to the fact that multiple biometric techniques exist. A general profile is described here, and the various biometric techniques are described further in BIOMETRICS DESIGN ALTERNATIVES (229).

Biometric techniques have the potential for high reliability, depending on the type of biometric selected. On the other hand, biometric techniques generally cost more and are not as easy to use as some other techniques. Biometric techniques often do well in recognizing legitimate users. However, environmental or aging factors may affect biometric readings. Such factors include poor lighting, sunglasses, facial hair, and change due to injury or disease.

Biometrics techniques are not suitable for software actors. Some biometric techniques may not be suitable for some types of mobile computing (for example cell phones). Safety depends on the type of biometric technique: retinal scans can cause damage to retina, so its safety is low. The cost is increased due to the need for biometric devices or scanners, as well as additional processor, storage, network loads and in some cases additional processing software. It is possible to steal biometric information, which has the potential for severe problems for a user. It is difficult and rather painful to change your biometric characteristics, such as fingerprints.

PKI

This technique depends somewhat on the population to which it is applied. It can score very highly on reliability with a relatively sophisticated user base, but has high cost. It may not be suitable for world-wide computing—that is, from locations where communications to registration servers have low availability. You not only have to trust the third party issuing the certificates, you also have to trust your computer hardware and software not to compromise your private keys or use weak encryption. In addition, you have to trust yourself or your employees to be able to validate the certificates and to actually do so.

Infrastructure impact is very high, including software development practices. It has moderate to high management costs, because of the third party involved. A PKI can work well with a defined user population where an established body issues certificates and carries a directory of public keys related to the individuals and organizations within that closed community. For example, it seems to work well within the Swiss medical community.

Hardware Token

The reliability of this technique can vary. The ability to avoid confirming imposters depends on the degree of protection of the token. Reliability is high if combined with password for use of the token. Stand-alone token ability to avoid denying legitimate users is high. If combined with password, this ability is medium, because of the possibility of mis-typed or forgotten passwords. Token techniques are not suitable for software actors. Some token types may not be suitable for some types of mobile computing (for example cell phones). Some types of tokens require moderate to high costs per connection, because they use token readers, while other types may only require installation of additional software. Authenticator protection depends on users to report lost tokens.

Unregistered Users

This technique generally scores highly on ease of use and cost effectiveness, but is low on reliability. The technique scales up to a very large user base. It is not suitable for software actors.

In Table 7.4, the requirements listed in the requirements column are described in detail in I&A REQUIREMENTS (192). The value or range of values indicates the extent to which a technique satisfies an I&A requirement. High indicates high satisfaction of the requirement, and Low indicates low satisfaction.

To determine the I&A technique(s) that will meet the I&A needs, a general approach is to compare the technique profiles with your results from applying I&A REQUIREMENTS (192) to find a technique that is most compatible with your specific requirements.

Considerations for Combining Techniques

From Table 7.4 it is clear that different techniques have different strengths and weaknesses. None of the techniques resolves all forces, and each one resolves certain forces better than others. In many situations, no single technique satisfies all important requirements. However, some techniques complement others, so that certain combinations of techniques can satisfy more requirements. It is often useful to combine techniques from different categories: what you know, what you have, what you are, where you are.

A common example of combined techniques is a hardware token combined with a user ID/password. Typically, a small hand-held device is synchronized with the target system's authentication scheme and displays a one-time password (OTP). To access the target system, the user enters an assigned user ID and password or PIN (personal identification number) followed by the OTP displayed on the hand-held device. Some implementations, such as SecurID are time-driven, that is, the OTP changes periodically, perhaps every minute. Other schemes are event-driven, using a button to press to get the next OTP. The latter have fewer problems with re-synchronization. The advantage of this strategy of combined token and password/PIN techniques is that it helps to prevent the replay of a compromised password. This combination increases accuracy by avoiding confirming imposters more than that of either individual technique. It also improves the protection of authenticators—unless of course you write the PIN on the token! This improvement is because the two part authenticator (OTP

Table 7.4 Summary of I&A technique profiles

REQUIREMENT	USER ID/ PASSWORD	BIOMETRICS	PKI	HARDWARE TOKEN	UNREGISTERED USERS
Avoid confirming imposters	Med–Low	High–Med	High	Med–High	Med–Low
Avoid denying legitimate users	Med	High–Low	High	Med–High	Med–Low
User types	Med–High	Med–High	High	Med–High	Med–High
User location	High	High	Med	High	High
User mobility	High	Low–Med	High	Low–Med	High
Easy to use	Med–High	Med	Med	High–Med	High
Speed of use	High	Med–High	Med	High	High
Safety of use	High	Low–High	High	High	High
Cost effective per user	High	Low–High	Med–Low	Med–High	High
Cost effective per connection	High	Low	High	Low–High	High
Infrastructure compatibility	High	Med–Low	Low	High–Med	High
Cost effective maintenance	High	Med–Low	Med–High	Med	High
Protection for authenticators	Low–Med	Med	High	Med–High	Med
Availability	High	Med–High	Med–High	Med–High	High

and PIN) means that an impostor must now obtain both parts, using different means, in order to fool the system. This strategy illustrates the technique of combining something you know (the password) with something you have (the token).

Other Considerations for Selecting a Strategy

While the scope of this pattern is the selection of a single strategy for one I&A domain, this decision does not occur in a vacuum. Decisions made about strategies in other similar I&A domains within the enterprise may influence the decision for a given I&A domain. A trade-off is involved in these decisions between a homogeneous and a heterogeneous approach across the organization. In a homogeneous approach, you use the same technique everywhere. The benefits of this include ease of single sign-on (SSO), efficiency of cost, training, and technical support, and establishing a standard for future application developments. On the negative side, this approach weakens the defence in depth achieved.

In a heterogeneous approach, you explicitly choose different I&A mechanisms for different I&A domains. The primary benefit of this is stronger defence in depth. On the negative side, this approach makes SSO more difficult and loses the efficiency of cost, training, and technical support. A small example of enforced heterogeneity is the Frontdoor product that is provided for HTTP and FTP. Since the FTP password is sent in plain text over an unencrypted TCP connection, the software requires a password that is not the same as the password for HTTP connections that are protected by SSL connections. If these passwords were the same, the 'weak' FTP-password would be the weak link for the (presumed) secure SSL-channel.

Example Resolved

How can Ivan the architect apply this pattern solution for I&A support of remote access to the museum intranet? The most important requirements for this museum I&A component are to have high accuracy, especially the ability to detect non-employees, to be easy to use, provide strong support of I&A from remote locations, and limit overhead. Based on the technique profiles, the high accuracy requirement suggests that PKI would be best, and biometrics and tokens may also be candidate techniques. The ease of use and low overhead requirements indicate that biometrics and PKI are not good candidates. Therefore, of the individual techniques, a token appears to be the best one, but it is not optimum.

To obtain a solution closer to optimum, Ivan considers combinations. He concludes that combining password and token techniques gives the best overall match with requirements, because the combination increases accuracy and protection, as discussed above in considerations for combining techniques. The combination also achieves the ease of use desired by Indiana Jones when he needs to log in from some exotic location. Ivan therefore chooses this combination as the I&A strategy for remote access to the museum intranet.

Known Uses

The approach to selection of I&A described in this pattern is a consolidation of MITRE Corporation's experience in working with multiple customers over several decades. The approach is generally used informally by those customers, as opposed to being codified or published. One discussion of trade-off factors for selecting an I&A strategy is presented in [Smith2002].

The individual techniques considered in this pattern are widely known and used. Passwords have been ubiquitous for decades in information systems. Hardware tokens are often used for remote access, and a common strategy is to combine a token with a pin or password (for example, the MITRE Corporation uses this strategy). Biometrics and PKI are becoming more widely used.

Consequences

The following benefits may be expected from applying this pattern.

- The pattern fosters engineer and manager awareness of the elements of the decision needed on selecting I&A techniques.

- It facilitates conscious and informed decision making about I&A to support identified I&A requirements, as well as clear traceability to requirements

- It encourages better balance among competing I&A selection forces and factors, by matching technique profiles to requirements in the context of your specific domain. The result is increased likelihood that an I&A technique will be selected that satisfies your most important requirements.

- It provides some assistance on how you can combine I&A techniques to provide a complete I&A service.

- It facilitates broader enterprise optimization by promoting integration of I&A choices across multiple domains and systems across the enterprise.

The following potential liabilities may result from applying this pattern.

- It requires an investment of resources to apply the pattern, including time to analyze I&A mechanisms.

- This pattern focuses on certain selected I&A techniques. Using the pattern may mean that other techniques applicable to your specific domain are ignored, and a sub-optimum strategy may be selected. You can mitigate this by explicitly bringing other selected techniques into the decision process.

- Perception of identification and authentication (I&A) needs can differ throughout an organization. This may make it difficult to reach agreement on priorities of I&A and therefore difficult to select a I&A mechanism. On the other hand, bringing such disagreements to the surface may be a benefit, because then they can be properly discussed and resolved. This is true of individual strategies for a given domain. It is even more true of organization-wide coordination of I&A strategies-for example, by having different domains use different I&A techniques.

See Also

A discussion of trade-off factors for selecting an I&A strategy is presented in [Smith2002].

The registration or enrolment function complements this pattern. The operation of most I&A techniques, and in this pattern all techniques except UNREGISTERED USERS I&A REQUIREMENTS (67), require that the domain of users for which I&A is to be performed must first be registered or enrolled, to obtain the independent user information. Although no registration pattern is described in detail this book, the registration function is part of the larger I&A picture (see Chapter 5, *The Security Pattern Landscape*).

7.3   Password Design and Use

This pattern describes security best practice for designing, creating, managing, and using password components in support of I&A REQUIREMENTS (192). This pattern can aid three audiences: engineers, in selecting or designing commercial products that provide password mechanisms, administrators, in the operation and management of password mechanisms, and users, in improving their selection and handling of passwords.

Example

Employees of the museum need to gain access to the museum intranet, which is based on passwords. Enforcement of security policy has been lax, and it has been common practice for employees to write down passwords and leave them by their workstations, or even tape them to the display monitor. As a result, several incidents have occurred in which unauthorized staff and even visitors have gained access to sensitive information. The system administrators want to correct this problem, specifically to create good passwords and keep them secure. There are two situations that require passwords as part of I&A whose results are used for access control. First, a low level of security is needed for I&A used to gain access to the overall intranet. Second, a high level of security is needed for I&A used to gain access to sensitive information, including employee salary data.

Context

A password mechanism has been selected for user authentication on a specified segment of an information system. The person applying this pattern understands the requirements for I&A, along with their relative importance—for example, from the results of applying I&A REQUIREMENTS (192).

Problem

How can passwords be created, managed, and used in a manner that retains password accessibility for their owners, but renders the passwords inaccessible to imposters?

In addition to forces relating to issues that apply to all I&A authenticators, the following forces specifically affect password practice:

- Stolen or guessed passwords can be used to masquerade as another person, which leads to false positives, that is, falsely confirming an unauthorized identity

- If passwords are stolen or compromised, assets whose protection relied on the confidentiality of the passwords can be damaged

- People need to remember their passwords in order to use them

- Passwords that are difficult to guess tend to be difficult to remember, which leads to false negatives, that is, falsely denying an authorized identity

- Passwords that are recorded can be intentionally or inadvertently discovered by someone else

- A person typically has many contexts in which a password is needed

- Using a single password in all contexts increases the potential scope of damage from password theft

- Using a different password in each context increases the difficulty of remembering each one, which in turn increases the pressure to record each one, reducing the protection of the passwords

- Passwords that are not changed periodically become increasingly susceptible to theft

Solution

Ensure that passwords are properly designed and defined, properly used and properly protected. More specifically, consider several factors that address each area—for example, consider the length of the password during design and definition. Determine how the factors can be used to best satisfy the I&A requirements for the specific domain being considered, such as a specific network or information system.

The following factors should be considered:

Design and Definition of Passwords

- Composition: the characters that are usable in a valid password

- Length range: the minimum and maximum acceptable number of characters in a valid password

- Source: the entities that can create or select a valid password from among all acceptable passwords

Use of Passwords

- Lifetime: the maximum acceptable period of time for which a password is valid
- Ownership: the set of individuals who are authorized to use a password
- Entry: acceptable methods by which a password may be entered by a user
- Authentication period: the maximum acceptable period between any initial authentication process and subsequent re-authentication processes during a single session

Protection of Passwords

- Distribution: acceptable methods for transporting a new password to its owner(s) and to all places where it will be needed
- Storage: acceptable methods of storing a valid password during its lifetime
- Transmission: acceptable methods for communicating a password from its point of entry to its point of comparison with a stored, valid password

Best practice details on each of these factors, as well as recent evolution of thinking on what is best practice, are provided in the Implementation section. See figure on page 220.

Structure

The general relationships among I&A requirements, password constraints, and passwords are illustrated in the figure above. A set of requirements for the specific domain under consideration clearly influences password constraints, which consist of several factors to be considered when selecting or designing passwords, as identified in the figure. The password constraints are used by engineers and administrators in building or selecting password systems, or configuring and managing passwords. The constraints constrain passwords that are defined by users.

Implementation

This section discusses classical best practice with respect to each of the factors introduced previously. It then briefly describes how some of the classical guidance is evolving to reflect the influence of the changing information technology environment.

1. Composition.

   Composition is the set of acceptable characters usable in a valid password.

   Consider the following good practice:

   Passwords should be composed from a defined set of ASCII characters.

   The password mechanism should verify that only characters in the defined set have been generated or selected whenever a password is created or changed.

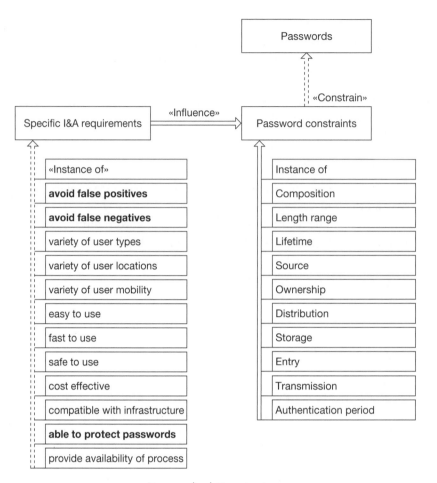

Password solution structure

Include a digit or punctuation.

Use upper and lower case.

Choose a phrase or combination of words to make the password easier to remember.

Two words separated by a non-letter non-digit character is acceptable.

Use different passwords on different machines.

When changing a password, don't reuse passwords or make only minor variations such as incrementing a digit.

Avoid the following bad practice:

> Do not use your account name or account data.

> Do not use any word or name that appears in any dictionary, reference or list regardless of case changes, and especially do not use character strings that appear in password cracking tools' word lists or bad password lists.

Do not use the following variations: phrases and slang with or without white space:

- Any mythological, legendary, religious or fictional character, object, race, place or event
- Acronyms
- Alphabetic, numeric or keyboard sequences—many such sequences are included in cracking tools word lists
- Titles of books, movies, poems, essays, songs, CDs or musical compositions

Do not vary the character sequences obtained from any of the foregoing items. Specifically, do not use any of the following methods:

- Prepend or append symbols, punctuation marks or digits to a word
- Use words with some or all the letters reversed
- Use conjugations or plurals of words
- Use words with the vowels deleted
- Use only the first or the last character in uppercase
- Use only vowels in uppercase
- Use only consonants in uppercase

Do not use any personally-related information (see below).

Do not use a publicly shown example of a good password.

Do not use vanity license plates.

Do not transliterate words from other languages.

Do not repeat any character more than once in a row.

Using personally-related information is poor practice. The most common examples of personal information include: names and initials, account name, names of immediate family members, names, breeds or species of pets, birthday, family member's birthdays, vehicle make, model, year, hobbies, interests, and job title. All permutations or combinations of the foregoing should also be avoided.

2. Length range.

Length range is the set of acceptable lengths of passwords, defined in terms of a minimum and maximum number of characters in a valid password.

Consider the following good practice:

> Passwords should have a length range, selected by the system manager and security officer, having a number greater than or equal to four as the minimum length and a maximum length. The maximum length should reflect the recognition that the average person can easily remember a maximum of seven items.
>
> The selected password composition and length range should allow for a minimum of 10,000 possible passwords, to make passwords less guessable.
>
> The selected password length range should provide a level of protection commensurate to the value or sensitivity of the resources or data it protects.
>
> A pass phrase—that is, a character sequence longer than the acceptable length of a password—should be transformed into a virtual password of acceptable length for storage.
>
> The password mechanism should verify that only passwords having a length within the acceptable length range are generated or selected whenever a password is created or changed.

3. Source.

Source is the set of acceptable entities that can create or select a valid password from among all acceptable passwords.

Consider the following good practice:

> The source of passwords should be selected by the Security Officer and System Manager, and should be one or more of the following: user, security officer, or automated password generator.
>
> All passwords that may be included in a new system when it is delivered, transferred or installed (for example passwords for the operator, system programmer, maintenance personnel or security officer) should be immediately changed by the security officer to one of the following:
>
> (a) Passwords that are invalid to the password system
>
> (b) Random passwords that may be subsequently changed
>
> (c) Valid passwords that are owned by authorized users of the system
>
> Passwords created by the security officer for new users of the system during initial system access should be selected at random from all acceptable passwords. Default passwords or formatted passwords related to the new user's identity or assignment should not be used.
>
> Users who create or select their own personal password should be instructed to use a password selected from all acceptable passwords at random, if possible, or to select one that is not related to their personal identity, history or environment.

Passwords selected or created by users or the security officer should be tested by the password system to assure that they meet the specifications of composition and length established for the system before they are accepted as valid passwords.

4. Lifetime.

Lifetime is the maximum acceptable period of time for which a password is valid.

Consider the following good practice:

Passwords should have a maximum lifetime of one year.

Passwords should have the shortest practical lifetime that provides the desired level of protection at the least possible cost.

Passwords should be replaced quickly if compromise of the password is suspected or confirmed.

Passwords should be deleted or replaced with an invalid password when an owner is no longer an authorized system user.

Passwords forgotten by their owner should be replaced, not reissued.

The password mechanism should allow the security officer, appropriately authenticated, to delete or replace a password.

The password mechanism should be capable of maintaining a record of when a password was created and changed.

5. Ownership.

Ownership is the set of individuals who are authorized to use a password.

Consider the following good practice:

Personal passwords used to authenticate identity should be owned (that is, known) only by the individual with that identity.

Each individual should be responsible for providing protection against loss or disclosure of passwords in their possession.

6. Entry.

Entry is the set of acceptable methods by which a password may be entered by a user for authentication or authorization purposes.

Consider the following good practice:

Passwords should be entered by the owner upon request by the password mechanism in a manner that protects the password from observation.

Users should be allowed more than one attempt to enter a password correctly to allow for inadvertent errors. However, the number of allowed password entry attempts—retries after incorrect password entry—should be limited to a number selected by the security officer. A maximum of three attempts is considered adequate for typical users of a computer system.

The response to exceeding the maximum number of retries should be specified by the security officer. The latter may include, for example, account lock-down, account suspension for a specified time, or account release by security officer only.

7. Authentication period.

Authentication period is the maximum acceptable period between any initial authentication process and subsequent re-authentication processes during a single terminal session.

Consider the following good practice:

Individual passwords should be authenticated each time a claim of identity is made, for example when logging on to an interactive system.

A system should have log-on time-outs established. That is, if there is no user activity for a specified period of time (the time-out period) the user is automatically logged off and must re-enter their password to continue work. Shorter time-outs offer better protection in theory, but may impact the business process unacceptably and try user patience to the point where users will find ways of bypassing I&A.

8. Distribution.

Distribution is the set of acceptable methods for providing (transporting) a new password to its owner(s) and to all places where it will be needed in the information system.

Consider the following good practice:

Personal passwords should be distributed from the password source in such a way that only the intended owner may see or obtain the password, for example in a separately-mailed envelope.

Passwords should be distributed in such a way that an audit record, containing the date and time of a password change, and the identifier associated with the password, but not the old or new password, can be made available to the security officer.

Passwords should be distributed from the password source in such a way that temporary storage of the password is erased, and long-term retention of the password is available only to the owner(s) and the protected-password system.

The password system that generates and distributes passwords should keep an automated record of the date and time of password generation and to whom it was distributed, but not the password itself.

9. Storage.

Storage is the set of acceptable methods of storing a valid password during its lifetime.

Consider the following good practice:

Stored passwords should be protected such that only the password mechanism(s) is authorized access to a password. Examples include:

■ Most systems have a password file that can be legitimately read only by the log-on process
■ Some systems separate the password file from the authorized user file
■ Some systems encrypt passwords, either reversibly (two-way) or irreversibly (one-way) using a data encrypting key.

Passwords that are encrypted before they are stored should be protected from substitution—that is, protection should be provided such that one encrypted password cannot be replaced with another unless the replacement is authorized.

10. Transmission.

Transmission is the set of acceptable methods for communicating a password from its point of entry to its point of comparison with a stored, valid password.

Consider the following good practice:

Passwords that are transmitted between the place of entry and the location for comparison against a stored password should be protected to the degree specified by the security officer, and at least equivalent to the protection required for the entities, such as the system or its data, that the password is protecting.

Passwords used as encryption keys should be selected at random from the set of all possible keys (for example, 236 keys for the Data Encryption Standard) and used either as data-encrypting keys or key-encrypting keys, but not both.

Unencrypted passwords should be transmitted as ASCII characters if interchanged between systems, while encrypted passwords and virtual passwords should be transmitted either as 64-bit binary fields, or as the ASCII representations of the hexadecimal character set [0-9, A-F].

Discussion: Evolution in password thinking

As noted in [Smith2002], the classical password selection rules can be summarized as follows: the password must be impossible to remember and never written down.

This illustrates the limitation of passwords as authenticators, and is compounded by the large number of passwords typically needed by a single individual-for example, for different computers, networks, and Web sites. It can be argued that the set of passwords that simultaneously conform to all the classic rules is a null set. Because of this limitation, and because of the trend toward more network use, the prohibition against writing down passwords is being reconsidered. The risk of having passwords compromised on the network has increased to the point where it significantly outweighs the risks of local compromise, that is, writing down passwords. One password guide [Geodsoft2002b] recommends recording sensitive passwords and protecting the recorded passwords, especially root or administrator passwords. This guidance may also apply when one person must remember a significant number of passwords. For example, multiple passwords could be stored and protected on a USB token.

[NIST800-63] defines four levels of assurance for authentication. Level 1 allows password challenge-response protocols, and does not require cryptographic methods. Level 2 allows passwords, but requires a secure authentication protocol and the use of cryptographic techniques. Level 3 requires at least two authentication factors, of which one can be a one-time password. Level 4 also requires multi-factor authentication, but does not allow passwords: both factors must be physical cryptographic tokens.

Example Resolved

The new museum wing's security officer, engineering team, and system manager determine that two different password systems are needed to deal respectively with the high and low security situations described in the Example and Problem sections.

1. Password system for low-protection requirements: I&A for access to museum intranet.

   Value for each factor:

   - Composition: Digits (0–9)
   - Length range: 4–6
   - Source: user
   - Lifetime: one year
   - Ownership: individual (personal password), group (access passwords)
   - Entry: non-printing keypad
   - Authentication period: each intranet session log-in, plus the end of each period of workstation inactivity that exceeds thirty minutes
   - Distribution: unmarked envelope by post
   - Storage: central computer on-line storage as plaintext
   - Transmission: plaintext

2. Password system for high-protection requirements: I&A for access to sensitive museum data.

   Value for each factor:

   - Length range: 6–8
   - Composition: full 95 character set
   - Source: automated password generator within the authentication system
   - Lifetime: one month
   - Ownership: individual
   - Entry: non-printing keyboards
   - Authentication period: log-in and after five minutes of terminal inactivity
   - Distribution: registered mail with receipt required
   - Storage: encrypted passwords
   - Transmission: encrypted communication with message numbering

Variants

Dirk Riehle and colleagues have defined a 'Password pattern language' that includes a few general security patterns and several specific password patterns [Riehle2002]. The language is a work in progress. Each pattern in the language addresses a very specific password issue such as a best practice item within the factors addressed in this pattern. For example, their DICTIONARY WORD pattern corresponds approximately to the 'Choose a phrase or combination of words to make the password easier to remember' item in this pattern under the composition factors.

Schumacher et al. introduced some password-related patterns [SRM03]. USER AUTHENTICATION PASSWORDS describes the general I&A approach that is based on passwords, a special case of 'something you know.' Another pattern, PASSWORD QUALITY, addresses the design and definition issues of passwords. Finally, there is also a general pattern that deals with PASSWORD PROTECTION. There are further related patterns that are used to implement password protection, namely 'Physical Protection,' a set of patterns that deals with SECURING LOCAL NETWORKS and a set of patterns that deal with SECURING WIDE AREA NETWORKS.

Known Uses

The factors are well-known, and passwords themselves are used in most information systems, including operating systems and file systems. The factors are taken from [FIPS112], and the good practice material is taken from [FIPS112], [NIST800-63], and [Geodsoft2002a]. [NIST800-63] is a partial replacement for [FIPS112].

Consequences

The benefits of applying this pattern are as follows:

■ Applying this pattern results in increased protection of passwords and consequently higher accuracy of I&A.

■ The potential number of false positives resulting from such things as password
guessing is expected to be reduced.

The pattern also suffers from the following liability:

■ Applying this pattern may lead you to conclude that passwords is the only I&A
technique that needs to be used. It is often better practice to adopt a strategy
that combines passwords with another technique.

You can find a discussion of password combination considerations in AUTOMATED
I&A DESIGN ALTERNATIVES (207) earlier in this chapter.

See Also

Other approaches to password patterns include Dick Riehle's password pattern language in [Riehle2002] and the patterns presented by Schumacher et al. [SRM03].
Other techniques that are alternatives to passwords are described by the following
patterns:

■ BIOMETRICS DESIGN ALTERNATIVES (229)

■ PKI DESIGN VARIABLES (66)

■ HARDWARE TOKEN DESIGN ALTERNATIVES (66)

■ UNREGISTERED USERS I&A REQUIREMENTS (67)

BIOMETRICS DESIGN ALTERNATIVES (229) is described in this chapter. Thumbnails
of the other patterns can be found in Chapter 5, *The Security Pattern Landscape*.

7.4 Biometrics Design Alternatives

This pattern aids the selection of appropriate biometric mechanisms to satisfy I&A requirements. Biometric mechanisms considered are face recognition, finger image, hand geometry, iris recognition, retinal scanning, signature verification, and speaker verification. Additional mechanisms, including DNA, are identified for completeness.

Example

The internal maintenance and research areas of the new gemstone wing of the museum essentially afford staff access directly to high-value assets and to the information on those assets. While physical entry for these activities is being tightly controlled, access to sensitive asset information must also be restricted. To gain access to the Web server with strictly controlled asset information, staff are required to log-on to the Web server. Part of the log-on process will be use of a biometric to provide additional verification of employee identities. Alvin the system architect must determine which biometric mechanism is most appropriate for the museum.

Context

The person applying this pattern understands the requirements for I&A, along with their relative importance, for example from the results of applying I&A RE-QUIREMENTS (192).

A decision has been made to use biometrics for I&A, for example from the results of applying AUTOMATED I&A DESIGN ALTERNATIVES (207), but which biometrics technique to use has not been decided. The decision to use some form of biometrics is typically made in the context of a user population of limited size, because of the enrolment effort required.

Discussion: What do all biometric mechanisms have in common?

All biometric mechanisms share an underlying methodology involving enrolment (which is outside the scope of this pattern) and verification or identification. At enrolment, the person offers a 'live sample' of the biometric, such as a finger image. This is scanned electronically, processed and stored as a template, which is a mathematical representation of the original sample. Once the template is captured, the original sample data is no longer used and is discarded. Alternatively, it might be wise to keep the original raw sample data, against the possibility that better template-algorithms and representations might become available in the future: in some areas such as fingerprint recognition, technology is changing and significant improvement can be expected. Keeping the raw sample data would allow one to benefit from newer algorithms without the need to re-enrol all users.

To confirm identity at a future time, the individual presents the live sample, which is matched against the stored template. In a 1:many search, the individual presents only the live sample, and the database is searched for a match. This is called *identification*. In a 1:1 search, the user presents a name or other identifier along with the live sample. The system checks the live sample only against templates stored under that identifier. This is called *verification*. [Seffers2001].

When biometrics are used for verification, the captured biometric record is matched against one biometric template in the data store to determine a match. The one biometric template in the data store is found by association with a presented identifier, acquired separately via non-biometric means such as a token. This is a 1:1 match, and answers the question 'Am I who I say I am'?

When biometrics are used for identification, the biometric capture and conversion are the same, but no separate identifier is acquired, and therefore the verifier matches the biometric record against all biometric records in the data store. If a match is found, the associated identifier is found. This is a 1:many match, and answers the question 'Who am I'? The result is still success or failure, and in the case of success, an identifier is produced. If the identifier is considered to be verified or authenticated, then in effect the biometric technique provides a full I&A solution.

Problem

Each technique has different strengths and weaknesses, which are described in the Implementation section. Therefore, no one technique or combination of techniques is best for all enterprises. Decisions are needed to determine the best biometric mechanisms for the given purpose.

It should be noted that biometrics, at least in human-readable form, have been available for a long time, even before the term 'biometrics' was used. For example, badges, licenses, and passports have often included photographs as well as physical characteristics such as height and eye color. Fingerprints have long been used in criminal justice and other security contexts.

Given that biometrics has been selected to perform some I&A purpose, what biometric mechanisms would best satisfy this purpose?

Selection of appropriate biometrics mechanisms needs to resolve the following forces:

Biometrics have Vulnerabilities and Limitations

■ Some biometric information can be stolen, for example, by obtaining and using pictures, images, imprints, or other models of another person's biometric information.

■ Biometric information can be erroneously associated with the wrong identity at enrollment: for example, actor B can enrol his biometric information with actor A's identity.

■ Stolen or erroneously enrolled biometric information can be used to masquerade as another person, which leads to false acceptance.

■ Some biometric measurements can vary due to environmental conditions, or can change over time due to age, or can change quickly due to injury, surgery, or other significant episode. Such variations can lead to false rejection.

Biometrics have Two Conflicting Error Types

■ False acceptance can lead to unauthorized access to assets, in cases in which an access control service relies on the biometric mechanism's results.

■ False acceptance can lead to lack of accountability, in cases in which an accounting service such as audit relies on biometric mechanism results. If actor B successfully masquerades as actor A, then actor A is erroneously held accountable for the actions of actor B.

■ False rejection can lead to reduced productivity and increased user frustration.

■ False rejection can also lead to lack of accountability. For example, actor A may take steps to change certain biometric characteristics via surgery with the goal of being falsely rejected as actor A. This may allow him to avoid accountability for an action such as a serious crime.

■ In general, low false acceptance rate (FAR) and low false rejection rate (FRR) are conflicting goals: configuring a biometric mechanism to achieve a very low FAR tends to increase the FRR. Conversely, achieving a very low FRR tends to increase the FAR. When comparing biometric systems, a low FAR is most important when security is the priority. On the other hand, a low FRR is most important when convenience is the priority. [Liu2001] discusses the inverse relation between these two error types.

Biometrics have Other Forces to Consider

■ Some biometric mechanisms cost more than others.

■ Some biometric mechanisms require more equipment and changes to the infrastructure than others.

■ Some biometric mechanisms are less safe than others.

■ Enterprise-wide optimization affects selection of biometric techniques. An enterprise may find it more efficient—for example, for cost, training, and maintenance reasons—if all I&A domains that select biometrics use the same biometrics technique. For example, an enterprise may decide that the biometrics used in granting physical access to all enterprise facilities throughout the country should use the same technique. Therefore, the selection of specific mechanisms may be a significant decision.

Solution

Systematically review the characteristics of available biometric mechanisms or techniques, and select a mechanism. Several well-known biometrics mechanisms exist. Different mechanisms have different strengths and weaknesses and emphasize different characteristics. Each technique resolves each force to a different degree than the others. The solution provides information about alternative biometric mechanisms that is intended to help differentiate them and to help select the best technique for a given purpose, enterprise, and I&A use.

All biometric techniques can be used for verification, but only a few are capable of performing identification, especially in a large population of users or actors. This is because the task of matching a live sample with one designated template is much simpler than finding a template from a large number of possible templates. According to [Ashbourn2000], the only biometric mechanisms with the capability to operate realistically in identification mode are finger image, iris recognition, retinal scan, and, to a lesser degree, facial scan.

Structure

Table 7.5 shows elements of the structure of this solution. Required capabilities and properties in the first column are derived from the general I&A REQUIREMENTS (192) pattern. Specialized selection criteria in the second column are additional factors related specifically to biometric mechanisms. Together, requirements and specialized criteria drive the selection of biometric mechanisms listed in the third column. Specialized criteria are further explained in the Implementation section.

Dynamics

This section describes the steps in the process of applying the pattern. Biometrics I&A inputs, including domain definition and requirements, are assembled first. Next, the specific characteristics of each biometric technique are defined, followed by selecting the best individual technique. If this technique is to be used as a stand-alone I&A mechanism, the process is then complete. If the technique is to be combined with another I&A technique—typically a non-biometrics technique, the combined strategy defined, for example, by AUTOMATED I&A DESIGN ALTERNATIVES (207)—then the selected biometric technique must be integrated with the other technique to form an integrated I&A solution.

Table 7.5 Elements of biometrics design solution structure

REQUIRED CAPABILITIES/ PROPERTIES	SPECIALIZED SELECTION CRITERIA	BIOMETRIC MECHANISMS
• Avoid false positives • Avoid false negatives • Variety of user types • Variety of user locations • Variety of user mobility • Easy to use • Speed to use • Safety of use • Cost effective • Compatible with infrastructure • Able to protect authenticators • Provide availability of process	• Devices needed • Obtrusiveness • Accuracy • Resistance to attack (secure) • Public acceptance • Biometric long-term stability • Potential interference • Template size	• Face recognition • Finger image • Hand geometry • Iris recognition • Retinal scanning • Signature verification • Speaker verification

Implementation

The description and characteristics of biometric mechanisms provided here is intended to help select appropriate biometrics for a specific context. Differentiating factors include degree of accuracy, ease of use, processing speed, and size of template—the amount of data to be captured and processed. The set of biometrics, and definition of each, are obtained primarily from [AfB1999].

Each technique is classified as being based on either a physical or a behavioral characteristic. In the set identified here, the behavioral biometrics are signature verification and speaker verification, although the latter is part behavioral and part physical. The remaining biometric techniques are classified as physical.

Additional biometric techniques that exist include:

■ DNA, which carries the unique genetic instructions for an individual

■ Keystroke dynamics, the typing rhythm when a user types onto a keyboard, ear shape, the outer ear, lobes, bone structure

■ Finger geometry, the shape and dimensions of one or more fingers

■ Palm geometry, the shape of the lines on the palm of the hand

■ Veincheck/Vein tree, which uses pattern of veins in the back of the hand

We do not consider these techniques further in this pattern because they are not yet commonly used for I&A. Keystroke dynamics shows promise, but has not yet reached a high level of accuracy.

Characteristics of the more common biometric mechanisms are summarized in Table 7.6. The value indicates the extent to which a technique satisfies a requirement for a particular factor. 'High' indicates high satisfaction of the factor, 'Low' indicates low satisfaction, and so on.

The potential interference factor identifies conditions that can inhibit successful operation of the mechanism. In general, one has to consider the basic characteristic of the concrete implementation of the technique. For example, background noise can interfere with voice recognition, or poor lighting can interfere with face recognition.

Table 7.6 Characteristics of common biometrics techniques. Reproduced by permission of ICSA Labs

TECHNIQUE FACTOR	FACE	FINGER	HAND	IRIS	RETINA	SIGNATURE	VOICE
Accuracy	High	High	Med/high	Very high	Very high	Medium	Medium
Ease of use	Medium	High	High	Medium	Low	High	High
Resistant to attack, secure	Medium	High	High	Very high	Very high	Medium	Medium
Public acceptance	Medium/ High	Medium	High	Medium	Medium	Very high	High
Long-term stability	Medium	High	Medium	High	High	Medium	Medium
Potential interference	Lighting, aging, glasses, hair	Dryness, dirt, age, race	Hand injury, age	Poor lighting	Glasses	Changing signatures	Noise, colds, weather
Safety	High	High	High	High	Medium	High	High

To determine the biometric mechanism that will best satisfy the biometric's purpose, you can compare the technique profiles with your results of applying I&A REQUIREMENTS (192) to find a mechanism that is most compatible with your specific requirements.

Characteristics of Each Biometric Mechanism

The more common techniques are now described in more detail, especially the features and considerations that affect their selection. The details are obtained primarily from [Tilton2002].

Table 7.7 describes the characteristics of face recognition, which is a physical biometric technique that analyzes distinguishing facial features.

Table 7.7 Face recognition. Reproduced by permission of the SAFLINK Corporation

	CAPTURE DEVICES	FEATURES (+)	CONSIDERATIONS (-)
	Still camera, video, thermal imaging	• Can use standard video camera input • Can be used passively (unobtrusively) and with existing photo databases • Socially acceptable • Compatible with existing ID systems such as drivers license, passport	• Can be affected by lighting and sometimes by skin tone, eyeglasses, facial hair, or expression • Twins harder to distinguish • Changes over time may require update/adaptation • Occasional religious objections and recent privacy objections to covert use • 600–3500 byte template size

Table 7.8 describes the characteristics of finger image, which is a physical biometric technique that looks at the patterns found on the tip of the finger. Finger images may be captured by placing a finger on a scanner, or by electronically scanning inked impressions on paper. It is one of the oldest biometric approaches.

Table 7.8 Finger image. Reproduced by permission of the SAFLINK Corporation

	CAPTURE DEVICES	FEATURES (+)	CONSIDERATIONS (-)
	Usually a small reader (sensor) embedded within a stand-alone device or a peripheral, such as a keyboard, PCMCIA card or mouse. Sensor types include optical, silicon chip, ultrasonic	• Significant proven use since largely easy to use and very quick • Relatively high accuracy • Variety of applications and products from numerous vendors	• Requires dedicated device • A small percentage of population have poor images due to injury, disease, or occupation • Dry skin can reduce accuracy • Some lingering criminal connotations • Overt action generally required, somewhat obtrusive • 250 B–1 Kbytes template size

Table 7.9 describes the characteristics of hand geometry, which is a physical biometric technique that involves analyzing and measuring the shape of the hand from a 3-D perspective. This is one of the oldest biometric approaches.

Table 7.9   Hand geometry. Reproduced by permission of the SAFLINK Corporation

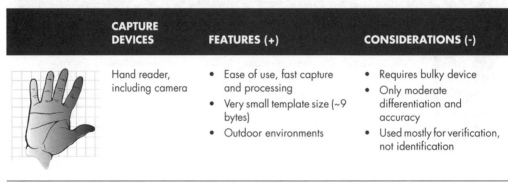

	CAPTURE DEVICES	FEATURES (+)	CONSIDERATIONS (-)
	Hand reader, including camera	• Ease of use, fast capture and processing • Very small template size (~9 bytes) • Outdoor environments	• Requires bulky device • Only moderate differentiation and accuracy • Used mostly for verification, not identification

Table 7.10 describes the characteristics of iris recognition. This is a physical biometric technique that analyses iris features found in the colored ring of tissue that surrounds the pupils.

Table 7.10   Iris recognition. Reproduced by permission of the SAFLINK Corporation

	CAPTURE DEVICES	FEATURES (+)	CONSIDERATIONS (-)
	Cameras, standard video technology	• Highly accurate, highly differentiating (each eye averages 266 unique features) • Can support identification as well as verification • Very stable over lifetime • Passive collection (non-obtrusive) • Not affected by common eye surgical procedures	• Requires dedicated device (some dual-use devices are available) • Mirrored sunglasses can interfere • Affected by some eye diseases such as cataracts • Limited focal length (4" to 3'), depending on device • 500 byte template size

Table 7.11 describes the characteristics of retinal scanning. This is a physical biometric technique that analyses the layer of blood vessels situated at the back of the eye.

Table 7.11 Retinal scanning. Reproduced by permission of the SAFLINK Corporation

CAPTURE DEVICES	FEATURES (+)	CONSIDERATIONS (-)
Low intensity light source (laser) with optical coupler	• High accuracy and stability, difficult to falsify • Minimal alignment and focus problems • Can support identification as well as verification	• User interface generally considered intrusive and uncomfortable • Safety concerns, possible damage if laser intensity too high • Capture can take several seconds • Devices still somewhat expensive • 96 byte template size

Table 7.12 describes the characteristics of signature verification. This is a behavioral biometric technique that analyses the way someone signs their name. The signing features such as speed, velocity and pressure exerted by the hand are as important as the static shape of the finished signature.

Table 7.12 Signature verification. Reproduced by permission of the SAFLINK Corporation

CAPTURE DEVICES	FEATURES (+)	CONSIDERATIONS (-)
Signature or graphics tablets, special pens	• Non-intrusive, natural act, highly acceptable • Particularly compatible with financial or legal transactions, orders, document signing • Many can already use built-in graphics devices, such as those in PDAs • Can work with Arabic lettering or Asian characters	• Requires multiple consistent captures for enrolment • Can be affected by behavioral factors such as stress, distractions • May change over time, require update/adaptation • Best used in 1:1 contexts, that is, verification, not identification • 1–3 Kbyte template size

Table 7.13 describes the characteristics of speaker verification. This is a part physical, part behavioral biometric that analyses patterns in speech. It compares live speech with a previously-created speech model of a person's voice.

Table 7.13 Speaker verification. Reproduced by permission of the SAFLINK Corporation

	CAPTURE DEVICES	FEATURES (+)	CONSIDERATIONS (-)
	Audio capture devices (sound cards, micro-phones)	• Socially acceptable and non-intrusive • Can use standard handset, sound cards, microphones, over existing audio channels such as telephone lines • Can be combined with challenge/response mechanisms • Algorithms are typically language independent • Generally cannot be defeated by tape recordings or mimics	• Can be affected by illness, stress, or background noise • Can be susceptible to high-quality digital audio playback attack • Requires similar microphones for enrolment and verification • May change over time, require update/adaptation • Best used in 1:1 contexts, that is, authentication, not identification • 6 Kbyte template size

Combining Mechanisms

If the purpose of the selected biometric mechanism is to perform verification, then the mechanism may need to be combined with a non-biometric I&A technique for a full I&A solution. The recommendation in this case is to apply AUTOMATED I&A DESIGN ALTERNATIVES (207) if you have made a decision to use only automated I&A, either prior to, concurrent with, or subsequent to, the application of BIOMETRICS DESIGN ALTERNATIVES (229).

Selecting a Biometric Mechanism

While the scope of this pattern is the selection of a biometric mechanism for one I&A use, this decision does not occur in a vacuum. Decisions made on biometric mechanisms for other similar I&A uses within the enterprise may influence the decision for a given biometric approach. In addition, more than one biometric may be needed and consideration will need to be given to the interaction of those mechanisms.

Example Resolved

Alvin the system architect determines that for the museum, part of the log-on process will use a biometric to provide additional verification of employee identities. The museum wants at least high confidence with regard to the accuracy, ease of use, and resistance to attack of the biometric selected. Only the iris scanning and

Table 7.14 Museum resolution for biometrics

TECHNIQUE FACTOR	IRIS	FINGER
Accuracy	Very high	High
Easy to use	Medium	High
Resists attack (secure)	Very high	High
Public accepts	Medium	Medium
Long-term stability	High	High
Potential interference	Poor lighting	Dryness, dirt, age, race
Safety	Medium	High

fingerprint approaches can provide high confidence for those important criteria, as shown in Table 7.14.

To address the concerns of their staff, Alvin chooses fingerprint detection as the preferred biometric mechanism, as the technology is known to be safe and easy to use, and the potential interference factors are not expected to be extreme for this environment.

Known Uses

Use of biometrics techniques is increasing, but the decision process for deciding among biometrics alternatives is generally tacit and informal, as opposed to being codified or published. However, discussion of the characteristics of various biometrics techniques does exist. [Smith2002] describes common characteristics and processes for biometrics I&A, as well as security of biometrics information. [Tilton2002] and [Liu2001] provide more details of variations among biometrics techniques, and are the sources of much of the implementation information in this pattern.

Consequences

The following benefits may be expected from applying this pattern:

- It fosters engineer awareness of the elements of the decisions needed for selecting biometrics techniques.
- It facilitates conscious and informed decision making about biometrics to support identified identification and authentication service needs.

■ It encourages better balance among competing biometrics selection forces and factors, including the inherent trade-off between the rates of false acceptance and false rejection, as well as theft, environmental impact, cost, and infrastructure impact. The result is increased likelihood that a biometrics technique will be selected that satisfies the most important requirements.

■ It provides some assistance about how you can combine biometrics with other mechanisms to provide a complete I&A service.

■ It facilitates broader enterprise optimization by promoting integration of biometrics choices across multiple domains and systems across the enterprise.

The following potential liabilities may result from applying this pattern:

■ It requires an investment of resources to apply the pattern, including time to analyze biometrics mechanisms.

■ Perception of identification and authentication (I&A) needs can differ throughout an organization. This may make it difficult to reach agreement on priorities for I&A, and therefore difficult to select a biometric mechanism. On the other hand, bringing such disagreements to the surface may be a benefit, because then they can be properly discussed and resolved.

■ Although biometric techniques work well today for authentication with a given ID, the techniques are less reliable for identification from a large user base. This point is often neglected by decision makers.

■ Users and organizations may have a false sense of increased security, because they are using technology that is more expensive and more sophisticated. The cautions of this pattern over theft and other limitations of biometrics may not overcome the general perception promoted in some of the literature that biometrics is infallible.

■ The enrolment process for biometrics can be expensive, because its users need to provide samples in a protected environment, otherwise an imposter might be able to submit their sample under a false identity.

■ If the biometrics sensor and the storage of the templates or the checking mechanism are coupled by a network, an intruder can either steal valid samples or templates for later misuse, or can perform a denial of service attack.

See Also

After applying this solution, the next step typically is to apply the selected technique, which might be any of these:

■ FACE RECOGNITION (65)
■ FINGER IMAGE (65)

- HAND GEOMETRY (65)
- IRIS RECOGNITION (65)
- RETINAL SCANNING (65)
- SIGNATURE VERIFICATION (65)
- SPEAKER VERIFICATION (66)

Each of these is a potential pattern, but none is included in this book. Thumbnails of these patterns can be found in Chapter 5, *The Security Pattern Landscape*.

Access Control Models

There was a Door to which I found no Key.
There was a Veil past which I could not see.

Omar Khayyam, 'The Rubaiyat,' translated by E.J. Fitzgerald

To develop secure systems, security should be considered at all stages of design, so that the design not only satisfies its functional specifications but also satisfies security requirements [Fer04]. To do this we need to start with high-level models that represent the security policies of the organization. Three basic models are used currently by most systems: the access matrix, the role-based access control (RBAC) model, and the multilevel model.

These models define security constraints at the highest architectural level, the application level, and are enforced by the lower levels. They have been extensively studied by the security community (for example [Pfl03] and [Sum97]) and we do not attempt here to add new models or extend the existing models. Our intention is to specify the accepted models as object-oriented patterns that can be used as guidelines in the construction of secure systems.

We first present AUTHORIZATION (245), which describes the rules that define allowed accesses to resources. We then describe ROLE-BASED ACCESS CONTROL (249), an extension of AUTHORIZATION (245) in which access rights are given to functional roles. We end with MULTILEVEL SECURITY (253), based on clearance levels to determine access. None of these patterns has dynamic sections because they are purely declarative. The last pattern, REFERENCE MONITOR (256), brings dynamics for evaluating requests according to the constraints defined by the declarative models. The combination of a declarative model and a reference monitor is called an 'access control model' [DeC02]. We also provide ROLE RIGHTS DEFINITION (259) in this chapter, to help in finding the rights associated with roles in an RBAC model.

All patterns in this chapter were written by Eduardo B. Fernandez: ROLE RIGHTS DEFINITION (259)was co-authored by Mei Fullerton. They are based on the patterns in [Fer01]. Rouyi Pan was the co-author of that paper. AUTHORIZATION (245) and ROLE-BASED ACCESS CONTROL (249) contain material from [Pri04]. Peter Sommerlad provided valuable comments.

8.1 Authorization

This pattern describes who is authorized to access specific resources in a system, in an environment in which we have resources whose access needs to be controlled. It indicates, for each active entity that can access resources, which resources it can access, and how it can access them.

Example

In a medical information system we keep sensitive information about patients. Unrestricted disclosure of this data would violate the privacy of the patients, while unrestricted modification could jeopardize the health of the patients.

Context

Any environment in which we have resources whose access needs to be controlled.

Problem

We need to have a way to control access to resources, including information. The first step is to declare who is authorized to access resources in specific ways. Otherwise, any active entity (user, process) could access any resource and we could have confidentiality and integrity problems.

How do we describe who is authorized to access specific resources in a system?

The solution to this problem must balance the following forces:

- The authorization structure must be independent of the type of resources. For example, it should describe access by users to conceptual entities, access by programs to operating system resources, and so on, in a uniform way.

- The authorization structure should be flexible enough to accommodate different types of subjects, objects, and rights.

- It should be easy to modify the rights of a subject in response to changes in their duties or responsibilities.

Solution

Indicate, for each active entity that can access resources, which resources it can access and how.

Structure

The Subject() class describes an active entity that attempts to access a resource (Protection Object) in some way. The ProtectionObject() class represents the resource to be protected. The association between the subject and the object defines an authorization, from which the pattern gets its name. The association class Right() describes the access type (for example, read, write) the subject is allowed to perform on the corresponding object. Through this class one can check the rights that a subject has on some object, or who is allowed to access a given object.

The figure below shows the elements of an authorization in form of a class diagram.

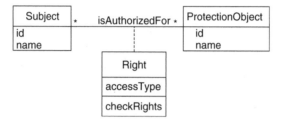

Class model for AUTHORIZATION (245)

Implementation

An organization, according to its policies, should define all the required accesses to resources. The most common policy is need-to-know, in which active entities receive access rights according to their needs.

This pattern is abstract and there are many implementations: the two most common approaches are Access Control Lists and Capabilities [Pfl03]. Access Control Lists (ACLs) are kept with the objects to indicate who is authorized to access them, while Capabilities are assigned to processes to define their execution rights. Access types should be application oriented.

Example Resolved

A hospital using an authorization system can define rules that allow only doctors or nurses to modify patient records, and only medical personnel to read patient records. This approach allows only qualified personnel to read and modify records.

Variant

The full access matrix model usually described in textbooks also includes:

■ Predicates or guards, which may restrict the use of the authorization according to specific conditions

■ Delegation of some of the authorizations by their holders to other subjects through the use of a Boolean 'copy' flag

The next figure extends AUTHORIZATION (245) to include those aspects. Right now includes not only the type of access allowed, but also a predicate that must be true for the authorization to hold, and a copy flag that can be true or false, indicating whether or not the right can be transferred. CheckRights is an operation to determine the rights of a subject or to find who has the rights to access a given object.

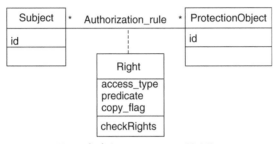

Extended AUTHORIZATION (245)

Known Uses

This pattern defines the most basic type of authorization rule, on which most more complex access-control models are based. It is based on the concept of access matrix, a fundamental security model ([Pfl03] and [Sum97]). Its first object-oriented form appeared in [Fer93]. Subsequently, it has appeared in several other papers and products ([Ess97] and [KBZ01]). It is the basis for the access control systems of most commercial products, such as Unix, Windows, Oracle, and many others. PACKET FILTER FIREWALL (405) implements a variety of this pattern in which the subjects and objects are defined by Internet addresses.

Consequences

The following benefits may be expected from applying this patter:

■ The pattern applies to any type of resource. Subjects can be executing processes, users, roles, user groups. Protection objects can be transactions, data, memory areas, I/O devices, files, or other resources. Access types are individually definable and can be application-specific in addition to the usual read and write.

■ It is convenient to add or remove authorizations.

■ Some systems separate administrative authorizations from user authorizations for further security, on the principle of separation of duties [Woo79].

- The request may not need to specify the exact object in the rule: the object may be implied by an existing protected object [Fer75]. Subjects and access types may also be implied. This improves flexibility at the cost of some extra processing time to deduce the specific rule needed.

The following potential liabilities may arise from applying this pattern:

- If there are many users or many objects, a large number of rules must be written.
- It may be hard for the security administrator to realize why a given subject needs a right, or the implications of a new rule.
- Defining authorization rules is not enough, we also need an enforcement mechanism.

See Also

ROLE-BASED ACCESS CONTROL (249) is a specialization of this pattern. REFERENCE MONITOR (256) complements this pattern by defining how to enforce the defined rights.

8.2 Role-Based Access Control

This pattern describes how to assign rights based on the functions or tasks of people in an environment in which control of access to computing resources is required and where there is a large number of users, information types, or a large variety of resources. It describes how users can acquire rights based on their job functions or their assigned tasks.

Example

The hospital has many patients, doctors, nurses, and other personnel. The specific individuals also change frequently. Defining individual access rights has become a time-consuming activity, prone to errors.

Context

Any environment in which we need to control access to computing resources and where there is a large number of users, information types, or a large variety of resources.

Problem

For convenient administration of authorization rights we need to have ways to factor out rights. Otherwise, the number of individual rights is just too large, and granting rights to individual users would require storing many authorization rules, and it would be hard for administrators to keep track of these rules.

How do we assign rights based on the functions or tasks of people?

The solution to this problem must balance the following forces:

- In most organizations people can be classified according to their functions or tasks
- Common tasks require similar sets of rights
- We want to help the organization to define precise access rights for its members according to a need-to-know policy

Solution

Most organizations have a variety of job functions that require different skills and responsibilities. For security reasons, users should get rights based on their job functions or their assigned tasks. This corresponds to the application of the need-to-know principle, a fundamental security policy [Sum97]. Job functions can be interpreted as roles that people play in performing their duties. In particular, Web-based systems have a variety of users: company employees, customers, partners, search engines, and so on.

Structure

A class model for ROLE-BASED ACCESS CONTROL (249) (RBAC) is shown in the figure below. The User and Role classes describe the registered users and the predefined roles respectively. Users are assigned to roles, roles are given rights according to their functions. The association class Right defines the access types that a user within a role is authorized to apply to the protection object. In fact, the combination Role, ProtectionObject, and Right is an instance of AUTHORIZATION (245).

Implementation

Roles may correspond to job titles, for example manager, secretary. A finer approach is to make them correspond to tasks—for example, a professor has the roles of thesis advisor, teacher, committee member, researcher, and so on. An approach to define role rights is described in ROLE RIGHTS DEFINITION (259).

There are many possible ways to implement roles in a software system. [KBZ01]considers the implementation of the data structures needed to apply an RBAC model. Concrete implementations can be found in operating systems, database systems, and Web application servers.

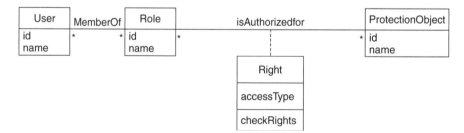

Class model for ROLE-BASED ACCESS CONTROL (249)

Example Resolved

The hospital now assigns rights to the roles of doctors, nurses, and so on. The number of authorization rules has decreased dramatically as a result.

Variants

The model shown in the figure on page 252 additionally considers composite roles—it is an application of COMPOSITE [GoF95]—and separation of administration from other rights, an application of the policy of separation of duties. The administrator has the right to assign roles to groups and users, and is a special user who can assign users to roles and rights to a role. Rights for security administration usually include:

- Definition of authorization rules for roles
- Creation/deletion of user groups
- Assignment of users to roles

The figure also includes the concept of a Session, which corresponds to the way to use a role and can be used to enforce role exclusion at execution time. Finally, the Group() class describes groups of users that can be assigned to the same role.

Known Uses

Our pattern represents in object-oriented form a model described in set terms in [San96]. That model has been the basis of most research papers and implementations of this idea [FBK99]. RBAC is implemented in a variety of commercial systems, including Sun's J2EE [Jaw00], Microsoft's Windows 2000, IBM's WebSphere, and Oracle, amongst others. The basic security facilities of Java's JDK 1.2 have been shown to be able to support a rich variety of RBAC policies [Giu99].

Consequences

The following benefits may be expected from applying this pattern:

- It allows administrators to reduce the complexity of security, because there are much more users than roles.
- Organization policies about job functions can be reflected directly in the definition of roles and the assignment of users to roles.
- It is very simple to accommodate users arriving, leaving, or being reassigned. All these actions require only manipulation of the associations between users and roles.
- Roles can be structured for further flexibility and reduction of rules.
- Users can activate more than one session at a time for functional flexibility—some tasks may require multiple views or different types of actions.
- We can add UML constraints to indicate that some roles cannot be used in the same session or given to the same user (separation of duties).
- Groups of users can be used as role members, further reducing the number of authorization rules and the number of role assignments.

The following potential liability may arise from applying this pattern:

■ Additional conceptual complexity—new concept of roles, assignments to multiple roles, and so on.

There are other possible structurings of roles [Fer94], which may be useful for specific environments. It is also possible to use roles to extend the multi-level model discussed in the next section.

See Also

Earlier versions of this pattern appeared in [Fer93] and [YB97], and a pattern language for its software implementation appears in [KBZ01], although this does not consider composite roles, groups, and sessions. The pattern shown in the figure below includes AUTHORIZATION (245) and COMPOSITE. Other related patterns are ROLE [Bau97], and ABSTRACT SESSION [Pry97].

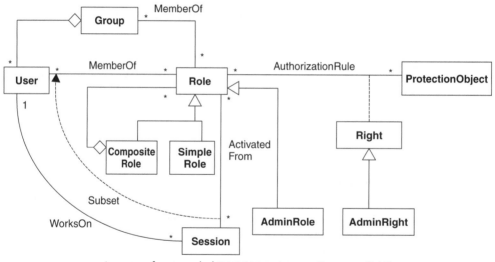

A pattern for extended ROLE-BASED ACCESS CONTROL (249)

8.3 Multilevel Security

In some environments data and documents may have critical value and their disclosure could bring serious problems. This pattern describes how to categorize sensitive information and prevent its disclosure. It discusses how to assign classifications (clearances) to users, and classifications (sensitivity levels) to data, and to separate different organizational units into categories. Access of users to data is based on policies, while changes to the classifications are performed by trusted processes that are allowed to violate the policies.

Example

The high command of an army has decided on a plan of attack in a war. It is extremely important that this information is not known outside a small group of people, or the attack may be a failure.

Context

In some environments data and documents may have critical value and their disclosure could bring serious problems.

Problem

How can you control access in an environment with sensitive documents so as to prevent leakage of information?

The solution to this problem must resolve the following forces:

- We need to protect the confidentiality and integrity of data based on its sensitivity.
- Users have to be allowed to read documents based on their rank or position in the organization.
- There should be a way to increase or decrease the ability of users to read documents and the sensitivity of the documents. Otherwise, people promoted to higher positions, for example, could not read sensitive documents, and we would end up with a proliferation of sensitive and obsolete documents.

Solution

Assign classifications (as clearances) to users and classifications (as sensitivity levels) to data. Separate different organizational units into categories. For example, classifications may include levels such as top secret, secret, and so on, and compartments may include units such as engDept, marketingDept, and so on. For confidentiality purposes, access of users to data is based on policies defined by the Bell-LaPadula model [BL73], while for integrity the policies are defined by Biba's model [Sum97]. Changes to the classifications are performed by trusted processes that are allowed to violate the policies of these models.

Structure

The next figure shows the basic structure of this pattern. The User Classification and Data Classification classes define the active entities and the objects of access, respectively. Both classifications may include categories and levels. Trusted Processes are allowed to assign users and data to classifications, as defined by the Assignment() class.

Implementation

Data classification is a tedious task, because every piece of information or document must be examined and assigned a classification tag. New documents may get automatic tags based on their links to other documents. User classifications are based on their rank and unit of work and are only changed when they change jobs. It is hard to classify users in commercial environments in this way: for example, in a medical system it makes no sense to assign a doctor a higher classification than a patient, because a patient has the right to see their record.

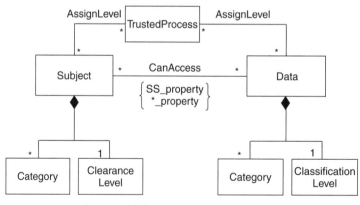

Class model for MULTILEVEL SECURITY (253)

Example Resolved

The group involved in planning attacks, as well as all the related documents it produces, are given a classification of Top Secret. This will prevent leakage towards lower-level army staff.

Known Uses

The model has been used by several military-sponsored projects and in a few commercial products, including DBMSs (Informix, Oracle) and operating systems (Pitbull [Arg] and HP's Virtual Vault [HP]).

Consequences

The following benefits may be expected from applying this pattern:

- The classification of users and data is relatively simple and can follow organization policies.
- This model can be proved to be secure under certain assumptions [Sum97].
- The pattern is useful to isolate processes and execution domains.

The following potential liabilities may arise from applying this pattern:

- Implementations should use labels in data to indicate their classification. This assures security: if not done, the general degree of security is reduced.
- We need trusted programs to assign users and data to classifications.
- Data should be able to be structured into hierarchical sensitivity levels and users should be able to be structured into clearances. This is usually hard, or even impossible, in commercial environments.
- Covert channels may break the assumed security.

See Also

The concept of roles can also be applied here, role classifications replacing user classifications.

8.4   Reference Monitor

In a computational environment in which users or processes make requests for data or resources, this pattern enforces declared access restrictions when an active entity requests resources. It describes how to define an abstract process that intercepts all requests for resources and checks them for compliance with authorizations.

Also Known As

Policy Enforcement Point.

Example

In the hospital example described in ROLE-BASED ACCESS CONTROL (249) we declared the accesses allowed to doctors and other personnel. However, we expected voluntary compliance with the rules. It has not worked, busy personnel bypass the rules and there is no way of enforcing them.

Context

A computational environment in which users or processes make requests for data or resources.

Problem

If we don't enforce the defined authorizations it is the same as not having them, users and processes can perform all type of illegal actions. Any user could read any file, for example.

The solution to this problem must resolve the following forces:

■ Defining authorization rules is not enough, they must be enforced whenever a user or process makes a request for a resource.
■ There are many possible ways of enforcement, depending on the specific architectural unit or level involved. We need an abstract model of enforcement that applies to every level of the system.

Solution

Define an abstract process that intercepts all requests for resources and checks them for compliance with authorizations.

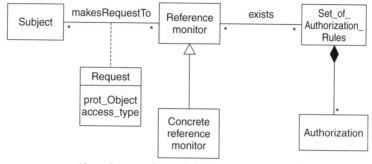

Class diagram for REFERENCE MONITOR (256)

Structure

The figure above shows a class diagram that describes a reified REFERENCE MONITOR (256). In this figure `Authorization Rules` denotes a collection of authorization rules organized as ACLs or in some other way.

Dynamics

The next figure is a sequence diagram showing how a request from a process is checked. The REFERENCE MONITOR (256) looks for the existence of a rule that authorizes the request. If one exists, the request is allowed to proceed.

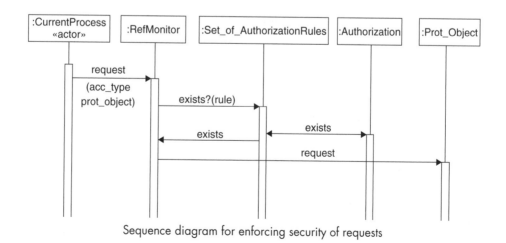

Sequence diagram for enforcing security of requests

Implementation

A concrete reference monitor is required at each section of the system that has resources that can be requested. Examples include a memory manager (to control access to main memory), and a file manager (to control use of files).

Example Resolved

The hospital bought a database system to store patient data. Now, when a user attempts to access patient data, their authorization is checked before giving them access to it. Actions such as read or write are also controlled, for example, only doctors and nurses are allowed to modify patient records.

Known Uses

Most modern operating systems implement this concept, including Solaris 9, Windows 2000, AIX, and others. The Java Security Manager is another example. Database management systems also have an authorization system that controls access to data requested by queries.

Consequences

The following benefits may be expected from applying this pattern:

- If all requests are intercepted, we can make sure that they comply with the rules.
- Implementation has not been constrained by using this abstract process.

The following potential liabilities may arise from applying this pattern:

- Specific implementations (concrete REFERENCE MONITOR (256)s) are needed for each type of resource. For example, a file manager is needed to control requests for files.
- Checking each request may result in intolerable performance loss. We may need to perform some checks at compile-time, for example, and not repeat them at execution time.

See Also

This pattern is a special case of CHECK POINT (287). INTERCEPTOR [POSA2] can act as a REFERENCE MONITOR (256) in some situations. Concrete versions of REFERENCE MONITOR (256) include file control systems (Chapter 10) and firewalls (Chapter 12).

8.5 Role Rights Definition

'Least privilege' is a fundamental principle for secure systems. Roles can directly support the least privilege principle, but a systematic approach to assigning only the required rights to each role is required. This pattern provides a precise way, based on use cases, of assigning rights to roles to implement a least-privilege policy.

Example

Multitronics is a company that sells on-line digital media such as video, sounds, or images. They have been advised that for security reasons they should use a ROLE-BASED ACCESS CONTROL (249) approach, in which they can apply a least-privilege policy. For this they need to first identify the roles required to perform the business functions. In this system a manager administers the items on sale, deciding what is to be sold, at what prices, and so on. He can also order items for future sale. Subscribers register and create accounts so that they can purchase copies of digital items and download them to a mobile device such as a cellular phone. Subscribers can also reserve items not yet in stock. A salesperson maintains a catalog of items for sale and bills the subscribers for their purchases. To apply the required policy, we need a systematic way to assign rights to these roles.

Context

Applications composed of a variety of roles in which it is not easy to assign proper rights to the roles.

Problem

The ROLE-BASED ACCESS CONTROL (249) model is used now in many systems. However, the different component frameworks (.NET, J2EE) provide support only to define roles and to write authorization rules, and do not say anything about where the rights come from. It is not easy for system designers or for administrators to define the required roles and their corresponding rights.

How can we assign appropriate rights to the roles when we want to implement a least privilege policy?

The solution to this problem must resolve the following forces:

■ Roles correspond to functional tasks in an organization, and we need to assign to these tasks sufficient rights to perform their work.

- Rights should be assigned according to the need-to-know (least privilege) principle, in which each role gets only the rights required to perform their duties.

- New roles appear and some roles may not be needed any more: changes to roles and their rights should be easy to perform.

- The assignment of rights should be independent of the system implementation.

Solution

Define the use cases of the system. The design of object-oriented systems always starts this way, but even systems that use other methodologies often define use cases as part of the requirements stage. As use cases define the interactions of actors with the system, we can interpret actors as roles. The roles that appear in a use case must be authorized for all the operations initiated by the role, or the role could not perform its functions. If we collect all the operations performed by a role over all use cases, they define the necessary rights for this role. To make this approach more detailed and systematic, we should build a use case diagram that displays all the use cases for the system, and sequence diagrams that show the interactions of roles with the system for each use case.

The figure below shows a generic sequence diagram indicating that actor role1 must use operations op1, op2, ... opN to interact with the system. This means that role1 should be given the rights to apply these operations to the system.

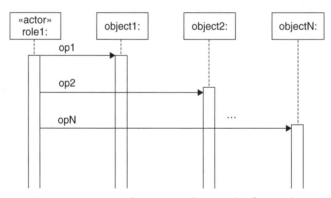

Generic sequence diagram to obtain rights for a role

Implementation

Consider the following steps in order to implement the solution:

1. Start by building a use case diagram to display all the use cases of the system. The actors in this diagram correspond to roles and we can capture all the required roles in this way.

2. Build sequence diagrams for each use case. There is a sequence diagram for the main flow and a few more diagrams for alternate flows [Lar05].

3. Analyze all the sequence diagrams to see what operations the actors (roles) need to apply to interact with the system. These operations correspond to the role rights. In fact, these rights could be generated automatically from the use cases—tools such as Rational Rose can keep track of use cases, and they could be extended to generate the required authorization rules. One can also find all this information in the textual descriptions of the use cases, but it is harder to see the interactions, the sequence diagrams make the interactions more explicit.

4. From the use case exceptions the administrator implements the actions needed for security violations.

5. Addition or deletion of authorization rules is only necessary if a use case is added or deleted, or some of the actions of a use case are changed.

In a centralized system, authorizations could be enforced at the user interface, while in a distributed system, authorization could be enforced in a centralized system component such as the application server. Object-oriented systems use approaches based on model-view separation, for example the MVC or PAC architectures [POSA1]. These two models separate the conceptual model objects—a digital item in our example—from user interfaces that can observe and modify these conceptual objects. The user views should be defined based on use cases [Losa97], and it is clear that they should be the only way to interact with the system. The user views should have access to the set of authorization rules to allow or deny access to the conceptual objects in the system.

Sequences of use cases can be used to define a workflow that requires a specific set of authorizations for different roles. For example, a digital item can only be added by the vendor, released by the administrator, purchased, and downloaded by the subscriber, in that order. This complete workflow could be authorized as a unit.

Example Resolved

The figure below shows a use case diagram for the Multitronics on-line digital item vending system, including the roles defined earlier.

A subscriber participates in four use cases. Any user, once authenticated, has the right to register, but only registered users have the right to reserve and purchase items. These are all the rights needed for a subscriber in this system. A salesperson registers users in the system, bills users for their purchases, and maintains the catalog of products. He can also order new items from vendors according to customers' requests. A manager manages items and approves ordered items. Vendors have the right to upload the ordered items.

However, this is not the whole story. As indicated in the solution, a use case may include several actions that may be performed by different roles. To capture all the

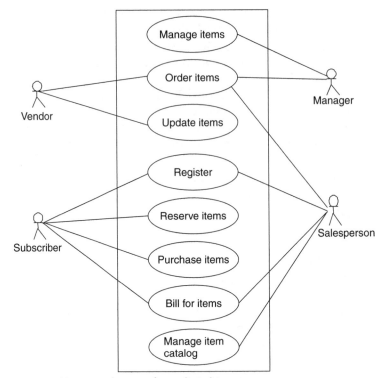

Use case diagram for a digital item management system

required rights, we need to look into the details of the use case or its corresponding sequence diagram. The figure below shows a sequence diagram to order an item. We can see that the salesperson initiates this use case and needs a right to order items. The manager has the right to approve the purchase, after which the salesperson has the right to send the order to the vendor.

The sequence diagram on page 263 shows the purchase of a digital item by a registered user.

From the two use cases shown, we can deduce that a salesperson role needs a right to order items, a manager role needs a right to approve orders, a registered subscriber role has the right to purchase and download an item. Sequence diagrams for the remaining use cases would provide the complete set of rights for all the roles.

Known Uses

Every complex object-oriented application using the RBAC model needs to define rights for its roles. Databases, for example Oracle, support user roles. Most modern frameworks, for example .NET and J2EE, support roles. Modern operating systems,

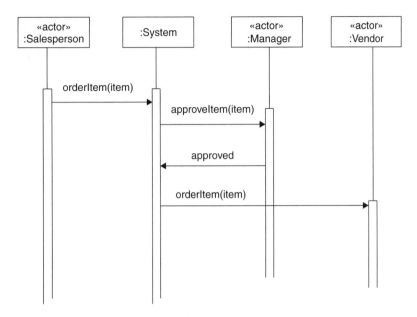

A sequence diagram for the use case Ordering a digital item

for example Trusted Solaris 7 and higher versions, also support roles. ROLE RIGHTS DEFINITION (259) indicates how to define rights for the roles in those systems.

Consequences

The following benefits may be expected from applying this pattern:

- Because roles correspond to functional tasks, their rights are defined according to the needs of the tasks.
- If these are the only rights given to the tasks, we have implemented a least privilege policy.
- Since all the use cases define all the interactions with the system, all the necessary rights can be generated in this way.
- A new use case just defines new rights that can be easily added to the existing set of rights.
- The approach is independent of the actual system implementation. Only the actor's commands to the system need to be authorized, not the internal object accesses triggered by these commands. As long as the external view of the system does not change, there is no need to change authorization rules when the implementation changes. This is consistent with the information-hiding property of object-oriented systems.

The following potential liability may arise from applying this pattern:

■ Building use cases requires specialized expertise, which may not be available in the organization.

See Also

ROLE-BASED ACCESS CONTROL (249) defines the structure of the security system, using classes such as User, Role, and others. ROLE RIGHTS DEFINITION (259) complements it, by providing a way to define the specific rights needed in a particular system.

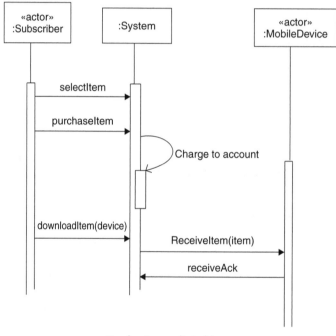

Purchasing a digital item

System Access Control Architecture

> *It's only when we truly know and understand that we have a limited time on earth—and that we have no way of knowing when our time is up—that we will begin to live each day to the fullest, as if it was the only one we had.*
>
> *Elisabeth Kubler-Ross*

An access control security service is essential to systems that explicitly permit or deny use. The first pattern in this chapter, ACCESS CONTROL REQUIREMENTS (267), explains why and how to gather the underlying requirements for a system under consideration from a generic set of access control requirements.

The remainder of the chapter contains patterns that deal with the architecture of software systems to be secured by access control. It deals with conceptual aspects with SINGLE ACCESS POINT (279), FULL ACCESS WITH ERRORS (305), and LIMITED ACCESS (312), as well as with concrete guidelines on how to implement security in a software system for all of the patterns presented here.

Joseph Yoder and Jeffrey Barcalow have already presented these patterns in a different form in [PLoPD4], but we edited and rewrote parts of them to fit into the context of this book and to provide more modern views.

SINGLE ACCESS POINT (279), CHECK POINT (287), and SECURITY SESSION (297) build on each other, showing how to implement an architecture that provides I&A and access control security services to an application or system.

The other two patterns, FULL ACCESS WITH ERRORS (305) and LIMITED ACCESS (312), demonstrate two opposite strategies for dealing with the problem of how to present a secured system to its users in which different users will have different access rights. Both approaches might seem to be extreme: however, knowing about these patterns allows you to more consciously design the interface, even if you opt to design somewhere in the middle ground.

Since the patterns in this chapter deal with very general problems, they might be too abstract for your concrete architecture or design. Please consult Chapter 12, *Firewall Architectures* and Chapter 13, *Secure Internet Applications* as well if you are designing the security aspects of a distributed or networked system. For example, DEMILITARIZED ZONE (449), PROTECTION REVERSE PROXY (457) and FRONT DOOR (473) provide more concrete technical guidance for implementing the patterns in this chapter for Web-based systems.

The author of ACCESS CONTROL REQUIREMENTS (267) was a team at the MITRE Corporation that consisted of Jody Heaney, Duane Hybertson, Susan Chapin, Ann Reedy, and Malcolm Kirwan, Jr. Helpful shepherding comments were provided by Munawar Hafiz, Ralph Johnson, Ed Fernandez, and Peter Sommerlad. The other patterns in the chapter have been rewritten for this book by Peter Sommerlad. Thanks to Joseph Yoder and Jeffrey Barcalow, the original authors, and Joseph for shepherding this version, and their colleagues, shepherds and workshoppers at PLoP '97 where the original version was workshopped [PLoPD4].

9.1 Access Control Requirements

The function of the access control security service is to permit or deny someone the right to perform an action on an asset, such as create, read, modify, or delete a data file. While each situation that calls for access control is unique, there are common generic requirements that apply to all access-control situations. This pattern provides a common generic set of access control requirements. The requirements address both the access control function and the properties of the access control service, such as ease of use and flexibility. The pattern also helps you to apply the general requirements to your specific situation, and helps you to determine the relative importance of conflicting requirements.

Example

A new wing of an existing museum of gemstones is to be opened. The wing will house gems of varying value, some of which are owned by the museum and some of which are on loan. Some of the gems are famous stones whose loss would involve much media publicity. The wing will house valuable gems on display, low-value gems in a hands-on exhibit, and gems of all values in working areas of the wing that are not open to the public.

Based on the results of applying ENTERPRISE SECURITY SERVICES (161), Samuel the museum's system engineer understands that the museum needs to control access to the gems and to the information related to gems. An obvious example is that an attempted access by Theo the thief to steal a gem should be denied. Another example is that the recorded carat weight for gems should not be modifiable by unauthorized people. An unauthorized change in recorded carat weight could change a gem's value, change insurance costs, or even signal the beginning of an attempt to carve off a piece of the stone.

But Samuel also understands that the need to deny unauthorized access must be balanced against the need to permit authorized access. For example, the best safeguard against theft of a gem is to lock it up in a vault and not tell anyone where it is. But this would interfere with a primary goal of the museum, which is to display gems for public viewing. Therefore, Samuel needs to specify a balanced set of requirements for access control and the relative importance of those requirements, as a means of driving and evaluating an appropriate access control service for the museum. How can Samuel define such a set of requirements?

Context

An organization understands how it plans to use access control, for example, from applying ENTERPRISE SECURITY SERVICES (161). An organization understands the general types of actors, assets and actions that are to be subject to access control. An access control rule permits an actor to perform an action on an asset—for example, user A is granted permission to modify file F. Actor types can include humans, software, business or automated processes, or information systems. Actors can be internal to an organization, such as an employee, or external, such as a supplier or customer. Action types include both physical and automated actions. Common actions include create, see, use, change, and destroy or delete. Asset types include both physical and informational assets.

Problem

You need a clear set of requirements to ensure that the strategy employed for access control actually satisfies the needs of the organization or system. Requirements for access control often conflict with each other, and trade-offs among them are often necessary. The conflict stated in the example is that the need to protect gems by denying unauthorized access must be balanced with the need to permit visitors to view the gems.

How can you determine the specific requirements for an access control service, and their relative importance?

The process of selecting and prioritizing access control requirements needs to balance the following forces:

- You can use access control to help achieve desired security properties, especially confidentiality and integrity.

- Access control has many associated costs, not only the money for its deployment, but also support personnel, software, latency, annoyance for users, and so on.

- Access control adds complexity for software, systems, users and administration.

- Access control should be consistent with the organization's security policies, and specifically with access control policies.

- The complexity of administering access control must be reasonable or the administrator will make errors, resulting in vulnerabilities.

- You cannot deploy access control as a stand-alone facility, it needs to interface or integrate with other security services, thus increasing complexity.

- Extremely high levels of control tend to achieve the desired result of denying most unauthorized access, but also tend to achieve the undesired result of denying more authorized access and making the asset or system harder to use.

- Moderate levels of control tend to achieve the desired result of allowing most authorized access, but also tend to achieve the undesired result of allowing more unauthorized access.

- The elements of the access control service need protection if the service is to perform its function.

Solution

Specify a set of access control requirements for a specific domain such as a system or organization, and determine the relative importance of each requirement. The solution has two aspects: a requirements process and a common set of generic requirements.

Requirements Specification and Prioritization Process

A system requirements engineer, in conjunction with an enterprise architect, typically perform requirements capture. An important first step is explicitly to define the domain for which you are specifying access control requirements, such as a specific system or facility. You also define factors that affect specialization and importance of requirements, such as organization constraints. You then specify access control requirements for the target domain, using the generic requirements provided below. The final activity is to define the relative importance of the specified requirements.

Generic Access Control Requirements

The following is a general set of requirements appropriate to access control services. An engineer will need to consider each of these and determine its priority based on criteria specific to the target domain, as well as on broader organization constraints. Additional requirements may be added to this list to address the system's unique characteristics. Some of the general requirements below represent access control functional requirements. The remaining requirements represent access control non-functional requirements, including requirements for security of the access control service.

- Deny unauthorized access

  One primary purpose of access control is to deny unauthorized access requests. No access control service is perfect, and therefore errors will be made in which unauthorized access will be permitted. The goal of this requirement is to keep such errors to a minimum. The importance of this requirement needs to be weighed against requirements for other functional services.

- Permit authorized access

  The second primary purpose of access control is to permit authorized access requests. The goal of this requirement is to keep to a minimum errors in which authorized access will be denied. Sometimes this type of error is caused by an operational error in the access control service; sometimes it is caused by the service's inability to support a desired authorizations policy, and sometimes it is caused by an incorrect access control service policy statement.

■ Limit the damage when unauthorized access is permitted

A strong security principle is to avoid relying on a single point of failure. This requirement says that a single error in which unauthorized access is permitted should not permit access to multiple actions. The well-known defence-in-depth approach, using multiple layers of security, could be used in addressing this requirement. This requirement needs to be weighed against the 'limit the blockage' and 'minimize burden' requirements below.

■ Limit the blockage when authorized access is denied

Consider an access control error in which authorized access is denied. This requirement says that a single failure of this type should not cause a serious interruption of business by denying many actions. This requirement needs to be weighed against the 'limit the damage' requirement above and the 'minimize burden' requirement below.

■ Minimize the burden of access control

The burden of access control is an issue that affects multiple players and activities, including system users, interaction with other security services, processing resources, and implementers of the access control service. Each of these will be discussed briefly.

The access control service should control similar actions in a similar way, to minimize the perceived complexity for human users and developers of non-human actors, and to minimize the likelihood of errors. The access control service functionality depends on effective I&A. I&A should therefore have an interface that accommodates the access control service easily.

Processing overheads can cause reduction in availability of operations on assets for authorized users. This reduction may be due to blocking requests that should be permitted, or due to interruptions of the request flow caused by the access control service. Latency can become a factor. For example, when every action needs to request permission from a remote access control server, overhead can be significant.

Factoring the commonalities among access control requirements to produce a small generic set, as in this pattern, has several purposes. One of them is to reduce the burden on access control implementers by enabling them to define the system with a minimal set of primitives.

■ Support desired authorization policies

The function of the access control service is to enforce the authorization policies defined to meet the business needs for the system or domain for which the service has responsibility. The access control service should be designed to enforce the required policies.

Definition and selection of access control policies is a key element. In fact, access control is about defining policies for authorization and then enforcing these policies through specific mechanisms. For example, a fundamental policy is 'open versus closed' systems. In an open system everything is allowed unless explicitly forbidden. In a closed system everything is forbidden unless explicitly allowed. Another set of fundamental policies is defined by the choices among the access control models discussed in Chapter 8: access matrix, role-based access control, multi-level control, and attribute-based control. Any access control system must implement one or more of these.

At the most generic level, therefore, the requirement is that an access control service must support all desired authorization policies. At a more specific level, authorization policies are selected that the implementation must enforce.

■ Make the access control service flexible

Authorization policy statements sometimes change. This requirement says that adaptation to those changes should be fast, easy, and reliable. That is, the access control service should accommodate policy changes without high cost, complex administration, or increased difficulty of validating that the access control service requirements accurately reflect the authorization policy statements.

Access control also needs to be flexible, to accommodate legitimate operational changes or exceptions. For example, when the threat of terrorist attack is perceived to be high the organization may require stringent checks at facility entry points at the cost of substantial delays. Employees and customers may tolerate such delays for a week or two, but not for months. An opposite example is the case of a hospital, where, if a patient's life is at stake, blocking access to normally-protected patient data may be wholly unacceptable. The system should make some provision that allows access, such as emergency override. At the same time, to provide protection in such incidents, the access control service should record the emergency activity automatically. This will enable a forensic activity or an audit to determine the facts about the violation of normal access rules, and to determine their legitimacy.

Another area of flexibility is granularity. An access control service must be able to support a policy that supports both fine-grained control, such as specific elements in a database, or coarse-grained control, such as a whole database or group of users. In addition, an access control service should be able to support conditional authorization, such as permitting access at certain times of the day but not at others.

An additional set of requirements applies to all service requirements patterns. Instead of duplicating the discussion of the same set in each requirements pattern, they are simply listed here, because they need to be considered in each requirements pattern. The requirements are: minimize time and effort to use, mismatch with users, risks to user safety, costs of per-user setup, costs of maintenance, management, and overhead, and changes needed to existing system infrastructure. The final requirement is to provide security protection of the service and its assets. Further discussion of each of these cross-cutting requirements, including implementation factors, is given in I&A REQUIREMENTS (192).

Implementation

This implementation section first provides more detail on the process that was summarized in the Solution section, then discusses factors for determining the relative importance of requirements.

Process Guidelines

The requirements process typically includes these steps:

1. Establish the domain for which the access control service is needed.

    Ensure that the domain has been identified and scoped. Typical access control domains include information system, physical facility, network, portal, or entire organization. Typical scope definition includes a defined set of actors, of assets, and of actions on those assets. Other constraints may bound the domain—for example, the access control requirements for entering a designated facility during normal work hours may differ from the requirements during out of work hours such as night-time and weekends: these would represent two domains.

2. Specify a set of factors that affect specialization and importance of requirements.

    The factors include uses of access control, access control needs, organization constraints, and priorities. You can find a general candidate set of factors in the next section.

3. Select one or more appropriate access control policies, such as a closed system policy and a role-based model, as discussed above.

    For security sensitive areas, it is generally considered better practice to follow a closed system policy, that is, to default to denial of access when it is not explicitly permitted. In less sensitive situations, an open system policy may be more appropriate, in which anything is permitted unless it is explicitly denied—for example, most information on public Web pages.

4. Specify the granularity levels at which access control will be applied.

   The level of granularity of the domain or asset to which access is specified can vary. For example, access to a physical facility such as a campus may be defined at the level of the entire facility, or a specific building, or a floor in the building, or a specific room. Access to a relational database may be defined at the level of the entire database, or to a specific partition or region, or a specific table, or specific rows in the table, or specific fields. The requirements need to specify the desired granularity, and often the requirement is to support multiple levels simultaneously.

5. Specify access control requirements for the target access control domain.

   To do this, specialize the set of generic requirements given in the Solution section.

6. Define the relative importance of specific requirements.

   You can find more details on the association of factors and requirements below.

Factors in Determining Relative Importance

Table 9.1 presents factors for judging the relative importance to the organization of the generic access control requirements that were identified in the Solution section. For each requirement, the table also describes how the factors affect the relative priority of the requirement. For an example of applying these factors to each requirement, see the Example section below.

Table 9.1 Access control requirements factors

GENERIC REQUIREMENT	FACTOR	IMPACT ON PRIORITY
Deny unauthorized access	When sensitivity of assets is very high, or ability to validate credentials of an actor is suspect, the preferred approach is to block all suspected unauthorized requests.	This requirement should have increased priority if allowing unauthorized access could cause significant damage to the system. This requirement needs to be balanced with the need to permit authorized access for business needs.
Permit authorized access	Users are a higher priority than assets and blocking authorized activities would create severe problems for the organization or system.	This requirement should have increased priority if denying authorized access would cause excessive levels of disruption of business functions, or excessive levels of user dissatisfaction with system. This requirement needs to be balanced with the need to deny unauthorized access.

Table 9.1 Access control requirements factors (*continued*)

GENERIC REQUIREMENT	FACTOR	IMPACT ON PRIORITY
Limit the damage when unauthorized access is permitted	Can use multiple levels of protection by increasing the number of actions required to achieve complete access.	This requirement should have increased priority if failure to block unauthorized access is likely to cascade into additional failures of security services. This requirement needs to be balanced with the need for ease of use: users may become frustrated with any multiple control paths they must navigate to gain access.
Limit the blockage when authorized access is denied	Consider high priority for this if user accessibility is of high importance.	This requirement should have increased priority if the controls are likely to cascade into excessive frustration and productivity loss of legitimate users due to erroneous denial of access. This requirement needs to be balanced with the need to deny unauthorized access.
Minimize burden of access control	System has tight constraints for performance and asset availability, as well as functionality of other services in the system	This requirement should have increased priority if a high burden of using the access control service would cause excessive levels of user dissatisfaction with system, or would disrupt business functions. This requirement needs to be balanced with the need to deny unauthorized access
Support desired authorization policies	The access control service is useful only if it supports the designated policies.	This requirement should always have high priority.
Make access control service flexible	Some organizations or domains have a diverse set of authorization policies, or the policies or access context change often, or policies need to operate in two or more modes, such as normal, increased security, and emergency override.	This requirement should have increased priority if your organization or domain has the characteristics described in this factor. Flexibility is important to permit users needed access in emergency situations, or to increase system protection when specific threats increase significantly. This requirement needs to be balanced with the need for ease of use and simplicity of design.

Example Resolved

Samuel the museum's system engineer defines the domain for access control to include the gem assets themselves, as well as sensitive information about the gems. Although these may be regarded as two different domains for some purposes, Samuel decided to define a single requirements set for both. A clear starting point is a closed authorization policy, in which access to both the gems and information about the gems is forbidden unless explicitly allowed.

Samuel, in consultation with Edward the museum architect, has also determined that the access control service will give greater importance to protection of the assets and sensitive asset information than to immediate satisfaction of user requests. The museum is inclined to disallow even valid requests if anything suspicious is detected in the activity. On the other hand, they will strive to make their unsophisticated user base less aware of the security controls by not presenting multiple rechecking at every step. The actual system policy approaches are known, and Samuel does not anticipate any need for expansion of the number or type of policies enforced. Samuel sees two potential modes of operation: normal conditions and an emergency lock-down.

Table 9.2 shows the requirements Samuel specified for the stated domain.

Known Uses

The general access control requirements and the process of specifying access control requirements described in this pattern are widely known, but are generally used informally, as opposed to being codified or published. The requirements as stated in this pattern represent a consolidation of MITRE Corporation experience in working with multiple customers over several decades. However, some publications on access control requirements exist. The examples that follow emphasize the value of defining access control requirements explicitly, and the separation of policy from mechanism while maintaining adherence of mechanism to policy, consistent with this pattern.

- [LDAP00] is a discussion of access control requirements for LDAP. In addition to LDAP access control requirements, it discusses policy requirements, granularity, and nonfunctional requirements, especially usability.

- [Coe03] discusses access control requirements in the context of virtual organizations. The authors discuss authorization and access control-related languages and standards, and access control policy requirements. They stress the importance of defining security domains for access control, and interoperability and composition among domains and their associated policies and models.

- [Eve04] is a case study used to motivate access control requirements. It discusses granularity and some of the nonfunctional requirements identified in this pattern.

Table 9.2 Museum requirements for access control service

GENERIC REQUIREMENT	MUSEUM REQUIREMENT AND PRIORITY
Deny unauthorized access	High priority – the museum requires access control to provide a certainty of at least 0.9999 for denying unauthorized access to high-value gems, meaning that the service shall allow no more than one successful access out of 10,000 unauthorized attempts. The museum requires that access control provide a certainty of at least 0.999 for denying access to the associated gems information.
Permit authorized access	Moderate priority – the museum regards user convenience as a lower priority than protecting the assets under its care. The museum requires access control to provide a certainty of at least 0.98 for permitting authorized access to gems or gem information, meaning that the service shall deny no more than one access out of 50 authorized requests for access.
Limit the damage when unauthorized access is permitted	High priority for gems – the museum places high priority on avoiding inadvertent access to all gems. If Theo the thief is successful at circumventing access control to get his hands on one gem, that success must not give him access to all the other gems. Moderate priority for gem information – the priority of this requirement for gem information is balanced by the need for access by gem researchers, with the assumption that the user base of researchers will not be overly knowledgeable with regard to the information system.
Limit the blockage when authorized access is denied	Low priority – the museum gives higher priority to asset protection than to user access. They would prefer to occasionally have to address a locked out user rather than lose an asset, or sensitive information about that asset.
Minimize burden of access control	Moderate priority – the museum will try to attain a middle ground with this requirement. They want effective access controls, but they don't want to impact other functional services, create bottlenecks, or create denial of service scenarios.
Support desired authorization policies	High priority – the museum has defined a closed system access control policy that focuses on the gems they protect and associated information. Samuel does not see that scenario changing over the long term.
Make access control service flexible	Moderate priority – the museum requires the access controls to change when they need to operate in emergency lock-down mode, as opposed to normal operating conditions, but the policy is not expected to change significantly.

- [ISO15408] is an international standard that defines evaluation criteria for information technology security. It includes a class or family of criteria that address the requirements for functions to define authorization or access control policy, and explicitly authorize or deny access of a subject to perform an operation on an object in conformance with that policy.

- [Vim03] identifies general desiderata or requirements for access control, and how they are expressed in policies. It discusses how the requirements are addressed in several current operating systems, database management systems, and network solutions.

Consequences

The following benefits may be expected from applying this pattern:

- It facilitates conscious selection of access control requirements, so that decisions about selecting access control mechanisms have a clear basis, rather than occurring in a vacuum.

- It promotes explicit analysis of trade-offs that encourages balancing and prioritizing of conflicting requirements. It helps avoid stronger than necessary access control that makes it difficult for valid users, and at the same time it helps avoid weaker than necessary access control that makes it easy for unauthorized actors to defeat.

- It results in documentation of access control requirements that communicates to all interested parties and also provides information for security audits.

- The pattern fosters a clear connection of requirements to authorization policies: this also encourages organizations to make their policies more explicit.

The following potential liabilities may arise from applying this pattern:

- An investment of resources is required to apply the pattern, including time to analyze domains and access control needs. In some cases the cost of applying the pattern may exceed its benefits.

- It poses a danger of over-engineering and complexity creep, if stakeholders are offered too many options. You can mitigate this by using the requirements as guidelines only for analysis, or by selecting parts of the pattern that give the most benefit.

- The formal selection process may be too long and costly and produce too much overhead. You can mitigate this in the same way as noted above.

- Specific circumstances might not be covered by generic access control requirements. You can mitigate this by adding specific requirements and including them in the trade-offs.

- Documentation of requirements implies that they must be maintained as they change over time. You can mitigate this by keeping the requirements in a form that is easy to update, integrated with other system documentation.

- Perception of access control requirements can differ throughout an organization or in a particular domain. This may make it difficult to reach agreement on priorities of requirements. On the other hand, bringing such disagreements to the surface may be a benefit of the pattern, because then they can be properly discussed and resolved.

See Also

After applying this solution, the next step typically is to apply architecture or design patterns that help satisfy the specified requirements for access control.

Patterns presented in this chapter include the following: SINGLE ACCESS POINT (279), CHECK POINT (287), and SECURITY SESSION (297) build on each other, showing how to implement an architecture providing I&A and access control to an application or system. The remaining two patterns, FULL ACCESS WITH ERRORS (305) and LIMITED ACCESS (312), demonstrate two opposite strategies for dealing with the problem of how to present a secured system to its users in which different users will have different access rights.

9.2 Single Access Point

If you need to provide external access to a system, but want to protect it from misuse or damage, define a single access point that grants or denies entry to the system after checking the client requiring access. The single access point is easy to apply, defines a clear entry point to the system, and can be assessed when implementing the desired security policy.

Also Known As

One Way In. Concrete implementations are called Login Window, Guard Door, or Validation Screen.

Example

Consider a small medieval village. It consists of a group of houses in close proximity. While there is little economic prosperity, there is little value in protection from burglars and little interest to robbery. Security for people means that each man protects his own belongings. Each man spends time building weapons and training in their use so that he can defend his family.

Somehow economy prospers (we do not speculate why and how), more and more people move to the village, and more and more value is accumulated within the village. However, since the people need more time for their prospering businesses, they have less time to spend practicing defence. Their level of protection becomes lower, while the threat from burglars grows. In addition, visitors must convince every individual shopkeeper that they are valuable customers instead of thieves before they can actually conduct business with them. The village dwellers wonder how they can simplify protection, so that everybody no longer needs to deal with it many times a day.

Context

You need to provide access to a system for external clients. You need to ensure the system is not misused or damaged by such clients.

Problem

Whenever a system is used by an external client such as a user, the system's integrity is in danger. Often such systems require some security property, like protection from misuse or damage. One means is to check every interaction with an external client to determine whether it is authorized. When the system has a non-trivial inner structure and consists of multiple parts or subsystems, an external interaction of the system can result in many different interactions of the client with the individual parts of the system. Checking each of these sub-interactions is required to protect all the parts, and thus the whole system. First, implementing all these checks can be a burden: second, if the same information has to be presented over and over, these checks can hinder performance and annoy a user: third, assessing the correct implementation of the overall security policy is hard, because of its complexity.

In addition it is a good practise to have a clearly-defined entry point to a system, as you are used to with the main entrance to a building. Such a prominent and well-known entry point makes using the system easier, because we do not need to spend time searching for the entrance.

The solution to this problem must resolve the following forces:

- You need to provide access to a system to make it usable.

- In a complex interconnected world, no system is an island.

- Most systems exhibit a non-trivial structure and are constructed from sub-systems that also need protection.

- Many entry points to a system reduce security, because the additional complexity makes it easier to bypass controls.

- Multiple entry points can have duplicate code for the same kind of checking.

- Repeated checks annoy clients or slow down the system.

- Uniform access to a system can lower its usability if different situations really require different means of access—for example, entering the Windows log-in password on a tablet PC is annoying if no actual keyboard is present on which to type it.

- Uniform access to a system is easier to control.

Solution

Define a single access point for clients using the system. At this access point you can check the legitimacy of the client according to your defined policy. Once clients passed the access point, they are free to use the system from that point on.

Protect the rest of the system's boundary, so that no circumvention of the single access point is possible. The inhabitants of our medieval village build a wall to serve as such a passive boundary protection: a computer operating system denies all activity from anonymous users not logged in.

Make the single access point prominent, so that it is easy to find and absolutely obvious where to enter the system. Nothing is more annoying than circling the city wall looking for a gate. A computer operating system usually shows a log-in window or prompt when no user is currently logged in.

If auditing is required, the single access point can record which clients entered the system and when. It might also record the termination of an client's use of the system.

This pattern applies to many levels of abstraction and technology. It further might apply within a more complex system to the system itself as well as its subsystems, which in turn can have additional single access points.

The above description is very generic: here is a list of some concrete examples:

- Function entry point with precondition check (for example in Eiffel)

- Windows operating system log-in screen

- Chapter 12, *Firewall Architectures*

- A security guard in an office building or military base

Structure

The single access point can be represented by the following UML diagram.

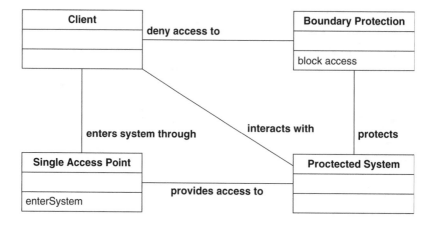

However it is more intuitive to presented it as shown in the accompanying sketch, since it is hard to show the boundary protection of the protected system. Boundary protection is essential to make the single access point efficient in checking clients and hindering intruders to access the system.

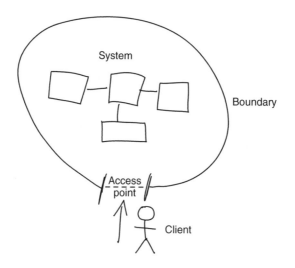

Dynamics

The sequence diagram illustrates a regular scenario of an client entering the system. The client logs in at the single access point and then uses the protected system. The passive protection given by the boundary (the city wall) cannot be shown here.

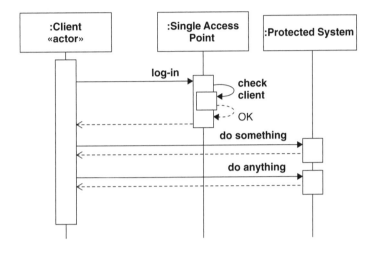

Implementation

To implement the SINGLE ACCESS POINT (279), several tasks are required:

1. *Define your security policy for the system at hand.* Before you start securing your system, you should know what you secure and why. Apply the patterns from this book to obtain the security requirements for the system to be protected. The security policy must contain the trust relationship between the internal subsystems. All of them need to trust the single access point and also each other. Even if such trust can be established, it might be wise to apply the Defence in Depth security principle (see Chapter 15, *Supplementary Concepts*) for extra-sensitive subsystems.

2. *Define a prominent or well-known position for the single access point, or make it transparent for its legitimate users.* Christopher Alexander's MAIN ENTRANCE [AIS+77] gives some guideline about where to place your main entrance, which SINGLE ACCESS POINT (279) definitely is. He writes, 'Therefore: place the main entrance of the building at a point where it can be seen immediately from the main avenues of approach and give it a bold, visible shape which stands out in front of the building.' Microsoft Window's classic

log-in screen with its 'Press ALT-CTRL-DEL to log in' is definitely not following the essence of that rule.

Another option is to make the single access point invisible, but impossible to circumvent. This makes the access transparent for clients, but nevertheless allows the system to be protected. The firewall patterns in this book are examples where the single access point is made transparent for legitimate uses but impassable for intruders.

3. *Optionally implement the entry check at the single access point.* If your system's security policy requires authentication and authorization, the single access point can play a major role in implementing it easily. A typical software system will provide a log-in window for the user to provide an identifier and password. If both match with corresponding stored values, the user is allowed to use the system. See the patterns in Chapter 7, *Identification and Authentication (I&A)*. CHECK POINT (287) shows how to make this checking flexible.

   If you apply CHECK POINT (287), you can also associate a SECURITY SESSION (297), or a so-called 'day pass,' with the client. Every client showing such a day pass is automatically trusted within the system once past the single access point. The single access point will initialize parameters and variables within the client's session to valid values on which the system can rely. In simple cases the 'day pass' can be implicit, by letting the client enter the system and trusting the boundary protection to hinder intruders.

4. *Implement the system initialization at the single access point.* Some protected systems need to be initialized corresponding to their user before they can be used. For example, the Unix log-in program initializes the user's process with their user and group identities, thus enforcing correct authorization later on. It also presets environment variables, as predefined by the system, and executes an initialization script before the user can start working with the system. SECURITY SESSION (297) shows details of how to identify the user throughout their use of the system and keep their related data in a convenient place.

5. *Protect the boundary of your system.* The single access point can only be effective if you provide a closed perimeter to your system. Especially, you need to look for potential 'back doors' that have been left open. It is in the sense of SINGLE ACCESS POINT (279) not to have these. For example, when you set up a firewall (see Chapter 12), you ensure that only those ports that are actually needed are open: all other network connections are disabled.

The boundary protection can be physical, like a city wall, or built into the system itself, such as operating systems not allowing anonymous users to start processes other than via the log-in program.

Example Resolved

The village people build a wall around their dwellings, effectively making it a walled town with a gate. The wall hinders burglar's access to the town, while the gate allows customers and townspeople to enter and leave the town. A single guard at the gate is now able to protect the whole town. The townspeople acquire more time for business by paying the trusted guard.

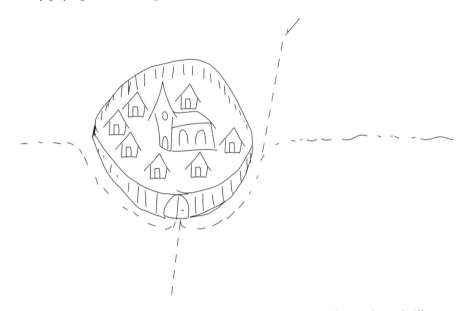

Despite their successful city wall and city gate protecting their enlarged village, our medieval folk still have some problems with theft from their open houses. They therefore apply the security principle of Defence in Depth, and re-apply SINGLE ACCESS POINT (279) at their individual houses. Each house gets a front door that can be locked, thus protecting its inhabitants, but still allowing them and their visitors in and out. The existing stone walls of their houses already provide good boundary protection, especially because, being medieval, their windows are made from iron bars instead of glass.

Known Uses

Many operating systems, such as Mac OS, Microsoft Windows, and Unix, require a user to log into the system before it can be used. All provide either a dedicated log-in program or a prominent log-in window for the user to provide their identity and password. The boundary protection is built into the operating system by not allowing programs to be run by unauthorized or anonymous users.

Other patterns in this book, such as the firewall patterns in Chapter 12 and PRO-TECTION REVERSE PROXY (457), provide examples of effective single access points, in which the clients are not always users, but can be network traffic that needs entry to the protected system.

Consequences

The following benefits may be expected from applying this pattern:

- It provides a single place to go for entering the system, a clearly defined entrance for users of the system, and a single place to set up the system or application properly.

- It provides a single place to guard your system: you only need to trust your gate guards at the single access point within your system. However, applying Defence in Depth might be required to improve security further.

- The inner structure of system is simpler, because repeated authorization checks are avoided. The system trusts the single access point.

- No redundant authorization checks are required: once the access point is passed, the system trusts the client.

- It applies to many levels of abstraction.

The following potential liabilities may arise from applying this pattern:

- Having just a single access point may make the system cumbersome to use, or even completely unusable. For a medieval city, if you arrive from the wrong direction, you have to walk right round the city just to reach its gate.

- You need to trust your gatekeeper and your city wall. However, it might be easier to check the single access point instead of multiple ones. Nevertheless, the boundary protection still can be a weak point of your system.

- The single access point might need to check the client on entrance more thoroughly than is required in the concrete situation, thereby annoying the client or slowing down entrance unacceptably.

- In a complex system, several single access points might be required for subsystems.

- The single access point might become a single point of failure. If the single access point breaks down, the system might become unusable, or its security compromised.

See Also

CHECK POINT (287) and SECURITY SESSION (297) both provide details of how to implement access control based upon SINGLE ACCESS POINT (279) in a flexible and effective way.

9.3 Check Point

Once you have secured a system using SINGLE ACCESS POINT (279), a means of identification and authentication (I&A) and response to unauthorized break-in attempts is required for securing the system. CHECK POINT (287) makes such an effective I&A and access control mechanism easy to deploy and evolve.

Also Known As

Policy Definition Point (PDP), Policy Enforcement Point (PEP), Access Verification, Holding off hackers, Validation and Penalization, Make the Punishment fit the Crime, Validation Screen, Pluggable Authentication.

Example

The mayor of our medieval town that established SINGLE ACCESS POINT (279) with their gate and guard is concerned about their protection during times when different threats come close to the town. For example, the merchants would like to have the gate freely open during daytime, to let traders in and out easily. However, they are concerned about burglars sneaking into their warehouses during night time.

Context

You have a system protected from unauthorized access in general, for example by applying SINGLE ACCESS POINT (279). Nevertheless, you want authorized clients be able to enter your system.

Problem

Whenever you introduce a security measure, you often do not know in advance about all its weaknesses. Also, you only learn how it influences usability if you deploy it to actual users.

A protected system needs to be secure from break-in attempts, and appropriate actions should be taken when such attempts occur. On the other hand, authorized clients should still be able to enter the protected system, and should not be impeded too much when they (in the case of a human) make a mistake when providing their credentials.

In addition, you want to consider the change of requirements for identification and authorization (I&A) that might occur over time, either because you need to address new threats, or because you learn from its use. One example for handling that situation is the development of a protected system in which a developer will use a dummy I&A implementation to test the system, without the hassle of logging into the system for every test. Later on, the deployed system needs to be protected by a log-in mechanism that authenticates and authorizes its users.

How can you provide an architecture that allows you to effectively protect system access while still being able to tune I&A to evolving needs without impact to the system you protect?

The solution to this problem must resolve the following forces:

- Having a way to authenticate users and provide validation about what they can do is important.

- Human users make mistakes and should not be punished too harshly for them. However, too many consecutive mistakes at authentication by a user can indicate an attack to the system and should be dealt with.

- Different actions need to be taken depending on the severity of the mistake and current context.

- Spreading checks throughout your protected system increase complexity and make it hard to change. It would be helpful to have a single place to which to refer for authentication and authorization of users.

- You might learn better ways and techniques for I&A after you have deployed an initial system, you might have to change your system after you recognized that it is vulnerable to specific attacks, or you might have to modify the protection because your risks have changed.

- Security-providing code is critical and requires thorough validation through reviews and tests. The smaller such components, the easier are these validations. Reuse of well-proven security components minimizes expensive validations.

Solution

Apply the STRATEGY design pattern [GoF95] to vary the checking behavior at the SINGLE ACCESS POINT (279). CHECK POINT (287) defines the interface to be supported by concrete implementations to provide the I&A service to the SINGLE ACCESS POINT (279). A separate configuration (mechanism) defines which concrete implementation of the CHECK POINT (287) interface to use.

The check point interface might provide further security-related functionality in addition to performing I&A. For example, it might define hooks for creating a SECURITY SESSION (297), checking access rights for a user or session by other system components, logging security-related information, or detecting attack patterns when unauthenticated access attempts occur.

By changing the configuration and thus the concrete CHECK POINT (287) implementation, the behavior at the SINGLE ACCESS POINT (279) changes. For example, Linux provides pluggable authentication modules (PAM) allowing the source of user identities and passwords to be changed [LinuxPAM]. PAM defines a module interface and a configuration mechanism in /etc/pam.d that allows system administrators to adapt the authentication mechanism easily by exchanging the corresponding modules.

The check point effectively encapsulates the security policy to be applied. This allows the development of systems to be independent of a concrete security policy, which might not be available during development. It also allows for easier later adaptation of the security policy of a system whenever external pressure or better knowledge require it.

If not all security decisions can be made at the time of passing the single access point, CHECK POINT (287) should supply an interface to be used later on by the system's applications. This interface can be used to determine application-specific access rights that might rely on values of application variables not within the scope of the initial access control at the single access point. For example, a bank's application might allow posting of transactions up to $10,000 for all internal users and up to $1,000,000 for managers, and require a director to acknowledge higher-valued transactions. Hard-wiring such decisions within the applications would hinder the evolution of the security policy.

Structure

The following structure shows the elements of CHECK POINT (287):

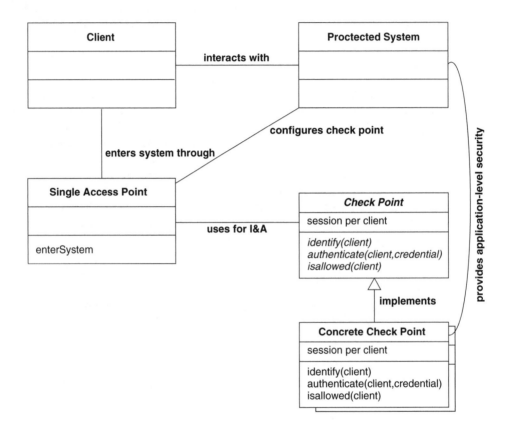

Dynamics

The scenario shows how a SINGLE ACCESS POINT (279) employs a CHECK POINT (287) implementation to identify, authenticate and authorize a client. The potential creation of a SECURITY SESSION (297) for a client successfully logged in is not shown.

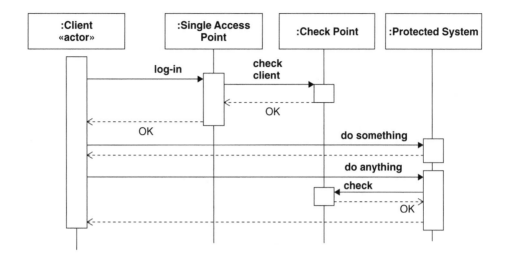

Implementation

To implement CHECK POINT (287), several tasks need to be done:

1. *Define or re-use an interface to be used by your* CHECK POINT (287) *components.* If implemented in an object-oriented language, this can be an abstract class or an interface. Other languages or implementation techniques might require different means appropriate for the chosen technology. For example, Linux PAM uses a object module with pre-defined function entry points in a table for different operations supported by PAM (authentication, access control, session management, password management).

   This CHECK POINT (287) interface corresponds to the abstract strategy in STRATEGY [GoF95]. The interface will provide hooks for I&A, authorization, handling unsuccessful attempts.

2. *Implement the entry check at the single access point.* A single access point ensures that CHECK POINT (287) is initialized and used correctly, and cannot be bypassed by intruders. SINGLE ACCESS POINT (279) usually calls CHECK POINT (287), providing a client's identification and the authentication information they provided. On successful authentication CHECK POINT (287) establishes SECURITY SESSION (297) for the client. If ROLE-BASED ACCESS CONTROL (249) is used, the SECURITY SESSION (297) gets initialized with the client's valid roles.

3. *Provide a configuration mechanism to select a concrete* CHECK POINT (287) *implementation.* To make it easy to adjust a system to use a different security policy, and thus a different concrete CHECK POINT (287) implementation, provide a means to configure it. This configuration mechanism must be protected as well, since changing the configuration effectively changes the security policy. Some implementations provide simple configuration files to be maintained by a privileged user.

   If different concrete CHECK POINT (287) implementations implement different parts of the CHECK POINT (287) interface, it can be handy to be able to combine these concrete CHECK POINT (287)s in a CHAIN OF RESPONSIBILITY [GoF95]. For example, if local Unix users should be authenticated by a system as well as users stored in a corporate LDAP directory, one can implement two concrete CHECK POINT (287)s, one accessing the /etc/passwd file and one accessing an LDAP directory. By configuring them to be applied one after the other and allowing access if either succeeds allows local users to log in as well as those in the directory. You can also change the configuration so that both checkpoints must be passed successfully. That way, only users that are registered both locally and in the corporate LDAP directory can pass. Such a change of the policy is possible without changing the code of any of the concrete check points—however, this is at the expense of increased configuration complexity.

4. *Implement required concrete* CHECK POINT (287). At least one concrete CHECK POINT (287) implementation is needed. More than one makes it useful for different use scenarios, or their combination by configuration in the system. For example, you can apply the NULL OBJECT pattern [Woolf96] to implement a CHECK POINT (287) that is always successful, allowing easier testing during development. A regular concrete CHECK POINT (287) will definitely authenticate clients accessing a system. Usually it stores the client's identification in a SECURITY SESSION (297) object. If ROLE-BASED ACCESS CONTROL (249) is used, the concrete CHECK POINT (287) initializes the session object with the corresponding role set of the client.

5. *Dealing with client errors by the check point.* Depending on the security violation or error, different types of failure actions may be taken. Failure actions can be broken down by level of severity. These types of failures and actions are contingent upon the security policy you are implementing. For example, the simplest action is to return a warning or error message to the user. If the error is non-critical, the security algorithm could treat it as a warning and continue. A second level of failure could force the user to start over. The next level of severity could force an abort of the log-in process or quit the program. The highest level of severity could lock out a machine or user name. In this case, an administrator might have to reset the user name and/or machine access. Unfortunately this could cause problems when a legitimate user tries to log in later, so if the violation is not extremely critical, the user name and

machine-disabled flags could be time-stamped and automatically re-enabled after an hour or so. All security failures could also be logged.

Sometimes, the level of severity of a security violation depends on how many times the violation is repeated. A user who types a password incorrectly once or twice should not be punished too harshly. Three or four consecutive failures could indicate that a hacker is trying to guess a password. To handle this situation, STRATEGY can include counters to keep track of the frequency of security violations and parameterize the algorithm.

The following diagram shows an example for such an algorithm [YB97].

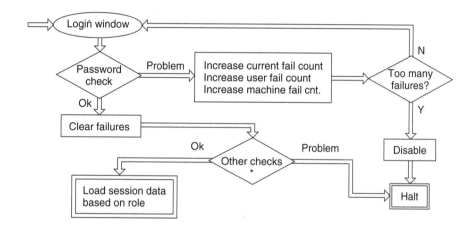

*   These other checks could include: Is the machine legal? Is the machne disabled? Is user's account disabled? Does user have valid role? Has the user's password expired? These other checks are related to the companies security policy.

6. *Provide application level API to check point.* If some security checks cannot be performed in the check point as the user enters the system, they must be deferred until later. For these cases, the check point could have a secondary interface for application components to use, or a separate authorization component will be required.

Because a consistent security concept is difficult to achieve in an application, it may be desirable to try to make a reusable security module for use in several applications. That goal is difficult when security requirements vary between the applications. All application teams will need to be involved to ensure the framework will satisfy each application's requirements.

One approach to reusing security code is to create a library of pluggable security components and a framework for incorporating these components into applications. However, the algorithm for putting together components will almost always be overridden, making the framework difficult to generalize. Another approach is to use the configuration mechanism explained above to allow small parts of the security algorithm to be combined.

Example Resolved

The growing medieval town does not yet know the best security policy to use at the gate that is its single access point, but they learn that a single one is insufficient for all their needs at different times.

The mayor decides to provide a more flexible policy at the city gate. During day time, the gate remains open, while the day-time guard observes the traffic and picks out suspicious-looking people and interrogates them to find out their objectives. During night time the gate remains strictly closed and observed by well-armed night guards. Only town dwellers are let in or out during night time.

The single gate with a newly-built watch house attached to it allows the town leaders to provide a more flexible security policy at their gate, and to change it if harder times require better protection, or prosperous times require easier access.

Known Uses

There are numerous systems and applications that implement CHECK POINT (287).

PAM [LinuxPAM] implements CHECK POINT (287). It allows different modules to implement different user authentication strategies. In addition, it allows different applications to be configured using different modules. Once a new technology for user authentication becomes available, for example storing user information in a new kind of database, a new corresponding PAM module allows this technology to be used immediately by all PAM-aware applications.

The Apache Web server implements CHECK POINT (287) with CHAIN OF RESPONSIBILITY within its modular extension mechanism. Extension modules get the chance to validate each HTTP request according to a configured and implicit activation sequence. Modules might reject a request (that is, its URL), modify it, or allow it for further processing.

The log-in process for an FTP server uses CHECK POINT (287). Depending on the server's configuration files, anonymous log-ins may or may not be allowed. For anonymous log-ins, a valid e-mail is sometimes required. This is similar for Telnet. Linux versions of these applications rely on PAM today.

Xauth uses a cookie to provide a CHECK POINT (287) that X-Windows applications can use for securely communicating between clients and servers.

A Swiss bank uses CHECK POINT (287) based on a CORBA interface throughout all their application systems. In addition to variation of access control by different implementations of the interface, they also allow variation by changing a corporate configuration of user roles, organizational structure, and access rights.

Consequences

The following benefits may be expected from applying this pattern:

■ *Concentrate implementation of a security policy.* All aspects of a security policy are implemented in a single place and are thus easily accessible for assessment.

■ *Flexibility in security policy.* The common interface to be used for CHECK POINT (287) allows for easy exchange of a concrete implementation if required.

■ *Easier testing and development.* Applying a null CHECK POINT (287) allows more efficient testing and development without the need to provide correct user credentials for every run.

■ *Independent testing of security policy implementation.* CHECK POINT (287) implementations can be tested independently of their surrounding system, allowing testing of this component more thoroughly than would be economic for the integrated system.

■ *Reuse of security components.* Applying CHAIN OF RESPONSIBILITY by configuration of concrete CHECK POINT (287) implementations allows for reuse of these components in different contexts or combinations, effectively providing different security policies with a single code base.

The following potential liabilities may arise from applying this pattern:

■ *Criticality.* Concrete CHECK POINT (287) implementations also localize critical sections. Vulnerabilities contained within concrete CHECK POINT (287)s can severely undermine security. Thus concrete CHECK POINT (287) implementations must be validated thoroughly.

■ *Algorithm complexity.* Dealing with invalid access attempts and detecting malicious users can require complex algorithms. While this complexity is unavoidable, CHECK POINT (287) at least concentrates it in a single defined location.

■ *State complexity.* Some security checks cannot be done at start-up. CHECK POINT (287) must have a secondary interface for parts of applications that require such checks. Usually the necessary information is already collected at login of a client and stored in its SECURITY SESSION (297) for reuse by these later checks.

■ *Interface complexity.* Designing a good and future-proof check point interface for applications can be challenging. Enforcing its use in the complex application landscape of a corporation can take years.

■ *Configuration complexity.* In addition to the implementations of concrete CHECK POINT (287)s and its user applications, the specific configuration also needs to be considered when assessing security. If CHAIN OF RESPONSIBILITY is applied, such as with Linux PAM, understanding the implications of such chaining of concrete CHECK POINT (287) implementations is no longer trivial.

See Also

CHECK POINT (287) uses STRATEGY [GoF95] for gaining flexibility in application security.

CHECK POINT (287) implementations can employ CHAIN OF RESPONSIBILITY [GoF95] to delegate decisions among several concrete CHECK POINT (287) implementations. PAM allows chaining of its modules in this way based on its configuration.

SINGLE ACCESS POINT (279) is used to ensure that CHECK POINT (287) gets initialized correctly and that none of the security checks are skipped.

CHECK POINT (287) usually configures a SECURITY SESSION (297) and stores the necessary security information in it.

ROLE-BASED ACCESS CONTROL (249) is often used to implement CHECK POINT (287)'s security checks. CHECK POINT (287) sets or evaluates a user's roles stored in its SECURITY SESSION (297).

For development purposes, or in domains in which security is not a requirement, NULL OBJECT can be used for implementing a concrete CHECK POINT (287) that permits everything.

9.4 Security Session

Verifying a user's identity and access rights for every system function can be tedious. To keep track of who is using the functions and their corresponding access rights, systems establish a security session after a user has logged in successfully. A unique reference to the session object is made available, instead of passing all access rights or re-authenticating a user repeatedly. Queries regarding a user's security properties are delegated to the attached session object via the session reference.

Also Known As

Session, User Environment, Namespace, Localized Globals

Example

Our medieval city is concerned about foreigners entering through its gate. Merchants are welcome, but burglars and thieves shouldn't be let in by the guards. Peasants looking for work in one of the city's workshops are allowed in depending on the demand of the guilds. On the other hand, once a person has entered the city, it is hard for the city dwellers to tell who that person is if they are not a well-known city dweller. Even the night watchman patrolling the city's streets has a hard time knowing how to deal with a stranger. A merchant should be welcomed and protected, while someone else lingering in the streets at night might need to be dealt with.

The problem of city inhabitants and the night watchman is that they do not have equivalent resources to the guards at the city gate, to interrogate and investigate people and check their identity. In addition, it would be annoying to visitors that are welcome if they had to answer the same questions over and over again, such as who they are, where they are going, and what their business is in the city.

The mayor summons the city council to discover a way to keep the city secure while making the city a welcoming as possible for merchants and other guests. Another requirement that comes up at the council meeting is that the city officials would also like to know when a visitor has left.

Context

Your system is shared by multiple users and system components need a way to share (security) data associated with a user. For example, you have already applied CHECK POINT (287).

Problem

Systems shared by multiple users, either via terminals or via a network, have become commonplace. Instead of single-user non-networked systems like the—now almost extinct—DOS PCs, shared or networked systems need to account for a user's actions and ensure users only have access to areas for which they have privileges. A user therefore needs to be identified and authenticated by the system, as described in Chapter 7, *Identification and Authentication (I&A)*. In addition, shared resources require controlling access to them, as described in Chapter 8, *Access Control Models*.

Different components acting on behalf of a user might need to know which user is activating them and what the user's permissions are. Having every individual component or program within the system identifying, authenticating and authorizing users is annoying to both users and developers. In addition, system components might call each other or work together, and thus need a way to share information about the user without compromising this global data to other users.

For example, when buying from a Web-based on-line store, you want to put items in a shopping cart that is associated with you. Later, the check-out process requires you to approve your credit card information and delivery address. The underlying protocol (HTTP) does not provide a context for multi-step interaction because it is stateless. Accordingly, the on-line store's software needs to associate every click you make in your browser with your identity, your shopping basket contents, and your billing information. In addition, you want the system to forget your credentials after the transaction is complete, either by an explicit sign-off mechanism or by a time-out after no interaction by you, thereby ensuring that forgetting to sign off will not compromise your private data such as your credit card account number.

How do you provide easy access for system components to the security properties and other values related with the current user, without requiring them to identify and authenticate every time they interact with the system or an individual component?

The solution to this problem must resolve the following forces:

- You need to provide access to global values shared by different system components. These values also need to be distinguished for individual users. Simple global variables will therefore not work.

- Such values might change during a user's interaction and might be different between several activity periods of the user's session—for example, the contents of the shopping cart in the on-line store.

- Different components or applications within your system can be interested in different values, and might want to change them or define new ones.

- Passing all shared values around the system for a given user can cause too much overhead and result in bloated interfaces.

- Asking a user for I&A over and over again is annoying, so the system needs a means of associating an action automatically with a user that was previously authenticated.

- After a long period of inactivity, the system needs to re-authenticate a user to prevent misuse and overhead. In other words, the system should automatically sign off inactive users.

Solution

Introduce a session object that holds all user-relevant shared data. Security information related to the user, especially, is kept in the session object. In addition to the session object that holds the values, the system needs to associate every action a user makes with this session. This can be either implicitly, such as associating every action coming over the user's connection with the session, or explicitly with an identifier like a session cookie that is sent to a user's browser by an on-line store site.

A system's CHECK POINT (287) is the usual place to instantiate the session object and set up its initial values. For systems with access control, the session object can be used to obtain access permissions at sign-on and cache them, to avoid multiple queries to an external database.

In addition, the session object can provide a scratch-pad area to allow different system components to share arbitrary data about the user between different actions within a log-on period. For example, classic mainframe systems provide a so-called 'terminal control block' that can be used by different interactive transaction programs to share data, such as the last values entered in a form. This allows otherwise independent transaction programs to be chained easily on behalf of the user. Web applications use cookies to share data for a given user.

Often a MANAGER [Som98] is used to keep track of active session objects and controls their life cycle. This MANAGER can also be used to provide the mapping of external session identifiers, such as those stored in a session cookie, to the session object and its data. Furthermore, it can collect obsolete sessions that were abandoned by their users.

Structure

The following diagram shows the component relationships assuming that there is a MANAGER. The CHECK POINT (287) uses the MANAGER to associate a Session object with the user. Later, the components accessed by the user rely on the associated Session object to access the user's access rights and further information. The Manager class uses the timestamp to keep track of stale session objects, and forces the user to re-authenticate if a session is either used for too long without authentication, or if it has not been used for a longer time.

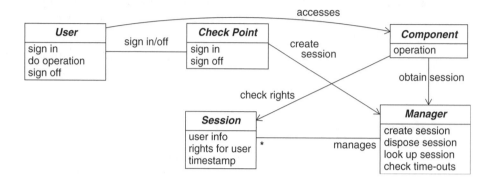

Dynamics

The following scenario shows a simplified interaction, in which a user logs into the system via the CHECK POINT (287). The CHECK POINT (287) uses the MANAGER to obtain a new `Session` object for the user. The manager does not return the object directly, but instead returns an external session identifier to be used by the user or CHECK POINT (287) for later reference. This scenario assumes that the user explicitly provides his session identifier instead, as would occur with a Web application's session cookie. Other systems can provide an implicit association of a user with his session object—this is not shown here.

Later on the user interacts with a system component, providing his session identifier for reference. The system component authorizes the user by asking the MANAGER for the underlying session object and checking the user's data stored there.

When the user logs off at the CHECK POINT (287), the MANAGER deletes the `Session` object belonging to the user, invalidating the corresponding session identifier, which no longer can be used. See figure on page 301.

Implementation

To implement SECURITY SESSION (297) several tasks are required:

1. *Create a session object* to hold all (security) variables associated with the user that may be needed by other components. Typical information kept in the session object are the user's identification, their access rights, the user's role (see ROLE-BASED ACCESS CONTROL (249)), and other system- or application-specific data, such as a shopping cart's content. In addition, you should add a time-stamp when the user logged in successfully, and a time-stamp of the user's last activity. For a flexible solution you might use a data container like PROPERTY LIST [FoYo98] or an ANYTHING [SoRu98] to keep track of varying data without changing code. Web applications might opt to keep the session

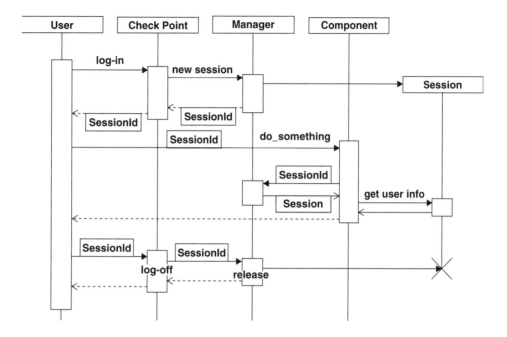

data in a cookie in encrypted form. Even when just storing the session identifier in a cookie or URL to keep track of users, such Web applications must ensure those identifiers are not easily guessable, to limit the risk of session hijacking.

2. *Introduce a* MANAGER *and unique session identifiers* to keep track of active session objects. If a user is only allowed to log in once, you might use a user's identification as the session identifier—otherwise a synthesized identifier is sufficient. A publicly-accessible session identifier must be protected against fraud, which in many cases disallows the user's identifier from use directly as their session identifier. Apply MANAGER [Som98] or RESOURCE LIFECYCLE MANAGER [POSA3] as a reference for implementing the MANAGER. The MAN-AGER provides an interface for other system components to access a session object corresponding to its identifier.

3. *Define session time-out semantics.* Lingering unused session objects carry risk, not only for security reasons, but also for memory management. The MAN-AGER should periodically check for inactive sessions and release them. If this inactivity time out is short, it effectively prohibits misuse of a session by an unidentified user. On the other hand, if it is shorter than the typical transaction time of a user, such a session time-out gets annoying.

4. *Define re-authentication time-out semantics.* In security-sensitive environ-ments, the MANAGER should also enforce re-authentication at the CHECK

POINT (287) for long-lived active sessions to protect a user's session from misuse and the user from forgetting his password. Appropriate values for such time-outs depend heavily on the given domain and use profile. For example, Yahoo! uses cookies that live for about five years to identify a user. However, from time to time, and whenever accessing sensitive data, a user needs to re-authenticate. In a system in which access rights management is separate, this re-authentication also provides a means of updating a user's access rights that are cached in the session object.

5. *Allow a user to log on and log off at the check point.* Even though it seems trivial, you shouldn't forget to provide the mechanism that allows a user to establish the security session and to allow them to cancel a session of their own will. This actively allows the user to care about security, which can be an important security measure. During log-in the MANAGER creates and initializes the session object with the user's access rights and other relevant data.

Example Resolved

Our medieval city council comes up with the concept of a day pass. This day pass is issued by the gate guards to every foreign visitor entering the city, and needs to be returned when leaving the city. To distinguish the more desirable guests from less-liked ones, the passes are color coded: peasants looking for work get a green pass, the private visitors of city inhabitants a white one, while merchants receive a bronze pass that they can keep for later visits.

A visitor is obliged to show his pass to everybody asking for it. Since the city is small enough for all citizens to know each other, the city does not need to issue passports for its inhabitants.

Known Uses

Netscape invented cookies as a means of keeping track of a user's session via the otherwise stateless HTTP protocol [RFC2109]. A user's browser automatically returns a cookie to the originating Web server, effectively passing the session object without the user needing to care about it. Cookies are the means of session tracking for Web applications.

Operating systems such as Unix or Windows use an implicit session object associated with each process in the system. This session object is copied or inherited when a new process is created by its parent process, and only privileged processes such as Unix' log-in program are allowed to set the corresponding session data. For example, in Unix this session object holds the user id and group id of the process owner, among other data. These two imply the corresponding permissions of the process.

Many classic Internet protocols such as FTP and Telnet, as well as many database systems like Oracle or MYSQL, use the TCP/IP connection between a client and a server as an implicit session mechanism. Each session is thus represented by an individual TCP connection. The termination of the connection also terminates the session. Operating systems and the 16-bit port numbers used in IPv4 place a hard limit on the number of usable sessions.

The open source implementation of SSL (Secure Sockets Layer), openSSL, uses a session id to avoid the expensive re-negotiation of certificates, encryption algorithms, and encryption keys for connections re-established between the same client and server. Some Web security systems use this SSL session mechanism instead of cookies to associate a security session with a user for HTTPS.

Consequences

The following benefits may be expected from applying this pattern:

- The session object provides a single, well-defined place to keep user and security-related data.
- Instead of passing different values around, the system can pass the single session object around for a user.
- Extending the session object to hold new data is straightforward and can be done without impacting unrelated system components.
- The system can use the session object to cache access permissions, thus improving performance.
- It is easy to externalize a session object's identifier when no implicit association between a user and a session object can be achieved, such as with a Web application.
- Checking the associations between sessions and users allows detection of multiple simultaneous uses of the same user credentials, which can be a security compromise, for example, if a user's password is used by several people.

The following potential liabilities may arise from applying this pattern:

- Developers thinking in terms of global variables, such as those the session objects provides, can imply badly-structured programs and uncoordinated or hidden coupling of system components.
- Keeping too many too large session objects around can limit system performance. Special means for collecting session garbage, for example session timeouts, might need to be implemented if users cannot be coerced to log off, or if a single user can initiate multiple sessions simultaneously.
- In a distributed system, session identifiers might be forged by attackers and thus lead to security compromises. Careful design of non-guessable and non-enumerable session identifiers is therefore a must. However, providing such

session identifiers must be automatic, or at least easier for a user than providing their original credentials.

- If all session data is sent to the user's browser in a cookie instead, the cookie needs to be encrypted and signed to avoid security compromises of the session data. Again, authenticating the cookie sent by a user must be easier for the user than providing their original I&A information.

- System components that initially do not need the session object might still keep a reference to it, since components instantiated or called might require it.

- Retro-fitting session objects to a (badly-designed) system relying on SINGLE-TONS or global variables can be difficult.

See Also

CHECK POINT (287) typically relies on SECURITY SESSION (297) to provide sign-on functionality for users. If a check point protects multiple systems and those share a single user session, it can provide effective single sign-on for users.

The session object plays the role of an ENCAPSULATED CONTEXT [Kell03] holding several parameters related to the user and their access rights. It is passed through the system as a single parameter, and components of the system can access the encapsulated data via the session object. The ENCAPSULATED CONTEXT avoids wide parameter lists for methods, and ripple effects on changing interfaces when additional user or session-related data is needed.

INTEGRATION REVERSE PROXY (465) and FRONT DOOR (473) rely on SECURITY SESSION (297) to keep track of Web users. They implement it via cookies, SSL session ids, or by encoding the session identifier into URLs.

9.5 Full Access with Errors

Designing the user interface for a system in which different users are granted different access rights can be challenging. At one end of the spectrum is the approach taken by this pattern, which provides a view of the maximum functionality of the system, but issues the user with an error when they attempt to use a function for which they are not authorized.

Also Known As

Full Access with Exceptions, Full View with Errors, Reveal All and Handle Exceptions, Notified View

Example

Consider you are developing an Internet site. The site should present your company on the World-Wide Web as well as provide downloads for brochures, user manuals, and demo software. However, to be able to track who downloaded such material, Internet surfers are required to provide their name and address before they can start a download. However, to avoid irritating returning users, they are granted privileges by the site via a cookie, and thus do not need to register again. See figure on page 306.

For example Yahoo! groups show a group's features to anonymous users, without letting them access the 'members only' menu. Once logged in and registered as a member of a group, the 'members only' menu is accessible.

How do you design the Web site so that it shows the possibility of downloads while still restricting access to registered users v?

Context

You are designing the interface of a system in which access restrictions such as user authorization to parts of the interface apply. While most of the applications of this pattern are within the domain of graphical user interfaces (GUI), it can also apply to other interface types as well.

Problem

When designing the user interface for a system with partial access restrictions, you face the challenge of whether to present functionality that a user might not be able to access within their current role or set of access rights, and how to do so. To complicate

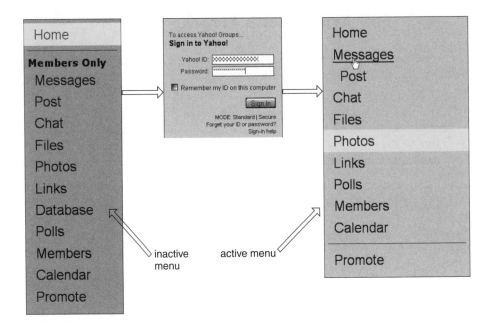

the issue, you might not know in advance what possible combinations of access rights will be used.

This problem generalizes to any interface you design whenever there are multiple modes of use, such as different access rights.

How do you present available functionality that might be partially inaccessible? The solution to this problem must resolve the following forces:

- Users should not be able to view data or perform operations for which they have no permissions.

- Hiding an available and accessible function is inappropriate, because users must be able to see what they can do.

- The visual appeal and usability of a graphical user interface (GUI) can be degraded by varying layouts depending on the (current) access rights of a user. For example, blank space might appear for some users where others see options they can access, or sequence and number of menu items might differ, depending on the current user's rights, and thus 'blind' operation of the menu by an experienced user is no longer possible.

- Showing currently unavailable functions can tease users to into upgrading their access rights, for example by paying for the access or buying a license after using a demo version.

- Trial and error are ineffective means of learning which functions are accessible. Invoking an operation only to learn that it doesn't work with your access rights is confusing.

- The privilege grouping of the typical user community might not be known at the design time of the GUI, and it might change over time, for example through organizational or business process changes, so that providing a few special modes of the GUI depending on the corresponding user roles is inappropriate.

- Checking whether a function is allowed by a user is most efficient, robust and secure, if done by the function itself—at least the code performing the checks is then closely related to the code performing the subsequent operation afterwards.

Solution

Design the system so that every available functionality is visible on its interface. When an operation or data is accessed by someone, the system first checks the access permission. If the access is allowed, the function is performed or data is displayed correspondingly. On lack of permission, an error notification is generated and presented to the user.

Often such an error notification gives the user a chance to upgrade or change access permission, or to provide further authorization for performing an otherwise failing operation. For example, a text editor might fail to save a file over an existing one with the same name. It will give the user an error message with the option of canceling the operation and thus accept the failure, or explicitly authorize the text editor to overwrite the file, thus raising the user's privileges for the current operation.

FULL ACCESS WITH ERRORS (305) works best when denial of an operation is sporadic and users are well aware of what they can and can not do.

The implementation of access right checks that are closely related to the function to be performed allows implementation of more sophisticated authorization schemas that depend on more than just a flag for an access right, such as data values used in the current transaction. For example, a bank might withhold the account statements of their bosses or of very rich clients from regular clerks, who could otherwise look at almost all accounts within their range of duty.

In this example the check not only involves the regular flag-based permissions of the current user, but also the organizational status of the account holder, as well as the current balance of the account. Such complex business logic for access rights is almost impossible to implement using a generic access rights management system. The benefit of implementing FULL ACCESS WITH ERRORS (305) is that there is a consistent error-handling mechanism in place that is readily available for developers to use and is also well known to the system's users.

Structure

The diagram shows the implementation of FULL ACCESS WITH ERRORS (305) in which the system code performing an operation checks the access rights before each operation, rather than the interface code. Usually such checking code is similar for each operation, and should be factored into a common routine, or, with modern programming approaches such as aspect-oriented programming, added as an aspect to each operation of the system.

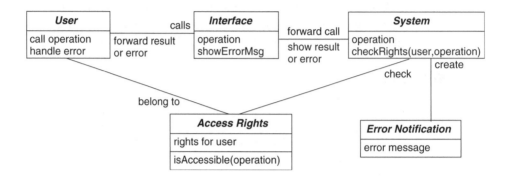

Dynamics

The sequence diagram shows two cases relevant for FULL ACCESS WITH ERRORS (305). The call of the first operation is granted to the user and thus after the check of the access rights is done, it returns successfully. The second case calling operation 2 shows the situation in which the user has insufficient rights and an error message is returned instead.

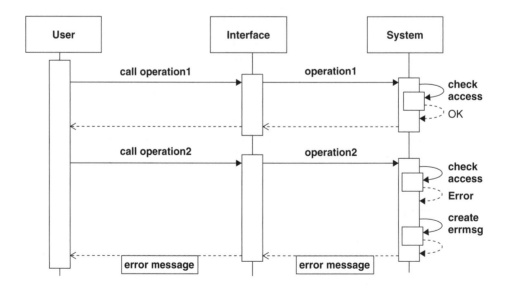

Implementation

To implement FULL ACCESS WITH ERRORS (305) several tasks need to be done:

1. *Implement the association of access rights with users.* CHECK POINT (287) and SECURITY SESSION (297) are typical means of providing a user log-in and attaching their access rights. In the case of FULL ACCESS WITH ERRORS (305) the modeling of access rights should follow closely the underlying operations of the system, so that is easy to associate them with the rights. Further details on I&A are given in Chapter 7, *Identification and Authentication (I&A)*. Modeling and management of access rights are discussed in Chapter 8, *Access Control Models*.

2. *Design the interface representing the full set of the system's functionality.* You should provide visual hints for novice users to recognize features that might be unavailable to them and show them how to achieve the corresponding access rights. Visual grouping of normally-available features versus those requiring authorization can be helpful.

3. *Design error notification for the user.* In simple cases this often allows the user to register or authenticate themselves, such as with Yahoo groups. In more complex settings with finer-grained access rights management, it might give a process description of how to obtain the corresponding access right. At the other end of the spectrum, an unauthorized access can be simply ignored. An additional means of security is to audit users, especially for unauthorized access. This can provide hints on potential for misuse, or on the lack of access rights for a given user role.

4. *Provide access rights checks for system components.* Before the execution of each system function, a user's right to do so must be checked. A combination of CHECK POINT (287) and SECURITY SESSION (297) provide a means of implementing the place where this checking is performed. Further details about how to ensure that such checks are carried out is beyond the scope of this pattern, but, for example, a COMMAND PROCESSOR [POSA1] can check access rights for issued commands centrally. Integrate checks and error notification mechanisms with the system.

Example Resolved

Following FULL ACCESS WITH ERRORS (305), the Web site initially contains all possibly available links. The download links are only available for registered users, so they point to a CGI script that first checks whether the user has registered already by checking whether the corresponding cookie is set in the request. In this case the Web site can also deal with bookmarks, links pointing to protected material issued by unauthenticated or unauthorized users.

Variants

LIMITED ACCESS (312) demonstrates the opposite strategy to FULL ACCESS WITH ERRORS (305) by presenting the user only the permitted functionality, thus avoiding surprising error messages. In many concrete cases neither of the extremes shown by these two patterns are used, but concrete designs lie somewhere in the middle. However, it is difficult to define 'somewhere in the middle.' As a starting point, you should chose a pattern according to the more visible forces in your context, and adapt it to suit the application domain.

A middle ground between FULL ACCESS WITH ERRORS (305) and LIMITED ACCESS (312) is to show all an application's features, but to 'gray out' menu items or buttons not available in the current situation. This allows a user to see what is available, but still provides instant feedback on what is really usable at the moment. Often this approach combines best of both worlds, as long as there aren't too many features to clutter the UI.

Known Uses

The Internet book-seller Amazon, as well as many other Internet sites, provide casual surfers with a view of almost all their functionality. For example, the links to a shopping cart and 'view my account' are active for everyone. When you open these, you can proceed. However, before checking out, or before you can actually see your orders, you have to either sign in or register yourself. This way, everybody sees what functionality is available, but only logged-in users can access their own data.

Under the Unix shell you can activate almost any program on any file in the file system. However, when your access rights are insufficient, accessing files or programs fails, often with a message saying 'permission denied.' Only the dedicate super user 'root' is unprotected from carelessly calling programs or overwriting files, giving access to everything and overriding all access rights set.

Oracle's SQLPlus interactive database access language allows you to execute any syntactically-valid SQL statement, displaying an appropriate error message if illegal access to data is attempted.

Most word processors and text editors, including Microsoft Word and vi, let the user try to save over a read-only file. The program displays an error message after the save has been attempted and has failed.

Consequences

The following benefits may be expected from applying this pattern:

- A system can be effectively secured, because a user's permissions for each individual operation are checked before the operation is executed.

- All possible functions are visible to a user, not only providing a consistent interface, but also demonstrating all available features, even when the user is not (yet) privileged to use them.

- It is easy to change access rights and groups for such a system without influencing the concrete implementation of the system or its interface.

- Retro-fitting this pattern into an existing system is straight forward: write an interface that will handle all possible functions, and whenever a problem happens with an operation, simply abort the operation and display an error message.

- Documentation and training material for an application can be consistent for each type of user.

- FULL ACCESS WITH ERRORS (305) fits well in situations in which users can upgrade their privileges for a otherwise unavailable operation on the fly, for example by confirming a dialogue, without breaking their flow of work.

- For Web applications applying the pattern allows stable URLs and links to a download area, even in the case in which a user must register first. A pre-registered user will be able to download directly using the same URL.

The following potential liabilities may arise from applying this pattern:

- Users can become confused and frustrated when they are forced to apply trial and error to learn and use a system that presents many things but then often just replies with an error message.

- Every operation needs to check permissions. This may cause complexity, duplicated code or—if omitted—lack of security.

- The user interface design becomes bloated when a system is serving disparate user roles. If you show everything to everybody, regardless of their interest in the system, it is very hard to find your way through the task. Too many features either remain hidden in deeply-nested menus or dialogs, or clutter available screen space.

See Also

CHECK POINT (287) and SECURITY SESSION (297) can be used to implement FULL ACCESS WITH ERRORS (305).

9.6   Limited Access

Designing the user interface for a system in which different users are granted different access rights can be challenging. This pattern guides a developer in presenting only the currently-available functions to a user, while hiding everything for which they lack permission.

Also Known As

Limited View, Blinders, Child Proofing, Invisible Road Blocks, Hiding the cookie jars, Early Authorization

Example

Extending the Web site example from FULL ACCESS WITH ERRORS (305): registered users are able to upload files to your Web site. After uploading they also need a means of deleting or changing the uploaded files. However, an individual user should only be able to change their own files. Only a user with administrative rights should be allowed to maintain files by all users.

Yahoo! groups provides a similar means of uploading files to groups for its group members. However, only the uploading member is able to delete or edit the file. The group owner can delete files uploaded by all users. If no permission is given, one can see the 'File' menu, corresponding to FULL ACCESS WITH ERRORS (305), but the file folder itself cannot be extended by adding files.

Context

You are designing the user interface of a system in which access restrictions such as user authorization apply to parts of the interface. While most of the applications of this pattern are within the domain of graphical user interfaces (GUIs), it can also apply to other interface types as well.

Problem

Presenting all potentially-available functionality to users not privileged to use it can represent a security problem. You might want users that don't have access to a functionality to not even be aware that it exists.

A system utilized by people with varying skills and access rights can be very hard to use if every possible option is presented to every user, as is proposed by FULL AC-CESS WITH ERRORS (305). It is much more user friendly if a user can only see or select the options actually available.

How can you present a system's functionality and ensure that users can only access those parts or data of a system to which they are entitled?

The solution to this problem must resolve the following forces:

■ Users should not be able to see or activate operations they cannot perform.

■ Users should not view data for which they have no permissions.

■ Users do not like being told what they cannot do and become annoyed by access violation messages.

■ Input validation can be easier when you limit users to see and operate only what they can access.

■ If options pop in and out dynamically because of changes to access rights or roles, users can become confused and the GUI's usability decreases.

Solution

Only let users see what they have access to. In a GUI, show them only the selections and menus that their current access privileges permit.

For example, if a user is not allowed to edit some data, do not present an edit button and use a read-only field to show that data.

When a user starts the system an I&A mechanism authenticates them and associates a SECURITY SESSION (297), typically within a CHECK POINT (287) architecture. The SE-CURITY SESSION (297) object caches the current privileges of the user that can then be used by the GUI implementation to decide what functions and data are permissible and may be presented to the user, independently of the function's implementation. In contrast to checking the access rights of a user after a request is issued, as would be done in FULL ACCESS WITH ERRORS (305), the system checks the access rights before presenting the user interface. Only functionality that is available to the user is rendered by the interface builder.

Details of GUI implementation are beyond the scope of this pattern, but patterns such as NULL OBJECT can be used to represent unavailable items or disable active GUI elements. The same mechanism that is used for hiding non-available GUI elements can be used to disable GUI elements, depending on the application's state. For example, if no document has been opened by a text editor, there is no active 'save the document' button—only buttons to open an existing document or create a new one might be available in that state of the application. If the user lacks the permission to create new documents, even the latter might be missing.

Structure

In contrast to FULL ACCESS WITH ERRORS (305), the interface is responsible for checking a user's access rights, even before the user interface is presented to the user. The protected system itself does not in general need to check rights, but may still rely on access rights for additional responsibilities such as logging and so on.

Dynamics

This scenario shows that when the user logs in or otherwise changes their access rights, the interface adjusts its appearance according to the current set of access rights. Later on when the user selects an operation, only valid operations can be accessed, so further checks are unnecessary and the operation is passed on directly to the system. See figure on page 315.

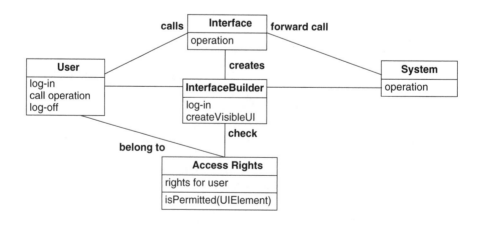

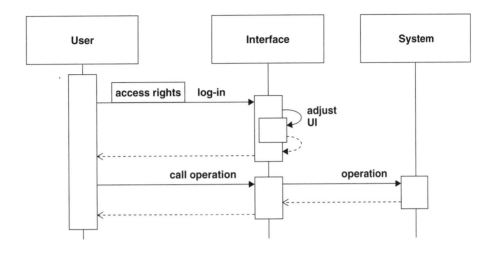

Implementation

To implement LIMITED ACCESS (312), several aspects need to be considered:

1. *Implement the association of access rights with users.* CHECK POINT (287) and SECURITY SESSION (297) are typical means of providing a user log-in and attaching their access rights. In the case of CHECK POINT (287) the interface can rely on the Check Point object to provide access to the set of enabled user interface elements. For further details about user identification and authentication, see Chapter 7, *Identification and Authentication (I&A)*. For the modeling and management of access rights, see Chapter 8, *Access Control Models*.

2. *Design the user interface and define the mapping of access rights to interface elements.* The issues surrounding the design of a good (graphical) user interface are far beyond the scope of this pattern. However, you should model your individual access rights close to the available user interface elements, so that management and checking of access rights for your application is straightforward. If your application requires complex rules to decide whether an option is valid for a user, evaluating these rules every time the interface is (re-) drawn can be too costly, so you should either use FULL ACCESS WITH ERRORS (305) in that case, or cache the results of such an evaluation, for example within the user's SECURITY SESSION (297). The latter approach is viable as long the user's rights will not change during a session.

A third way to optimize a LIMITED ACCESS (312) user interface is to provide an individual design for each role in ROLE-BASED ACCESS CONTROL (249). This works if your system only needs to support a few defined, stable and clearly-distinguished user roles. You can opt to design separate visual user interface layouts for each user role. However, you should rely on common layouts for functionality that is available across the different roles.

Regardless of the approach chosen, the interface builder is the component to implement the mapping of access rights to the UI.

3. *Decide how to present and implement accessible versus inaccessible interface elements.* Most UI toolkits already provide the Boolean attributes 'enabled/ disabled' or 'show/hide.' Either of these can be used to control the appearance of user interface elements that depend on the access rights of a user. Hiding is more appropriate for data elements that a user should not access, whereas disabling is better for operational elements such as buttons, menus, or menu items. If possible, you should refrain from creating your own visual appearance mechanism for enabling and disabling options, instead follow the mechanisms suggested by your GUI platform's guidelines, to avoid confusing your users.

For Web applications, rendering of interface elements mainly consists of string concatenation, so disabling an element often means rendering an empty string or an alternative to the active representation. Since such rendering is mainly sequential, the checks for permissions can be done on the fly during that sequential process.

4. *Take care of security issues in a distributed environment.* If the interface and the protected system are separate, for example as is the case with a Web application, then LIMITED ACCESS (312) can fall short in protecting the system. An attacker in the middle might trick the system into thinking that an access comes from the interface, where it already would have been checked, but instead is actually crafted by the attacker to force access without proper permission.

Even on a single machine on which your system consists of individual components, for example Windows COM components, just relying on the user interface to check every access is dangerous, because compromised parts of the system might access the components without encountering the user interface checks.

In those situations it is wise to combine LIMITED ACCESS (312) with the checks close to the functionality, as proposed by FULL ACCESS WITH ERRORS (305). For Web applications especially, it is crucial to re-check every request sent to the system for validity and permission before it is handled, even when the user interface already checked for parameters.

Variants

The opposite strategy to LIMITED ACCESS (312) is FULL ACCESS WITH ERRORS (305). While both approaches are proven and practical, it is often the case that in a concrete system you need to combine them. This may be either because both sets of forces apply, or because you need to re-check access rights within a called operation, for example when you cannot trust your limited access interface to ensure no invalid call is made.

The Yahoo! groups example shows both patterns applied together. Using FULL ACCESS WITH ERRORS (305), you see the complete menu of group features. However, a group without access rights for its regular members doesn't allow use of the File folder after it is selected.

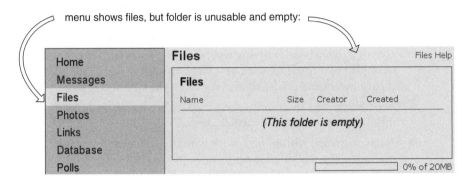

Known Uses

Most current operating systems' and applications' GUIs provide LIMITED ACCESS (312) with user- and context-specific menus and buttons that are enabled when usable and disabled when their use is impossible in the current context. For example, most word processors don't allow a file to be re-saved if it hasn't changed since the last save.

Firewalls implement LIMITED ACCESS (312), by restricting network traffic to the point at which only allowed network connections can be seen from the outside, all other network packets being silently dropped by the firewall.

Eclipse JDT, the Java development, environment shows only those refactorings, in a pop-up menu, that are applicable to the currently-selected source code portion. While this allows efficient use by experienced programmers, it makes it hard for novices to learn about all available automatic refactorings without studying Eclipse's documentation.

Unix' restricted shell /usr/lib/rsh[1] provides a user interface with limited access. Using the chroot command with a carefully-crafted restricted Unix environment can provide an even more restricted LIMITED ACCESS (312). The simplest, but insecure, variation of LIMITED ACCESS (312) in Unix is the hiding of files by starting their name

---

[1] Do not confuse with today's more popular remote shell, /usr/bin/rsh.

with a dot, making them invisible to the casual user through not being listed in ls commands without specific options.

Consequences

The following benefits may be expected from applying this pattern:

■ LIMITED ACCESS (312) disables access to restricted operations and data by providing no means by which the user can even try to access it.

■ Since the user can only access permitted data and operations, developers don't have to worry about verifying rights for every access. Note that in the case of a decoupled user interface such as a Web browser, this is careless, and re-checking of parameters and access rights is necessary on the server side.

■ Security checks can be simplified, as only the interface depends on it. The rest of the system can neglect further checks.

■ Users are guided within their work with the system and won't become confused or annoyed by unavailable options, or by the system barking error messages at them.

The following potential liabilities may arise from applying this pattern:

■ Users can become confused and frustrated when options appear and disappear. For example, if when viewing one set of data, an editing button is available, while when viewing another set of data, it disappears. A user might not be aware that a security issue is triggering the hiding of the option, but might assume the application is broken, or that there is something wrong with the data.

■ A graphical user interface built on the principle of LIMITED ACCESS (312) can look ugly and weird if it blanks out unavailable options and data without changing its layout. On the other hand, it might be completely confusing if the arrangement of UI elements changes whenever operations appear or disappear. To achieve stability in such cases, often icons, options and buttons are still displayed, but disabled and given a visual hint that they are unusable by reducing their contrast or coloring (graying them out).

■ Training and documentation must be tailored for different user groups, since the mode of operation and available options differ with their permissions. References to non-existent UI elements should be avoided, while all accessible ones need to be explained.

■ Retrofitting LIMITED ACCESS (312) into an existing system can be difficult, because data for limiting and enabling access, as well as code for doing so, could be spread throughout the system.

■ Relying solely on LIMITED ACCESS (312) for checking access rights at the front end of a system carries the danger of someone in the middle tricking a back end into performing operations without the front end having checked permissions. The security principle of Defence in Depth (see Section 15.1, *Security Principles and Security Patterns*) should be applied when an architecture (such as Web applications) is vulnerable in such a situation.

See Also

CHECK POINT (287) and SECURITY SESSION (297) should be considered for designing and implementing the user I&A and association of access rights.

ROLE-BASED ACCESS CONTROL (249) can be used to provide several pre-built incarnations of the user interface for the different user roles. This allows you to avoid the dynamic rendering of available options, with all its problems of layout automation.

Operating System Access Control

The superior man, when resting in safety, does not forget that danger may come. When in a state of security he does not forget the possibility of ruin. When all is orderly, he does not forget that disorder may come.

Confucius (551 BC–479 BC)

Operating systems are fundamental to the provision of security to computer systems. The operating system supports the execution of applications, and any security constraints defined at that level must be enforced by the operating system. A weak operating system would allow hackers access not only to data in the operating system files, but also data in database systems that use the services of the operating system. The operating system performs this function by protecting processes from each other and protecting the permanent data stored in its files [Sil03]. For this purpose, the operating system controls access to resources such as memory address spaces and I/O devices. The operating system isolates processes from each other, protects the permanent data stored in its files, and provides controlled access to shared resources. Most operating systems use the access matrix as security model (see Chapter 8). An access matrix defines which processes (or subjects in general) have what types of access to specific resources (resources are represented as objects in modern operating systems).

To apply this model, we need to make sure that subjects are authenticated before they perform any access, by using AUTHENTICATOR (323). Processes are the active units that perform computational work and use resources, and we need to control the rights given to each process when it is created, using CONTROLLED PROCESS CRE-ATOR (328), and to let processes execute in a controlled environment in which they cannot exceed their rights, using CONTROLLED EXECUTION ENVIRONMENT (346). We also need to define rights of access to new objects, using CONTROLLED OBJECT FACTORY (331), and to control access to objects at execution time, using CON-TROLLED OBJECT MONITOR (335). This latter pattern performs access control by in-tercepting requests and checking them for authorization.

This chapter was written by Eduardo B. Fernandez and is based on [Fer02] and [Fer03a]. John Sinibaldi was the coauthor of [Fer03a]. Markus Schumacher and Rick Dewar made valuable comments.

10.1   Authenticator

This pattern addresses the problem of how to verify that a subject is who it says it is. Use a SINGLE ACCESS POINT (279) to receive the interactions of a subject with the system and apply a protocol to verify the identity of the subject.

Example

Our system has legitimate users that use it to host their files. However, there is no way to make sure that a user who is logged in is a legitimate user. Users can impersonate others and gain illegal access to their files.

Context

Operating systems authenticate users when they first log in, and maybe again when they access specific resources. The operating system controls the creation of a session in response to the request by a subject, typically a user. The authenticated user, represented by processes running on its behalf, is then allowed to access resources according to their rights. Sensitive resource access may require additional process authentication. Processes in distributed operating systems also need to be authenticated when they attempt to access resources on external nodes.

Problem

A malicious attacker could try to impersonate a legitimate user to gain access to her resources. This could be particularly serious if the impersonated user has a high level of privilege. How can we prevent impostors from accessing our system?

The solution to this problem must resolve the following forces:

- There is a variety of users that may require different ways to authenticate them. We need to be able to handle all this variety, or we risk security exposures.

- We need to authenticate users in a reliable way. This means a robust protocol and a way to protect the results of authentication. Otherwise, users may skip authentication or illegally modify its results, exposing the system to security violations.

- There are trade-offs between security and cost—more secure systems are usually more expensive.

- If authentication needs to be performed frequently, performance may become an issue.

Solution

Use a SINGLE ACCESS POINT (279) to receive the interactions of a subject with the system, and apply a protocol to verify the identity of the subject. The protocol used may imply that the user inputs some known values, or may be more elaborate.

Structure

The figure below shows the class diagram for this pattern. A Subject, typically a user, requests access to system resources. The Authenticator receives this request and applies a protocol using some Authentication Information. If the authentication is successful, the Authenticator creates a Proof of Identity, which can be explicit, for example a token, or implicit.

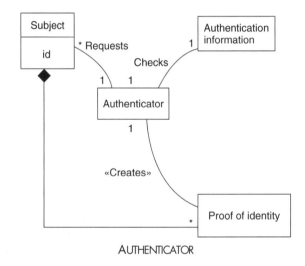

AUTHENTICATOR

Dynamics

The figure on page 326 shows the dynamics of the authentication process. A user requests access to the AUTHENTICATOR (323). The AUTHENTICATOR (323) applies some authentication protocol, verifies the information presented by the user, and as a result a proof of identity is created. The user is returned a handle for the proof of identity.

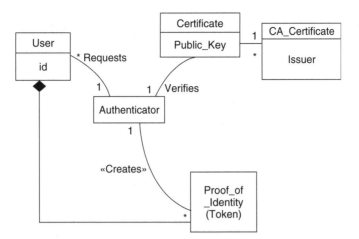

Variant of AUTHENTICATOR: PKI authentication

Implementation

Assuming a centralized system, we need to carry out the following tasks to implement the pattern:

- Define authentication requirements, considering the number of users, degree of security required, and so on—see I&A REQUIREMENTS (192)
- Select an authentication approach
- Build the list of registered users—the authentication information.

Example Resolved

We adopted the use of passwords for authenticating our users. While not a perfect solution, we can keep out most of the impostors.

Variants

Single Sign-On (SSO) is a process whereby a subject verifies its identity, after which the results of this verification can be used across several domains and for a given amount of time. The result of the authentication is an authentication token used to qualify all future accesses by the user.

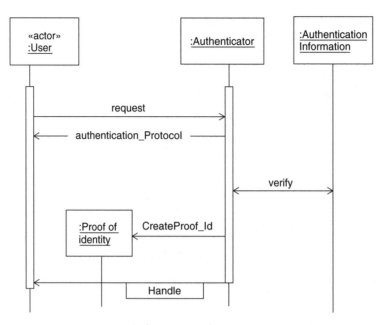

Authentication dynamics

PKI Authenticator. Public key cryptography is a common way to verify identity. This authentication can be described with a slight modification of the pattern in the first figure, as shown in the second figure above. An `Authenticator` class performs the authentication using a certificate that contains a public key from a certificating authority that is used to sign the certificate. The result of the authentication could be an authentication token used to qualify all future accesses by this user. In this case this is also a variant of SSO.

Known Uses

Most commercial operating systems use passwords to authenticate their users. RADIUS provides a centralized authentication service for network and distributed systems [Has02]. The SSL authentication protocol uses PKI for authentication. SAML, a Web Services standard for security, provides a way to implement an SSO architecture as one of its main uses [SAML].

Consequences

The following benefits may be expected from applying this pattern:

- Depending on the protocol and the authentication information used, we can handle any types of users and we can authenticate them in diverse ways.

- Since the authentication information is separated, we can store it in a protected area to which all subjects may have read-only access at most.
- We can use a variety of algorithms and protocols of different strength for authentication. The selection depends on the security and cost trade-offs.

  Three varieties include: something the user knows (such as passwords), something the user has (such as an identity card), something the user is (their biometrics), or where the user is (the terminal or node).
- Authentication can be performed in centralized or distributed environments.
- We can produce a proof of identity to be used in lieu of further authentication. This improves performance.

The following potential liabilities may arise from applying this pattern:

- The authentication process takes some time.
- The general complexity and cost of the system increases with the level of security.

See Also

DISTRIBUTED AUTHENTICATOR [Bro99] discusses an approach to authentication in distributed systems. SINGLE ACCESS POINT (279) (see Chapter 8) is an abstract pattern applied here: AUTHENTICATOR (323) is a concrete application of it. SINGLE SIGN ON is a variant implemented in many systems. REMOTE AUTHENTICATOR (and AUTHORIZER) [Fer03b] is intended for remote access to shared resources in a distributed system. Passwords are a specific authentication protocol—see PASSWORD DESIGN AND USE (217).

10.2 Controlled Process Creator

This pattern addresses how to define and grant appropriate access rights for a new process.

Example

Most operating systems create a process with the same rights as its parent. If a hacker can trick an operating system into creating a child of the supervisor process, this runs with all the rights of the supervisor.

Context

An operating system in which processes or threads need to be created according to application needs.

Problem

A user executes an application composed of several concurrent processes. Processes are usually created through system calls to the operating system [Sil03]. A process that needs to create a new process gets the operating system to create a child process that is given access to some resources. A computing system uses many processes or threads. Processes need to be created according to application needs, and the operating system itself is composed of processes. If processes are not controlled, they can interfere with each other and access data illegally. Their rights for resources should be carefully defined according to appropriate policies, for example 'need-to-know.'

The solution to this problem must resolve the following forces:

- There should be a convenient way to select a policy to define process' rights. Defining rights without a policy brings contradictory and non-systematic access restrictions that can be easily circumvented.

- A child process may need to impersonate its parent in specific actions, but this should be carefully controlled, otherwise a compromised child could leak information or destroy data.

- The number of child processes created by a process must be restricted, or process spawning could be user to carry out denial-of-service attacks.

- There are situations in which a process needs to act with more than its normal rights, for example to access data in a file to which it doesn't normally have access.

Solution

Because new processes are created through system calls or messages to the operating system, we have a chance to control the rights given to a new process. Typically, operating systems create a new process as a child process. We let the parent assign a specific set of rights to its children, which is more secure because a more precise control of rights is possible.

Structure

The figure below shows the class diagram for this pattern. The Controlled Process Creator is a part of the operating system in charge of creating processes. The Creation Request contains the access rights that the parent defines for the created child. These access rights must be a subset of the parent's access rights.

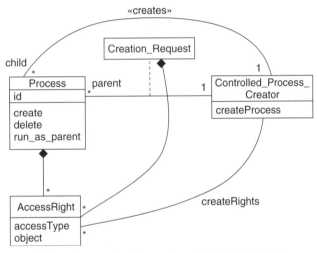

Class diagram for CONTROLLED PROCESS CREATOR

Dynamics

The figure on page 331 shows the dynamics of process creation. A process requests the creation of a new process. The access rights passed in the creation request is used to create the new access rights for the new process.

Implementation

For each required application of kernel threads, define their rights according to their intended function.

Example Resolved

There is now no automatic inheritance of rights in the creation of children processes, so creating a child process confers no advantage for a hacker.

Known Uses

In some hardened operating systems such as Hewlett Packard's Virtual Vault, a new set of rights must be defined for each child [HP].

Consequences

The following benefits may be expected from applying this pattern:

- The created process can receive rights according to required security policies.
- The number of children produced by a process can be controlled. This is useful to control denial of service attacks.
- The rights may include the parent's id, allowing the child to run with the rights of its parent.

The following potential liability may arise from applying this pattern:

- Explicit rights transfer takes more time than using a default transfer.

See Also

CONTROLLED EXECUTION ENVIRONMENT (346) could use this pattern to define the execution domain of new processes.

10.3 **Controlled Object Factory**

This pattern addresses how to specify the rights of processes with respect to a new object. When a process creates a new object through a factory (see FACTORY METHOD and ABSTRACT FACTORY [GoF95]), the request includes the features of the new object. These features include a list of rights to access the object.

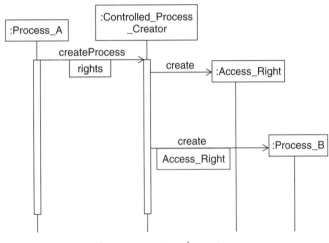

Process creation dynamics

Example

In many operating systems the creator of an object gets all possible rights to the object. Other operating systems apply predefined sets of rights: for example, in Unix all the members of a file owner's group may receive equal rights for a new file. These approaches may result in unnecessary rights being given to some users, violating the principle of least privileges.

Context

A computing system that needs to control access to its created objects because of their different degrees of sensitivity. Rights for these objects are defined by authorization rules or policies that are enforced when a process attempts to access an object.

Problem

In a computing environment, executing applications need to create objects for their work. Some objects are created at program initialization, while others are created dynamically during execution. The access rights of processes with respect to objects must be defined when these objects are created, or there may be opportunities for the processes to misuse them. Applications also need resources such as I/O devices and others that may come from resource pools: when these resources are allocated, the application must be given rights to them.

The solution to this problem must resolve the following forces:

- Applications create objects of many different types, but we need to handle them uniformly with respect to their access rights, otherwise it would be difficult to apply standard security policies.

- We need to allow objects in a resource pool to be allocated and have their rights set dynamically: not doing so would be too rigid.

- There may be specific policies that define who can access a new object, and we need to apply these when creating the rights for an object. This is a basic aspect of security.

Solution

Whenever a new object is created, define a list of subjects that can access it, and in what way.

Structure

The figure on page 333 shows the class diagram for the solution. When a `Process` creates a new object through a `Factory`, the `Creation_Request` includes the features of the new object. Among these features is a list of rights that define the access rights for a `Subject` to access the created `Object`. This implies that we need to intercept every access request: this is done by CONTROLLED OBJECT MONITOR (335).

Dynamics

The figure on page 334 shows the dynamics of object creation. A process creating an object through a FACTORY defines the rights for other subjects with respect to this object.

Implementation

Each object may have an associated access control list (ACL). This will list the rights each user has for the associated object. Each entry specifies the rights that any other

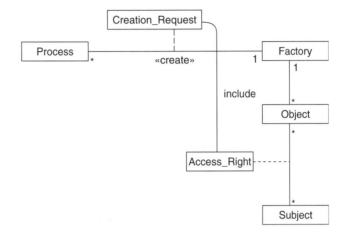

Class diagram for CONTROLLED OBJECT FACTORY

object within the system can have. In general, each right can be an 'allow' or a 'deny.' These are also known as Access Control Entries (ACE) in the Windows environment (see [Har01], [Mic00], and [Zac87]). The set of access rules is also known as the Access Control List (ACL) in Windows and most operating systems.

Capabilities are an alternative to an ACL. A capability corresponds to a row in an access matrix. This is in contrast to the ACL, which is associated with the object. The capability indicates to the secure object that the subject does indeed have the right to perform the operation. The capability may carry some authentication features in order to show that the object can trust the provided capability information. A global table can contain rows that represent capabilities for each authenticated user [And01], or the capability may be implemented as a lists for each user which indicates which object each user has access to. [Kin01]

Example Resolved

Our users can now be given only the rights to the created objects that they need. This prevents them from having too many (possibly unnecessary) object rights. Many misuses occur through processes having too many rights.

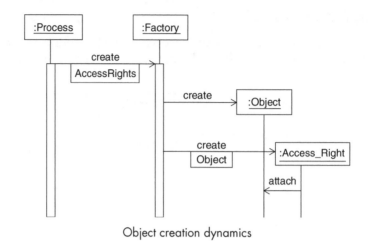

Object creation dynamics

Known Uses

The Win32 API allows a process to create objects with various `Create` system calls using a structure that contains access control information (DACL) passed as a reference. When the object is created, the access control information is associated with the object by the kernel. The kernel returns a handle to the caller to be used for access to the object.

Consequences

The following benefits may be expected from applying this pattern:

- There will be no objects that have default access rights because somebody forgot to define rights to access them
- It is possible to define access rights to an object based on its sensitivity
- Objects allocated from a resource pool can have rights attached to them dynamically
- The operating system can apply ownership policies: for example, the creator of an object may receive all possible rights to the objects it creates. The following potential liabilities may arise from applying this pattern:
- There is a process creation overhead
- It may not be clear what initial rights to define

See Also

BUILDER and other creation patterns [GoF95].

10.4 Controlled Object Monitor

This pattern addresses how to control access by a process to an object. Use a reference monitor to intercept access requests from processes. The reference monitor checks whether the process has the requested type of access to the object.

Example

Our operating system does not check all user requests to access resources such as files or memory areas. A hacker discovered that some accesses are not checked, and was able to steal customer information from our files. He also left a program that randomly overwrites memory areas and produces serious disruption to the other users.

Context

An operating system that consists of many users, objects that may contain sensitive data, and where we need to have controlled access to resources.

Problem

When objects are created we define the rights processes have to them. These authorization rules or policies must be enforced when a process attempts to access an object.

The solution to this problem must resolve the following forces:

■ There may be many objects with different access restrictions defined by authorization rules: we need to enforce these restrictions when a process attempts to access an object

■ We need to control different types of access, or the object may be misused

Solution

Use a REFERENCE MONITOR (256) to intercept access requests from processes. The REFERENCE MONITOR (256) checks whether the process has the requested type of access to the object according to some access rule.

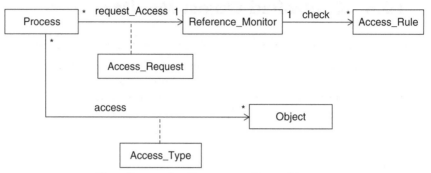

Class diagram for CONTROLLED OBJECT MONITOR

Structure

The figure above shows the class diagram for this pattern. This is a specific implementation of REFERENCE MONITOR (256). The modification shows how the system associates the rules to the secure object in question.

Dynamics

The next figure shows the dynamics of secure subject access to a secure object. Here the request is sent to the REFERENCE MONITOR (256) where it checks the Access Rules. If the access is allowed, it is performed and result returned to the subject. Note that here, a handle or ticket is returned to the Subject so that future access to the secure object can be directly performed without additional checking.

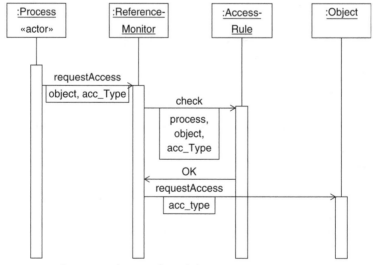

Sequence diagram for validating an access request

Example Resolved

A REFERENCE MONITOR (256) mediates all requests. There are now no unchecked requests, so a hacker cannot get access to unauthorized files or memory areas.

Known Uses

Windows NT. The Windows NT security subsystem provides security using the patterns described here. It has the following three components (see [Har01], [Kel97], and [Mic00]):

- Local Security Authority
- Security Account Manager
- Security Reference Monitor

The Local Security Authority (LSA) and Security Account Manager (SAM) work together to authenticate the user and create the user's access token. The security reference monitor runs in kernel mode and is responsible for the enforcement of access validation. When an access to an object is requested, a comparison is made between the file's security descriptor and the Secure ID (SID) information stored in the user's access token. The security descriptor is made up of Access Control Entries (ACE's) included in the object's Access Control List (ACL). When an object has an ACL the SRM checks each ACE in the ACL to determine if access is to be granted. After the Security Reference Monitor (SRM) grants access to the object, further access checks are not needed, as a handle to the object that allows further access is returned the first time.

Types of object permissions are no access, read, change, full control, and special access. For directory access, the following are added: list, add, and read.

Windows use the concept of a handle for access to protected objects within the system. Each object has a Security Descriptor (SD) that contains a Discretionary Access Control List (DACL) for the object. Each also process has a security token that contains an SID which identifies the process. This is used by the kernel to determine whether access is allowed. The ACL contains Access Control Entries (ACE's) that indicate what access is allowed for a particular process SID. The kernel scans the ACL for the rights corresponding to the requested access.

A process requests access to the object when it asks for a handle using, for example, a call to `CreateFile()`, which is used both to create a new file or open an existing file. When the file is created, a pointer to an SD is passed as a parameter. When an existing file is opened, the request parameters, in addition to the file handle, contain the desired access, such as `GENERIC_READ`. If the process has the desired rights for the access, the request succeeds and an access handle is returned, so that different handles to the same object may have different accesses [Har01].

Once the handle is obtained, additional access to read a file will not require further authorization. The handle may also be passed to another trusted function for further processing.

Java 1.2 Security. The Java security subsystem provides security using the patterns described here. The Java Access Controller builds access permissions based on permission and policy. It has a `checkPermission` method that determines the codesource object of each calling method and uses the current `Policy` object to determine the permission objects associated with it. Note that the `checkPermission` method will traverse the call stack to determine the access of all calling methods in the stack. The `java.policy` file is used by the security manager that contains the grant statements for each codesource.

Consequences

The following benefits may be expected from applying this pattern:

■ Each access request can be intercepted and accepted or rejected depending on the authorization rules.

■ The access rules can implement an access matrix defining different types of access for each subject. We can add content-dependent rules if required.

The following potential liabilities may arise from applying this pattern:

■ There is a need to protect the authorization rules. However, the same mechanism that protects resources can also protect the rules.

■ There is an overhead involved in controlling each access. This is specially heavy for content-dependent rules. However, some accesses may be compiled for efficiency.

See Also

The REFERENCE MONITOR (256) is the pattern from which this pattern is derived.

10.5 Controlled Virtual Address Space

This pattern addresses how to control access by processes to specific areas of their virtual address space (VAS) according to a set of predefined access types. Divide the VAS into segments that correspond to logical units in the programs. Use special words (descriptors) to represent access rights for these segments.

Example

Our operating system improved by using a reference monitor. However, hackers discovered that the unit of access control to memory was coarse. By taking advantage of the lack of precision in controlling access they were able to access other processes' areas.

Context

Multiprogramming systems with a variety of users. Processes executing on behalf of these users must be able to share memory areas in a controlled way. Each process runs in its own address space. The total VAS at a given moment includes the union of the VASs of the individual processes, including user and system processes. Typical allowed accesses are read, write, and execute, although finer typing is possible.

Problem

Processes must be controlled when accessing memory, otherwise they could overwrite each other's memory areas or gain access to private information. While relatively small amounts of data can be directly compromised, illegal access to system areas could allow a process to force a higher execution privilege level and thus access files and other resources.

The solution to this problem must resolve the following forces:

- There is a need for a variety of access rights for each separate logical unit of VAS (segment). In this way security and controlled sharing are possible.
- There is a variety of virtual memory address space structures: some systems use a set of separate address spaces, others a single-level address space. Further, the VAS may be split between the users and the operating system. We would like to control access to all of these types in a uniform manner.

- For any approach to be efficient, hardware assistance is necessary. This implies that an implementation of the solution will require a specific hardware architecture. However, the generic solution must be hardware-independent.

Solution

Divide the VAS into segments that correspond to logical units in the programs. Use special words (descriptors) to indicate access rights that show the starting address of the accessible segment, the limit of the accessible segment, and the type of access permitted (read, write, execute).

Structure

The figure below shows a class diagram for the solution. A process (the Process class) must have a descriptor (the Descriptor class) to access segments in the VAS.

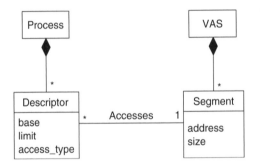

Class diagram for CONTROLLED VIRTUAL ADDRESS SPACE

Implementation

Some implementation aspects include:

- The limit check when accessing an address must be done by the instruction microcode or the overhead would not be acceptable. This check is part of an instance of REFERENCE MONITOR (256)—see Chapter 8.

- The same idea applies to purely paging systems, except that the limit in the descriptor is defined by the page size. In paged systems pages do not correspond to logical units and cannot perform a fine security control.

■ There are two basic ways to implement this pattern:

- Property descriptor systems. The descriptors are loaded at process creation by the operating system. The descriptors are handled through special registers and disappear at the end of execution.

- Capability systems. A special trusted portion of the operating system distributes capabilities to programs. Programs own these capabilities. To use them, the operating system loads them into special registers or memory segments.

In both cases, access to files is derived from their ACLs.

Example Resolved

Descriptors can control areas of memory of any size. A process without a descriptor for an area cannot access it. If sharing is required, several processes can have a descriptor with the same addresses but with different access rights.

Known Uses

The Plessey 250 [Ham73], Multics [Gra68], IBM S/38, IBM S/6000, Intel X86 [Chi84], and Intel Pentium use some type of descriptors for memory access control. The operating systems in these machines must use this approach for memory management. Specific uses include the Choices operating system [Rus89] and AIX [Cam90].

Consequences

The following benefits may be expected from applying this pattern:

■ The pattern provides the required segment protection, because a process cannot access a segment without a descriptor for it. Two processes with descriptors with the same memory address base–limit pair[1] can conveniently share a segment.

■ The pattern applies to any type of virtual address space: single, segregated, or split.

■ If all resources are mapped to the virtual address space, the pattern can control access to any type of resource, including files.

---

[1] This relates to a simple method of enforcing memory protection by adding two registers to the CPU, a base address and a size limit, which together demarcate a range of memory to which valid references can be made. References outside that range trigger a memory exception. This works well as long as all memory is allocated contiguously, but non-contiguous memory is harder to protect, as is sharing memory between more than two processes.

The following potential liabilities may arise from applying this pattern:

- Segmentation makes storage allocation inefficient because of external fragmentation [Sil03]. In most systems segments are paged for convenient allocation.
- Hardware support is needed, which puts an extra requirement on this solution.
- In systems that use multiple separate address spaces, it is necessary to add an extra identifier to the descriptor registers to indicate the address space number.

See Also

This pattern is a direct application of AUTHORIZATION (245) to the processes' address space.

10.6 Execution Domain

Unauthorized processes could destroy or modify information in files or databases, with obvious results, or could interfere with the execution of other processes. Therefore, define an execution environment for processes, indicating explicitly all the resources that a process can use during its execution, as well as the type of access to the resources.

Example

In our operating system we know now how to assign access rights to processes and how to enforce these rights at execution time. However, a process may have different functions and in each functional mode it may need different rights. For example, if a process needs to read some files to collect some data, this should happen only at the specific time of access to the file, otherwise a hacker could take advantage of the extra rights to perform illegal accesses.

Context

A process executes on behalf of a user, group, or role (a subject). A process must have access rights to use the resources defined for its subject during execution. The set of access rights given to a process define its execution domain. At times the process may also need to enter other domains to perform its work: for example, for example, to extract data from a file in another user's domain. Frequently, users structure their domains as a hierarchical tree of domains with one root domain.

Problem

Restricting a process to a specific set of resources is a basic step towards controlling malicious behavior. Otherwise, unauthorized processes could destroy or modify information in files or databases, with obvious results, or could interfere with the execution of other processes.

The solution to this problem must resolve the following forces:

- There is a need to restrict the actions of a process during its execution; otherwise it could perform illegal actions.
- Resources typically include memory and I/O devices, but can also be system data structures and special instructions. Although resources are heterogeneous, we want to treat them uniformly.

- A process needs the flexibility to create multiple domains and to enter inner domains for specific purposes.
- There should be no restrictions on how to implement the domain.

Solution

Attach a set of descriptors to the process that represent the rights of the process. Collect them into an execution domain. Execution domains can be nested.

Structure

In the figure below, the Domain class represents domains, and, in conjunction with COMPOSITE, it describes nested domains. The operation enter() in Domain lets a process enter a new domain. A domain includes a set of descriptors that define rights for resources.

Example Resolved

Using the concept of execution domain, we have a set of well-defined environments with explicit rights. A process can change domains according to its tasks and acquire only the needed rights in each domain.

Known Uses

The concept of domains comes from Multics [Gra68]. Segments or pages (as in EROS [Sha02]) are structured as tree directories. The Plessey 250 and the IBM S/6000 running AIX [Cam90] are good examples of the use of this pattern. The Java Virtual Machine defines restricted execution environments in a similar way [Oak01].

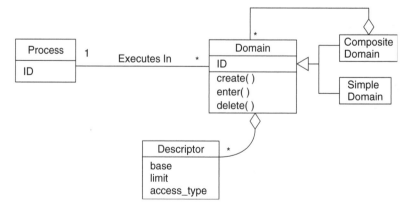

Class diagram for EXECUTION DOMAIN

Consequences

The following benefits may be expected from applying this pattern:

- The pattern lets users apply the principle of least privilege to processes— they can be given only the rights they need to perform their functions.
- It could be applied to describe access to any type of resource if the resource is mapped to a specific memory address.
- Processes may have several execution domains, either peer or nested.
- The model does not restrict the implementation of domains. A domain could be represented in many ways. For example, the Plessey 250, IBM S/38, and IBM S/6000 use capabilities. The Intel X86 and Pentium series and their corresponding operating systems use descriptors for memory access control.
- One can define special domains with predefined rights or types of rights. For example, Multics and the Intel X86 series use Protection Rings, in which each ring is assigned to a type of program, for example Supervisor, Utilities, User programs, and External programs. The rings are hierarchically structured based on their level of trust. Descriptors are used to cross rings in program calls.
- As shown, the descriptors refer to VAS segments, which is the most usual implementation. However, they could indicate resources not mapped to memory.

The following potential liabilities may arise from applying this pattern:

- Extra complexity—special hardware is needed to handle descriptors and set up domains.
- Performance overhead in setting up domains and in entering and leaving domains. Because of this, some operating systems for Intel processors use only two rings, improving performance but reducing security.
- Setting up the execution domain is implementation-dependent. In descriptor systems the operating system creates a descriptor segment with the required descriptors. In capability systems the descriptors are part of the process code and are enabled during execution.

See Also

CONTROLLED PROCESS CREATOR (328) and CONTROLLED OBJECT MONITOR (335) work in conjunction with this pattern.

10.7   Controlled Execution Environment

If a process execution environment is uncontrolled, processes can scavenge information by searching memory and accessing the disk drives where files reside. They might also take control of the operating system itself, in which case they have access to everything. Use AUTHORIZATION (245) to define the rights of a subject. From these rights we can set up the rights of processes running on behalf of the subject. Process requests are validated by CONTROLLED OBJECT MONITOR (335) or REFERENCE MONITOR (256) respectively.

Example

Jim the hacker discovers that the customer's files have authorizations and cannot be accessed directly, so he tries another approach. He realizes that processes are not given only the rights of their owners, but also have rights with which they can access memory and other resources belonging to other users. He systematically searches areas of memory and I/O devices being used by other processes until he can scavenge a few credit card numbers that he can use in his illicit activities.

Context

A process executes on behalf of a user or role (a subject). A process must have access rights to use these resources during execution. The set of access rights given to a process define its execution domain. Processes must be able to share resources in a controlled way. The rights of the process are derived from the rights of its invoker.

Problem

Even if direct access to files is restricted, users can do 'tunneling,' attacking them through a lower level. If the process execution environment is uncontrolled, processes can scavenge information by searching memory and accessing disk drives. They might also take control of the operating system itself, in which case they have access to everything.

The solution to this problem must resolve the following forces:

- We need to constrain the execution of processes and restrict them to use only resources that have been authorized based on the rights of the activator of the process.
- Subjects can be users, roles, or groups. We want to deal with them uniformly.

■ Resources typically include memory and I/O devices, but can also be files and special instructions. We want to consider them in a uniform way.

■ A subject may need to activate several processes, and a process may need to create multiple domains. Execution domains may need to be nested. We want flexibility for our processes.

■ Typically, only a subset of a subject's rights needs to be used in a specific execution. We need to provide to a process only the rights it needs during its execution (on the principle of least privileges).

■ The solution should put no constraints on implementation.

Solution

Use the AUTHORIZATION (245) pattern to define the rights of a subject. From these rights, we can set up the rights of processes running on behalf of the subject. Process requests are validated by CONTROLLED OBJECT MONITOR (335) or REFERENCE MONITOR (256) respectively.

Structure

The figure on page 348 shows the UML class diagram of CONTROLLED EXECUTION ENVIRONMENT (346). This model combines AUTHORIZATION (245), EXECUTION DOMAIN (343), and REFERENCE MONITOR (256) to let processes operate in an environment with controlled actions based on the rights of their invoker. Process execution follows EXECUTION DOMAIN (343)—as a process executes it creates one or more domains. Domains can be recursively composed. The descriptors used in the process' domains are a subset of the authorizations that the subject has for some `Protection-Objects` (defined by an instance of AUTHORIZATION (245)). `ProtectionObject` is a superclass of the abstract `Resource` class, and `ConcreteResource` defines a specific resource. Process requests go through a `ReferenceMonitor` that can check the domain descriptors for compliance.

Dynamics

The figure on page 348 shows a sequence diagram representing the use of a right after entering a domain. Here x denotes a segment requested by the process. An instance of REFERENCE MONITOR (256) controls the process requests. This diagram assumes that the descriptors of the domain have been previously set up.

Example Resolved

A new operating system was installed, with mechanisms to make processes operate with the rights of their activator. Jim does not have access to customer files, which makes his processes also unable to access these files. Now he cannot scavenge in other users' areas, so his illicit actions are thwarted.

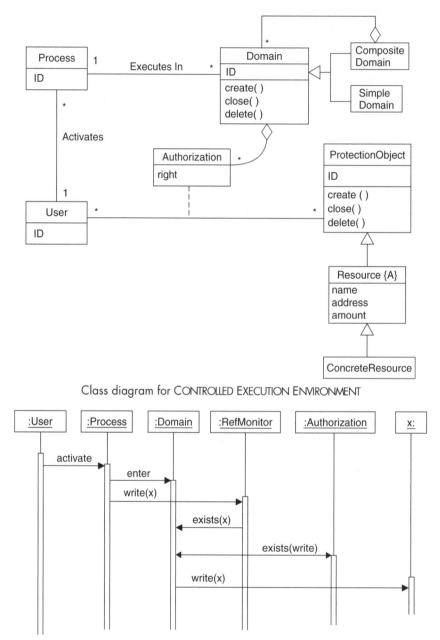

Class diagram for CONTROLLED EXECUTION ENVIRONMENT

Sequence diagram for entering a domain and using a right in that domain

Known Uses

The IBM S/38, the IBM S/6000 running AIX, the Plessey 250 [Ham73], and EROS [Sha02] have applied this pattern using capabilities. Property descriptor systems such as the Intel architectures may use this approach although their operating systems not always do so.

Consequences

The following benefits may be expected from applying this pattern:

- We can apply the principle of least privileges to processes based on the rights of their activators. This also provides accountability.
- It can be applied to any type of resource.
- Subjects may activate any number of processes, and processes may have several execution domains.
- The same structure can also provide fault tolerance [Ham73].
- Execution domains are defined according to DOMAIN, and may include any subset of the subject's rights.

The following potential liabilities may arise from applying this pattern:

- Some extra complexity and performance overhead may be required.
- It can be dependent on the hardware architecture.

See Also

This pattern uses AUTHORIZATION (245), EXECUTION DOMAIN (343), and REFERENCE MONITOR (256). CONTROLLED VIRTUAL ADDRESS SPACE (339) pattern may be indirectly used by EXECUTION DOMAIN (343).

10.8 File Authorization

This pattern describes how to control access to files in an operating system. Authorized users are the only ones that can use a file in specific ways. Apply AUTHORIZATION (245) to describe access to files by subjects. The protection object is now a file component that may be a directory or a file.

Example

Jim is an application programmer in a bank. He has a user account and some files in the bank's operating system. He realizes that the same system also stores files with customer data. These files have no authorization controls. Jim reads several of these files and finds customer information such as SSNs and credit card numbers. He uses this information to charge some items bought at mail-order shops.

Context

The users of operating systems need to use files to store permanent information. These files can be accessed by different users from different workstations, and access to the files must be restricted to authorized users who can use them in specific ways. Because of the needs of the organization, some (or all) of the files must be shared by these subjects. Use cases for a file system include creation and deletion of files, opening and closing of files, reading and writing files, copying files, and so on. A subject has a home directory for each authorized workstation, but the same home directory can be shared among several workstations or among several subjects. The home directory is used to search the files for which a subject has rights. Files are organized using directories, usually in a tree-like structure of directories and files. This facilitates the search for specific files.

Problem

Files may contain valuable information and access to them must be controlled carefully. In several recent attacks, hackers obtained lists of credit card numbers by accessing customer data illegally. Because files need to be shared, security becomes harder to enforce.

The solution to this problem must resolve the following forces:

- There may be different types of subjects, for example users, roles, and groups. The rights for users in groups or roles are derived from the group or role rights (they are implicit rights). Groups of groups are possible, which makes deducing access rights even harder. All these subjects must be handled uniformly.

- Subjects may be authorized to access files or directories, and to exercise their file rights from specific workstations. To prevent illegal actions, we may need ways to apply these two types of authorization.
- Each operating system implements file systems in a different way. We need to abstract implementation details.
- Not all operating systems use workstations, groups, or roles. We need a modular system in which features not used can be cut easily from the model.

Solution

We apply AUTHORIZATION (245) first to describe access to files by subjects. Typically, file systems use Access Control Lists that are sets of authorizations. The protection object is now a file system component that may be a directory or a file. To reflect the fact that files may be accessed only from some workstations, we use AUTHORIZATION (245) again with the same subject and with workstations as protection objects. The tree structure of files and directories can be conveniently described by applying COMPOSITE [GoF95].

Structure

The figure below combines two versions of AUTHORIZATION (245) with COMPOSITE. File access is an extension of AUTHORIZATION (245) 1 by replacing `ProtectionObject`

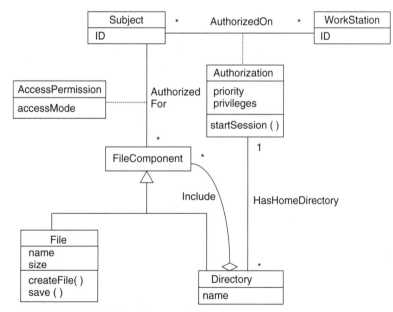

Class diagram for FILE AUTHORIZATION

by `FileComponent` and `Right` by `AccessControlListEntry` (ACLE). Workstation access is defined by a similar application of AUTHORIZATION (245).

Dynamics

The next figure shows the opening and writing of a file. A user actor opens the file, the directory locates it, and when found, opens it. Opening results in the file access permission being set up for future reference. When the user later tries to write to the file, their rights to write the file are checked and the write operation proceeds if authorized.

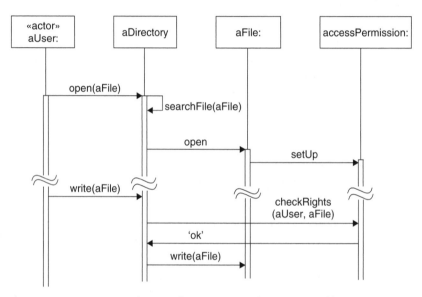

Sequence diagram for opening and writing to a file

Implementation

Typically directories are organized in a tree or directed graph structure [Sil03]. A file control block (FCB) describes the characteristics of each file, including its access permissions.

Example Resolved

A new operating system is installed that has authorization controls for its files. Now a need-to-know policy is set up in which only users that need access to customer files are given such access. This is the end of Jim's illicit activities.

Known Uses

This file system pattern can be found in most current operating systems such as Windows, Unix, and Linux. Not all of these systems uses all the concepts of the pattern.

Consequences

The following benefits may be expected from applying this pattern:

- The subjects can be users, roles, and groups by proper specialization of the Subject class. Roles and groups can be structured recursively [FP01]—that is, there can be role and group hierarchies that permit more flexibility in the assignment of rights.

- The protection objects can be single files, directories, or recursive structures of directories and files.

- Most operating systems use read/write/execute as access types, but higher-level types of access are possible. For example, a file representing students in a university could be accessed with commands such as list, order alphabetically, and so on.

- Implied authorization is possible: for example, access to a directory may imply a similar type of access to all the files in the directory [Fer94]. This approach allows an administrator to write fewer authorization rules, because some access rights can be deduced from others.

- Workstation access is also controlled and workstations can be homes for directories.

- This is a conceptual model that doesn't restrict implementation approaches.

- Workstation authorization is separated from file authorization, and systems that do not need workstation authorization can just ignore the relevant classes.

- In some operating systems, for example Inferno [Rau97], all resources are represented as files. Other systems represent resources by objects with ACLs. This means that this pattern could be used to control all the resources of the operating system.

The following potential liabilities may arise from applying this pattern:

- Implementations of the pattern are not forced to follow the access matrix model. For example, Unix uses a pseudo-access matrix that is not appropriate for applying the need-to-know policy. However, constraints can be added to the pattern to force all the instances of the pattern to conform to an access matrix model.

- Typically, access permissions are implemented as Access Control Lists (ACLs).

■ [Gol99] and [Sil03]. These are data structures associated with a file in which each entry defines a subject that can access the file and its permitted access modes. The pattern models the entries of the ACLs but not the fact that they are associated with the file components.

Other aspects of using this pattern include:

■ Some systems use the concept of Owner, who has all rights on the files they create. The Owner in this model corresponds to a special type of subject. When roles are used, there are no owners and when groups are used, ownership is not inherited in subgroups.

■ In some systems, files are mapped to the virtual memory address space. The pattern still applies to this case, although a more uniform solution is then possible (see CONTROLLED VIRTUAL ADDRESS SPACE (339)).

■ In some systems, the directory is not strictly a tree, because it is possible to have links between files in different subtrees [Sil03]. Modeling this case would require adding some associations to the model shown in the figure AUTHENTICATOR (324).

See Also

This pattern uses AUTHORIZATION (245). If roles are used, ROLE-BASED ACCESS CONTROL (249) is also relevant. The file structure uses COMPOSITE [GoF95]. It can use CONTROLLED EXECUTION ENVIRONMENT (346) for implementation.

CHAPTER

11

Accounting

Distrust and caution are the parents of security.

Benjamin Franklin

Events are groups of operational activities that may occur on a cyclic basis, on a daily or weekly basis, or may occur sporadically. Security events are violations that occur during operational activities. There is a need for decision makers to be aware of security events that occur involving their assets. This need is addressed by security accounting.

The function of security accounting is to track security-related actions or events, such as damage to property, attempts at unauthorized database access, or transmission of a computer virus, and provide information about those events. The information provided includes identifying those who participated in the events, so that they may be held accountable. The primary security property supported by security accounting is accountability.

How do you determine what is a security event? In many cases, a security event is clearly definable as a violation or attempted violation, such as breaking a window or a lock on the door of a building, transmitting a computer virus through a firewall, or obtaining unauthorized access to a sensitive asset. In other cases, events that are not in themselves violations must be recorded or tracked to be able to detect potential future violations. A good example of this is non-repudiation. A perfectly valid transaction that occurs today is recorded so that we can detect at some future time if one of the parties to the transaction denies that they participated. In general, it is easier to define a security event than to detect whether a security event has occurred. Security accounting is a service area that performs four functions:

- Capture: acquire data about a security event
- Store: hold data about an event
- Review: discern information from the data
- Report: communicate information about an event

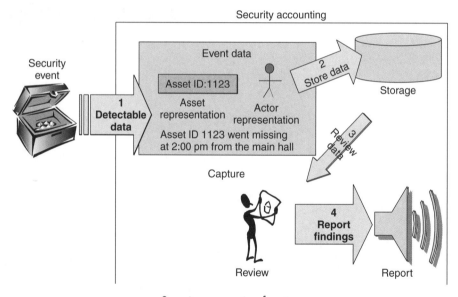

Security accounting functions

The term *audit* is sometimes used informally to encompass these four functions. In this chapter we use the more formal definition of audit, which is limited to review and analysis of captured information after the fact.

The figure illustrates the basic security accounting service in terms of the four functions and their typical sequence. An event occurs and accounting captures detectable data from the event (1), makes representations of the event, actors, and assets (2), attempts to identify the who, what, when, where, why, and how of the event (3), and reports on the findings (4). The representation can be stored for review at a later time. The review mechanism is active. It scrutinizes the representation, and the report mechanism makes the accounting users aware of the security relevance of the event, along with any other information that it can give. A key point to understand is that accounting works with the *representations* of events, not the events themselves. Any link that is established is between representations of actors and events, and not the physical actor and events.

The *capture function* is responsible for acquiring detectable data from an event and providing information related to the who, what, when, where, why, and how of an event. For some security events, the capture function cannot determine the actual values of these elements directly, but it may be able to provide information that the review function can use to identify the actual values. Attempts to capture detectable data related to security events should focus on trying to retrieve the following pieces of information:

- Who (what actors) were involved in the event? In many cases an actor is a human, but an actor may also be elements such as the weather or a software program. Sensors provide a useful example of security accounting capture mechanisms. Sensors are used to detect when activities are occurring.

- What assets were affected during the event? Assets may include elements such as jewels, secret documents, or employees.

- When did the event occur? Date and time of occurrence may be extremely important depending on the data's later use. Sufficient granularity is needed, in some cases to the nearest second or even fraction of a second.

- Where did the event occur? This piece of information is often overlooked. Depending on the situation, location might be geographic, or a network location such as the IP addresses of system nodes where an event occurred.

- Why did the event occur? While motivation is usually not information captured directly, the association between a security event and other events occurring at the same time or in the same location may support added insights to support later audit services.

- How did the event occur? As with the motivation issue, all the particulars of how an event occurred are seldom accessible to the capture process. However, links to other events that preceded or succeeded the event of interest could also support later audit services.

The *storage mechanisms* keep and hold the representations that the capture mechanism(s) produce, so that the representations may be used at a later date. There are many ways to store information, such as files, databases, tapes, disks and memory—either computer or human. Storing security event captured information is useful, because it allows for repeated scrutiny of events to facilitate the discovery of additional security relevant information.

Lengths of time to retain event information can vary greatly, from a very brief time to years or even decades. This can have a significant effect on storage requirements, especially when coupled with amount of data captured. If data is only captured for specific security events, the amount of data is much less than if general logs of all routine activities need to be captured. Since we often do not know when a security event occurs until after the fact, logging all activities—not just security-related ones—is typically required to support later auditing. This is especially true of computer and network activities.

The *review mechanism* supports analysis of the internal representation created by the capture mechanism and, usually but not always, stored by the store mechanism. The review mechanism attempts to establish relationships between the who, what, when, where, why, and how of the event. The review mechanism seeks to accurately describe the event by:

- Verifying the accuracy of what was captured
- Discerning facts by examining what was captured

During this analysis, the review function attempts to assert one or more of the following three types of links:

- Actor–event link: this establishes a relationship between an actor and some event, and determines the role of the actor in the event.
- Event–asset link: this establishes a relationship between an event and some asset, and that the event was the cause of the effect on the asset.
- Actor–event–asset link: this builds on the previous links to establish a relationship between an actor, an event, and an asset. The review mechanism provides some degree of confidence that the actor was present or caused a change in the asset's state.

Two examples of security accounting review mechanisms are audit and intrusion detection system (IDS) analysis (including process signature analysis). Audit is the review of events stored in logs, sometimes called *audit logs* or *audit trails*, to determine inadequacies during operation or non-compliance with policy. Audit specifically scrutinizes information for security relevance.

There are some cases in which reviews happen fairly quickly, without storing the captured information outside of current memory. In the case of IDS analysis mechanisms, the goal is quickly to determine the semantic content of data captured on the front end of an IDS capture mechanism. For example, an IDS detects that a new program has started and is beginning to delete files in a directory. This analysis may take a few seconds to determine whether the program is behaving appropriately.

The *report mechanism* takes information from the review mechanism and delivers it to an accounting user. The user can be human or software. The delivery can be automatic, or initiated by a request from the user. A report can be in the form of a written report, briefing, formatted message, an audible alarm or some other form that is intended to get the attention of someone/something so that corrective actions can take place.

Two examples of security accounting report mechanisms are alerts and analysis reports. An alert is an automatically-generated signal used to call the attention of a user to an event. Examples are fixed-formatted messages, electronically-triggered phone calls to a pager, and visual or audible signals. An analysis report can be generated from stored captured events. Typically a user's request for a report first invokes the review mechanism to extract and analyze requested event types, then a report mechanism to present the review results to the user.

There is a wide variety of contexts in which security accounting can be used to accomplish a task. This context, together with other factors, will shape the designs of security accounting services. The accounting mechanisms (capture, store, review and report) have constraints on their functionality, depending on how they are being used:

- Only events that relay information that is usable directly or indirectly by the review mechanism should be captured.

- Capture mechanism may need to provide the ability selectively to include different information threads, depending on the security status of the organization.

- The storage mechanism needs consideration over the term of storage. When appropriate, long-term repositories should be established for retaining accounting information.

- The storage mechanism must provide flexible capabilities that are usable by the review and report mechanisms.

- When review must occur immediately, capabilities that can support near real-time or real-time must be considered.

- The report mechanism may require the ability to report or send alerts immediately.

- The report mechanism should be flexible enough to enable human reviewers to create their own reports dynamically.

The patterns in this chapter were written by a team at the MITRE Corporation consisting of Jody Heaney, Duane Hybertson, Susan Chapin, Ann Reedy, and Malcolm Kirwan Jr. Malcolm Kirwan and Duane Hybertson wrote the introductory material for the chapter, and Duane Hybertson integrated the material into the chapter. Peter Sommerlad provided shepherding comments for the MITRE patterns. Markus Schumacher provided comments on integrating the material into the chapter.

11.1 Security Accounting Requirements

A security accounting service must satisfy a set of requirements for both the service and the quality of service. The function of security accounting is to track security-related actions or events, such as damage to property, attempts at unauthorized database access, or transmission of a computer virus, and provide information about those actions. While each situation that calls for security accounting is unique, there are common generic requirements that apply to all security accounting situations. This pattern provides a common generic set of security accounting requirements. The pattern also helps you apply the general requirements to your specific situation, and helps you to determine the relative importance of conflicting requirements.

Example

Gemstones within a museum are objects used in archeological research. They are also cleaned, transported and handled by several authorized personnel. The museum is interested in protecting museum assets from theft, damage or any mishandling. The museum is serious about assigning responsibility for any asset compromise or attempts to compromise assets. The museum needs to identify the requirements for the key components of a security accounting service that will help them protect their valuable gems and help assign responsibility for attempts to compromise their assets.

Based on the results of applying ENTERPRISE SECURITY SERVICES (161), Samuel the museum system engineer understands that the museum needs accountability of actions and events when the gems are transported or handled, and accountability of actions on the information about the gems, which is stored in a database. The museum needs to be able to assign responsibility for any asset compromise or attempts to compromise assets. For example, the museum needs to know who is responsible for transporting a gem. When information about a gem, such as its current location or its recorded carat weight, is entered or modified, the museum needs to know who made the addition or change. But Samuel also understands that the need to track and account for these actions and events must be balanced with the need for privacy and ease of operations. Therefore, Samuel needs to specify a balanced set of requirements for security accounting and the relative importance of those requirements, as a means of driving and evaluating an appropriate security accounting service for the museum. How can Samuel define such a set of requirements?

Context

The planned uses of security accounting are understood, for example, from applying ENTERPRISE SECURITY SERVICES (161). Asset types with a need for security accounting services are known, and the general types of actors that are to be held accountable are known. Actor types can include humans, software, business or automated processes, or information systems. Actors can be internal to an organization, such as an employee, or external, such as a supplier or customer. Asset types include both physical and information assets. The degree of confidence needed for the security accounting services by general asset types is known in relative terms. For example, a museum needs a very high degree of confidence in knowing who broke into the museum and stole a valuable gem, but it needs a lower degree of confidence in knowing who defaced the outside of the museum building.

Problem

Security accounting is an activity that takes in the detectable data from an event and provides some security-relevant information about that event to a human. A basic accounting sequence is completed when security-relevant information associated with an event of interest is provided to the accounting user. You need a clear set of requirements to ensure that the strategy employed for a security accounting system actually satisfies the needs of the organization or system. Requirements for security accounting often conflict with each other, and trade-offs between them are often necessary. You need to prioritize these requirements to determine under what circumstances you should put more emphasis on one requirement over another.

How can you determine specific requirements for a security accounting service, and their relative importance?

Below are examples of different security accounting use situations that define different security accounting needs for an organization. Many other security accounting service use scenarios are possible.

1. Security accounting is used to establish how well financial assets are being protected over a five-year period. The organization suspects that authorized access to the records is being used to misdirect funds, so security accounting is employed to help identify any perpetrators.

2. Security accounting is used to search for any intrusions into the organization's network. Security accounting monitors network traffic and compares that information to authorized traffic. Security accounting issues an alert if there is activity that is unwanted or unexpected.

3. Security accounting is used to establish a documented trail of evidence for global, very large, financial transactions. Security accounting must capture transaction terms, and the identities of parties that engage in such transactions. The terms and party identities must be accessible for review and reported to decision makers. There is a risk of large financial loss, and therefore the security accounting service must be as accurate as possible.

The process of selecting and prioritizing accounting requirements needs to balance the following forces:

- You can use security accounting to help achieve desired security properties, especially accountability

- Applying accounting has many associated costs (support personnel, software, additional processing time, and so on) that are counter to the organization goal of minimizing total costs

- Collecting extensive relevant raw accounting data increases the likelihood of achieving accountability

- Collecting extensive raw accounting data increases the risk of violating privacy laws, or of abusing such data, or of damaging the reputation of the collector

- The range of time in which accounting may be needed for an event is very broad, ranging from near-real-time to years after the event

- Types of events for which accounting is needed may include repeatable, consistent events, as well as ad-hoc events

- Applying accounting adds complexity to the administration processes, which is counter to the organization goal of minimizing and simplifying administrative and maintenance processes

- Accounting needs to interface with other security services (for example, access control, I&A), thereby increasing the complexity of the software, which is counter to the organization engineering goal to maximize service independence

- Supporting multiple types of accounting policies across an organization increases complexity, which is counter to reducing overall costs

- The elements of the security accounting service need protection if the service is to perform its function

Solution

Specify a set of accounting requirements for a specific domain such as a system or organization, and determine the relative importance of each requirement. The solution has two aspects: a requirements process and a common set of generic requirements.

Requirements Specification and Prioritization Process

A system requirements engineer, in conjunction with an enterprise architect, typically perform the requirements process. An important first step is explicitly to define the domain for which you are specifying security accounting requirements, such as a specific system or facility. You also define factors that affect specialization and importance of requirements, such as organization constraints. Then you specify security accounting requirements for the target domain, using the generic requirements provided below. The final activity is to define the relative importance of the specified requirements.

Generic Requirements Description

Security accounting is a security service that involves the capturing, storage, reviewing and reporting of security-relevant information from an event. The following is a general set of requirements appropriate to security accounting services.

- Provide information about specific events.

  A security accounting service must allow information to be obtained about events that are undesirable or harmful to the organization. The time of day, day, month and year are all pieces of information that should be included in details of an event. The details provided by security accounting can either be given as they are captured or made available for scrutiny at a later date. This information will be used to help protect assets by allowing an accounting user to determine what the event was, who was involved, when and where the event happened, why and how the event happened, and how an asset was affected by an event. It also allows actions to be taken to preserve the confidentiality, integrity and availability of an asset based on the type of event.

- Provide information about who engages in activities.

  This requirement is essential for accounting for user actions. The security accounting service should allow information to be obtained that can be used to establish links between user activity and some event. Security accounting needs to allow its users to determine who the actors are who engage in a malicious or undesired event, and a description of their activities at the time the event was captured. This information will be used to help assign responsibility to an actor for the event and its consequences.

- Provide a degree of confidence that its service will function when needed.

  This requirement is essential to support security availability. Security accounting needs to be able to provide its services during times when the tracking of events is absolutely important. During operation the security accounting service should be aware of events that could cause significant damage to the organization, and it needs to be able to continue functioning during those high-impact events. Whether the information needed from security accounting is in real-time or non-real time, security accounting is required to be ready to perform its function.

- Provide a degree of confidence that the information it provides is accurate.

  This requirement is essential to support integrity. Security accounting should provide information about the accuracy of the data it provides to a user. This information gives decision makers insight into the trustworthiness of the security accounting information.

An additional set of requirements applies to all service requirements patterns. Instead of duplicating the discussion of the same set in each requirements pattern, they are simply listed here, because they do need to be considered in each requirements pattern. The requirements are: minimize time and effort to use, minimize mismatch with user characteristics, risks to user safety, costs of per-user set-up, costs of maintenance, management, and overhead, and changes needed to existing system infrastructure. Further discussion of each of these cross-cutting requirements, including implementation factors, is given in I&A REQUIREMENTS (192).

The remainder of this pattern focuses on the access control-specific requirements identified and discussed above.

Implementation

This section first provides more detail about the process summarized in the Solution section, then discusses factors in determining the relative importance of requirements.

Process Guidelines

The requirements process typically includes these steps:

1. Establish the domain for which the accounting service is needed.

   Ensure that the domain has been identified and scoped. Typical security accounting domains include information system, physical facility, network, portal, or entire organization. The domain consists of at least three parts: a defined scope of actors, a defined scope of assets, and a defined scope or set of events that involve actions on those assets. Note that other terms are also used in place of actor, asset, action. For example, [ISO15408] uses subject, object, and operation, respectively. Other constraints may also bound the domain—for example, the accounting requirements for real-time service may differ from those for multi-year service. These might represent two distinct domains.

2. Specify a set of factors that affect the specialization and importance of requirements.

   The factors include uses of accounting, accounting needs, organization constraints, and priorities. You can find a general candidate set of factors below.

3. Specify accounting requirements for the target accounting domain.

   To do this, specialize the set of generic requirements given in the Solution section.

4. Define the relative importance of specific requirements.

Requirement Priority Factors and Impacts

Table 11.1 reiterates the generic requirements described in the Solution section, along with factors for judging their relative importance to the organization. For each requirement, positive and negative impacts of the factors on importance or priority of the requirement are also provided.

Table 11.1   Accounting service requirements importance factors

GENERIC REQUIREMENT	FACTOR	RESULTING PRIORITY
Provide information about events (what, when, where, why and how)	Required by law or other mandate outside of the organization, or events involve highly-sensitive or valuable assets.	High
	Internal organization concern rather than external mandate, or events involve assets of medium value.	Medium
	Only prevention approach used, not detection or response, or events involve low value assets.	Low
Provide information about who engages in activities (who)	Assigning responsibility is a high priority, because it is required by law, or events involve highly sensitive or valuable assets.	High
	Accountability is an organization concern and not a legal or external mandate, or events involve assets of medium value, or losses are covered by insurance, or fall within the boundaries of acceptable risk.	Medium
	No action will be taken against individuals, or events involve low value assets.	Low
Provide a degree of confidence that the service will function when needed	The need for accountability is high, and security accounting is the only source of this information.	High
	The need for accountability is moderate, or alternative sources of accounting information are available.	Medium
Provide a degree of confidence that the information the service provides is accurate	The need for accountability is high, or security accounting information must be provided to an outside organization.	High
	The need for accountability is moderate, and only required inside the organization.	Medium

Example Resolved

Samuel the museum systems engineer defines several domains, because the importance of accounting requirements varies for different asset types. The domains include high value gemstones, the database system that records information about gems, and the physical facilities that house the gem exhibits. Table 11.2 shows the requirements ratings Samuel has specified for the high-value gems domain. Not surprisingly, all security accounting requirements are rated High for this domain.

Known Uses

The general accounting requirements and the process of specifying accounting requirements described in this pattern are widely known, but are generally used informally, as opposed to being codified or published. The requirements as stated here represent a consolidation of MITRE Corporation's experience in working with multiple customers over several decades. However, some publications on accounting requirements also exist.

For example, the Common Criteria [ISO15408] is an international standard that defines evaluation criteria for information technology security. It includes some discussion of accounting requirements, especially in the context of the potential conflict between accounting and privacy, or in some cases between accounting and availability. An example of the latter is specifying the required action when an audit trail is full: should you make the associated asset unavailable, or should you retain availability of the asset and allow collection of accounting data to lapse?

Table 11.2 Museum requirements for security accounting service

REQUIREMENT	MUSEUM REQUIREMENT RATING
Provide information about events (what, when, where, why and how)	HIGH – The museum decision makers want to track all activities and events regarding high value gems across the organization.
Provide information about who engages in activities (who)	HIGH – The museum decision makers want information that can hold people responsible for malicious activities regarding high value gemstones.
Provide a degree of confidence that its service will function when needed	HIGH – The museum would like to have a high level of certainty that accounting will perform its function, and specifically requires a 0.9999 availability rating.
Provide a degree of confidence that the information it provides is accurate	HIGH – The museum would like to have certainty that it can rely on the information that security accounting provides.

Consequences

The following benefits may be expected from applying this pattern:

- It facilitates conscious selection of security accounting requirements, so that decisions about selecting security accounting mechanisms have a clear basis rather than occurring in a vacuum.

- It promotes explicit analysis of trade-offs that encourages balancing and prioritizing of conflicting requirements and forces. This includes balancing the need for accountability with the need for privacy. This helps to avoid stronger than necessary security accounting mechanisms that would make it difficult for valid users, and at the same time it helps to avoid weaker than necessary security accounting that makes it easy for unauthorized actors to avoid.

- It results in documentation of security accounting requirements which communicates to all interested parties, and is useful in determining the adequacy of accounting services such as audits.

- The explicit requirements resulting from the pattern foster a clear connection of requirements to security accounting policies: this also encourages organizations to make their accounting policies more explicit.

The following potential liabilities may arise from applying this pattern:

- It requires an investment of resources to apply the pattern, including time to analyze domains and security accounting needs. In some cases the cost of applying the pattern may exceed its benefits.

- It poses a danger of over-engineering and complexity creep if stakeholders are offered too many options. You can mitigate this by using the requirements only as guidelines for analysis, or by selecting parts of the pattern that give the most help.

- The formal selection process may be too long and costly and produce too much overhead. You can mitigate this in the same ways as noted above.

- Specific circumstances might not be covered by generic security accounting requirements. You can mitigate this by adding specific requirements and including them in the trade-offs.

- Documentation of requirements implies that they must be maintained as they change over time. You can mitigate this by keeping the requirements in a form that is easy to update, integrated with other system documentation.

- Perception of security accounting requirements can differ throughout an organization or in a particular domain. This may make it difficult to reach agreement on the relative priorities of requirements. On the other hand, bringing such disagreements to the surface may be a benefit of the pattern, because then they can be properly discussed and resolved.

See Also

After applying this pattern, the next step typically is to apply AUDIT REQUIREMENTS (369), AUDIT TRAILS AND LOGGING REQUIREMENTS (378), INTRUSION DETECTION REQUIREMENTS (388), or NON-REPUDIATION REQUIREMENTS (396).

11.2 Audit Requirements

An audit service must satisfy a set of requirements for both the service and the quality of service. The audit function is to analyze logs, audit trails or other captured information about an event, such as entering a building or accessing resources on a network, to find and report any indication of security violations. While each situation that calls for an audit is unique, there are common generic requirements that apply to all audit situations. This pattern provides a common generic set of audit requirements. The pattern also helps you to apply the general requirements to your specific situation, and helps you determine the relative importance of conflicting requirements.

Example

The museum's research department has a network that they use for messaging and collaboration with various universities around the world. Among the types of information exchanged and stored are details about the location of various gemstone mines. Every six months the museum must present a report of the information exchanges to the board of trustees. The museum wants to take six months' worth of activity and summarize it into the critical and non-critical events that occurred over that six month period, and who was involved in those events. Samuel the museum system engineer understands this goal, but at the same time he understands that capturing extensive audit information can degrade system performance and require significant resources for storage and analysis. Privacy considerations are also a constraint on the capture and use of audit data. Samuel needs to identify requirements for an audit service that will help the museum achieve the goals while balancing the constraints.

Context

Accounting requirements and their relative importance are understood, for example, from applying SECURITY ACCOUNTING REQUIREMENTS (360). The planned uses of audit are understood.

Problem

Audit is a security service that scrutinizes logs, audit trails or other captured information and attempts to discern more detailed information about an event. It analyzes the event information for any indication of security violations. You need a clear set of requirements to ensure that the audit strategy employed actually satisfies the needs of the organization or system. Requirements for audit often conflict with each other, and trade-offs among them are often necessary. The conflict stated above in the example is that the need to provide an audit trail must be balanced with resource and privacy constraints. What types of information are appropriate or required for an audit system to analyze?

How can you determine a balanced set of specific requirements for an audit service, and their relative importance?

The process of selecting and prioritizing audit requirements needs to balance the following forces.

- Collecting extensive relevant audit raw data increases the likelihood of achieving the desired security properties, especially accountability.

- Collecting extensive audit raw data increases the risk of violating privacy laws, or of abusing such data, or of damaging the reputation of the collector.

- Applying audit has many associated costs (support personnel, software, additional processing time, and so on) that are counter to the organization goal of minimizing total costs.

- Audit errors can result in lack of accountability in two ways. If person A commits an act that violates security, and the audit concludes that person B committed this act, then (1) person A is not held accountable for his action, and (2) person B is incorrectly held accountable and suffers consequences for an act he did not commit.

Solution

Specify a set of audit requirements for a specific domain such as a system or organization, and determine the relative importance of each requirement. The solution has two aspects: a requirements process and a common set of generic requirements.

Requirements Specification and Prioritization Process

A system requirements engineer, in conjunction with an enterprise architect, typically perform the requirements process. An important first step is explicitly to define the domain for which you are specifying audit requirements, such as a specific system, or types of activities and events. You also define factors such as organization constraints that affect the specialization and importance of requirements. Then you specify audit requirements for the target domain, using the generic requirements provided below. The final activity is to define the relative importance of the specified requirements.

Generic Requirements Description

The audit function is to analyze logs, audit trails or other captured information about an event, such as entering a building or accessing resources on a network, to find and report any indication of security violations. The following is a general set of requirements appropriate to an audit service.

- Provide information about malicious and unwanted events.

  An audit service must provide information about events that are actually or potentially harmful to the organization. The information is used to determine what the event was, when and where the event happened, and why and how the event happened. It is also used to determine where organization vulnerabilities exist, and help the organization determine how a threat may have become a reality. The circumstances of an undesirable event, including the location and time of day and date, should be captured. The location of the event needs to be included in the details so that planners and investigators of the event can examine the area for more clues about the event. Location might be physical, such as a building, room or gate, or 'virtual,' such as a network or a Web site. Other event information may include whether or not any elements of the attack were detected in advance, and responses that ensued. This requirement implies an ability to distinguish desirable or normal events from undesirable ones. Such a distinction is often not possible until after the data is captured and analyzed.

- Provide information that associates actors with events.

  An actor may be a person, or a hardware or software element. The audit service needs to provide information not only on events that occur, but also what actors were involved in the events. A minimum requirement is to provide actor identification. Other actor information may include the location of the actor during the event and role of the actor in the event. The information is used eventually to assign the responsibility of the event to the actors. Information on thwarted attacks will need to be fed back to security officers to ensure awareness about what does work.

- Provide information on actor activity over a period of time.

  Predicting behavior can be used to prevent malicious activity from harming the organization. Over the course of time users develop habits when using a system, and those habits can be gathered into a user profile. An audit system can be used to provide details of these habits to distinguish one user from another. This information can also be used to better understand the vulnerabilities in the system, and allow decision makers the opportunity to dictate what vulnerabilities should be addressed. Decision makers want to be sure that actors who engage in activity in the organization are performing their duty in a manner that does not violate or threaten security.

- Be able to determine what captured information is relevant.

  An audit usually takes place over an extended period of time. Audit also examines information about events that have been captured over an extended period of time. In order to identify security violations that have occurred over that time, an audit activity must take care to examine the information carefully and thoroughly to ensure that the relevant information has been discerned from the captured events. Audit logs typically contain a large amount of captured information, but the information that pertains to an event of interest is by comparison very small. Finding the relevant information is often not an easy task. Sometimes even determining which events are of interest is not easy.

■ Perform its service when needed.

An audit system needs to be able to provide its services during times when the tracking of events is absolutely important, yet the ability to do so may be hampered by attacks. This requirement is essential to support availability, and concerns the readiness of the audit service.

■ Provide reliable and accurate information.

An audit system provides information relative to a specific event, and the user of the audit information wants to have confidence in the reliability and integrity of the information. Although audit was not responsible for capturing or storing the raw logging information that was input to the audit process, it may also need to provide information about the reliability and integrity of that information as well. Those working with the audit mechanisms must be trusted not to alter any information previously captured. In addition, any automated tools supporting the audit process need to be fully understood with regard to how they process the information and the rules used for establishing associations between disparate pieces of information. This requirement is essential to support integrity, and concerns the trustworthiness of the information the audit service provides.

An additional set of requirements applies to all service requirements patterns. Instead of duplicating the discussion of the same set in each requirements pattern, they are simply listed here, because they do need to be considered in each requirements pattern. The requirements are: minimize time and effort to use, minimize mismatch with user characteristics, risks to user safety, costs of per-user set-up, costs of maintenance, management, and overhead, and changes needed to existing system infrastructure. Further discussion of each of these cross-cutting requirements, including implementation factors, is given in I&A REQUIREMENTS (192).

The remainder of this pattern focuses on the audit-specific requirements identified and discussed above.

Implementation

This section first provides more detail about the process that was summarized in the Solution section, then discusses factors in determining relative importance of requirements.

Process Guidelines

The requirements process is typically performed by a system requirements engineer, in conjunction with an enterprise architect, and includes several steps:

1. Establish the domain for which the audit service is needed.

    Ensure that the domain has been identified and scoped: typical audit domains include information system, physical facility, network, portal, category of events, or entire organization. The domain consists of at least three parts: a defined scope of actors or users, a defined scope of assets, and a defined scope or set of events that involve actions or operations on those assets. Other constraints may bound the domain—for example, the audit requirements for a real-time service may differ from those for a multi-year service: these might represent two domains.

2. Specify a set of factors that affect the specialization and importance of requirements.

    The factors include use of audit, audit needs, organization constraints, and priorities. You can find a general candidate set of factors below.

3. Specify the audit requirements for the target audit domain.

    To do this, specialize the set of generic requirements given in the Solution section.

4. Define the relative importance of specific requirements.

Factors in Determining Relative Importance

Table 11.3 reiterates the generic requirements described in the Solution section, and identifies factors for judging their relative importance to an organization or system. For each factor, the table also indicates the resulting requirement priority, in terms of High, Medium, and Low.

Example Resolved

Samuel the museum systems engineer defines the museum's research network as an audit domain. Table 11.4 shows the requirements ratings Samuel has specified for this domain.

Known Uses

The general audit requirements and the process of specifying audit requirements described in this pattern are widely known, but are generally used informally, as opposed to being codified or published. The requirements as stated in this pattern represent a consolidation of MITRE Corporation's experience in working with multiple

Table 11.3 Audit service requirements factors

GENERIC REQUIREMENT	FACTOR	RESULTING PRIORITY
Provide information about malicious and unwanted events	Required by law or other mandate outside of the organization, or events involve highly-sensitive or valuable assets.	High
	Internal organization concern rather than external mandate, or events involve assets of medium value	Medium
	Only prevention approach used, not detection or response, or events involve low value assets.	Low
Provide information associating actors with events	Assigning responsibility is high priority, because it is required by law, or events involve highly sensitive or valuable assets.	High
	Accountability is an organization concern and not a legal or external mandate, or events involve assets of medium value, or losses are covered by insurance or fall within the boundaries of acceptable risk.	Medium
	No action will be taken against individuals, or events involve low value assets.	Low
Provide information on actor activity over a period of time	Actor behavior is a concern to boards, customers, or regulatory entities, who require the organization to provide this information.	High
	Accountability is an organization concern and not a legal or external mandate, or activities and behavior patterns involve assets of medium value.	Medium
	Actions are not long-lasting and are of minimal impact.	Low
Be able to determine what captured information is relevant	Event information is to be used by boards, customers or regulatory entities who require the organization to provide this information.	High
	Accountability is an organization concern and not a legal or external mandate, or activities and behavior patterns involve assets of medium value.	Medium
	Only a small amount of audit log information is captured, or the overall need for audit service is low.	Low

Table 11.3 Audit service requirements factors (*continued*)

GENERIC REQUIREMENT	FACTOR	RESULTING PRIORITY
Perform its service when needed	The need for accountability is high, and security accounting is the only source of this information.	High
	The need for accountability is moderate, or alternative sources of accounting information are available.	Medium
Provide reliable and accurate information	The need for accountability is high, or security accounting information must be provided to an outside organization.	High
	The need for accountability is moderate, and only required inside the organization.	Medium

Table 11.4 Resolution of example problem for AUDIT REQUIREMENTS

REQUIREMENT	MUSEUM PRIORITY AND CONCERN
Provide information about malicious and unwanted events	HIGH – The museum decision makers want to audit all activity across the organization.
Provide information associating actors with events	HIGH – The museum decision makers want information that can hold people responsible for malicious activities.
Provide information on actor activity over a period of time	HIGH – The museum decision makers want information audited over a six-month period.
Be able to determine what captured information is relevant	MEDIUM – It is important for the museum to get as much factual data as possible. However, they would not expend a large amount of resources to do so.
Perform its service when needed	LOW – Although important to have audit ready when it is needed, the museum decision makers need audit every six months. They would not need to expend resources to make audit highly available.
Provide reliable and accurate information	HIGH – The integrity of data is critical to the museum obtaining an accurate report. The museum would allocate resources to ensure that the information they start with is in fact accurate.

customers over several decades. However, some publications on security audits and audit requirements exist:

- ISO standards [ISO13335-4] and [ISO17799] discuss security audits as one of the primary safeguards.
- [ISO15408] is an international standard that defines evaluation criteria for information technology security. It includes a class or family of criteria that address audit requirements, including data to be generated, analysis to be performed, and event storage.
- [COBRA02] discusses the COBRA method of security audit that includes questionnaires, checklists, and a tool to help automate audits.

Consequences

The following benefits may be expected from applying this pattern:

- It facilitates conscious selection of audit requirements, so that decisions about selecting audit mechanisms have a clear basis, rather than occurring in a vacuum.
- It promotes explicit analysis of trade-offs that encourages balancing and prioritizing of conflicting requirements and forces. This includes balancing the need for accountability with the need for privacy. This helps to avoid stronger than necessary audit mechanisms that would make it difficult for valid users, and at the same time it helps to avoid weaker than necessary audit that makes it easy for unauthorized actors to avoid.
- It results in documentation of audit requirements that communicates to all interested parties and is useful in determining the adequacy of accounting services such as audits.
- The explicit requirements resulting from the pattern foster a clear connection of requirements to audit policies. This also encourages organizations to make their accounting policies more explicit.

The following potential liabilities may arise from applying this pattern:

- It requires an investment of resources to apply the pattern, including time to analyze domains and audit needs. In some cases the cost of applying the pattern may exceed its benefits.
- It poses a danger of possible violation of privacy rights if extensive data is captured and analyzed. You can mitigate this by capturing and analyzing the minimum amount of data, and by working closely with your legal department.
- The formal selection process may be too long and costly and produce too much overhead. You can mitigate this in the same ways as noted above.

- Specific circumstances might not be covered by generic audit requirements. You can mitigate this by adding specific requirements and including them in the trade-offs.

- Documentation of requirements implies that they must be maintained as they change over time. You can mitigate this by keeping the requirements in a form that is easy to update, integrated with other system documentation.

- Perception of audit requirements can differ throughout an organization or in a particular domain. This may make it difficult to reach agreement on the relative priorities of requirements. On the other hand, bringing such disagreements to the surface may be a benefit of the pattern, because they can then be properly discussed and resolved.

See Also

After applying this solution, or in parallel, you can apply AUDIT TRAILS AND LOGGING REQUIREMENTS (378). This pattern captures the information used by AUDIT REQUIREMENTS (369).

11.3 Audit Trails and Logging Requirements

A service that captures security audit trails and audit logs must satisfy a set of requirements for both the service and the quality of service. The audit trails and logging function is to capture audit logs and audit trails about events and activities that occur within an organization or system, to enable reconstruction and analysis of those events and activities. While each situation that calls for an audit trail is unique, there are common generic requirements that apply to all audit trails and logging situations. This pattern provides a common generic set of audit trail requirements. The pattern also helps you to apply the general requirements to your specific situation, and helps you to determine the relative importance of conflicting requirements.

Example

The new museum wing for gemstones keeps its most precious gems in a room with limited access. The room's access is controlled by electronic badge access. Cleaning personnel, scientists and other authorized personnel need special badges to access the room. As an extra precaution, the museum would like a way to track access to the room by individuals and by roles. Samuel the museum system engineer needs to specify the requirements for audit trails and logging (AT&L) of activities related to this limited access room, and the relative importance of those requirements, as a means to drive and evaluate an AT&L service.

Context

Audit requirements and their relative importance are understood, for example, from applying AUDIT REQUIREMENTS (369). The planned uses of audit trails and logging are understood.

Problem

An organization needs to observe events and to revisit data related to those events to help achieve security properties in a system or domain, and to understand when and how security properties have been compromised. Audit trails and logging (AT&L) is a security service that automates the capturing of information about events and activities that occur within the organization. Audit trails are a series of records about system events or user activities. Audit trails can be used to reconstruct events, determine who is responsible for events, what malicious or unwanted activities have occurred, and analysis of any problems. Logs are individual trails of information that may be combined into an audit trail.

You need a clear set of AT&L requirements to guide selection or implementation of an AT&L service and to determine if it is adequate to address organization or system needs. These requirements need to be prioritized to determine under what circumstances an organization should put more emphasis on one requirement over another.

How can you determine a balanced set of specific requirements for an AT&L service, and their relative importance?

The process of selecting and prioritizing AT&L requirements needs to balance the following forces:

- Capturing logs and audit trails increases the likelihood of achieving desired security properties, especially accountability
- Capturing logs and audit trails requires resources and entails cost
- Capturing logs and audit trails increases the risk of violating privacy laws, or of abusing such data, or of damaging the reputation of the collector
- A higher capacity of logs and audit trails enables greater volume and frequency of data acquisition, and a greater length of time for which data is available, which in turn supports increased accounting capability
- A higher capacity of logs and audit trails requires greater processing and storage resources
- Following accepted community AT&L requirements tends to save implementation cost, because tools are available to use
- Following accepted community requirements on collecting AT&L data may not give your organization exactly what you need
- AT&L data compression reduces required storage but requires compression and decompression tools

Solution

Specify a set of AT&L requirements for a specific domain such as a system or organization, and determine the relative importance of each requirement. The solution has two aspects: a requirements process and a common set of generic requirements.

Requirements Specification and Prioritization Process

A system requirements engineer, in conjunction with an enterprise architect, typically performs the requirements process. An important first step is explicitly to define the domain for which you are specifying audit trails and logging requirements, such as a specific system, or type of activities and events. You also define factors, such as organization constraints, that affect the specialization and importance of requirements. You then specify AT&L requirements for the target domain, using the generic requirements provided below. The final activity is to define the relative importance of the specified requirements.

Generic Requirements Description

The following is a general set of requirements appropriate to an AT&L service.

- Acquire information about designated types of activities and events.

  An AT&L service must support the capture and storage of information related to security events that are potentially harmful or undesirable to the organization in audit trails or logs. This requirement is essential for stakeholders, who use the details provided to determine what the event was, when and where the event happened, and why and how the event happened. Significant related information should be stored along with the event information. For example, the time of day and date should be included in details of an event. Best practice does not require audit trails or logs to be provided for immediate viewing, although sometimes they are streamed to available workstations. Generally, audit trails and logs are subjected to audit analysis after the fact.

- Ensure that information acquired can help establish links between users and events.

  The AT&L service should ensure that the information acquired can be used to establish links between user activity and some event. The AT&L service needs to allow its users to acquire identifiers that represent the identity of a user uniquely and a description of their activities at the time the event was captured. This requirement is essential for accounting for user actions. Stakeholders use the provided details to determine who the actors are who engage in malicious or unwanted activity, and eventually assign the responsibility of the event to those actors.

- Ensure that information acquired is in a form that users can interpret.

  An AT&L service must not only capture information about events, but also ensure that the information is in a form that the user can understand. This requirement is essential for facilitating understanding of events and making informed decisions.

- Enable users to reconstruct events captured from disparate sources.

  Regardless of where or when parts of an event are captured, an audit trail creates a comprehensive view of the event. The audit trail may come from disparate sources, but collectively it forms a more complete view of the event. Users of the AT&L service should be able to acquire information as a single view about events even though parts of the information are gathered from multiple sources. This requirement is essential for determining what an event was, performing investigations into malicious events, and piecing together information to determine event history.

■ Enable users to repeatedly examine the information derived from an event.

Scrutinizing events can help address future security breaches. Audit trails and logs gathered by this service need to be generally available for all accounting mechanisms and for extended periods of time, for potential event clarification or elaboration, as necessary. This requirement is essential to support users who need to revisit events to derive more information or re-examine conclusions drawn from earlier scrutiny.

■ Perform its service when needed.

An AT&L service needs to be able to provide its services during times where the tracking of events is absolutely important. During operation the AT&L service is processing information about events that could cause significant damage to the organization, and the AT&L service needs to be able to continue functioning during those high-impact events. This requirement is essential to support availability, and concerns the readiness of the AT&L service.

■ Protect the information it captures.

The AT&L service needs sufficient protection for its activity within the organization, and must afford a reasonable level of protection for the information being processed. The AT&L service should ensure that information intended for authorized users is not accessible to malicious actors. The AT&L service should also ensure that the information it provides to a user retains its accuracy. This information gives decision makers insight into how well the AT&L information is protected from malicious actors and how reliable the AT&L information is to use. This requirement is essential to support confidentiality, integrity, and privacy, and concerns the trustworthiness of the information the AT&L service provides.

■ Provide accountability for changes to audit trails and logs.

The AT&L service should provide information about an event that resulted in unauthorized or authorized access to information that the AT&L service provides. Event information needs to include all actor identifiers and events that occurred. This requirement is essential to support accountability.

An additional set of requirements applies to all service requirements patterns. Instead of duplicating the discussion of the same set in each requirements pattern, they are simply listed here, because they do need to be considered in each requirements pattern. The requirements are: minimize time and effort to use, minimize mismatch with user characteristics, risks to user safety, costs of per-user set-up, costs of maintenance, management, and overhead, and changes needed to existing system infrastructure.

Further discussion of each of these cross-cutting requirements, including implementation factors, is given in I&A REQUIREMENTS (192).

Implementation

This section first provides more detail on the process that was summarized in the Solution section, then discusses factors in determining the relative importance of requirements.

Process Guidelines

The requirements process is typically performed by a system requirements engineer in conjunction with an enterprise architect, and includes several steps:

1. Establish the domain for which the AT&L service is needed.

   Ensure that the domain has been identified and scoped: typical AT&L domains include information system, physical facility, network, portal, or entire organization. The domain consists of at least three parts: a defined scope of actors or users, a defined scope of assets, and a defined scope or set of events that involve actions or operations on those assets. Other constraints may bound the domain—for example, the AT&L requirements for a real-time service may differ from those for a multi-year service: these might represent two domains.

2. Specify a set of factors that affect the specialization and importance of requirements.

   The factors include uses of AT&L, AT&L needs, organization constraints, and priorities. You can find a general candidate set of factors below.

3. Specify AT&L requirements for the target AT&L domain.

   To do this, specialize the set of generic requirements given in the Solution section.

4. Define the relative importance of specific requirements.

   You can find more details about the association of factors and requirements below.

Factors in Determining Relative Importance

Table 11.5 reiterates the generic requirements described in the Solution section, and identifies factors for judging their relative importance to an organization or system. For each factor, the table also indicates the resulting requirement priority, in terms of High, Medium, and Low.

Table 11.5 Audit trail and logging service requirements factors

GENERIC REQUIREMENT	FACTOR	RESULTING PRIORITY
Acquire information about designated types of activities and events	Required by law or other mandate outside of the organization, or events involve highly-sensitive or valuable assets.	High
	Internal organization concern rather than external mandate, or events involve assets of medium value.	Medium
	Only prevention approach used, not detection or response, or events involve low-value assets.	Low
Ensure that the information acquired can help establish links between users and events	Assigning responsibility is high priority, because it is required by law, or events involve highly-sensitive or valuable assets.	High
	Accountability is an organization concern and not a legal or external mandate, or events involve assets of medium value, or losses are covered by insurance.	Medium
	No action will be taken against individuals, or events involve low value assets.	Low
Ensure that information acquired is in a form that users can interpret	Immediate response is needed to a critical event, and precise understanding is essential.	High
	Event responses allow for reasonable delay in reaction, or only general understanding is needed.	Medium
	Event responses are not time critical.	Low
Enable users to reconstruct events captured from disparate sources	Insurance or recoup of financial losses is critical.	High
	Organization is aware that it has events that span multiple areas.	Medium
	Events are localized or do not have multiple sources.	Low
Enable users repeatedly to examine the information derived from an event	Events and the information derived from event capture are critical to organization operations.	High

Table 11.5 Audit trail and logging service requirements factors (*continued*)

GENERIC REQUIREMENT	FACTOR	RESULTING PRIORITY
	Event information can be derived with a reasonable amount of scrutiny.	Medium
	Events are short-lived and simple.	Low
Perform its service when needed	Available AT&L is critical to event traceability.	High
	Losses due to unavailable AT&L are covered by insurance or fall within the boundaries of acceptable risk.	Medium
	No immediate need to respond to events.	Low
Protect the information it captures	Information found in audit trails is sensitive or information must be provided to an outside organization.	High
	Information is used only internally, or the information is not sensitive.	Medium
Provide accountability for changes to audit trails and logs	Legal mandate to provide that information, or needed for insurance purposes.	High
	Internal organization decision determines the consequences for the malicious actors.	Medium

Example Resolved

Samuel the museum systems engineer defines the museum rooms where precious gems are kept as an AT&L domain. Table 11.6 shows the museum concerns and associated requirements priorities Samuel has specified for this domain.

Known Uses

The general AT&L requirements and the process of specifying AT&L requirements described in this pattern are widely known, but are generally used informally, as opposed to being codified or published. The requirements as stated in this pattern represent a consolidation of MITRE Corporation's experience in working with

Table 11.6 Problem example resolution for audit trails and logging requirements

REQUIREMENT	MUSEUM PRIORITY AND CONCERN
Acquire information about designated types of activities and events	HIGH – The museum decision makers want to enforce AT&L services for this domain across the organization.
Ensure that information acquired can help establish links between users and events.	HIGH – The museum decision makers want information from the AT&L service to be immediately usable to substantiate user involvement with events.
Ensure that information acquired is in a form that users can interpret	MEDIUM – Obviously, the museum would want the information to be as coherent as possible, but the priority is tracking of activities. The museum would be willing to trade off users taking a bit longer to understand information against having all information available to scrutinize.
Enable users to reconstruct events captured from disparate sources	LOW – In general this is an important requirement, but in this case the museum is interested in tracking the activity of access to the badge-protected room specifically, so logs from this room are most important.
Enable users repeatedly to examine the information derived from an event	MEDIUM – The ability to scrutinize the information facilitates the tracking of activities in the long term. This is useful but not critical for this domain.
Perform its service when needed	HIGH – The museum absolutely wants to have this ability to track activities for this domain even under emergency conditions. AT&L needs to be able to demonstrate that it can do this.
Protect the information it captures	HIGH – To have trust in the tracking information, AT&L needs to demonstrate that its information can be trusted.
Provide accountability for changes to audit trails and logs	MEDIUM – The museum wants to know who changes the information, but this is less important than acquiring and protecting the information.

multiple customers over several decades. However, some publications on security AT&L and AT&L requirements exist. Examples are:

- ISO standard [ISO13335-4] discusses AT&L as one of the primary safeguards.
- [ISO15408] is an international standard that defines evaluation criteria for information technology security. It includes a class or family of criteria that address AT&L requirements, including event storage and audit trail availability.

Other more general discussions of AT&L practice are available in [Abrams95], [Bace01], [Cugini00], [DCD+02], [NIST800-12], and [Wheel99].

Consequences

The primary benefit is the existence of a set of explicit AT&L requirements for a given system or security domain. The relative importance of the requirements is identified. You may expect the following benefits from applying this pattern:

- It facilitates the conscious selection of AT&L requirements, so that decisions about selecting AT&L mechanisms have a clear basis, rather than occurring in a vacuum.

- It promotes explicit analysis of trade-offs that encourages balancing and prioritizing of conflicting requirements and forces. This includes balancing the need for accountability with the need for privacy. This helps to avoid stronger than necessary AT&L mechanisms that would make it difficult for valid users, and at the same time it helps to avoid weaker than necessary AT&L that makes it easy for unauthorized actors to avoid.

- It results in documentation of AT&L requirements that communicates to all interested parties and is useful in comparing the adequacy of alternative implementations of AT&L services.

- The explicit requirements resulting from the pattern foster a clear connection of requirements to audit and logging policies: this also encourages organizations to make their accounting policies more explicit.

The following potential liabilities may arise from applying this pattern:

- It requires an investment of resources to apply the pattern, including time to analyze domains and AT&L needs. In some cases the cost of applying the pattern may exceed its benefits.

- It poses a danger of possible violation of privacy rights if extensive data is captured and analyzed. You can mitigate this by capturing and analyzing the minimum amount of data, and by working closely with your legal department.

- The formal selection process may be too long and costly and produce too much overhead. You can mitigate this in the same ways as noted above.

- Specific circumstances might not be covered by generic AT&L requirements. You can mitigate this by adding specific requirements and including them in the trade-offs.

- Documentation of requirements implies that they must be maintained as they change over time. You can mitigate this by keeping the requirements in a form that is easy to update, integrated with other system documentation.

■ Perception of AT&L requirements can differ throughout an organization or in a particular domain. This may make it difficult to reach agreement on the relative priorities of requirements. On the other hand, bringing such disagreements to the surface may be a benefit of the pattern, because then they can be properly discussed and resolved.

11.4 Intrusion Detection Requirements

An intrusion detection system (IDS) must satisfy a set of requirements for both the service and the quality of service. IDS is a security service that automates the monitoring of events occurring in a computer system or network, and analyzes these events for any indication of security violations. While each situation that calls for intrusion detection is unique, there are common generic requirements that apply to all intrusion detection situations. This pattern provides a common generic set of intrusion detection requirements. The pattern also helps you to apply the general requirements to your specific situation, and helps you to determine the relative importance of conflicting requirements.

Example

The museum's research department has a network that they use for messaging and collaboration with various universities around the world. Among the information exchanged and stored are details about the location of various natural gemstone mines. Samuel the museum system engineer wants the museum immediately to detect unauthorized and successful attempts to gain access to the network and to any hosts that contain sensitive information. Once alerted, Samuel would like information that can be used to hold accountable the individual(s) that have breached their perimeter. In addition, Samuel would like to have information recorded and available on unsuccessful attempts to gain access. Samuel understands that trade-offs are involved, because stopping intruders and capturing information about attempted intrusions can require significant resources that degrade system performance, and which may make legitimate access more difficult. Privacy considerations are also a constraint on intrusion detection efforts. Samuel needs to identify requirements for an IDS service that will help the museum achieve the goals while balancing the constraints.

Context

Accounting requirements and their relative importance are understood. The requirements might have been selected by applying SECURITY ACCOUNTING REQUIREMENTS (360). The planned uses of IDS are understood.

Problem

IDS is a security service that automates the monitoring of events occurring in a computer system or network. It analyzes these events for any indication of security violations. You need a clear set of requirements to ensure that the intrusion detection strategy employed actually satisfies the needs of the organization or system. Requirements for intrusion detection often conflict with each other, and trade-offs among them are often necessary. The conflict stated in the example is that the need to detect intrusion must be balanced with resource and privacy constraints.

What types of information are appropriate or required for an IDS to analyze? How can you determine a balanced set of specific requirements for an IDS service, and their relative importance?

The process of selecting and prioritizing intrusion detection requirements needs to balance the following forces:

- Applying intrusion detection increases the likelihood of achieving the desired security properties, especially accountability and integrity.

- Applying intrusion detection has associated costs, such as software, additional processing time and resources, and risks, such as privacy violations.

- Intrusion detection errors can result in two different types of problems. First, if an intrusion occurs that violates security, and the IDS service does not detect it or prevent it, then damage can occur, and it might not be discovered until a later time. Second, if no intrusion occurs but the IDS incorrectly believes an intrusion has occurred, then resources are wasted trying to respond to a problem that does not exist.

Solution

Specify a set of intrusion detection requirements for a specific domain such as a system or network, and determine the relative importance of each requirement. The solution has two aspects: a requirements process and a common set of generic requirements.

Requirements Specification and Prioritization Process

The requirements process is typically performed by a system requirements engineer in conjunction with an enterprise architect, and includes several activities. An important first step is explicitly to define the domain for which IDS requirements are to be specified, such as a specific system or facility. Factors that affect specialization and importance of requirements are also defined, such as organization constraints. IDS requirements for the target domain are then specified, using the generic requirements provided below. The final activity is to define the relative importance of the specified requirements.

Generic Requirements Description

The following are general requirements that drive the design of an IDS Service:

- Detect intrusion events.

  An IDS service must detect intrusion attempts. This information is used to determine organization vulnerabilities. By its very need to provide immediate information, IDS services will only be able to provide information about security events as it is received. While some IDS services can provide a degree of correlation between events, there is an inherent time delay before such information can be reported.

- Report on successful intrusions and thwarted intrusion events.

  Reported information includes actor identities and any distinguishing characteristics of the events. The information should also include, but not be limited to: the location of the actor, software or hardware used in the attack, discussion of whether or not any elements of the attack were detected in advance, and the responses that ensued.

- Provide countermeasures against intrusions.

  An IDS service has the responsibility to try to thwart intrusion attempts. An IDS service will need to perform some event correlation so that it will be able to recognize attack patterns and warn security officers and system administrators. Compiling user profiles based on behavior patterns can also help to recognize and thwart attacks. If reasonable, the IDS service should be permitted to shut down avenues of access when attack patterns indicate that an attack is beginning to happen. In some cases, the known presence of an IDS may in itself deter actors from engaging in malicious activity.

- Support the capability for repeated examination of information derived from an event.

  The IDS service needs to provide the security events and information it detects to the normal audit trail and logging mechanisms for capture and storage for the longer term.

- Perform its service when needed.

  The IDS service will itself require protection. An IDS needs to be available to provide its services when the tracking of events is absolutely important. During operation the IDS should be aware of events that could cause significant damage to the organization, and the IDS service needs to be able to continue functioning during those high-impact events.

- Provide reliable and accurate information.

  Malicious actors should not be able to tamper with information the IDS service obtains or generates: the IDS should protect its own information as far as possible. Decision makers will need to judge how well the IDS information is protected from malicious actors. This requirement is essential to support confidentiality and integrity.

An additional set of requirements applies to all service requirements patterns. Instead of duplicating the discussion of the same set in each requirements pattern, they are simply listed here, because they do need to be considered in each requirements pattern. The requirements are: minimize time and effort to use, minimize mismatch with user characteristics, risks to user safety, costs of per-user set-up, costs of maintenance, management, and overhead, and changes needed to existing system infrastructure. Further discussion of each of these cross-cutting requirements, including implementation factors, is given in I&A REQUIREMENTS (192).

Implementation

This section first provides more detail on the process that was summarized in the Solution section, then discusses factors in determining relative importance of requirements.

Process Guidelines

The requirements process is typically performed by a system requirements engineer in conjunction with an enterprise architect, and includes several steps:

1. Establish the domain for which the intrusion detection service is needed.

    Ensure that the domain has been identified and scoped. Typical intrusion detection domains include [ISG00]:

    - Trespass: gaining unauthorized physical access to sensitive data by circumventing a system's protections
    - Penetration: gaining unauthorized logical access to sensitive data by circumventing a system's protections
    - Reverse engineering: acquiring sensitive data by disassembling and analyzing the design of a system component
    - Cryptanalysis: transforming encrypted data into plaintext without having prior knowledge of encryption parameters or processes

    Other constraints may also bound the domain.

2. Specify a set of factors that affect specialization and importance of requirements.

    The factors include use of IDS, intrusion detection needs, response needs, organization constraints, and priorities. You can find a general candidate set of factors below.

3. Specify the intrusion detection requirements for the target domain.

To do this, specialize the set of generic requirements given in the Solution section.

4. Define the relative importance of specific requirements.

You can find more details on the association of factors and requirements below.

Factors in Determining Relative Importance

Table 11.7 reiterates the generic requirements described in the Solution section, along with factors for judging their relative importance to the organization. For each requirement, positive and negative impacts of the factors on importance or priority of the requirement are also provided.

Table 11.7 Intrusion detection system service requirements factors

GENERIC REQUIREMENT	FACTOR	RESULTING PRIORITY
Detect intrusion events	Potential intrusions could give access to highly-sensitive or valuable assets, or could cause significant damage.	High
	Intrusions would not cause significant loss or damage, or the loss is covered by insurance.	Low
Report on successful intrusions and thwarted intrusion events	Strong need to assess quality of IDS and patterns of intrusion attempts.	High
	Information needed only for insurance claims.	Medium
Provide countermeasures against intrusions	Potential intrusions could cause loss of or damage to highly-valuable assets that could not be replaced or repaired.	High
	Assets could easily be replaced or repaired.	Low
Support the capability for repeated examination of information derived from an event	IDS is the only accounting service deployed, and understanding of patterns that emerge over time is needed.	High
	An audit trail and logging service is deployed, or the primary need for IDS is to detect and thwart current attacks.	Low
Perform its service when needed	Potential intrusions could give access to highly-sensitive or valuable assets, or could cause significant damage.	High

Table 11.7 Intrusion detection system service requirements factors (*continued*)

GENERIC REQUIREMENT	FACTOR	RESULTING PRIORITY
	Intrusions would not cause significant loss or damage, or the loss is covered by insurance.	Low
Provide reliable and accurate information	Strong need to assess quality of IDS and patterns of intrusion attempts.	High
	Information needed only for insurance claims.	Medium

Example Resolved

Samuel the museum systems engineer defines the museum research network as an IDS domain. Table 11.8 shows the requirements ratings Samuel has specified for this domain.

Table 11.8 Resolution of example problem for IDS requirements

REQUIREMENT	MUSEUM PRIORITY AND CONCERN
Detect intrusion events	HIGH – The museum wants immediately to detect unauthorized and successful attempts to gain access to the network and to any hosts that contain sensitive information.
Report on successful intrusions and thwarted intrusion events	HIGH – Once alerted, the decision makers would like information that can be used to hold the individual(s) that have breached their perimeter accountable.
Provide countermeasures against intrusions	MEDIUM – The museum wants to thwart intrusions, but for this domain, the benefit-to-cost ratio for this capability is less than detection and reporting.
Support the capability for repeated examination of information derived from an event	LOW – The museum is most interested in current attacks rather than long-term analysis.
Perform its service when needed	HIGH – The problem statement clearly states that the museum needs the IDS to capture malicious activity. The museum must have confidence that the IDS can perform this task
Provide reliable and accurate information	MEDIUM – Information on malicious actors is important, but protecting other tracking information is only moderately important.

Known Uses

The general IDS requirements and the process of specifying IDS requirements described in this pattern are widely known, but are generally used informally, as opposed to being codified or published. The requirements as stated here represent a consolidation of MITRE Corporation's experience in working with multiple customers over several decades. However, some publications on intrusion detection and IDS requirements exist. Examples are:

- [ISO13335-4] discusses intrusion detection as one of the primary safeguards.

- [ISO15408] is an international standard that defines evaluation criteria for information technology security. It includes criteria that address IDS requirements, although the discussion is tangential and in the context of audit and system monitoring activities.

- [IDWG02] discusses requirements for IDS message exchange in the context of the Internet.

- [Farshchi03] discusses requirements for wireless IDS.

- [Liesen02] discusses criteria for organization-wide IDS products.

Consequences

The following benefits may be expected from applying this pattern:

- It facilitates conscious selection of IDS requirements, so that decisions about selecting IDS mechanisms have a clear basis, rather than occurring in a vacuum.

- It promotes explicit analysis of trade-offs that encourages balancing and prioritizing of conflicting requirements and forces. This includes balancing the need for accountability with the need for privacy. This helps to avoid stronger than necessary IDS mechanisms that would generate excessive false warnings or cost too much, and at the same time it helps to avoid a weaker than necessary IDS that makes it easy for malicious actors to penetrate.

- It results in documentation of IDS requirements that communicates to all interested parties, and is useful in determining the adequacy of accounting services such as IDS.

- The explicit requirements resulting from the pattern foster a clear connection of requirements to audit and intrusion policies: this also encourages organizations to make their accounting policies more explicit.

The following potential liabilities may arise from applying this pattern:

- It requires an investment of resources to apply the pattern, including time to analyze domains and IDS needs. In some cases the cost of applying the pattern may exceed its benefits.

- It poses a danger of possibly violating privacy rights if extensive actor data is captured and analyzed. You can mitigate this by capturing and analyzing the minimum amount of data, and by working closely with your legal department.

- The formal selection process may be too long and costly and produce too much overhead. You can mitigate this in the same ways as noted above.

- Specific circumstances might not be covered by generic IDS requirements. You can mitigate this by adding specific requirements and including them in the trade-offs.

- Documentation of requirements implies that they must be maintained as they change over time. You can mitigate this by keeping the requirements in a form that is easy to update, integrated with other system documentation.

- Perception of IDS requirements can differ throughout an organization or in a particular domain. This may make it difficult to reach agreement on the relative priorities of requirements. On the other hand, bringing such disagreements to the surface may be a benefit of the pattern, because then they can be properly discussed and resolved.

See Also

AUDIT TRAILS AND LOGGING REQUIREMENTS (378) describes requirements for capturing and storing information that could be passed from an intrusion detection system.

11.5 Non-Repudiation Requirements

A non-repudiation service must satisfy a set of requirements for both the service and the quality of service. The function of non-repudiation is to capture and maintain evidence so that the participants of a transaction or interaction cannot deny having participated in that activity. While each situation that calls for non-repudiation is unique, there are common generic requirements that apply to all non-repudiation situations. This pattern provides a common generic set of non-repudiation requirements. The pattern also helps you to apply the general requirements to your specific situation, and helps you to determine the relative importance of conflicting requirements.

Example

The museum seeks to increase the publicity of its new wing for gemstones. To do this, the museum seeks to have many exotic gems on display for the grand opening. The Crown Jewels of England are scheduled to be a part of the display. Manuela the museum manager would like to have a high degree of confidence that the receipt of the jewels by the museum and the release of the jewels after the opening are protected. Samuel the museum system engineer needs to specify the requirements for non-repudiation and the relative importance of those requirements, as a means of driving and evaluating a non-repudiation service that will support events such as this grand opening. How can Samuel define such a set of requirements?

Context

Accounting requirements and their relative importance are understood, for example, from applying SECURITY ACCOUNTING REQUIREMENTS (360). The planned uses of non-repudiation are understood. A common transaction type is the sending and receiving of materials such as merchandise or contracts. Non-repudiation is used to prevent the receiver from denying that they received the materials when in fact they did receive them. Sometimes non-repudiation is used to prevent the sender from claiming that they sent the materials when in fact they did not send them.

Problem

Non-repudiation is a security service that captures and maintains evidence so that the participants of a transaction or interaction cannot deny having participated in that activity. The need is to identify the common requirements that drive the design of this service. The model in the figure places non-repudiation in the context of the identity of the participants, in terms of the activity that it collects, and the facts and evidence that it provides. This ensures that the participants cannot deny having engaged in the activity. Non-repudiation needs information about the event that will disallow the participants from denying their participation. If the participants are allowed to deny their involvement in the activity, then the integrity of the activity will be jeopardized and other participants may suffer negative consequences. For example, if a purchaser receives a book that they ordered from Amazon.com, and then denies receiving it, Amazon may need to send another copy of the book, which is a financial loss to them.

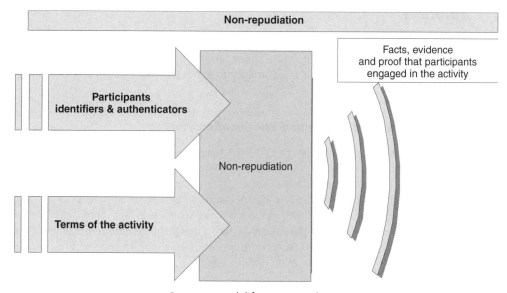

Common model for non-repudiation

How can specific requirements for a non-repudiation service, and their relative importance, be determined?

The process of selecting and prioritizing non-repudiation requirements needs to balance the following forces:

- You can use non-repudiation to help achieve the desired security properties, especially integrity and accountability.

- Obtaining evidence that a person or organization participated in a transaction can have significant benefits in cases in which they deny participation, including favorable resolution of both economic and legal disputes.

- Applying non-repudiation has associated costs, including the time and resources required for continuously capturing identifiers and authenticators and explicitly defining the terms of an event. This is counter to the organization goal of minimizing total costs.

■ High need for non-repudiation often involves intrusive or inconvenient constraints on participants.

■ There may be legal constraints that mandate that participants have access to the facts and evidence of their activities.

■ The elements of the non-repudiation service need protection if the service is to perform its function.

Solution

Specify a set of non-repudiation requirements for a specific domain such as a system or organization, and determine the relative importance of each requirement. The solution has two aspects: a requirements process and a common set of generic requirements.

Requirements Specification and Prioritization Process

A system requirements engineer, in conjunction with an enterprise architect, typically perform the requirements process. An important first step is explicitly to define the domain for which non-repudiation requirements are being specified, such as a specific system or facility. You also define factors such as organization constraints that affect specialization and importance of requirements. You then specify non-repudiation requirements for the target domain, using the generic requirements provided below. The final activity is to define the relative importance of the specified requirements.

Generic Non-repudiation Requirements

The following is a general set of requirements appropriate to non-repudiation services. An engineer will need to consider each of these and determine its priority based on criteria specific to the target domain, as well as on broader organization constraints. Additional requirements may be added to this list to address system-unique characteristics. Some of the general requirements represent non-repudiation functional requirements. The remaining requirements represent non-repudiation non-functional requirements, including requirements for security of the non-repudiation service.

■ Provide information that an actor took specified actions in an activity or event.

  Non-repudiation needs to have the ability to form strong links between the participants who engage in an activity and the activity itself. The evidence and facts that are derived from capturing information about the event need to be explicit and detailed enough to help assign accountability. This requirement has increased priority when the events are of high importance. 'High' importance may mean critical to business functions or operations, providing legal or financial evidence, or otherwise significant.

■ Provide identifiers, authenticators and the terms of an event when requested.

Non-repudiation should examine any legal or external considerations regarding the gathering of information about participants of an event. There may be consequences for the organization if laws are not followed regarding the collection of identifiers and authenticators.

■ Minimize the time it takes participants to provide their identifiers and authenticators.

You need to consider that if events require non-repudiation and the events must happen for other business reasons, participants in these events should not be discouraged from joining due to complexities associated with identifiers and authenticators.

■ Protect all non-repudiation information associated with an event.

The confidentiality, integrity, and availability of facts and evidence need to be maintained. Due to the need to help to assign accountability, it is imperative that the information gathered by the non-repudiation service be uncorrupted. The better the non-repudiation service can maintain and provide a degree of confidence about the protection of the information, the more the service user can rely on the information that it provides. Non-repudiation also needs to verify that the information that it collects is not forged or misrepresented.

An additional set of requirements applies to all service requirements patterns. Instead of duplicating the discussion of the same set in each requirements pattern, they are simply listed here, because they do need to be considered in each requirements pattern. The requirements are: minimize mismatch with user characteristics, risks to user safety, costs of per-user set-up, costs of maintenance, management, and overhead, and changes needed to existing system infrastructure. Further discussion of each of these cross-cutting requirements, including implementation factors, is given in I&A REQUIREMENTS (192).

Implementation

This section provides more detail about the process that was summarized in the Solution section. The requirements process typically includes these steps:

1. Establish the domain for which the non-repudiation service is needed.

   Ensure that the domain has been identified and scoped: typical non-repudiation domains include categories of transactions or interactions. For example, transactions at a company's public Web portal may be a different domain from transactions involving contracts with suppliers. Other constraints or distinctions may bound the domain as well, such as separating transactions that occur outside the organization from internal transactions.

2. Specify a set of factors that affect the specialization and importance of requirements.

   Factors can include uses of non-repudiation, non-repudiation needs, organization constraints, and priorities.

3. Specify non-repudiation requirements for the target domain.

   Specialize the set of generic requirements given above.

4. Define the relative importance of specific requirements.

   Priority is increased when the transactions or their consequences are of high importance. 'High' importance may mean critical to business functions or operations, providing legal or financial evidence, or otherwise significant.

Example Resolved

Samuel the museum system engineer defines the domain for non-repudiation to be transactions in which the museum lends or borrows gems of high value. Borrowing the Crown Jewels for an exhibit is an example of a transaction in this domain. To ensure protection of the reception and dispatch of the Crown Jewels, the museum defines specific non-repudiation requirements. Table 11.9 shows the specific requirements and relates them to the general requirements defined in the Solution section.

Although many aspects of this exchange will be time-consuming, it will also provide a very high degree of confidence that the parties exchanged the Crown Jewels and that the Crown Jewels were returned in the same condition as that in which they were received.

Known Uses

The general non-repudiation requirements and the process of specifying non-repudiation requirements described in this pattern are widely known, but are generally used informally, as opposed to being codified or published. The requirements as stated in this pattern represent a consolidation of MITRE Corporation's experience in working with multiple customers over several decades. However, some publications on non-repudiation requirements exist.

- [ISO13335-4] discusses non-repudiation as one of the primary safeguards, in the context of integrity.

- [ISO15408] is an international standard that defines evaluation criteria for information technology security. It includes non-repudiation requirements in the context of communication.

Table 11.9 Museum specific requirements for non-repudiation

GENERAL REQUIREMENT	SPECIFIC REQUIREMENT FOR THIS TRANSACTION
Provide information that an actor took specified actions in an activity or event	Capture, store, and record the receipt and return of the Crown Jewels by video taping the event or having it done with witnesses from both the sender and the receiver.
Provide identifiers, authenticators and the terms of an event when requested	• Identify and authenticate the individual(s) from whom the Crown Jewels should be received and to whom they should be given after the opening. • Explicitly outline the terms of the exchange and have all participants provide an authenticated signature. • Provide copies of this agreement to the sender and the receiver.
Minimize the time it takes participants to provide their identifiers and authenticators	Prepare everything, including video taping preparations and writing down the agreement, to make it as efficient and unobtrusive as possible. Document the process and have standard forms available for use in similar transactions.
Protect all non-repudiation information associated with an event	Store this agreement, the signatures, and the videotape in a secure location.

- [ISO13888] is an international standard on non-repudiation.

- [Louridas00] discusses non-repudiation protocol guidelines and stresses the need to match protocols with requirements.

- [IETF99] discusses requirements for non-repudiation in the context of the Internet.

- [Gindin01] discusses technical requirements for non-repudiation, in contrast with legal requirements.

Consequences

The following benefits may be expected from applying this pattern:

- It facilitates conscious selection of non-repudiation requirements, so that decisions about selecting non-repudiation mechanisms have a clear basis, rather than occurring in a vacuum.

■ It promotes explicit analysis of trade-offs that encourages balancing and prior-itizing of conflicting requirements. This helps to avoid stronger than necessary non-repudiation which places increased burden on the parties to a transaction, and at the same time it helps to avoid weaker than necessary non-repudiation, which would make it easy to deny participation.

■ It results in documentation of non-repudiation requirements which communi-cates to all interested parties and also provides information for security audits.

■ The pattern fosters a clear connection of non-repudiation requirements to se-curity accounting policies. This also encourages organizations to make their policies more explicit.

The following potential liabilities may arise from applying this pattern:

■ It requires an investment of resources to apply the pattern, including time to analyze domains and non-repudiation needs. In some cases the cost of applying the pattern may exceed its benefits.

■ It poses a danger of over-engineering and complexity creep if stakeholders are offered too many options. You can mitigate this by using the requirements only as guidelines for analysis, or by selecting those parts of the pattern that give the most help.

■ The formal selection process may be too long and costly and produce too much overhead. You can mitigate this in the same ways as noted above.

■ Specific circumstances might not be covered by generic non-repudiation re-quirements. You can mitigate this by adding specific requirements and includ-ing them in the trade-offs.

■ Documentation of requirements implies that they must be maintained as they change over time. You can mitigate this by keeping the requirements in a form that is easy to update, integrated with other system documentation.

Firewall Architectures

The Great Wall of China was built over 2,000 years ago, by Qin Shi Huangdi, the first emperor of China. Armies were stationed along the wall as a first line of defence against the invading nomadic tribes north of China (the Huns). Signal fires from the Wall provided early warning of an attack.

www.enchantedlearning.com/subjects/greatwall/Allabout.html

In the case of computers connected to a local network, attacks may come from hosts in external networks or in other local sub-networks. Network traffic has a layered structure and we need to protect against attacks that may come through any layer. This means that we need different types of defensive structures. Accessing a mistrusted site is a risk, and we also need to protect the traffic going out from a local network. A common solution to the protection of local networks is to incorporate a firewall to filter unwanted traffic [Zwi00].

Firewalls have been shown to be very effective in providing security by creating a 'choke point' of entry and exit for a local network [Bar99]. A firewall therefore restricts unauthorized clients from access to the local network, and local networks from accessing external sites that are considered untrustworthy. A firewall can be used as a mechanism to enforce security policies, and also allows a limited exposure of the protected network to outsiders.

PACKET FILTER FIREWALL (405) defines a basic filtering function at the IP layer based on packet inspection, typically of network addresses. PROXY-BASED FIREWALL (411) (also called APPLICATION-LEVEL FIREWALL) is used at the network application layer to control access to application services through the use of a proxy that represents the service. This firewall can be combined with PACKET FILTER FIREWALL (405). Both PACKET FILTER FIREWALL (405) and PROXY-BASED FIREWALL (411) can be complemented with a STATEFUL FIREWALL (417), where the state of the connection is also used to decide access. There are also application firewalls, intended for filtering user application inputs: these are discussed elsewhere [Del04].

A firewall is implemented as software or a combination of software and hardware that enforces an access control policy between networks. The basic underlying architectures of the various types of firewalls are similar and we try here to capture their generic structures, leaving out implementation details. In this chapter we consider the architecture of the firewalls themselves, while Chapter 13 considers their use in filtering configurations for Web-based systems.

The patterns in this chapter have been jointly written by Eduardo B. Fernandez, Maria M. Larrondo-Petrie, Naeem Seliya, Nelly Delessy-Gassant, and Markus Schumacher. We received valuable comments from Munawar Hafiz, Andy Longshaw, Peter Sommerlad, and Dan Thomsen. The first two patterns appeared in [FLS+03c]. Angela Herzberg was a co-author of that paper.

12.1 Packet Filter Firewall

Some of the hosts in other networks may try to attack the local network through their IP-level payloads. These payloads may include viruses or application-specific attacks. We need to identify and block those hosts. A packet filter firewall filters incoming and outgoing network traffic in a computer system based on packet inspection at the IP level.

Example

Our system has been attacked recently by a variety of hackers, including somebody who penetrated our operating system and stole our clients' credit card numbers. Our employees are wasting time at work by looking at inappropriate sites on the Internet. If we continue like this we will soon be out of business.

Context

Computer systems on a local network connected to the Internet and to other networks with different levels of trust. A host in a local network receives and sends traffic to other networks. This traffic has several layers or levels. The most basic level is the IP level, made up of packets consisting of headers and bodies (payloads). The headers include the source and destination addresses as well as other routing information, while the bodies include the message payloads.

Problem

Some of the hosts on other networks may try to attack the local network through their IP-level payloads. These payloads may include viruses or application-specific attacks. How can we identify and block those hosts?

The solution to this problem must resolve the following forces:

- We need to communicate with other networks, so isolating our network is not an option. However, we do not want to take a high risk for doing so.
- The protection mechanism should be able to reflect precisely the security policies of the organization. A too coarse defence may not be useful.
- Any protection mechanism should be transparent to the users. Users should not need to perform special actions to be secure.

- The cost and overhead of the protection mechanism should be relatively low or the system may become too expensive to run.

- Network administrators deploy and configure a variety of protection mechanisms; hence it is important to have a clear model of what is being protected.

- The attacks are constantly changing; hence it should be easy to make changes to the configuration of the protection mechanism.

- It may be necessary to log input and/or output requests for auditing and defence purposes.

Solution

A PACKET FILTER FIREWALL (405) intercepts all traffic coming and going from a port P and inspects its packets (see the figure below). Those coming from or going to mistrusted addresses are rejected. The mistrusted addresses are determined from a set of rules that implement the security policies of the organization. A client from another network can only access the Local Host if a rule exists authorizing traffic from its address. Specific rules may indicate an address or a range of addresses. Rules may be positive (allow traffic from some address) or negative (block traffic from some address). Most commercial products order these rules for efficiency in checking. Additionally, if a request is not satisfied by any of the explicit rules, then a default rule is applied.

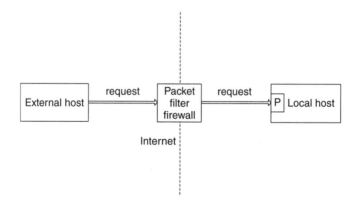

The concept of the packet filter firewall

Structure

The figure on page 407 shows an external host requesting access to a local host (a server) through a packet filter firewall. The organization policies are embodied in the objects of class Rule collected by the RuleBase. The RuleBase includes data structures and operations to manage rules in a convenient way. The rules in this set are ordered, and can be explicit or default.

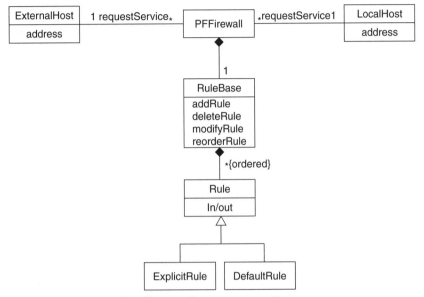

Class diagram for PACKET FILTER FIREWALL

Dynamics

We describe the dynamic aspects of the PACKET FILTER FIREWALL (405) using a sequence diagram for one of its basic use cases. There is a symmetric use case, filtering an outgoing request, which we omit for briefness. We also omit use cases for adding, removing, or reordering rules, because they are straightforward. See the figure on page 408.

Filtering a Client's Request

- *Summary.* A host in a remote network wants access to a local host to either transfer or retrieve information. The access request is made through the firewall, which according to its set of rules determines whether to accept or deny the request—that is, it filters the access request.
- *Actors.* A host on an external network (client).
- *Precondition.* An existing set of rules to filter the request must be in place in the firewall.

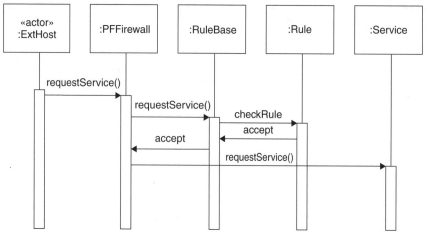

Sequence diagram for filtering a client's request

■ *Description*:

1. An external host requests access to the local host.

2. A firewall filters the request according to a set of ordered rules. If none of the explicit rules in the rule set allows or denies the request, a default rule is used for making a decision.

3. If the request is accepted, the firewall allows access to the local host.

■ *Alternate flow.* The request is denied.

■ *Postcondition.* The firewall has accepted the access of a trustworthy client to the local host.

Implementation

1. Define an organization policy about network access, classifying sites according to our trust in them.

2. Convert this policy into a set of access rules. This can be done manually, which may be complex for large systems. An alternative is using an appropriate commercial product, such as Solsoft [Sol].

3. Note that the idea of a single point of access is virtual: there may be several physical firewalls deployed at different places. This means that it is necessary to install firewalls at all external boundaries, such as routers or gateways.

4. Write the rules in each firewall. Again, products such as Solsoft and others automatically propagate the rules to each registered firewall.

5. Configure the corresponding firewalls according to standard architectures. A common deployment architecture is the DEMILITARIZED ZONE (449) (DMZ).

Example Resolved

We were able to trace the addresses of our attackers and we installed a firewall to block requests from those addresses from reaching our system. We also made a list of addresses of inappropriate sites and blocked access to them from the hosts in our network. All this reduced the number of attacks and helped control the behavior of some employees.

Known Uses

This model corresponds to an architecture that is seen in commercial firewall products, such as ARGuE (Advanced Research Guard for Experimentation), which is based on Network Associates' Gauntlet Firewall [Eps99], OpenBSD Packet Filtering Firewall [Rus02], which is the basic firewall architecture for the Berkeley Software Distribution system, and the Linux Firewall [Zie02], which is the basic firewall architecture used with the Linux operating system. PACKET FILTER FIREWALL (405) is used as an underlying architecture for other types of firewalls that include more advanced features.

Consequences

The following benefits may be expected from applying this pattern:

- A firewall transparently filters all the traffic that passes through it, thus lowering the risk of communicating with potentially hostile networks.

- It is possible to express the organization's filtering policies through its filtering rules, with different levels of protection for different parts of the network.

- It is easy to update the rule set to counter new threats.

- Because it intercepts all requests, a firewall allows systematic logging of incoming and outgoing messages. Because of this, a firewall facilitates the detection of possible attacks and helps to hold local users responsible for their actions when interacting with external networks.

- Its low cost enabled it to be included as part of many operating systems and simple network devices such as routers.

- It offers good performance, only needing to look at the headers of IP packets rather than the complete packet.

- It can be combined with intrusion detection systems (IDS) for greater effectiveness. In this case, the IDS can tell the firewall to block suspicious traffic.

The following potential liabilities may arise from applying this pattern:

■ The firewall's effectiveness and speed may be limited due to its rule set (order of precedence). Addition of new rules may interfere with existing rules in the rule set, so a careful approach should be taken in adding and updating access rules.

■ The firewall can only enforce security policies on traffic that goes through the firewall. This means that one must make changes to the network to ensure that there are no other paths into its hosts.

■ An IP-level firewall cannot stop attacks coming through the higher levels of the network. For example, a hacker could put malicious commands or data in header data not used for routing, or in the payload.

■ Each packet is analyzed independently, which means that it is necessary to analyze every packet. This may reduce performance.

■ A packet filter cannot recognize forged addresses (IP spoofing) because it only examines the header of the IP packet. This can be corrected (at some extra cost) using link layer filtering, in which each IP address is correlated to its hardware address [Fra01].

See Also

AUTHORIZATION (245) defines the standard security model for PACKET FILTER FIREWALL (405). This pattern is also a special case of SINGLE ACCESS POINT (279) and is the basis for other, more complex, types of firewalls described later in this chapter. DEMILITARIZED ZONE (449) (DMZ) defines a way to configure this pattern in a network. This pattern can also be combined with STATEFUL FIREWALL (417).

12.2   Proxy-Based Firewall

A proxy-based firewall inspects and filters incoming and outgoing network traffic based on the type of application service to be accessed, or performing the access. This pattern interposes a proxy between the request and the access, and applies controls through this proxy. This is usually done in addition to the normal filtering based on addresses.

Also Known As

Proxy Firewall, Application Firewall

Example

After we started using a PACKET FILTER FIREWALL (405) most of our problems were reduced. However, some of the messages sent from sites we don't consider suspicious contain malicious payloads, because hackers were spoofing trusted addresses. These payloads sometimes contained incorrect commands or the wrong type and length of parameters. Our PACKET FILTER FIREWALL (405) cannot stop these attacks, because it doesn't look at the message payload, and as a result we are experiencing new problems. It is also hard to block every malicious site.

Context

Computer systems on a local network connected to the Internet and to other networks, where a higher level of security than the one provided by packet filters is needed. Specifically, we want to control attacks at the application layer of the network protocol. Incorrect commands or parameters can produce buffer overflows and other conditions that can be exploited for attacks. In some cases we might also want to authenticate the client to avoid spoofing. Outgoing flows (to malicious sites) can also be damaging in this environment.

Problem

PACKET FILTER FIREWALL (405) only inspects the network addresses when deciding whether to allow access for a request. We can only block supposedly malicious sites. It is hard to know about all of those sites, and we need further defences. Also, how do we protect our network from potential attacks that might be embedded within the data segment of the packets?

The solution to this problem must resolve the following forces:

■ We need to let external networks access our services and local users access external sites. Isolation is not acceptable.

■ There are a variety of application services in a system, for example mail, file transfer, and others. Hackers can plan specific attacks against them and we need to be prepared for a variety of attacks.

■ Network administrators deploy and configure a variety of protection mechanisms, so it is important to have a clear model of what is being protected and what types of attacks are possible.

■ The protection mechanism should be able to reflect precisely the security policies of the organization.

■ The types of attacks are constantly changing, so it should be easy to make changes to the configuration of the protection mechanisms.

■ It may be necessary to log requests for auditing and defence purposes.

Solution

Make the client interact only with a proxy of the service requested, which in turn communicates with the protected service (see the figure below). The client can only receive service from the server if an application proxy exists for the requested service. Each application proxy has its own access rules pre-defined by the administrator that may be used to authenticate, inspect, change, and filter the incoming (or outgoing) messages.

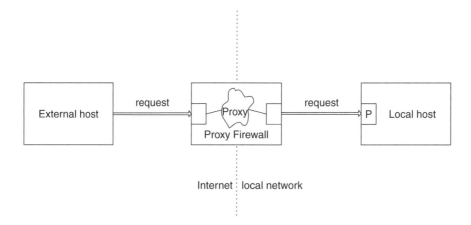

The concept of the proxy-based firewall

Structure

The figure below shows the class diagram for this pattern. We show here only the proxy aspects: the classes shown in the figure on page 407 can be part of this firewall or can be provided separately. This firewall contains `Proxies`, which in turn contain `Rules`, collected in a `RuleBase`. All the hosts of a local network share the firewall. Each local host provides a set of services. The rules may now specify specific constraints for the use the available services.

Dynamics

We illustrate a use case for filtering requests for services. See the sequence diagram on page 414.

Providing Service to a Client

- *Summary.* An external client wants access to a service from a local host. The access request is made through the firewall, which according to its application proxies and their rules determines whether to deny or accept the request.
- *Actors.* External client.
- *Precondition.* None.

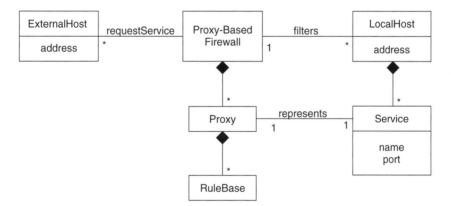

Class diagram for PROXY-BASED FIREWALL

- *Description.* An external network requests a service to the PROXY-BASED FIREWALL (411). The firewall filters the request according to its application proxies and their access rules. If none of the rules in the rule set are satisfied, then a default rule is used to filter the request. If the request is accepted, the client is allowed to access the service through the proxy.

- *Alternate flow.* If the service request is not supported by the PROXY-BASED FIREWALL (411), or the firewall considers the client untrustworthy, the firewall will block the access.

- *Postcondition.* The firewall has accepted the service request from a trustworthy client to the local host.

Implementation

1. According to organization policies, define which services will be made available to clients of the network.

2. Write, reuse, or buy a proxy for each service and assign a location or address to it.

3. Define who can have what type of access to which service and other restrictions on their use.

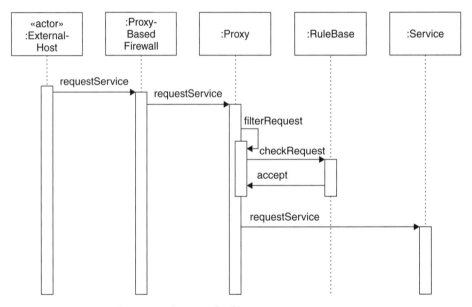

Sequence diagram for filtering service requests.

4. Implement these constraints in the rule base.

5. Consider configurations such as PROTECTION REVERSE PROXY (457), INTEGRATION REVERSE PROXY (465) or a combination with a PACKET FILTER FIREWALL (405) in a distributed configuration [Cyb03].

Example Resolved

We bought a PROXY-BASED FIREWALL (411) and now every request for a service is authenticated and checked. We can verify that the requests are authentic and filter out some payload attacks, for example, a wrong command for a service, wrong type parameters in the service call, and so on.

Known Uses

Some specific firewall products that use application proxies are Pipex Security Firewalls [Pip03] and InterGate Firewall. The SOCKS Protocol from IETF, although not intended as a firewall, uses a similar principle [Socks]. Postfix filters act as proxy and packet filter firewalls [Haf05].

Consequences

The following benefits may be expected from applying this pattern:

- The firewall inspects and filters all access requests based on predefined application proxies that are transparent to the users of the services. In some cases, it may even modify a request—for example, doing network address translation.
- It is possible to express the organization's filtering policies through its application proxies and their rules.
- The implementation details of the local host can be hidden from the external clients. This also improves security.
- A firewall permits systematic logging and tracking of all service requests going through it. This facilitates the detection of possible attacks and helps hold local users responsible of their actions.
- It provides a higher level of security than packet filters, because it inspects the complete packet including the headers and data segments. This global view may control attacks in the payload and attacks based on the structure and size of the packets.

The following potential liabilities may arise from applying this pattern:

- Possible implementation costs due to the need for specialized proxies. The proxies also need to be configured correctly. On the other hand, proxies already exist for common services.
- Performance overhead due to the need for inspection of the data segment of packets and maybe additional checking.

■ Increased complexity of the firewall. A PROXY-BASED FIREWALL (411) may require a change in applications and/or the user's interaction with the system. This is not necessary, however, in a well-designed system.

See Also

This pattern uses the PROXY pattern from [GoF95]. It can be combined with PACKET FILTER FIREWALL (405) and STATEFUL FIREWALL (417).

12.3   Stateful Firewall

A stateful firewall filters incoming and outgoing network traffic in a computer system based on state information derived from past communications. State information generally describes whether the incoming packet is part of a new connection, or a continuing communication whose connection was approved previously. In other words, states describe a context for each packet.

Example

We have been able to contain many attacks with PACKET FILTER FIREWALL (405) and PROXY-BASED FIREWALL (411). However, we are still plagued with distributed denial of service attacks that prevent customers from reaching our site. We also have performance problems for high-speed streams. In addition, a more sophisticated group of hackers is attacking us, sending us viruses whose bodies are assembled from parts included in message data and commands.

Context

Computer systems on a local network connected to the Internet and to other external networks. A higher level of network security is needed than static packet or proxy filtering. A PACKET FILTER FIREWALL (405) only inspects the address of the packet, without the knowledge of previous communications of the same network. Similarly, a PROXY-BASED FIREWALL (411) filters based on proxy restrictions for each packet. The knowledge of whether a connection is a new connection or an established connection is important for improved security: in particular, denial of service attacks could be identified more conveniently if we knew the relationship between packets [Nou00].

Problem

How can we correlate incoming packets? This correlation may be useful to see if they include portions of commands or data needed for attacks, or to avoid redundant checks and improve performance.

The solution to this problem must resolve the following forces:

■ Network administrators deploy and configure a variety of firewalls, so it is important to have a clear model of what packet correlations are required to be inspected and filtered, and what level of stateful inspection is desired. Otherwise, configuration errors and extra overhead may result.

- The configuration of the firewalls must reflect the organization's security policies, otherwise it would be difficult to decide on what to filter and what stateful features to include.
- What is being inspected and filtered is constantly changing, so it should be easy to make changes to the configuration of the firewall.
- It may be necessary to log client requests for auditing and defence purposes.

Solution

Keep a list or table (a dynamic rule set) with the connections that have been opened, and correlate the type of messages received or sent. This gives the option of not inspecting the packets of a well-established connection.

Structure

The figure below shows the `Stateful Firewall` class as including a `StateTable` class that describes the existing network connections. The new client (an external host) can only access our local network if a rule exists for authorizing traffic from its address. In addition, if it is a continuing communication from the same client, access is allowed based on whether a corresponding entry is in the `StateTable`. Each association link between the client and local network is therefore controlled by a `Rule` and/or an entry in the `StateTable`. The `Stateful Firewall` includes a set of access rules defined for the organization or local network according to its policies. If a particular request is not satisfied by any of the explicit rules, then the default rule is applied. For every new connection, an entry is made into to `StateTable`.

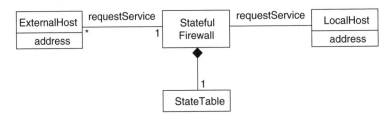

Class diagram for STATEFUL FIREWALL

Dynamics

In the figure on page 419 the dynamic aspects of the STATEFUL FIREWALL (417) are described by a sequence diagram that corresponds to the basic use case of filtering a client's request using states.

Filtering a Client's Request

Summary. A remote network requests access to the local network to either transfer or retrieve information. The access request is made through the firewall, which according to a state table, and if necessary a set of rules, determines whether to accept or deny the request.

Actors. External client.

Precondition. The state table contains the list of previously-established connections or connection attempts. If the state table does not allow a request, rules must be consulted as in PACKET FILTER FIREWALL (405).

Description:

1. An external network requests access to the local network.

2. A firewall filters the request according to a state table. If the connection exists in the state table, the request is accepted without further inspection.

3. If the connection does not exist in the state table, the request may be filtered based on a set of rules, assuming a packet firewall is part of the combination—see Variants below. If none of the rules are satisfied, then the default rule is used to filter the request, as in PACKET FILTER FIREWALL (405).

4. If the request is accepted, the firewall allows access to the local network.

■ *Alternate flow.* If the request if denied, the firewall rejects the access request by the external network to the local network.

■ *Postcondition.* The firewall has filtered the access of a client to the local network.

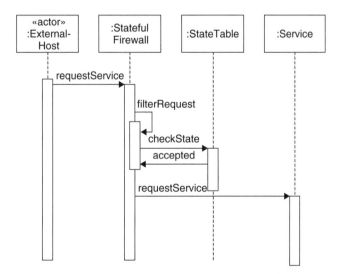

Sequence diagram for providing service to a client via a state table

Implementation

1. Make a list of the types of attacks we want to prevent.
2. Set the state tables to correlate packets according to these attacks.

Example Resolved

Typical denial of service attacks start by sending a connection request not followed by an establishment of the connection after its acknowledgement. Our state table keeps a list of all open connections, and if the connections are not established within a given time period, we just cancel them. We also have a catalog of virus patterns and we can make our firewall inspect sequences of messages to detect these attacks.

Variants

A STATEFUL PACKET FILTER FIREWALL (shown in the next figure) combines address-based filtering with state information, that is, it filters based on the address of the packet and the information in the state table.

The STATEFUL PROXY-BASED FIREWALL (not illustrated here) inspects and filters incoming and outgoing network traffic based on the type of network application they are accessing, and the state of the communication between the networks.

Known Uses

This pattern can be found in commercial firewall products from organizations such as Software Technologies [Sof03], Check Point Technologies, and CyberGuard [Hen01]. Some specific firewall products that use stateful application proxies are Pipex Security Firewalls [Pip03] and InterGate Firewall [Vicom].

Consequences

The following benefits may be expected from applying this pattern:

- It is relatively easy to set up the state table once we know what attacks we are expecting.
- It has a low implementation cost, as it requires only a state table.
- If offers good performance. It only needs to look at packet headers for new connections. For existing connections it looks only at the state table.
- It can enhance the security of the other types of firewalls by adding information from different levels about correlated packets.

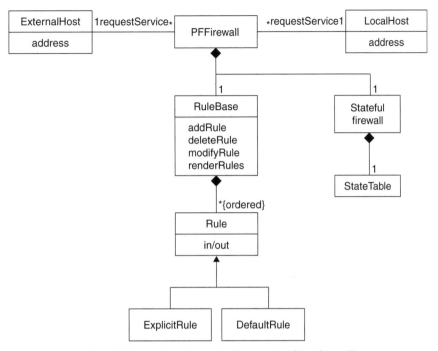

Stateful Firewall combined with a packet filter firewall

- New attacks only require more ways to correlate packets.
- It allows connection-based logging of traffic. This may be useful for detecting patterns of attack that can be used by intrusion detection systems.

The following potential liabilities may arise from applying this pattern:

- The state table may fill and allow some attacks that take advantage of this fact [Fra01].
- Attack patterns must be defined and coded so they can be recognized.

See Also

This firewall is usually combined with one or both of the previous types of firewalls, PACKET FILTER FIREWALL (405) and PROXY-BASED FIREWALL (411).

CHAPTER

13

Secure Internet Applications

> *I'm not interested in security through obscurity. I want real security*
> *mechanisms, solutions that work for **everybody**. Yes, that's a lot more*
> *difficult than randomly blowing away 'suspicious' portions of the Internet*
> *mail infrastructure, but it's the Right Thing To Do.*
>
> Daniel J. Bernstein (aka 'djb')

This chapter deals with patterns mined from Internet applications. They specialize patterns from Chapter 9, *System Access Control Architecture* and the firewall patterns in Chapter 12 within the domain of Internet applications. Dealing with such applications, they can give more concrete implementation guidance than those more generic patterns.

In cryptography 'security by obscurity' is usually a bad idea, because the security of an algorithm must not depend on its secrets, but only on the length of the key. However, in a system context this is less true: there is no need to disclose internal details, as any sensitive, internal information can be useful to an attacker.

INFORMATION OBSCURITY (426) helps to protect sensitive information using the data itself, for example through some form of encryption, and obscuring information about the environment surrounding the data.

Messages that leave a system can passing across any public network. The information contained in such messages is potentially available to an eavesdropper. For sensitive communication across a public network, create encrypted SECURE CHANNELS (434) to ensure that data remains confidential in transit.

In the case of interactions that are commercially sensitive or of a high value, we want to be sure that the users with whom we are interacting are who we think they are, and the users themselves want to be sure that our system is what they think it should be. By introducing a system of KNOWN PARTNERS (442), identified uniquely in a way that can be authenticated, we can be sure of who is interacting with our system. We can also prove to users that we are who they think we are.

A DEMILITARIZED ZONE (449) (DMZ) separates the business functionality and information from the Web servers that deliver it and places the Web servers in a secure area. This reduces the 'attack surface' of the system.

Implementing an application-level server-side proxy[1] [GoF95] [POSA1] can also result in a large number of positive consequences. However, the aspects of network security, single sign-on and integration imply different forces upon such a reverse proxy. Attaching the surrounding infrastructure can create additional roadblocks for a successful deployment.

PROTECTION REVERSE PROXY (457), INTEGRATION REVERSE PROXY (465), and FRONT DOOR (473) try to structure these forces on the different security aspects into three patterns that can be studied to understand reverse proxy solutions, and applied to design reverse proxy architectures.

The most popular reverse proxies implement the hypertext transfer protocol (HTTP), therefore the reverse proxy patterns in this chapter just refer to HTTP. Nevertheless, the underlying patterns are also applicable for any other Internet protocols, for example FTP.

PROTECTION REVERSE PROXY (457) shows how to protect your servers at the application protocol level on the network perimeter. An INTEGRATION REVERSE PROXY (465) allows a collection of servers to be integrated under a common entry point, thus hiding the network and host internals. FRONT DOOR (473) gives guidance for single sign-on and access control to a set of Web applications.

INFORMATION OBSCURITY (426), SECURE CHANNELS (434), KNOWN PARTNERS (442), and DEMILITARIZED ZONE (449) were written by Andy Longshaw and Paul Dyson. They would like to thank the original workshoppers of their pattern material at OT2002 and the subsequent peer reviewers at EuroPLoP 2002 and EuroPLoP 2003. They would particularly like to thank their shepherds at various times: Klaus Marquardt, Peter Sommerlad, Michael Stal, and the incredible rapid

---

[1] In contrast to a regular proxy configured within a user's browser, such a transparent server-side proxy is called a 'reverse proxy.'

shepherding skills of Frank Buschmann. PROTECTION REVERSE PROXY (457), INTEGRATION REVERSE PROXY (465), and FRONT DOOR (473) were written by Peter Sommerlad. Peter would like to thank his EuroPLoP 2003 shepherd Kevlin Henney and the writers' workshop participants in Irsee. The work presented is based on work of Peter's former colleagues, who have implemented Telekurs' Frontdoor solutions: Andreas Birrer, Bruno Büchel, Marcel Huber, Ulf Leonhardt, Alessio Montorfano, Markus Pfister, Jürgen Wothke. Thanks to Lara Beraha, Lukas Buzzi, and Felix Gähler of Telekurs Financial Information Ltd, who allowed Peter and his former colleagues to implement Frontdoors and learn with them about the issues, benefits and drawbacks of operating reverse proxies.

13.1 Information Obscurity

All systems are potentially liable to attack, whether from internal or external sources. If the information held by a system is sensitive, it should be protected. Part of this protection can take the form of obscuring the data itself, probably through some form of encryption, and obscuring information about the environment surrounding the data.

Example

A typical Internet technology system will use a combination of Web and application servers, together with a COMMON PERSISTENT STORE [Dys04], usually in the form of a common database, in which application data is stored. All these parts of the system will be protected from external attack by a firewall and possibly a DEMILITARIZED ZONE (449). However, this is no guarantee of security—what if the attacker breaches these external measures, or if an attack is internal to the organization?

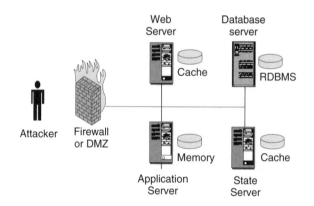

Protection using a firewall or DMZ

The system will gather user information, such as credit card details, and store this in the database. The user information in the database is an obvious target for any attacker who wishes to steal or alter such information. Hence extra security measures may be put in place for the database. However, user information may also be retained temporarily by other parts of the system, in memory, in a cache, or in session state server, as shown in the figure on the previous page.

Application data can be protected by encrypting it, but such encryption is comparatively slow. Widespread use of encryption for all data in the system will impact system performance. Even then, there is no guarantee of security, as the system must have access to the keys required to decrypt the data when it is needed by the application. This means that such keys are also vulnerable to attack. If the intruder can find and identify the encryption keys used for particular purposes, then all benefit from the encryption is lost. This can be addressed by designating one server to hold and distribute the keys. This server can then be specially protected. However, if an intruder can obtain credentials to access this server, then it too may be compromised, hence anywhere the application has access to such credentials (or equivalent privilege must also be protected).

Context

An APPLICATION SERVER ARCHITECTURE [Dys04] has been adopted to deliver Internet technology application servers together with a COMMON PERSISTENT STORE [Dys04]. The business logic and dynamic Web content generation of the application resides on application servers, while all static content is provided by Web servers that also act as a PROTECTION REVERSE PROXY (457) or an INTEGRATION REVERSE PROXY (465) for the dynamic Web content. The application gathers information on users and holds this in its database. The application is protected from external attack by a DEMILITARIZED ZONE (449).

Problem

How do we ensure that sensitive data gathered and stored by our system is protected from unauthorized access?

The solution to this problem must resolve the following forces:

- Much application data is non-sensitive, but the data that is sensitive needs to be protected in parts of the system that are vulnerable to attack. The degree of protection should be commensurate with the sensitivity of the data, and the data must still be readily accessible by the system itself.

- Encryption and decryption are comparatively slow and expensive in resource terms and so should be avoided unless necessary.

- To encrypt and decrypt information you need the appropriate encryption key. However, you must then guard this encryption key from unauthorized access.

Solution

Grade the information held by the system for sensitivity. Obscure the more sensitive items of data using an encryption mechanism in situations in which it might be exposed to attack, while leaving the bulk of the application data unencrypted. Take appropriate measures to protect the encryption artifacts, such as encryption keys, from direct attack.

Structure

INFORMATION OBSCURITY (426) requires the following elements:

- Encryption keys, to encrypt and decrypt sensitive data.
- A key storage mechanism, to store and possibly distribute the keys. This could be anything from a system registry to an off-the-shelf key management server.
- An encryption mechanism, used with the encryption key to obscure data.
- An application component or components obtain and use encryption keys to secure application data in various parts of the system.
- A protected location, a place to store encryption artefacts used by the system. This location should itself be defended by obscurity and/or other defence mechanisms.

The following relationships govern the encryption of data to obscure its contents:

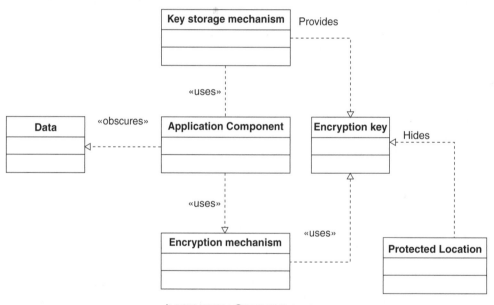

INFORMATION OBSCURITY structure

The application component uses an encryption mechanism, seeded with an appropriate key, to obscure the data it uses.

Implementation

Only part of the data held needs to be obscured, as only part of it is sensitive. The first task is therefore to categorize the data held and used by the system. This process of identification and classification is a form of SECURITY NEEDS IDENTIFICATION FOR ENTERPRISE ASSETS (89), in this case based on considerations such as:

- The impact should that data be accessed by an unauthorized third party, for the user, for the company, and for the relationship between the two: for example, a list of HIV-infected patients on a medical system.

- The incentive for a third party to find this data: for example, credit card details.

- The accessibility of the place where the data is stored: for example, in a cache file on disk.

- Whether this data can be used to compromise further data.: for example, an encryption key.

- The data protection rules governing the specific type of data.

The last point should be well noted, as in many countries there are legal requirements for organizations to take due care in the management and protection of information gathered from customers and clients. Failure to conform to the appropriate set of rules will not only be insecure, but also illegal.

> Discussion: password protection in operating systems.
>
> A suitable example of how to categorize and manage sensitive data is the way in which passwords are managed by the operating systems on which our applications run. An obvious piece of data to protect is a user's password. The first thing to note about the way that Unix and Windows handle user and password data is that they only encrypt a small part of the information. The rest of the information, for example the user name, home directory, shell, and so on in the Unix /etc/passwd file remains in clear text, which means that it is far easier and faster to manipulate it than if it were encrypted. Only the sensitive part—the password itself—is encrypted: the level of encryption for passwords has increased markedly over time in Unix, and even more markedly in Microsoft Windows, which was originally a single-user system. The second thing to note is that in both cases, a one-way algorithm is used to encrypt the sensitive information (the password) and the security subsystem never decrypts the password back into plain text. The password remains obscured throughout its use in the system—the only time that it is in plain text is when it is typed in by the user. In cases in which we are using a piece of data to authenticate a user—a password, pass phrase, or the ubiquitous 'mother's maiden name'—it may be quite sufficient to store it in obscured form without the ability to retrieve the original plaintext.

Because part of the sensitivity assessment is based on the location of the data in the system, and hence its exposure to attackers, this audit should be repeated whenever the system architecture changes in a major way as the system evolves—for example, the introduction of a DEMILITARIZED ZONE (449). Ideally you should make the decisions about the sensitivity of the data independently of the decision about the obscurity mechanism to be applied. If you find that you have lots of data that needs to be obscured to a high level, then the project's sponsors should be persuaded to make the budget available to do this.

Most sensitive user data will still be stored in a database. Small amounts of information can be encrypted and stored in character- or byte-based fields, while larger amounts of ciphertext would be stored as BLOBs (binary large objects). Whether you store your encrypted data in the database or on the file system, you will need metadata to describe it in order to identify the user with which it is associated, used as a primary key in the database, or the file name on the file system. For custom software elements you can use the encryption APIs provided in the Java and .NET world to manipulate encrypted data, although you need to be aware of some limitations built into cryptographic products exported from the USA, which limit key lengths for 'foreign' implementations. Alternatively you can buy third-party cryptographic libraries from many places that achieve the same purpose.

If any part of your system is not enabled for encrypted data, you may need to build a custom adapter. One way of reducing the need for obscurity is to increase the number of the strength of the 'locks' through which a cracker must pass to be able to access the data. You might find that it is easier in overall terms to implement a stronger DEMILITARIZED ZONE (449) and use less encryption within the internal network than to make many parts of your application encryption-aware.

One thing to remember here is that INFORMATION OBSCURITY (426), when applied to data, is concerned with the protection of information inside the application. Once it moves outside the application, or even onto the network between elements in the application, this data is still potentially vulnerable. For this reason you often find INFORMATION OBSCURITY (426) used in combination with SECURE CHANNELS (434), so that data is protected both inside the system and in transit.

As noted earlier, it is not just user data that needs to be protected, but also the configuration information used by the application. To be flexible, information used by the application for its own purposes is often held externally, for example in configuration files. However, some of this configuration information is in itself sensitive information. An example of such application configuration data would be an encryption key. The application needs the encryption key to access encrypted user data, but you do not want an intruder to obtain it easily. Information-based security artefacts such as encryption keys are particularly sensitive, as they can just be stolen—copied—without your knowledge if you don't spot the intrusion.

To secure this type of data, you could secure your external configuration file from unauthorized access. In addition, you could use an obscured name to identify the key in the configuration file. This makes it more difficult for an attacker to identify their target information. If you are still not happy with the level of security—for example, the file could be accessed over the network if the system is configured incorrectly—you could move the sensitive data into a location that is only accessible to local principals, such as the Windows system registry. Alternatively, you can embed the information in a binary artefact such as a compiled class or resource component to make it more difficult to retrieve. In a late-bound environment such as Java or .NET, you might even want to obfuscate your bytecode or intermediate language to make it even less obvious which bit of data is the key.

Obviously, most of the considerations for the encryption key relate to the strength of the 'lock' protecting it. In the case of other sensitive information, such as a database connection string containing credentials for the database, encryption can be used to obscure the contents of the string to help prevent the discovery and use of the embedded credentials. This encrypted information can then be placed in a suitable location, as discussed above for encryption keys.

Once you have decided what is to be encrypted, you need to consider the impact on the rest of the system. The main issue with encryption is speed. Encryption and decryption on general purpose computer systems requires resource-intensive cryptographic algorithms to be run using the standard processor and memory. Although these resources are suitable for general application server usage, they are quite slow compared to what you would ideally want for cryptographic purposes. If you only require a small amount of cryptographic processing, this is usually acceptable. However, the more cryptographic processing you require, the more impact is caused by running it on sub-optimal hardware.

One solution would be to upgrade all the systems to have faster processors, for example, more on-board cache and faster memory. However, this would increase the cost of each system noticeably. The alternative is to buy dedicated hardware that performs the encryption and decryption. Depending on the level and type of encryption required, this would probably be cheaper than upgrading the processor and memory. It would almost certainly be faster.

One final aspect to consider is infrastructure security, as application security can be undermined by an insecurely-configured infrastructure. To address this, INFORMATION OBSCURITY (426) can also be used to help to improve the security of the infrastructure. Some parts of the system already use obscurity, for example when storing passwords. However, this can be undermined if a suitable password policy is not enforced. Other steps can be taken to make a system less vulnerable to attack, such as using obscure host names rather than, say, 'dataserver,' 'kerberos1' or 'keymanager.'

Example Resolved

All public data, such as catalog information held in caches and in memory on the Web servers, is held in plain text. However, any credit card details are held in encrypted form. The only place in the system where such details appear in plaintext is in memory on the application server as it is delivering this information to the credit card processing agency.

After weighing the possible consequences of data disclosure against the risk of intrusion, it is considered that the system contains other data worth encrypting explicitly—customer information. The passwords used by customers for personalization are encrypted anyway by the personalization and customization engine, but their personal details however are not. The encryption used for the customer information is not too strong, as we don't want to impact system performance too much. The main intention is to make it difficult for any intruder to break this encryption casually.

One point to note is that there is a single encryption key used for all customer information, not one per customer. There is little benefit (and much complexity) in the use of multiple keys, as the intention is that the application server software is authorized to view this data, as it has the decryption key. The authentication and authorization of each customer is a separate matter —see KNOWN PARTNERS (442).

Known Uses

Web application components that cache sensitive data on the Web server will obscure the data in those caches. User authentication mechanisms apply INFORMATION OBSCURITY (426) to the data they need to maintain by only encrypting the user's password.

Consequences

The following benefits may be expected from applying this pattern:

- Security is improved by data obscurity because, even in the event of an attack during which the attacker gains access to the file system, system memory and application database, sensitive data is not usable by the attacker.

- The impact on system performance is minimized, because only a small percentage of the application and system data is typically encrypted in order to deliver a reasonable level of security.

- Security is also improved by configuration obscurity, because any attacker will find it more difficult to obtain the information they need to crack the system.

The following potential liabilities may arise from applying this pattern:

- Performance is impacted if an obscurity mechanism is introduced, due to the processing overhead associated with the mechanism. This is particularly true of complex encryption algorithms with long key lengths.

- Manageability is impacted, as additional configuration will be needed for any encryption mechanism, such as key management.

- Components that use obscured data may need to encrypt and decrypt that data themselves, so adding to the cost and effort of developing them.

■ Cost is probably increased, as the extra requirements for encryption may require either additional general capability to support software encryption, or dedicated encryption hardware. You may also need to buy additional encryption software, depending on what comes with your existing platforms and tools.

13.2   Secure Channels

Messages passing across any public network—particularly the Internet—can be intercepted. The information contained in such messages is thus potentially available to an eavesdropper. For sensitive communication across a public network, create encrypted SECURE CHANNELS (434) to ensure that data remains confidential in transit.

Example

A typical Internet-based application will exchange a variety of information with its users. Some of this information about people, products and services will be sensitive in nature. Typical examples include credit card numbers when making on-line purchases or bookings, or product plans and shipment schedules exchanged between business partners.

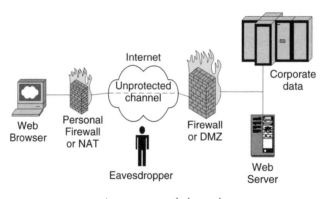

An unprotected channel

It is relatively straightforward to secure data on the client and the server. The client and server can be protected by different firewall mechanisms, in the case of the server maybe even a fully-fledged DEMILITARIZED ZONE (449), to make it difficult for an attacker to penetrate the systems and gain access to the data they hold. If the data is of a particularly sensitive nature, such as credit card numbers, it may even be stored in encrypted form following INFORMATION OBSCURITY (426). However, data on the Internet itself has no protection from intruders, and straightforward encryption mechanisms that can be used in a managed environment cannot be applied between two unrelated machines across the Internet. Because of this, data is passed across an unprotected channel, as shown in the figure on the previous page.

A private channel could be set up between client and server, but this would rely on a private networking mechanism, which defeats the object of delivering services cheaply and conveniently across a public network such as the Internet.

Context

The system delivers functionality and information to clients across the public Internet through one or more Web servers. Larger systems may use multiple Web servers and multiple application servers to deliver this functionality, all protected by a DE-MILITARIZED ZONE (449). The application must exchange data with the client. A percentage of this data will be sensitive in nature.

Problem

How do we ensure that data being passed across public or semi-public space is secure in transit?

The solution to this problem must resolve the following forces:

- Much application data is non-sensitive, but data that is sensitive needs protection when it is made available outside the system's defence mechanisms.
- Encrypting data is a significant overhead on system performance.
- It is easier to provide encryption solutions with known partners, but many customers of the system cannot or will not install specific software or hardware for this purpose.

Solution

Create secure channels for sensitive data that obscure the data in transit. Exchange information between client and server to allow them to set up encrypted communication between themselves. Reduce the associated overhead on the system by using ordinary communication channels for non-sensitive data.

Structure

SECURE CHANNELS (434) requires the following elements:

- A Web server, which provides access to the application's functionality and information. The Web server software could be one of many common types such as Apache or Internet Information Services, but it must support the encryption and key exchange mechanisms being employed.

- A client browser, the universal client used to access the system. The browser can be any generic browser such as Internet Explorer or Netscape, but it must support the encryption and key exchange mechanisms being employed.

- A shared encryption key. To exchange encrypted data in a secure but efficient manner, the client browser and Web server must share a secret value. This usually takes the form of a symmetrical encryption key that can be used to both encrypt and decrypt data.

- A key exchange mechanism such as an agreed protocol that the client browser and Web server use to exchange the shared encryption key securely.

- An encryption mechanism. The client browser and Web server use an agreed encryption mechanism that is applied to sensitive data. Armed with the shared encryption key and an algorithm to implement this encryption mechanism, both client and server can encrypt and decrypt confidential data.

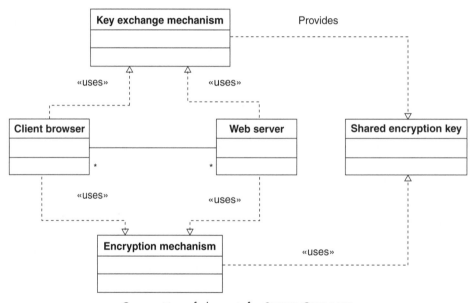

Composition of elements for SECURE CHANNELS

Dynamics

Most of the time the client and server exchange information over a normal, unencrypted channel. When they wish to exchange sensitive data, they set up a secure channel using encryption. This section focuses on such an encrypted exchange. In a typical encrypted exchange, two parties, Alice and Bob, wish to exchange information. They can use a shared, symmetric encryption key to pass information privately across a public space, such as the Internet. Eve, the eavesdropper trying to intercept the message, cannot decrypt the message even if she captures it, because she does not possess the shared key. This is the basic privacy mechanism used by Secure Sockets Layer (SSL), the most prevalent secure channel mechanism on the Internet.

In Internet terms, the roles of Bob and Alice are played by the Web server and the browser or other client software. However, this presents us with a problem: usually the client and server do not know each other well enough to have established a shared key. The shared key cannot just be built into the Web server and browser software, otherwise everyone could decrypt everybody else's messages. Each SSL session uses a unique shared key—hence it is also called the 'session key' in SSL. What we need is a way for the Web server and the client to exchange the session key to be used.

The exchange of session keys is based on the use of a digital certificate. The owner of the Web server must obtain a server certificate that associates a given public key with the server's DNS name, for example www.securitypatterns.org. Once the server certificate has been installed on the Web server, a client requests a secure channel by accessing a resource using a URL that starts with 'https:' rather than 'http:' This request causes the server to send the client its digital certificate to prove its identity, and to provide the client with its public key. The client then checks the digital certificate to make sure that it is issued by a trusted third party and that it matches the DNS name with which it is accessing the server.

If the certificate looks valid, the client generates a symmetrical encryption key (the session key) and uses the public key in the certificate to encrypt it. The server uses its private key to decrypt the session key, then starts using the session key to exchange encrypted messages with the client. This exchange has achieved two things: the client now believes that the server is genuine, and the client and server now have a shared, secret key with which to exchange private messages—in this case, the contents of HTTP POST requests. This key exchange can be extended to allow the client to authenticate itself with the server, which is important for KNOWN PARTNERS (442), but is not essential for most SECURE CHANNELS (434) across the Internet. The essence of the key exchange is shown in the figure below, with Bob in the role of the Web server. For a more detailed description of how the whole exchange works, see [And01]. See figure on page 438.

You may at this point be wondering why we do not just use the public/private key pairs to encrypt the data passing back and forth. The answer is that the symmetrical session key and its associated algorithm are respectively shorter and quicker to run than those for public/private key encryption. Most machines do not currently have the necessary resources to encrypt the amount of data passing between a Web client and server in an appropriate time using public key cryptography. This is a trade-off between performance and security.

Because the session key is shorter and its algorithm simpler, ciphertext based on it is easier to crack than ciphertext based on public key cryptography. If the same session key is used all the time between a client and server, it becomes increasingly

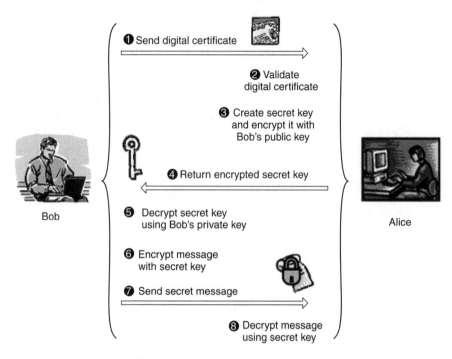

❶ Send digital certificate

❷ Validate digital certificate

❸ Create secret key and encrypt it with Bob's public key

❹ Return encrypted secret key

Bob

❺ Decrypt secret key using Bob's private key

❻ Encrypt message with secret key

❼ Send secret message

Alice

❽ Decrypt message using secret key

Key exchange for SECURE CHANNELS

possible to work out the shared key using statistical analysis of the messages being passed based on the number of times particular words appear in the language in which the messages are written. To counter this, the session key is changed on a regular basis using a mechanism similar to the initial exchange of the session key described earlier.

Implementation

Because much information provided by the system is non-sensitive, it can be distributed by normal Internet mechanisms such as HTTP. When the system need to exchange sensitive data with a user, a SECURE CHANNEL is set up specifically for that exchange. The most common mechanism for creating SECURE CHANNELS (434) across the Internet is the Secure Sockets Layer (SSL). SSL capabilities are built into all major current Web browsers, and also into popular development platforms such as J2EE and .NET. Any application that wishes to use these capabilities merely needs to obtain a server certificate for SSL that can then authenticate the server to the client and can be used as the basis for secure session key exchange.

One issue to consider is that the increased security delivered by SECURE CHANNELS (434) may conflict with other desired non-functional characteristics. One obvious conflict is between the use of SSL and performance. In theory we could use SSL for all exchanges between client and server—in practice, this imposes too great an overhead on the exchange of non-sensitive information. Another less obvious conflict is between SSL and the application of LOAD BALANCED ELEMENTS [Dys04] to the Web servers to improve availability and scalability. When load balancing is combined with SECURE CHANNELS (434) it presents a problem, because if the client were to be routed to a different server than the one that began the SSL session, the new server would not possess the session key for that SSL exchange. One solution here is to 'pin' a particular client to a particular server for the duration of its SSL exchange, a technique that is sometimes termed 'server-affinity.' However, this impacts on the availability and scalability of the solution.

To use load balancing and SECURE CHANNELS (434) in combination, it is best to use load balancing hardware that understands secure channels and that can itself participate in the secure channel on behalf of the server. This solution avoids issues of server-affinity, but does open up a further security gap, as unencrypted information is exchanged between the load balancer and the servers. To address this problem we introduce a totally new set of Web servers and load balancers. Any traffic that enters the outermost switch will either arrive on port 80, the default HTTP port, or port 443, the default HTTPS port. Traffic on port 80 is switched to a standard Web server via the standard load balancer. Traffic on port 443, however, can only go to a secure Web server via a secure load balancer. The packets passed between the secure load balancer and the selected secure Web server are still unencrypted, but we now have the opportunity to put in place additional security measures to harden the channel from secure load balancer to secure Web server. This effectively extends the secure channel from the browser right down to the secure Web server.

The use of SSL between the client and the Web server is fairly standard and is the obvious place to apply SECURE CHANNELS (434): this applies for both B2C e-commerce and B2B[2] e-commerce. However, this is not the only place that such security should be considered. Even if a site has been protected as described in DEMILITARIZED ZONE (449), it may be possible for an attacker to penetrate one of the routers, or even a Web server on the DMZ. From this vantage point they can potentially monitor traffic within the DMZ as it passes between the Web servers and the application servers. If this traffic is not encrypted, it is then available to the eavesdropper. To avoid this possibility, you can set up a virtual private network (VPN) between the Web servers and the application servers. This VPN makes sure that data is encrypted as it passes through the DMZ, the firewall and the internal router.

[2] B2B: business-to-business, B2C: business-to-customer.

Example Resolved

The Internet application uses SSL between browser and Web server to create a SECURE CHANNEL. Such channels are used to protect application data in transmission in different scenarios:

- Passing payment information between client and server
- Viewing of order status by customers
- Logging in by customers
- Changing of details by customers

For a high-availability system, load balancing content switches would be used to process SSL so that the SSL session is between the client browser and the load balancer (as opposed to between the client and the server). Although a VPN using IPSec would provide peer-to-peer security between the Web and application servers, this would be an unnecessary overhead for most applications given the sensitivity of the information passed back and forth.

Variants

Asynchronous Secure Channel. So far this pattern has discussed synchronous secure channels between clients and Web servers. However, there are other ways to implement secure channels. One option is to use an asynchronous messaging system and to encrypt the contents of the messages. Asynchronous operation gives us better performance and availability characteristics, at the expense of the additional processing that is required to correlate messages and to recover from failure.

In terms of Internet technology, we can use MIME-encoded e-mail messages with encrypted payloads as a secure, asynchronous channel. Alternatively, we can use encrypted XML/SOAP messages, as defined in the WS-Security specification [OASIS]. These messages can be delivered synchronously (HTTP), pseudo-asynchronously (one-way HTTP message), or asynchronously (e-mail). While the use of asynchronous messaging is generally useful, you may well need to write more custom code to support this unless you find some good products to help you out.

Known Uses

SECURE CHANNELS (434) is implemented in all mainstream Web browsers (Internet Explorer, Netscape, Mozilla, Opera, Firefox) and Web servers (IIS, Apache) through the provision of SSL functionality. Support for SSL is also included in development platforms such as .NET and J2EE. There are other, less commonly-used variations on SECURE CHANNELS (434), such as IPSec, TLS and various VPN protocols.

Consequences

The following benefits may be expected from applying this pattern:

- Security is improved, because even in the event of an attack that captures data in transit, the data is not usable by the attacker.
- Common implementations of SECURE CHANNELS (434) are built into most Internet software.
- Key exchange allows previously-unknown partners to conduct confidential conversations.
- The mechanism does not impact the exchange of non-sensitive data, because it is only used when sensitive data is to be exchanged.

The following potential liabilities may arise from applying this pattern:

- Performance is impacted by the processing overhead associated with the encryption mechanism.
- Scalability is potentially impacted if the encryption mechanism causes server-affinity, which would undermine effective load balancing.
- Availability is potentially impacted if the encryption mechanism causes server-affinity, which would undermine effective fail-over.
- Cost is increased and maintenance overhead is added, because you must obtain and maintain one or more server certificates for your SECURE CHANNELS (434). Also, you may need to increase the hardware specification of your Web servers or buy dedicated encryption hardware to mitigate the associated performance overhead.

13.3   Known Partners

An organization conducting e-commerce, offering services, or publishing information using Web technologies must make their service easily accessible to their users. However, if these interactions are commercially sensitive or of a high value, we want to ensure that the users with whom we are interacting are who we think they are, and the users themselves want to be sure that our system is what they think it is. By introducing a system of KNOWN PARTNERS (442), identified uniquely in a way that can be authenticated, we can be sure of who is interacting with our system. We can also prove to users that we are who they think we are.

Example

A commercial Internet system offers two Web-technology interfaces: one for the general public and the other for business partners. The business partner interface allows the users to place orders for goods, often with a value that runs to many tens of thousands of dollars. Once the order is placed with the Web-technology system, it is sent to the corporate ordering facility. This initiates a number of supply-chain-management functions, culminating in the goods being shipped to the business partner along with an invoice for the goods.

If we allowed anyone to access this system anonymously, we would run the risk that, either maliciously or accidentally, orders would be placed by users not authorized to do so. This could result in goods being shipped in error, invoices being issued incorrectly, and business partners claiming that orders shipped to them were never placed by them.

Equally, users will be less willing to use the system and to submit information such as credit details and user information for an order, if there is a chance that someone is 'spoofing' the system, for example offering something that looks like our system, but is in fact an operation set up to collect information that can be used to commit fraud.

Context

An APPLICATION SERVER ARCHITECTURE [Dys04] has been adopted to deliver an Internet technology application. The business logic and dynamic Web content generation of the application resides on application servers, while all static content is provided by Web servers that also act as reverse proxies (see PROTECTION REVERSE PROXY (457), INTEGRATION REVERSE PROXY (465), and FRONT DOOR (473)) for the dynamic Web content. The application provides commercially-sensitive or high value services to a restricted set of users.

Problem

We want to provide a system that allows us to collaborate with an organization either as a customer or as a business partner. How can we validate the identity of an organization so that we can be sure they are who we think they are, and they can be sure that we are who we say we are?

Solving this problem requires you to resolve the following forces:

- We want to make the system as easy to access as possible to encourage business: this is probably one of the reasons we chose to offer the system via Web technologies in the first place. However, we need to balance accessibility against the need to identify and authenticate users, and to protect users from anyone who is trying to spoof our system.

- Lightweight security mechanisms such as user-name and password combinations are typically one-way: they identify the user to the system, but not vice-versa. We could adopt a lightweight approach, but these types of mechanisms are relatively easy to break, and the user is often required to provide information that is valuable to anyone that has gone to the trouble of setting up a spoof system.

- The cost of an extensive security solution will be high, but the cost of invalid system use may also be high in terms of theft and loss of customer confidence. If the potential rewards from the attack are high in terms of financial gain or publicity, the risk of such an attack will be higher. The scope, and hence cost, of any countermeasure must be commensurate with the level of perceived threat and the potential cost of the fraud.

Solution

Ensure that access to system functionality and data is restricted to known partners who must authenticate themselves in a secure manner. This 'secure manner' should involve some form of two-way exchange such that the user is identified to the system and the system is shown to be what the user thinks it is. In effect, the user and the system are both identifying each other as KNOWN PARTNERS (442) with whom they want to interact.

Structure

This pattern requires the following elements:

- System identity. The system has an identity that verifies to the user that the system is what they think it is.
- User identity. The user has an identity that verifies to the system that the user is who it thinks it is. This identity can be passed through the system to provide

non-repudiation of interaction: that is, the user cannot claim that an interaction was performed by someone else, and that they should not be responsible for the consequences of the interaction, because the interaction is effectively 'signed' with their identity.

■ User identity verification service, a service either provided by the system or by a trusted external agency that verifies that any user identity submitted to the system is valid.

■ SECURE CHANNELS (434)—identities are usually exchanged via a secure channel, as well as any further interactions between the user and the system.

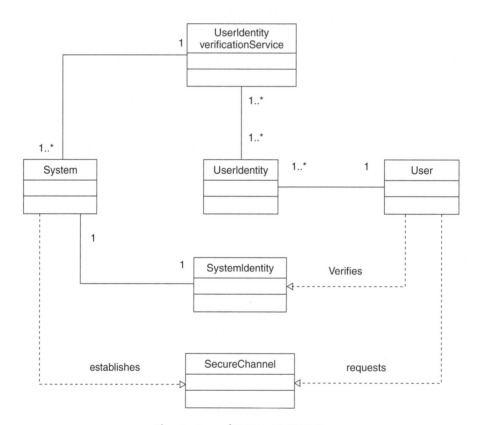

The structure of KNOWN PARTNERS

Dynamics

The first scenario shows a successful interaction between the user and system. The user wants to send the message Message to the system which requires access to restricted

functionality. First, both the User and the System need to establish that they are each
KNOWN PARTNERS (442).

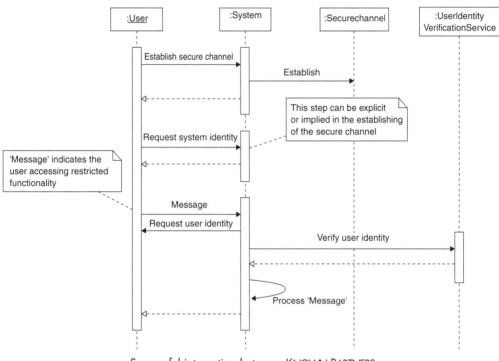

Successful interaction between KNOWN PARTNERS

The second scenario shows an invalid client identity being detected and blocked
by the system. See figure on page 446.

Implementation

One of the commonest implementations of KNOWN PARTNERS (442) is to use digital
certificates for both the system and client identities. In this case the system provider
obtains a certificate from a known certification authority (CA). This certificate has
the domain name of the system embedded in it. When the user first connects to the
system, the system provides the certificate, while the browser verifies that it is correct
for the domain name and has been authorized by a known CA. This prevents spoofing, as a spoof organization should not be able to obtain a CA-authorized certificate
and, if they do, it will not be tied to the domain name of the system provider.

To access any restricted functionality, the user also needs to obtain a CA-authorized
certificate. This certificate is installed directly into the browser, where it is secure from

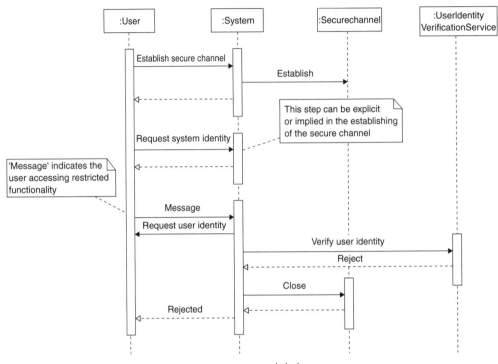

Rejecting an invalid client

tampering—although the machine on which browser is installed may not itself be secure. When the user's browser has verified that the system provider's certificate is valid, the user must then provide their certificate to the system. The user identity verification service then checks that the user certificate is also valid—that is, it is CA-authorized and has not been revoked or expired by the CA. If the certificate is valid, the user is given access to the restricted functionality.

To ensure non-repudiation, it is not uncommon for the system to require that the user certificate is passed to the system for every interaction or culmination of interaction, such as the confirmation of order placement. This means that the certificate's details can be stored with the results of the interaction (or passed to back-end systems). As long as the system provider can demonstrate that there is no way within the system for one user's certificate details to be replaced by another, it is very hard for the user to contend that the interaction was not carried out by them, and that they therefore should not be liable for its consequences.

How the client obtains their certificate is dictated by the level of security required by the system provider. One option is for the system provider to act as their own CA: they provide the certificate to the user and maintain the set of valid user certificates. Another option is to partner with a recognized CA and outsource the verification of user identity, issuing of certificates, and maintenance of the revocation list to them. CAs will offer different levels of user identity verification, from a simple check of on-line identity through to a face-to-face identity verification.

Example Resolved

The commercial organization implements a certificate-based KNOWN PARTNERS (442) mechanism. It obtains a certificate from a recognized CA which it uses to set up an SSL-based SECURE CHANNELS (434). All access to restricted functionality must take place over that SECURE CHANNELS (434).

The organization decides to act as its own CA because it already has a lot of face-to-face interaction with its business partners. Each business partner that requires access to the on-line functionality is issued an individual certificate signed by the organization. When the user accesses the restricted functionality, they are required to provide the certificate, which the system then checks against its own revocation list.

At the culmination of an interaction such as the confirmation of order placement, the individual user ID embedded in the certificate is passed with the order details to the corporate ordering facility.

Known Uses

KNOWN PARTNERS (442) mechanisms are becoming increasingly common for commercially sensitive or high-value online interactions. The authors have worked with several companies that implement a certificate-based KNOWN PARTNERS (442) scheme to provide access to 'extranet systems' as well as internal resources such as document and code repositories. The UK government also uses a certificate-based scheme for its 'government gateway' (http://www.gateway.gov.uk/), which provides access to functionality such as on-line filing of business tax returns.

Variants

Multi-part user identity. The use of digital certificates actually ties the interaction to a browser on a machine rather than to an individual user. This is advantageous if we want to allow multiple users to act on behalf of a business partner and we don't care which individual, but is a liability if we want to identify individual users. A common variant of certificate-based user identification is the addition of a password or PIN individual to each user, that must be supplied at the same time as the certificate. Multi-part user identities are also useful in the case of machine theft, as possession of the certificate alone is not sufficient to access the restricted functionality of the system.

Hardware token. Rather than using certificates for user identification, a hardware 'token' is issued to each user. The token usually provides a key that changes frequently and must be provided to the system on log in—either the key is displayed and the user types it in, or the hardware token is physically connected to the machine and provides the key automatically. Hardware-token based systems also frequently use a multi-part user identity, as theft of the token is usually easier than theft of the client machine, and less readily noticed by the user.

Consequences

The following benefits may be expected from applying this pattern:

- Security is improved, because the system can be sure that any user accessing the system is who it thinks they are.
- User confidence is improved, because they can be sure they are not accessing a 'spoof' system.

The following potential liabilities may arise from applying this pattern:

- Performance is slightly impacted, because exchanging and verifying system and user identities introduces overhead in processing a user's request.
- Availability is potentially impacted, because the user identity verification service becomes a single point of failure for access to restricted functionality.
- Manageability is impacted, because system and user identities must be actively managed to maintain the required level of security.
- KNOWN PARTNERS (442) is significantly more expensive to implement and maintain than a lightweight mechanism based on passwords.

13.4 Demilitarized Zone

Any organization conducting e-commerce or publishing information over Web technologies must make their service easily accessible to their users. However, any form of Web site or e-commerce system is a potential target for attack, especially those on the Internet. A Demilitarized Zone (DMZ) separates the business functionality and information from the Web servers that deliver it, and places the Web servers in a secure area. This reduces the 'surface area' of the system that is open to attack.

Example

A commercial Internet system holds customer profiling information, dealer order information and commercially-sensitive sales information, any of which could be stolen or corrupted by an attacker. This information must be shared with the organization's corporate systems, making them liable to attack as well.

You could use a firewall to control access to your systems from the outside world as shown below.

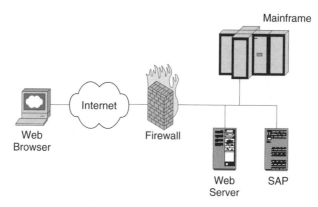

Firewall protection against outside attacks

The firewall would be configured to allow only inbound traffic to access the Web server. However, this places a large onus on the system administrators to configure the firewall correctly, and on the firewall software to operate correctly. If the firewall fails, an attacker could potentially have direct access to other business resources such as the SAP system or mainframe shown in the diagram. The configuration of the firewall is further complicated by the fact that for any highly-available Web-based system, multiple servers must be exposed to support either load balancing or failover. If the Web-based system is also high-functionality, additional protocols must be allowed through the firewall. All of this makes a configuration error more likely.

Context

An APPLICATION SERVER ARCHITECTURE [Dys04] has been adopted to deliver an Internet technology application. The business logic and dynamic Web content generation of the application resides on application servers, while all static content is provided by Web servers that also act as a PROTECTION REVERSE PROXY (457) for the dynamic Web content. The application holds information on users and provides important functionality for users, but the application is exposed to an environment that contains potential attackers.

Problem

Internet technology systems, particularly those facing the public Internet, are regularly subject to attacks against their functionality, resources and information. How do we protect our systems from direct attacks?

Solving this problem requires you to resolve the following forces:

- The cost of an extensive security solution will be high, but the cost of an intrusion may also be high in terms of system damage, theft and loss of customer confidence. If the potential rewards from the attack are high in terms of financial gain or publicity, the risk of such an attack will be higher. The scope, and hence cost, of any countermeasure must be commensurate with the level of perceived threat and the potential cost of the intrusion.

- To prevent attack, we must make intrusion into any part of the system as difficult as possible, especially an organization's internal business systems. However, increasing the level of security will generally make the system more difficult to use, which conflicts with the goal of making the system open and easy for legitimate users.

Solution

Provide a region of the system that is separated from both the external users and the internal data and functionality—commonly known as a demilitarized zone (DMZ). This region will contain the servers, such as Web servers, that expose the functionality of the Web-based application. Restrict access to this region from the outside by limiting network traffic flow to certain physical servers. Use the same techniques to restrict access from servers in the DMZ to the internal systems.

Structure

A DMZ requires the following elements:

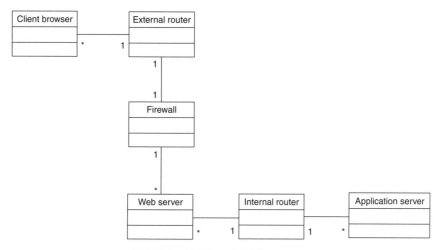

DEMILITARIZED ZONE (DMZ) structure

- External router, a filtering router whose principal responsibility is to ensure that all inbound traffic is directed to the firewall. Its secondary responsibility may be to keep out random traffic generated by attackers.

- Firewall, responsible for receiving inbound requests from the external router and subjecting them to more sophisticated analysis, such as stateful inspection. If a request is judged to be legitimate, it will be forwarded to an appropriate Web server.

- Web servers, providing access to the application's functionality and information. There may be multiple Web servers that are accessed through a load balancer. A Web server will receive a request from the firewall and service that request. A request for a static resource, such as a fixed page of HTML or an image, may be delivered from a cache held on a local disk. A request for a dynamic resource will be proxied through to an application server that is shielded from the outside world in the style of a PROTECTION REVERSE PROXY (457). No application functionality, such as servlets or ASP.NET pages, will run on the Web servers, as this makes them open to direct attack. Although described here as 'Web' servers, these servers may support access through other protocols such as FTP.

- Internal router, a filtering router whose principal responsibility is to ensure that it only passes legitimate traffic from the Web servers through to the internal network.

■ Application servers, a platform on which the application's code runs, typically in the form of Web components such as servlets and business components such as EJBs.

Dynamics

The first scenario shows a successful client request for some business functionality. The client browser request is filtered by the external router to ensure that it is destined for a valid server. The request is forwarded to the firewall to undergo more rigorous checking. If the firewall is happy with the protocol use, the request goes onwards to the server requested by the client.

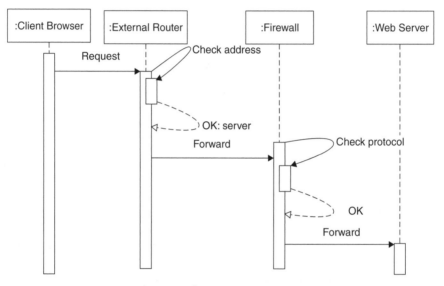

Filtering a client request in a DMZ

The second scenario shows a malicious client call being blocked by the firewall. The client browser request is again filtered by the external router to ensure that it is destined for a valid server. The request is then forwarded to the firewall to undergo more rigorous checking. At this stage, the firewall detects invalid protocol use—maybe some form of protocol-based attack, or an attempt to flood the server. The request is rejected and the suspicious activity is logged. See figure on page 453.

Implementation

Since the request handling and business functionality must be separated by a filter, it is best to use DEDICATED WEB and APPLICATION SERVERS [Dys04] where any

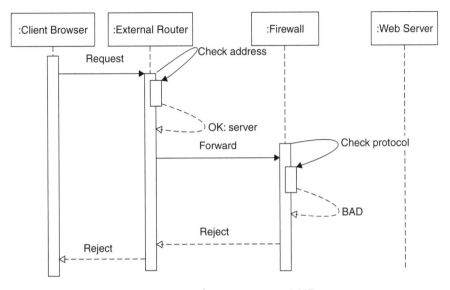

Rejecting a client request in a DMZ

programmatic functionality, whether business or presentation, is deployed on an application server that is physically separate from the Web server. These application servers can be placed on a more protected network than the Web servers. This protected network will have easier (possibly direct) access to the corporate information and services required by the Web-based application.

The external router should be configured to deny any attempted access to any network addresses outside of those known in the DMZ. To increase security, any requests with a destination address that does not match the Web server address (or that of the Web server cluster) may be rejected. The external router may also reject requests based on the port number of the request, for example rejecting any request that is not for port 80. The external router will therefore block direct attacks on the internal router, and possibly the firewall.

The Web servers will be built solely for the purpose of delivering static Web content or proxying requests through to the application servers. These Web servers should be locked down (or 'hardened') by removing unnecessary functionality. Such hardening helps to prevent other, unintended, access to the servers.

The internal router will limit network traffic to connections between the Web servers on the DMZ and specific internal servers, such as the application servers, using a fixed set of protocols. This restriction reduces the risk of attack on other internal systems. The use of an internal router helps to reduce the risk of attack should the external router be breached. Because of this threat, no traffic should be allowed directly from the external router to the internal router.

The whole operation of the routers and the traffic filtering may be controlled from a machine running specific firewall software. This makes it easier to apply consistent rules to the routers and to use statistical analysis to detect potential attacks. The firewall applies more sophisticated traffic filtering rules to detect more complex attacks. Depending on the type of firewall, the network traffic may or may not pass through the firewall itself.

Because the number of servers exposed to the outside world is reduced, it means that fewer parts of the system need a high level of security. In the scenario described, the application servers will not need to be hardened to the same level as the Web servers. To access those servers not directly exposed (and hence less securely configured), any attacker will have to breach several security elements that form part of the DMZ. Hopefully, they will set off various intruder alerts as they do so—if, indeed, they are capable of doing so.

Applying a DMZ to a system is a good way to provide protection for the system. However, you must remember that protecting the platforms on which the system is built is only part of the solution. Since security is a matter of policy as well as technology, all protection mechanisms—such as a DMZ— must be backed up with appropriate procedures and processes to ensure that the level of security remains high— see the patterns in Chapter 6, *Enterprise Security and Risk Management*. If there is a high level of concern about possible attacks on the system, an intrusion detection system (IDS) (see INTRUSION DETECTION REQUIREMENTS (388)) may also be used. An IDS monitors the traffic on the network, or on specific hosts, looking for suspicious activity. If the IDS identifies a pattern of network or host traffic that indicates an attack is underway, it will notify the system administrators. An IDS could be used on the DMZ itself, on the internal network, or both.

Example Resolved

The commercial organization implements a typical DMZ configuration. The system only allows HTTP and FTP traffic into the organization, and even then such traffic is only allowed to the Web servers. The external router drops any traffic that tries to reach the internal router, firewall, or the external router itself. This rogue traffic is also logged at the firewall and notified to the system administrators to assist in the detection of potential intruders.

The internal router allows inbound traffic only from the Web servers, and even then it limits it to specific protocols (IIOP), specific hosts and specific port ranges. This means that any hacker who achieves a beachhead within the DMZ must either attack the internal router directly (and risk setting off alarms from the router) or they must be literate in IIOP to the degree that they could use it to gain access to one of the servers on the other side of the internal router.

The firewall acts as a clearing house for security alerts and as a management console for the DMZ. The organization chose Firewall-1 software based on its track record and traditional association with Sun, on whose hardware it is deployed. The Firewall software gets alerts from the two routers and provides a unified view of security on the DMZ. The firewall software also controls the configuration of the two routers, to avoid inconsistencies creeping in between the three main parts of the firewall system.

Variants

Multi-homed firewall. The number of machines involved in implementing the DMZ will vary according to the level of protection required (based on anticipated risk) and the amount of money available. In the simplest case, the DMZ may be partitioned using a single firewall machine. This machine will have three network cards: one connected to the Internet, one connected to the internal network and one connected to a dedicated LAN containing only the Web servers and any other 'public facing' parts of the system. The firewall software running on the machine will manage the traffic between the three networks to maintain three separate security zones. The benefits of such an 'multi-homed host' implementation include reduced cost and ease of maintenance. However, this system creates a single point of failure, both in terms of security and availability. It also means that any attacker is only one system away from gaining access to the sensitive internal systems.

Firewall as filter. A multi-homed firewall host may be used in place of the external or internal router. This means that all traffic must pass through the firewall (and its filtering rules) to reach the internal network or the DMZ itself.

Stealth firewall. Rather than relaying traffic, the firewall may simply be attached to the demilitarized network and act in 'stealth' mode, simply monitoring traffic for potential intrusion. This can make the firewall itself more difficult for an intruder to detect.

Known Uses

DMZs are extremely common for almost all Internet sites and advice on the creation of DMZ configurations is offered by almost all major network hardware and software vendors, such as:

- Sun `http://www.sun.com/executives/iforce/solutions/SecuritySolnII-Final3.pdf`
- Microsoft `http://www.microsoft.com/windows2000/techinfo/reskit/en-us/default.asp?url=/windows2000/techinfo/reskit/en-us/deploy/dgcf_inc_icku.asp`
- Cisco (variously described as part of their SAFE Blueprint)

Consequences

The following benefits may be expected from applying this pattern:

- Security is improved, because fewer systems are exposed to attack and multiple firewall artefacts must be breached to compromise security.

- The level and depth of protection can be varied to match the anticipated risk and the cost limitations.

- The additional security is transparent to the users of the system functionality and to the developers of such functionality.

- Fewer hosts must be hardened to withstand attack than if they were all exposed to the outside world.

The following potential liabilities may arise from applying this pattern:

- Availability may be impacted, because the firewall becomes a single point of failure. The standard procedure is therefore for a firewall to 'fail closed'—that is, in the event of failure, it will deny all connections to the protected systems.

- Manageability is impacted, because the very restrictions that limit access to internal data may make it difficult to access the application from an internal monitor.

- Cost is increased, because extra elements must be procured to build the DMZ. These include not only the filtering routers, firewall software and firewall host, but also the extra network equipment, such as switches and cabling, used on the DMZ itself.

- Performance is impacted due to the overhead of network traffic filtering. Performance is also impacted as it becomes necessary physically to separate the Web servers from the application servers. If this has not already been done to improve another non-functional characteristic, it must be done to implement a DMZ, and so will add multiple extra network hops for each user transaction.

13.5 Protection Reverse Proxy

Putting a Web server or an application server directly on the Internet gives attackers direct access to any vulnerabilities of the underlying platform (application, Web server, libraries, operating system). However, to provide a useful service to Internet users, access to your server is required. A packet filter firewall shields your server from attacks at the network level. In addition, a PROTECTION REVERSE PROXY (457) protects the server software at the level of the application protocol.

Example

You are running your Web site using a major software vendor's Web server software. Your Web site uses this vendor's proprietary extensions to implement dynamic content for your visitors, and you have invested heavily in your Web site's software. Your server is protected by a PACKET FILTER FIREWALL (405).

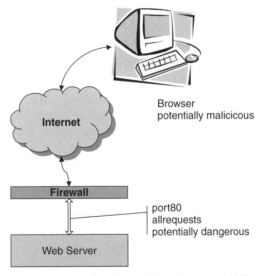

Protection using a PACKET FILTER FIREWALL (405)

You must open this firewall to allow access to the public port (80) of your Web server. Attacks from the Internet that exploit vulnerabilities of your server software frequently burden your system administrator with patch installation. Switching to another vendor's Web server is not possible, because of the existing investment in the Web server platform, its content and your own software extensions. In addition, with every new patch you install, you run the risk of destabilizing your configuration so that your system and software extensions cease to work. How can you escape the dilemma and keeping your Web site up without compromising its security?

Context

Any kind of service accessible through the Internet or a through another potentially-hostile network environment. Usually the access protocol is HTTP or HTTPS.

Problem

Even if you install a simple PACKET FILTER FIREWALL (405) your Web server can remain vulnerable to attacks that exploit weaknesses in its protocol implementation. How can you protect your Web server infrastructure in the light of its potential vulnerability to attacks using its protocol?

The solution to this problem must resolve the following forces:

- A simple packet filter firewall is not enough to protect your Web server, because access to its protocol (for example port 80) must be provided to the Internet.

- Attack scenarios often employ extra long or extra crafted request parameters to exploit buffer overflows. Most firewalls work at the network packet level and cannot detect attacks using such invalid requests.

- Hardening your Web server might be beyond your capabilities, for example because it comes as a black box from your vendor, or because it is too complex.

- Installing patches to your Web server platform helps avoid exploitation of known vulnerabilities. But with each patch, you risk your system extensions ceasing to work. You need to re-run your integration tests at each patch level, and might need to keep your extensions up to date with each patch level. It might even be impossible to upgrade your Web server in a timely manner because the extensions aren't ready.

- Switching to another Web server software by a different source is also potentially expensive, risky and time consuming. A new Web server might have fewer vulnerabilities, but you are less familiar with it. In addition it might also require you to adapt your own system extensions.

- You cannot know about vulnerabilities that might be detected in the future.

Solution

Change your network topology to use a PROTECTION REVERSE PROXY (457) that shields your real Web server. Configure this reverse proxy to filter all requests, so that only (mostly) harmless requests will reach the real Web server. Two PACKET FILTER FIREWALLS (405) ensure that no external network traffic reaches the real Web server.

The resulting network topology provides a DEMILITARIZED ZONE (449) containing only the reverse proxy machine, and a secured server zone containing the Web server.

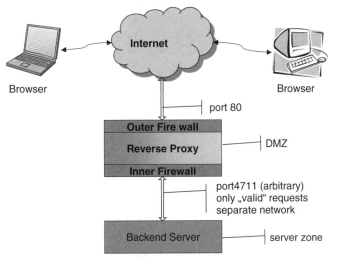

Protection using a PROTECTION REVERSE PROXY

Although this solution discusses only Web servers, it applies to other protocols like FTP, IMAP, and SMTP as well. A PROTECTION REVERSE PROXY (457) for FTP, for example, might scan files for viruses or executable content and prohibit upload of such files, or limit the available FTP commands and prohibit third-party host data connections, which are allowed by the FTP standard.

Structure

The class diagram for this pattern is shown below:

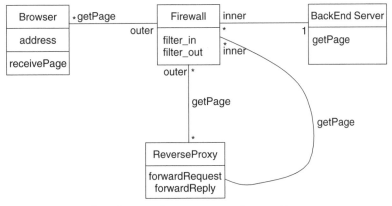

Class diagram for PROTECTION REVERSE PROXY

Dynamics

The first scenario shows how a valid request is checked and passed on by the protection reverse proxy. The inner and outer firewall components are assumed to be transparent in that case and thus are not shown. Post processing a back-end server's reply is optional, but can be used to adjust protocol header fields, for example. Note that the access log is only written after the reply was sent, to improve the responsiveness of the system.

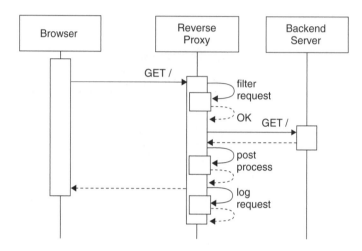

Allowing a client request in PROTECTION REVERSE PROXY

The second scenario demonstrates the blocking mechanism of the protection reverse proxy by ignoring an invalid and thus potentially malicious request. Nevertheless, even though the browser will not get an answer, the attempt will be logged. According to the official hypertext transfer protocol, the reverse proxy should return an error code (typically '403 forbidden' or '404 not found'). It depends on your security policy whether you give an error reply, or silently ignore the attempt and close the connection at the Protection Reverse Proxy. See figure on page 461.

Implementation

To implement this pattern, several tasks need to be carried out:

1. *Plan your firewall and network configuration.* Even if the firewall update is done after every other part is in place, it is good to start with a plan, so that configuration of the other components can rely on the firewall plan. Often the concrete configuration needs to consider more than just one protocol, and

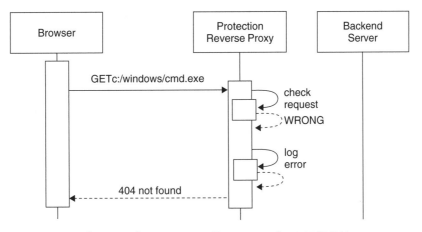

Refusing a client request in PROTECTION REVERSE PROXY

some explicit 'holes' in your firewall may be needed. Find out what protocol your reverse proxy solution needs to support. Typically only HTTP (port 80) is needed, but you might want to allow other protocols through your reverse proxy as well.

2. *Select a reverse proxy platform.* You might create your own reverse proxy, for example by configuring the Apache Web server with `mod_rewrite` and `mod_proxy` modules—several vendors offer professional reverse proxy solutions—or you might need to implement your own reverse proxy, for example because you are using a special protocol not supported by other solutions.

   Showing the implementation details of your own reverse proxy server software is beyond the scope of this pattern. Nevertheless, there are cases in which you might not trust a solution provider, or not have one and rely on your own skills.

   When selecting a vendor or source for your protection reverse proxy, you should opt for a simple and proven solution. For example, by using Apache you risk all the Apache Web server vulnerabilities being present in your protection reverse proxy. On the other hand, the Apache Web server is deployed so often that most vulnerabilities and countermeasures are known.

3. *Configure your back-end Web server(s).* The Web content should rely on relative path names and not use its internal name or IP address to refer to itself. Otherwise links might not work, because the browser can no longer access the machine it is running on directly.

4. *Configure your protection reverse proxy.* For the security to work you need to define which requests should be mapped to your back-end Web server, and define what should happen if invalid requests occur. For example, you might

want to log requests that were denied by the reverse proxy. There are two approaches to request filtering: 'black lists' and 'white lists.'

- A *black list* filter only blocks requests that its list of malicious requests knows of, but passes all others. Black list filters are easier to deploy, but riskier. They are often used by 'higher-level' firewalls.
- A *white list* filter is more restrictive and only lists allowed requests. It needs to be configured with detailed knowledge of the back-end server and allowed URLs. A white list filter needs to be adapted every time your back-end server changes significantly in its URL space. Nevertheless, it is the better choice for a PROTECTION REVERSE PROXY (457).

If your back-end server relies on redirects or other mechanisms that use its host address and you cannot change that, you need to configure your reverse proxy to modify server responses accordingly.

5. *Deploy everything.* Initial deployment, setting up firewalls, network and routers, host IP addresses, and so on requires good planning. If you have a system up and running already, this re-configuration might mean some service interruption. Nevertheless, later changes to the topology need only consider the reverse proxy and eventually the inner firewall.

Example Resolved

Following these implementation guidelines, we are able to protect our vulnerable Web server with a PROTECTION REVERSE PROXY (457).

Variants

INTEGRATION REVERSE PROXY (465) and FRONT DOOR (473) can (and should) be combined in their function with PROTECTION REVERSE PROXY (457), and thus vary this pattern by adding functionality.

Known Uses

PROTECTION REVERSE PROXY (457) are popular. Some organizations in the financial industry have as a guideline to use a reverse proxy for every protocol provided over the Internet (with some exceptions, such as DNS). They can thus ensure that a vulnerable server is never directly accessible from the 'wild.'

Vendors of security infrastructure provide PROTECTION REVERSE PROXIES as part of their broader infrastructure. Examples of such infrastructures are Bull Evidian's Access Master and PortalXpert [Evidian] as well as IBM's Tivoli Access Manager [Tivoli].

Consequences

The following benefits may be expected from applying this pattern:

- Attackers can no longer exploit vulnerabilities of the back-end server directly. Even when the back-end server is compromised, the firewalls hinder further spreading of Internet worms and so on by blocking outgoing requests from the back-end server.

- Even with known vulnerabilities, you might be able to keep your Web server configuration stable, because the PROTECTION REVERSE PROXY (457), with its request filtering capability, can prohibit exploitation of the Web server's vulnerabilities.

- Easier patch administration. Only one machine remains connected to the Internet directly, needs to be monitored for potential vulnerabilities, and have existing patches applied. However, you cannot blindly trust your PROTECTION REVERSE PROXY (457). A back-end server still needs to be configured with your brain switched on, to avoid exploitation of vulnerabilities with 'allowed' requests.

- More benefits apply when combined with more functionality—see INTEGRATION REVERSE PROXY (465) and FRONT DOOR (473).

The following potential liabilities may arise from applying this pattern:

- Black list filtering can give you a false sense of security. Like patches, black lists can only be constructed after a vulnerability is known.

- White list filtering can be fragile when back-end servers change. Adding functionality, or rearranging content structure on the back-end Web server, can imply additional work to re-configure the white list filter of the PROTECTION REVERSE PROXY (457).

- Latency. A reverse proxy adds latency to the communication, not only because of the additional network traffic, but also because of the filtering and validation of requests.

- Some loss of transparency: some restrictions are imposed on the back-end servers. However, these are typically good practice anyway, such as relative paths in URLs. Nevertheless, the back-end servers no longer see the communication end partner directly at the network level. The protocol may therefore need to provide a means of identifying the original communication end point (which HTTP allows).

- An additional point of failure. If the reverse proxy stops working, access to your Web site is impossible. Any additional component that can fail increases the overall risk of system failure. To reduce this risk, you can provide a hot or cold stand-by installation with hardware or software fail-over switches.

■ Hardware, software and configuration overhead. PROTECTION REVERSE PROXY (457) requires you to configure an additional packet filter firewall, as well as another machine to run the reverse proxy on.

See Also

PROTECTION REVERSE PROXY (457) is a special implementation of SINGLE ACCESS POINT (279).

In conjunction with regular firewalls, PROTECTION REVERSE PROXY (457) builds on the principle of 'defence in depth'—see Section 15.1, *Security Principles and Security Patterns* and Schneier [Sch03b].

13.6 Integration Reverse Proxy

A Web site constructed from applications from different sources might require several different servers because of the heterogeneous operating requirement of the different applications. Because of the Internet addressing scheme, this distribution across several hosts is visible to the end user. Any change of the distribution or switch of parts of the site to a different host can invalidate URLs used so far, either cross-links to the Web site or bookmarks set up by users. An INTEGRATION REVERSE PROXY (465) alleviates this situation by providing a homogenous view of a collection of servers, without leaking the physical distribution of the individual machines to end users.

Example

Consider a typical Web site of a company Myshop.com that sells goods and services. Their on-line presence was established with an interface to their support group, giving users access to static documentation such as a FAQ and a simple e-mail interface to contact support personnel. This Web server runs on a machine support.myshop.com. The marketing department the purchase an on-line catalog software vendor that displays their offerings on the server catalog.myshop.com.

Later on they implement a simple on-line ordering system with a small development company, because orders need to be routed to their home-grown ERP system automatically. Because they use a different platform for development for cost reasons, this order-taking system again needs to run on a separate server, order.myshop.com.

To avoid problems with late-paying customers and ease operation of their on-line business, they add credit card on-line payment software from yet another vendor. Again an additional machine is needed, pay.myshop.com. They end up with the structure shown in the diagram.

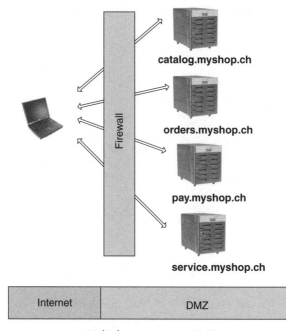

Multiple servers in a DMZ

The business flourishes and their original infrastructure hits some limits. However, their practice of having every server known on the Internet makes shifting applications to another server or running an application on two different systems hard. The complexity of the infrastructure and the cross-linking of the different application servers make every change a complex endeavor, with the risk of many broken links. How can the IT organization shield end users and servers from changes in the infrastructure? How can they extend functionality or processing power without breaking links or invalidating bookmarks of users?

Context

A Web site consisting of several Web servers or Web applications.

Problem

You want to implement your Web site using different servers, or use different vendors solutions for your Web site. How do you provide everything in a consistent Web application space without showing your server topology to users? How do you gain flexibility in network topology, for example by adding or removing servers without surprising users? How do you provide fail-over switching or load balancing if an application server gets overloaded?

The solution to this problem must resolve the following forces:

- You cannot implement your complete Web site with a single server and platform because of complexity, performance, robustness, or reuse reasons.

- You want to hide network topology from your users, so that changes in machine configuration do not break their bookmarks or links to your Web site.

- In addition back-end cross-server links should continue to work regardless of network topology. This ensures that individual back-end applications continue to work unchanged, even when one back-end application is moved to some other machine.

- You want to be able to exchange parts of the Web site's implementation without breaking links.

- You want to add new elements and functionality to your Web site easily.

- You want to be able to switch a request for an application between hosts, either for fail-over or load balancing.

- You want only a single SSL certificate, because certificates are expensive, especially coordinating their renewal.

Solution

Use a reverse proxy to integrate all your Web servers as back-end servers with a common host address (that of the reverse proxy).

Map URL paths below the common host address to individual back-end server functions, so that any modification of the association of a function to a specific back-end host can easily be changed at the reverse proxy. Optionally provide your INTEGRATION REVERSE PROXY (465) with an SSL certificate for your Web site domain.

Structure

You end up with the following structure when you place the INTEGRATION REVERSE PROXY (465) machine in the DEMILITARIZED ZONE (449). See figure on page 468.

Dynamics

The dynamics of INTEGRATION REVERSE PROXY (465) are very similar to those of PROTECTION REVERSE PROXY (457) or PROXY-BASED FIREWALL (411). In addition to checking the permission, the INTEGRATION REVERSE PROXY (465) also calculates the network address and URL of the back-end server it should use as request target.

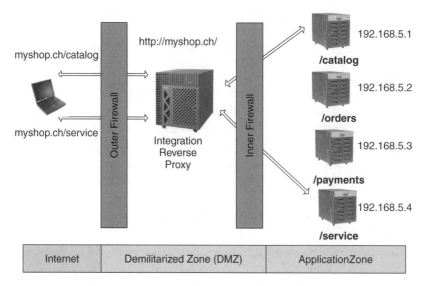

Protection using an INTEGRATION REVERSE PROXY

The parameters of this mapping are the original request URL and the application zone's network topology and addresses. Optionally you might chose to implement load balancing or a back-end failover strategy at the integration reverse proxy. See figure on page 469.

Implementation

The implementation of an INTEGRATION REVERSE PROXY (465) follows most of the steps explained for PROTECTION REVERSE PROXY (457). Additional steps to be considered are:

1. *Design your Web site's name space*. This is a step that requires some planning, to allow for future extensibility. In our example, a path prefix maps to a specific server implementing the functionality. Several prefixes might also map to the same machine. Nevertheless, try to keep the mapping simple. There is one special case regarding the entry point '/': one back-end server can handle this, or the reverse proxy itself can show a navigation page to the user consisting of a menu of configured back-end services. This can change automatically with changes in configuration of the reverse proxy.

   An alternative to the path prefix mapping is to use virtual hosts for the reverse proxy, where a host name still designates a back-end service. This allows Myshop.com to continue to provide their original host names, even after they switched to a reverse proxy architecture.

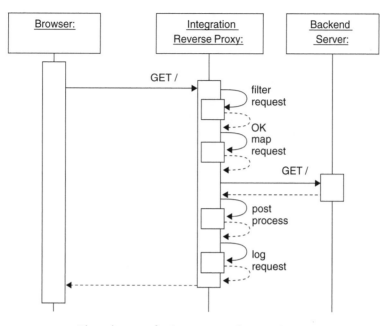

Class diagram for INTEGRATION REVERSE PROXY

A combination of prefixes and virtual hosts allows a service provider to host similar functionality for several clients without the need to duplicate all infrastructure, and with easy extension of infrastructure if the need for it arises. Our example company can use this combination to provide a shop service (catalog, order, payment) for resellers under their reseller's domain address with My-shop.com's servers.

2. *Configure back-end Web servers.* In addition to the issues mentioned in PRO-TECTION REVERSE PROXY (457), you want links from one back-end service to another. For example, the /catalog back-end server will want to link to /orders and vice versa. Following your name space schema, adapt your Web pages and applications to create correct links without referring to the internal host addresses.

3. *Implement back-end server fail-over.* If your Web site must remain operational in the face of hardware or software failures, or when a new version of some back-end needs to be installed, you can provide a fail-over switch to a different back-end server machine implementing the same functionality. Such a switch can be automatic, when the reverse proxy cannot connect to the primary back-end server, or manually configured by operating personnel.

4. *Implement back-end server load balancing.* Similarly to fail-over, you can also implement some load balancing for back-ends if you need it. Several strategies

are possible. The simplest one is passing requests in a round robin fashion among several back-end servers that implement identical functionality. More sophisticated strategies can make use of statistics collected at the reverse proxy, such as response times of back-ends or special queries to the back-ends while collecting their respective loads.

Load balancing becomes more complicated in the case of Web applications on the back-ends that carry a user's session context, because a session's request need to be passed to the same back-end when more than one is available ('session stickiness'). See FRONT DOOR (473) for ideas on how to resolve these issues.

Variants

Integration Protection Reverse Proxy. It is easy (and wise) to combine the INTEGRATION REVERSE PROXY (465) with the PROTECTION REVERSE PROXY (457) and gain the benefits of both.

You can also use INTEGRATION REVERSE PROXY (465) in an intranet integration scenario. Simple intranet applications (for example, those using PHP or Perl) can be deployed quickly behind the reverse proxy without the need to publicize the servers' address explicitly to all users. In addition, external Web applications can be similarly integrated into the workspace without users recognizing the external nature. Combined with a menu of available back-end services generated on the reverse proxy, deployment of tools can thus be instantaneous. This style of integration, relying only on HTTP, is much easier than using a fully-fledged portal server platform. In addition you can gain security, because the back-end servers can operate in a separated network zone that is not accessible directly from the potentially hostile corporate intranet (think about e-mail worms).

A combination of two INTEGRATION REVERSE PROXY (465), one facing the Internet and one for the intranet sharing of the back-end servers, is also possible. This reduces cost if the same functionality must be available on both networks.

Known Uses

Pound (`http://www.apsis.ch/pound/index.html`) is an INTEGRATION REVERSE PROXY (465) that provides SSL wrapping and load balancing with a simple form of session stickiness.

Consequences

The following benefits may be expected from applying this pattern:

- Only one externally-known host: only one name and one IP address for the reverse proxy need be known and accessible outside, except when virtual hosts are used. You also increase security, because fewer machines need to operate in the DEMILITARIZED ZONE (449).

- The network topology of back-end servers is hidden. You can move back-end Web servers from one machine to another without invalidating external URLs or cross-application links.

- Ease of integration and extension. Mix and match of Web applications and technology becomes feasible for back-end Web servers and is transparent to end users.

- Bookmarks and cross-back-end links continue to work, even when a back-end is moved to another host.

- Load balancing of back-end servers by the reverse proxy is possible. However, if your back-end servers carry session, the reverse proxy must take stickiness into account. See FRONT DOOR (473) for more optional features.

- Centralized logging. The INTEGRATION REVERSE PROXY (465) provides a good hook on which to implement access and error logging. Ideally back-end servers no longer need to perform logging. A single log is easier to evaluate—for example, a user's navigation path can be followed easily even if more than one back-end server is used.

- You can save money and effort on SSL certificates and maybe also on IP addresses or host names, because only one host is connected to the Internet. Virtual host-to-service mapping is infeasible with a single SSL certificate. You then need to configure multiple IP addresses for the reverse proxy to make it possible to use valid SSL certificates, or you need to use an expensive 'wildcard' SSL certificate.

However, INTEGRATION REVERSE PROXY (465) also has its **liabilities**. It shares the last three liabilities with PROTECTION REVERSE PROXY (457): latency, some loss of transparency for back-ends, and introducing an additional point of failure.

- It is a potential single point of failure. If everything runs through your reverse proxy, this becomes a single point of failure. Additional redundancy is required for risk minimization. Without the reverse proxy, a single server outage can reduce available functionality, but might not bring everything down completely. Using a redundant hardware load-balancing switch and a redundant reverse proxy configuration can alleviate this problem.

- The number of concurrent connections is limited. IP imposes a hard limit on the number of usable ports and thus the number of concurrent connections that is possible. On really heavy loaded sites with relatively slow back-ends this might imply that you need additional means such as multiple reverse proxies with DNS round robin to stretch these limits.

- Complexity. There may be simpler means to gain one or the other benefit. For example, you can use a hardware load-balancing switch.

- Session stickiness with load balancing can be problematic when back-end servers rely on sessions. See FRONT DOOR (473) for more details and resolutions of this problem.

- Testing individual applications can be harder. You may need to set up a 'dummy' INTEGRATION REVERSE PROXY (465) to be able to test new applications. There can even be the need for a complete testing environment consisting of all back-ends to validate all possible cross-links.

See Also

FRONT DOOR (473) is an even more sophisticated application of INTEGRATION REVERSE PROXY (465) using user authentication, authorization and session management.

13.7 Front Door

Web applications and services often need to identify a user and keep track of a user's session. Integrating several such services allows a single log-in and session context to be provided. A reverse proxy is an ideal point to implement authentication and authorization, by implementing a Web entry server for your back-ends. A sophisticated reverse proxy can even access external back-ends, providing the user's id and password automatically from a 'password wallet.'

Also Known As

Web Entry Server, Web Single Sign On.

Example

Let us continue with the Myshop.com example. Soon after the INTEGRATION RE-VERSE PROXY (465) was deployed, users complained that they had to re-enter their identity several times on the Web site. Myshop.com's IT personnel recognized that each Web application carried its own user database. Adding an application that required user authentication only meant adding another user data base. Providing support services to their customers and resellers via the Web required more sophisticated authentication, and they wanted to allow access only to those users who paid for the service. See figure on page 474.

How can Myshop.com provide access control to their Web applications easily, without requiring users to sign on several times, and with support for extensibility?

In addition, the CIO recognizes that new means of user authentication can become popular in the future, so doesn't want the different applications to depend on a single authentication schema. For example, Myshop.com might give security tokens that generate one-time passwords to their resellers, to add a more secure authentication for users who place bulk orders.

Context

A Web site consisting of multiple Web applications that require user authentication.

An INTEGRATION REVERSE PROXY (465) where applications need to authenticate users, and where only authenticated users are authorized to access a defined subset of applications, a PROTECTION REVERSE PROXY (457) where user authentication is required, and where only authenticated users will get access to the underlying Web application, or a combination of both.

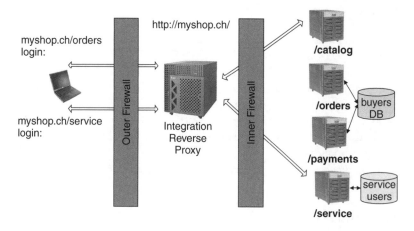

Supporting multiple databases through an INTEGRATION REVERSE PROXY

Problem

How do you provide a single sign on for several Web applications or services?
The solution to this problem must resolve the following forces:

- You want a single user identity for all applications, even when existing Web applications already carry their own user data base.

- You do not want users to have to provide their password for each application separately, depending on your security policy.

- You might want to force users to identify themselves several times, to avoid misuse of a user's session that is left alone for some time.

- You want your applications to be independent of the authentication schema used. Depending on your security policy, you might even require different schema. For example, strong authentication with a one-time password from a security token for payment service, or weak authentication using a regular id-password combination for service access.

- Different users have different access rights to your systems. You want to be able to handle these differences with a single solution.

- You want new applications to easily integrate into your authentication– authorization schema.

- You want both a single sign-on and a single log-off. That means that a user should keep his session as long as he is active, regardless of the concrete back-end he interacts with. On the other hand, when a user logs off, his session should be terminated, so that even when the browser is left open, nobody else can connect to the back-end servers without re-authentication.

Solution

Implement a FRONT DOOR (473) server as a specialization of the INTEGRATION RE-VERSE PROXY (465) that identifies users and keeps track of user sessions. This server passes user identity and session identification to all of the back-ends. The FRONT DOOR (473) can log all user activity in a central log. Depending on the nature of the complete solution, some back-end servers might be accessible by everyone, and the FRONT DOOR (473) only protects some back-end servers from unauthenticated users. Nevertheless, remember that it can also act as a PROTECTION REVERSE PROXY (457) for the public part of the Web site.

You need to consolidate user identities held in existing back-end applications. Store the resulting user profiles by combining a user's identities and access rights in a single user directory. Currently an LDAP directory server is the popular solution for that, but another kind of data base might also be appropriate.

A system for managing user identities and access rights is beyond the scope of this pattern, but is often required. In large solutions that use a vendor's solution for access rights, management can be effective, or you might be able to extend an Active Directory when you are using Windows.

Structure

You end up with the following structure if you apply FRONT DOOR (473) to the scenario from our example. The usual place for the machine hosting the FRONT DOOR (473) service is the DEMILITARIZED ZONE (449). See figure on page 476.

Dynamics

In addition to INTEGRATION REVERSE PROXY (465)s mapping to back-end servers, FRONT DOOR (473) adds another pre-processing step by first checking a user's permissions. Depending on the result of this check, the request is either routed to the desired back-end server, to a log-in page for a user to authenticate themselves, or, in the case of access denial, to an error page. As with PROTECTION REVERSE PROXY (457), FRONT DOOR (473) might chose to silently drop unauthorized requests and just log the access attempts.

Implementation

To implement a FRONT DOOR (473) reverse proxy the following must be considered in addition to the issues given in the preceding patterns:

1. *Unify user representations and data base*. This is easiest if you have a clean start, or if only one user database exists. An LDAP directory server is a popular

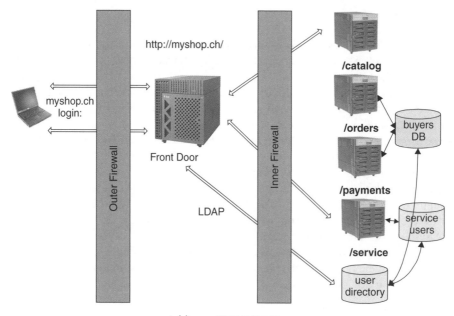

Adding a FRONT DOOR

means for storing user identities, passwords and access rights. If you want to integrate existing back-ends that you cannot change, you might need to add an identity and password wallet to each user object in the directory, to enable automatic replay of id and password when accessing such a back-end.

2. *Define authentication mechanism(s).* Popular mechanisms are id-password, one-time passwords, one-time token based password, challenge-response with token, biometrics, certificates, or any useful combination of these. Since now only the FRONT DOOR (473) needs to implement user authentication, it is easy to change or extend authentication mechanisms later without any impact on existing applications. See Chapter 7, *Identification and Authentication (I&A)* for more information.

3. *Define access rights schema if needed.* Different approaches exist for representing access rights and the mapping of users to the set of allowed services. For the purpose of the FRONT DOOR (473), a coarse-grained model is sufficient, but individual applications might need fine-grained control to internal functionality. A sophisticated implementation will provide a complete model applicable not only for the FRONT DOOR (473), but also for all an application's needs. Chapter 8, *Access Control Models* provides some insights into these issues.

4. *Design user and session representation* as passed to back-ends via header fields. This can be a specifically-named header field, or you can use HTTP's

basic authentication mechanism to pass on the user identity. If there is no single user representation, FRONT DOOR (473) might need to map the user id to the one specific to the back-end. This mapping needs to be stored in the user data base as designed in step 1. Optionally define additional header fields for inter-back-end communication. Those header fields are analyzed by FRONT DOOR (473), kept in its session store and automatically passed to all interested back-ends.

This and the following three steps correspond roughly to activities described in SECURITY SESSION (297)'s Implementation section.

5. *Design and implement how* FRONT DOOR (473) *keeps track of user sessions.* Some solutions that rely on SSL for browser-FRONT DOOR (473) communication use the SSL session id for that purpose. Using a session cookie is also popular. Rewriting all URLs to add a session id in the content of back-end replies, if cookies are disabled, seems too great an overhead and too complex. Using cookies, it is even possible to be able to keep the session context when switching between HTTP and HTTPS, either for performance or security reasons. FRONT DOOR (473)'s session cookies should be encrypted and cryptographically signed to ensure that they cannot be manipulated. If FRONT DOOR (473)'s cookies are secured like this, and they also contain some identification of their source, FRONT DOOR (473) can even accept such a cookie as a valid user identification after a crash without the user being aware of the session's re-authentication.

6. *Design and implement* FRONT DOOR (473)*'s session context.* The session cookie can be the means to store all session context. However, because of a cookie's size limitation and security issues, it might be better to keep the session context on the server side. One solution is to keep a session list with all session contexts in memory. This is the most efficient solution, especially if the access rights of a user are also cached there, but it carries the risk of losing session state on a crash. Another option is to use persistent storage in a data base for session context. However, this tends to be an order of magnitude slower, but allows for several FRONT DOOR (473) instances to share session context. Which solution for keeping session context is best depends on the concrete requirements. For more explanations for keeping session state, refer to the chapter *Session State Patterns* in [Fow03].

7. *Implement a cookie jar.* If back-end servers use their own session cookies, FRONT DOOR (473) can keep those session cookies in its own session context and not pass them to the user's browser. This ensures single log-off. If this is not done, a browser might send an old application session cookie after a new user logged into FRONT DOOR (473), confusing the back-end server.

8. *Design and implement log-in and portal pages.* FRONT DOOR (473) can delegate user identification to a special back-end server, or it can implement its

own log-in page. As with INTEGRATION REVERSE PROXY (465), a portal page that consists of a menu of all services available to the logged-in user is a possible poor-man's portal solution. In addition, a special service link (for example, /logoff) should be implemented by FRONT DOOR (473) to allow applications to give the user the ability to consciously terminate their session.

Apart from its visual nature, this corresponds to CHECK POINT (287) in a FRONT DOOR (473) user's experience.

Variants

As with INTEGRATION REVERSE PROXY (465) you can deploy two FRONT DOOR (473)s that share back-end servers, one for the Internet (effectively making it an extranet) and one for intranet users.

Known Uses

Peter Sommerlad's former company's Frontdoor solution for Telekurs Financial Services Ltd. implements most of the issues given here, in addition to being able to be configured as a PROTECTION REVERSE PROXY (457). The underlying application framework in C++ should be available as open source software when this book is in print.

Bull Evidian PortalXpert [Evidian] implements a Web Entry Service.

IBM Tivoli Access Manager [Tivoli] provides FRONT DOOR (473) reverse proxy functionality with its Web Seal product.

Consequences

In addition to the consequences of PROTECTION REVERSE PROXY (457) and INTEGRATION REVERSE PROXY (465), this pattern implies the following **benefits**:

- *Single sign-on and single log-off*, because FRONT DOOR (473) keeps track of a user's session, and back-ends automatically obtain the user id from FRONT DOOR (473) instead of asking the user for it again.

- *One user profile is possible across back-end applications.* This is not necessarily the case, for example if you start with several existing Web applications and integrate them, but FRONT DOOR (473) facilitates the mechanisms that enable you to move implement a solution that uses one user profile and one administration application.

- *Applications are relieved from implementing access control and user authentication.* This gives you the opportunity to deploy Web applications quickly that readily integrate with FRONT DOOR (473)'s access control. Experience shows that such an architectural guidance for Web applications can be a great benefit, especially on an intranet.

■ *Centralized logging* allows user tracking and reporting. Marketing departments might die for such logs, which keep a detailed track of user activity.

However, in combination with the previous patterns' liabilities, FRONT DOOR (473) carries the following additional **liabilities:**

■ Applications might enforce their own user database, increasing the risk of inconsistencies. For example, RSA's ACE/Server has its own user database for managing tokens for its strong authentication. If you implement FRONT DOOR (473) using both RSA SecureID and another user authentication schema, you end up with two user databases you need to synchronize.

■ A central management application for user identities and access rights is needed. Without a single sign-on, this need can exist already, but might not be recognized. Deploying FRONT DOOR (473) makes this need prominent. Also a lack of corresponding organizational processes is more easily shown up.

■ Password aging policies across back-end applications can conflict. You then need to auto-generate new passwords when they expire, or let the user worry about changing their password on the back-end application and in their FRONT DOOR (473) profile.

■ Conflicting session time-outs of FRONT DOOR (473) and applications can confuse users.

See Also

You can view FRONT DOOR (473) as adding CHECK POINT (287) and SECURITY SESSION (297) to an INTEGRATION REVERSE PROXY (465) or PROTECTION REVERSE PROXY (457), and thus also providing a SINGLE ACCESS POINT (279) to a company's Web applications and services.

Case Study: IP Telephony

'Mr. Watson. Come here. I want you.'

Alexander Graham Bell—the first words spoken on the telephone.

In this chapter IP telephony systems have been chosen as an emerging application that plays an important role in today's business. Despite the fact that it is a new technology, it has inherited many well-known concepts from other Internet applications. However, known flaws of these applications have surfaced again in the design and products of IP telephony systems. That is clearly a case where the pattern approach would have been extremely helpful in avoiding these flaws.

In this chapter the most appropriate patterns from this book have been applied to several use cases in IP telephony systems.

14.1 IP Telephony at a Glance

IP telephony has followed the same 'hype-curve' of many previous new technologies. Early experiments in the transmission of voice packets over Ethernet cables were conducted as long ago as 1983 [Swi83]. Expectations for IP telephony systems in recent years have varied between different groups of potential users, ranging from IP telephony as another Web application to the complete replacement of traditional telephony systems. Traditional systems use circuit-switched time-division multiplexing (TDM) networks, while IP telephony systems transmit voice traffic, together with other data traffic, over IP networks. A huge cost saving was expected from sharing the same network infrastructure, but these high expectations had not been met, despite hype, by the end of the 90s. Available products did not satisfy the required levels of stability, security and feature set. The use of IP backbones for voice transmission was adopted by a number of providers, but IP telephony for end users was not made widely available.

After a phase of disillusionment the products matured and have since been deployed for a professional use. The solutions offered were characterized by an improved system design, but still only a reduced feature set. Nevertheless, a shared IP network platform promises more advanced integrated communication services. This is achieved by incorporating and combining different communication technologies such as e-mail, instant messaging and video conferencing.

In our analysis the focus is not on the 'amateur' view of IP telephony, such as setting up a voice conversation with a friend, where the participants are often served by the same provider and are using 'soft' clients and no specialized hardware. Rather, telephony is considered as an essential and business-critical application. Such a system must be able to provide the necessary scalability for supporting a very large number of end systems and simultaneous calls. The use cases provided focus on applying IP telephony in carrier-grade applications.

IP telephony systems have to satisfy several requirements if they aim to be a serious competitor to existing telephony systems. Customers request a level of telephone functionality and telephony services similar to the Public Switched Telephone Network (PSTN). Additionally, IP telephony must provide particular economic efficiency for the users and for the providers. The customer's trust in the attributes of availability, reliability, predictability, and security have to be satisfied to make an impact on the telephony market.

Without a specific grade of security, IP telephony will not be successful in a carrier-grade environment. People exchange sensitive and often private information over the telephony network. A high level of protection against eavesdropping is expected from the system. The security is based on the 'trust-by-wire' principle in which the users have confidence in the carrier. Subscriber also trust the correctness of the PSTN in terms of billing (a billion dollar market) and call routing (approximately 7,000 billion calls per year). Security is therefore an essential feature in this domain.

A first (public) view of attacks against IP telephony components can be found in [ASR+01]. The analysis show conceptual weaknesses, as well as flaws in the implementation of specific products. A remarkable result of the analysis was that a lot of the flaws found have been known for years, and were simply re-implemented in this 'new' technology. IP telephony components are related to the more general concept of network appliances, which has existed for much longer. Knowledge gained from building these appliances from a security viewpoint has clearly not been considered to its fullest extent.

The conceptual weaknesses are mostly due to the fact that the feature set of the telephony components has a higher priority than security issues or resistance to misuse. One of the reasons for this is competition against existing telephony systems and their large and established feature set. The basic call-control services such call forwarding and call transfer have been merely implemented in IP telephony signaling protocols and systems. Further features such as call hunting or voice mail are missing. A rich feature set becomes the main distinction between products from different vendors, while a shorter time-to-market cycle increases the possibility of error-prone products.

IP telephony was picked as a demonstration application for security patterns, as it provides functionality that has been known for many decades, but using a different underlying technology. It is of particular relevance because errors known from the design and implementation of similar network applications have been made again. Use cases are used to show how to apply security patterns: the application of these patterns in the design phase of IP telephony applications and products would have reduced the number of flaws.

14.2 The Fundamentals of IP Telephony

The principles of IP telephony are explained to give a better understanding for the discussion of security patterns later. The network characteristics and various components are shown in a typical set-up in the figure on page 484, and are described in the next section.

IP telephony systems use IP networks for the transmission of packetized voice as well as for the transport of signaling messages. Only one type of shared network is therefore required. The transmission concept follows an end-to-end behavior in which the end systems initiate the calls and handle the call states. The core IP network is considered to be fast but dumb, while the end systems are considered 'intelligent.' This is a fundamental difference from the network concept used in the PSTN and the Intelligent Network[1] (IN), in which the network provides the services, while the attached end systems (mainly telephones) have only limited functional capabilities.

---

[1] The Intelligent Network (IN) is a network architecture for fixed and mobile telecommunication networks that allows operators to provide value-added services as well as standard telecommunication services such GSM for mobile phones.

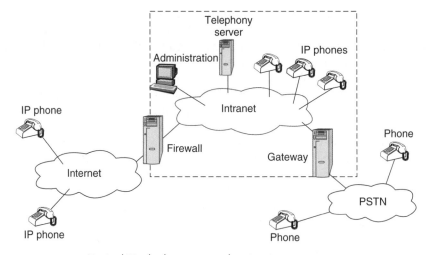

Typical IP telephony set-up showing its components

IP Telephony Components

IP telephony network components such as IP phones are usually assumed to be intelligent, in the sense of being a fully-qualified Internet host, as defined in [Bra89]. Additionally, the entities are aware of their call state. Several IP telephony components are found typical set-ups.

End Systems

IP phones are the most common end systems in IP telephony systems. They are network elements that offer a direct interface for users. These equivalents to traditional telephone are available as a variety of hardware devices, often with graphical output capabilities for call-related information, or as software clients such as Windows XP Messenger or kphone.

IP Telephony Server

IP telephony servers are intermediate network entities that handle application-level routing control. The servers are placed within the IP telephony network and fulfill supplementary services similar to the PSTN. Both H.323 and Session Initiation Protocol (SIP) use a conceptual server that provides functionality for end-device registration, maintenance and administrative support.

User custom services are a noticeable distinction from traditional telephony systems. These services are created by (ambitious) users to fulfill specific call-control functionalities. The functionalities of these services go beyond the parameterization-only services supported by the PSTN. Call Processing Language (CPL) [LS00] is a prominent method to create such services. The individual scripts are executed on a telephony feature server.

Several additional server components can be found in IP telephony systems. Feature Servers provide mechanisms that allow users to create and deploy customized services. Redirect Servers play a key role in supporting personal mobility for SIP. To allow conferencing facilities, Multipoint Control Units (MCU) offer floor control and mixing capabilities. All these servers are also vulnerable to threats, but are not covered in detail in this section.

Gateways

Gateways form a translation point between two networks with different characteristics. Media gateways perform transcoding between different codecs, while signaling gateways translate between different signaling protocols. The gateway acts as a logical combination of two end systems for each protocol 'cloud' in a back-to-back manner. An extensive analysis on the various signaling gateways for heterogeneous IP telephony networks can be found in [Ack03].

Another gateway that is often found in IP telephony set-ups is a gateway to the PSTN. This component allow calls from within IP telephony networks to be routed to participants on the traditional telephone network and vice versa.

IP telephony signaling and media streaming

The signaling messages convey basic information to set up, modify and take down multimedia sessions. Additionally, media descriptions are exchanged between the components. An IP telephony system architecture comprises a signaling and a media transport plane as well as several telephony components. Signaling in IP telephony systems usually traverses a number of telephony servers. These perform application-layer routing and address lookup operations. The media streams are usually exchanged directly between the end systems. This forms the typical trapezoid routing in IP telephony scenarios—a typical setup is shown in the figure on page 486.

High-level scenario overview

The following scenario is assumed for the use cases:

An organization with several subsidiaries is planning to expand, and a new site has been built. The IT infrastructure is connected to the headquarters computing center over a dedicated network. The IT and telecommunication officer decides to use the same kind of network for data and voice traffic.

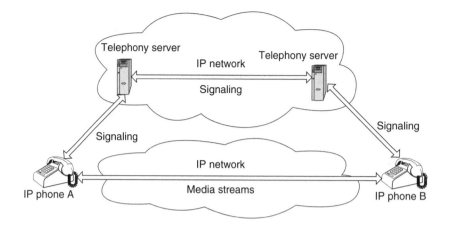

Typical trapezoid routing in IP telephony.
Signaling and media transport are using different routes.

The company chooses to use an IP telephony system for internal voice communication, as well as for the communication between the various branches and the headquarters. Gateways to the PSTN should allow calls to be made via the traditional telephone network. Calls traversing this gateway are billed.

The reasons to introduce IP telephony are:

- Cost saving on installed network infrastructure
- Cost saving on calls between the branches
- Supporting user mobility and flexible offices

Assumptions

Branches are connected via leased lines, for example T 1 connections from the existing ISP. Data is exchanged using this dedicated IP network connection. Additionally, voice traffic is transported over the same connection. A gateway to the PSTN is available in every branch.

Within this use case SIP [RSC+02] is assumed as signaling protocol. However, the case also applies to IP telephony systems using the H.323 protocol suite [ITU03]. Both are application-layer protocols that use the processing power of the end systems. Media streams are transported using Real-time Transport Protocol (RTP) [SCF+96]. A different approach is offered by MEGACO (MEdia GAteway COntrol) [ADE+99], a protocol that uses a master/slave architecture. This assumes limited intelligence at the edges and concentrates intelligence in the core.

The deployed IP telephony components offer administration of network entities and via a remote interface. This interface can be accessed by Telnet or through an

HTTP interface. The device settings are divided into administrator settings and personal settings, such as short-dial numbers or displayed names. IP phones often have a graphical display that also allows direct administration from the device. User input is typed using a numerical or an alpha-numeric keypad.

Business Requirements

IP telephony systems provide seamless integration of the computer network and communication infrastructure of the company. The IP telephony infrastructure is also used for internal calls between subsidiaries. The system also provides the ability to place calls via the traditional telephone network. The devices provide auto-configuration, such that the phones use DHCP to obtain their IP address and register at the registration servers. This allows flexible for working and user mobility. Moreover, the end systems are remotely manageable.

Two different kinds of groups will use the IP telephony infrastructure: administrators and users. Both user types and their assigned actions are defined within a set of policies. The users group can be further subdivided into *regular* users and *anonymous* users.

An anonymous user can perform the following action:

■ Placing calls. The user can place calls from the phone if the phone is not locked by the legitimate user.

The regular user can perform the following actions:

■ Log-in to the IP phone. After successful authentication, the user is granted access to the user configuration menu.

■ Phone configuration. After successful log-in, the menu is displayed to the user. The menu allows the user to edit personal settings and address books on the current device.

■ Place calls. The user can initiate and receive calls to or from any destination within the policy settings. Calls to specific (such as costly) service numbers, or long-distant calls via the PSTN, might be rejected.

■ Register. The phones possess an auto-configuration feature. The user can plug the phone into any Ethernet network access point in building, and call routing will be automatically changed accordingly. The user must therefore be allowed to register the network address of their phone with a symbolic name (or number) at the company's registration server.

In addition to user task, the administrator can perform the following actions:

■ Log-in to IP telephony server. After successful authentication an administrator session is created, giving access to the system-wide configuration menu.

- System Configuration. After successful log-in the administrator is able to configure the IP telephony system's components. This includes the settings of all IP telephony servers, such as the registration server, proxy or gateways, as well as the network and signaling settings of the end systems.

- Log-out, terminate the administrator session.

14.3   Vulnerabilities of IP Telephony Components

Signaling and media transport both rely on the same network infrastructure, the IP network, compared to conventional telephony via the PSTN, where there is a certain level of isolation, for example the B- and D-channels in ISDN. This increases the risk of system misuse. In IP telephony systems there is no physical separation between the signaling plane and the media plane—both run over the IP network, which is also used by other services. Additionally, both end system and infrastructure components are often fully-featured computers that are able to fulfill many other tasks, such as providing HTTP-based management interfaces.

Further, the network infrastructure used for IP telephony is not maintained or controlled by a single authority or a small set of trustworthy providers. Instead, rather the signaling and media plane might rely partly on untrusted networks, components and operators.

Based on these facts, one can conclude that not only telephony-related security problems, for example possible loss of conversation privacy, can occur. IP telephony systems are based on normal network and computer systems and interfere with them. The resulting security problem domain is considerably larger when compared to a standard PSTN-based telephony system, as physical access to the network is required.

While the traditional telephone networks offer 'trust-by-wire' to ensure a certain grade of confidentiality, IP telephony therefore needs to use cryptographic methods to achieve protection. In contrast to the switched telephone network, signaling in IP telephony applications is transported through the public Internet. This leads to easy access that can allow intruders to perform packet sniffing and injection of malicious signaling.

The use cases here will further concentrate on IP telephony-specific problems, however, and not mention for example that routers or other general infrastructure components are also vulnerable.

14.4   IP Telephony Use Cases

Based on the functional requirements, the following actors have been identified:

- Anonymous user
- Regular user
- Administrator

The following uses cases have been identified:

- Place calls
- Log in to the IP phone application
- Log in to the IP telephony server
- Log out from the IP telephony server

In the following we outline each use case in order to discover in which scenarios security is important.

Placing Calls

The use case describes the trivial action of placing a call with an IP phone. The phones are termed *Terminals* in H.323 terminology and *User Agents* in the SIP context. These devices originate messages to establish and control calls. Additionally, they are able to send and receive media data. In these end systems the signaling and media path must come together. The phones might be locked by the legitimate user. If not, then anonymous user are also allowed to call from the device. This use case is shown in the figure below.

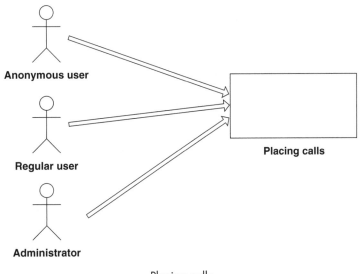

Placing calls

The anonymous user picks takes the hone off hook and enters the desired address of the communication partner. Regular users or administrators can also use the phone after unlocking a locked phone.

Log In

Several IP telephony components require authentication before they can be accessed. This is most likely for SIP servers or an infrastructure component, but can also apply to end systems such as IP phones. The user and the administrator respectively are prompted for their user name and password. On successful validation the application creates the required user session. The end system can be configured through the keypad at the devices itself. Additionally, most phones provide a Web interface, such as Telnet or HTTP.

1. The user is prompted for their user name and the password.
2. The user enters the requested information and submits it to the application running on the IP telephony device.
3. The application validates the user name and the password. If both items match, the application creates a user session.

Log Out

To terminate a user session, the user requests a log out from the application. This action is only available if the user has successfully logged into the application and has a valid user session.

1. The user selects the log-out function.
2. The application terminates the session.

Configuring Personal Settings

Modern IP phones offer a variety of settings for the user. The configuration plane is divided into an area for personal settings and a restricted area with administrative settings. After a successful log in, the relevant configuration menu is displayed to the user. This use case, as shown in the figure on page 491, shows the first case for the regular user.

1. The application running on the IP telephony device verifies that the user has a valid session. If not, the user has no access to the configuration menu.
2. The application displays the configuration menu.
3. The user edits the configuration and the application receives the changes and stores them on request.

Configuring Administration Settings

The administrator of the IP telephony system has the ability to configure the IP phone network settings. These settings specify for example which registration server

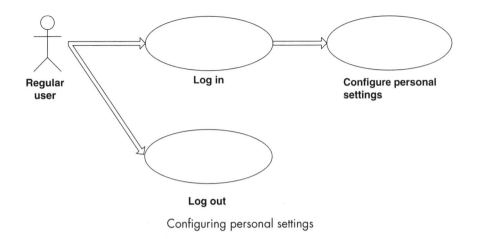

Configuring personal settings

or gateway to use. The access to this configuration is protected by an administrator password. After a successful log in, the administrator can choose between the personal settings and the network settings menu. Protection of specific configuration types is crucial. For example, while pure IP telephony calls might be charged at a fixed volume base price, detailed billing of costly calls via the PSTN is often needed. This billing information can be collected at these transition points. Unauthorized changes to the gateways might lead to fraud: calls could be routed over a gateways that bills at a higher rate, or to a gateway of a competitor where the calls can be eavesdropped. The use case is shown in the figure below.

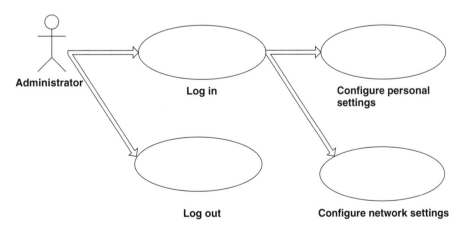

Configuration administrator settings

1. The application verifies that the administrator has a valid session. If not, the user has no access to the administration configuration menu.

2. The application displays the menu that allows configuration and personalization of the phone. Additionally, an administration settings menu is shown.

3. The administrator edits the configuration, the application receives the changes and stores them on request.

Configuring Systems

Gatekeepers (H.323) and registration server/SIP Proxy (SIP) play central roles in IP telephony systems even though they are optional components, because end systems can establish calls directly. However, these entities provide a means of mapping individual subscriber identities to system IP addresses. Additionally, they offer functionalities for admission control and bandwidth control. Their central role makes them sensitive to malicious attacks.

The individual IP telephony servers are managed through their Web interfaces. The administrator has to authenticate to gain access the settings. After log-in the administrator can choose which component (registration server, proxy, and gateway) to configure. The next figure shows the use case diagram with three example kinds of IP telephony server.

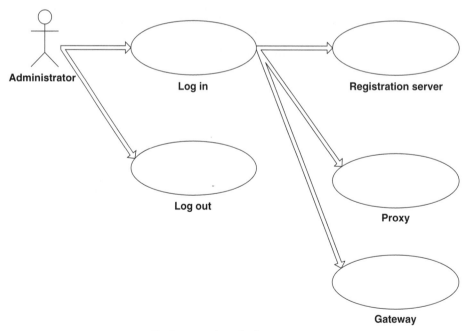

Configuring the telephony system

1. The application verifies that the administrator has a valid session. If not, the user has no access to the administration configuration menu.
2. The application displays the menu for the administrator.
3. The administrator edits the configuration, the application receives the changes, and stores them on request.

14.5   Securing IP telephony with patterns

The scenario described above will now be analyzed using the concepts and pattern described in this book. The use cases provide the basis for this analysis. The root pattern is SECURITY NEEDS IDENTIFICATION FOR ENTERPRISE ASSETS (89) which should be applied first. It is assumed that the process of identifying security needs is done by a planner who has knowledge of IP telephony systems and their risks.

Identifying Assets

The process starts with the identification of the business assets of the organization. Two asset types are distinguished: information assets and physical assets. Both are shown in Table 14.1 and Table 14.2, respectively.

Identifying Business Factors

In this step the business factors that influence the security protection requirements of assets are identified. The results are shown in Table 14.3. The factors can be both external and internal to the organization.

Table 14.1   Information asset type

ASSET TYPE	DESCRIPTION
Configuration data	Any data that is needed to set up the system: registration information, server configuration, and so on.
Media data	Audio or video packets sent over the network carrying a phone call's content.
Billing information	Information that is collected to provide billing mechanisms.
Signaling data	Signaling packets that are needed to set up and maintain a session.
User services	Services that users create to personalize their communication processes. CPL scripts are typical user services.

Table 14.2 Physical type

ASSET TYPE	DESCRIPTION
End points	H.323 terminals or SIP user agents. These can be soft client (XP Messenger, NetMeeting) or IP phone devices.
Server	Any intermediate system as described in the previous section, such as redirect server, registration server, gatekeeper.
Gateways	Entities that allow translation from one protocol or codec into another. Such an entity could be an SIP/PSTN gateway.
Conferencing units	Devices that provide audio or video stream mixing and conference floor control.

Table 14.3 Business factors

BUSINESS FACTOR	DESCRIPTION
Accounting	To provide proper accounting the system must have access to the called number information. Additionally, the time and the duration of the call are important assets. This information is required to ensure correct billing.
Confidentiality	Cryptographic methods are used to encrypt the signaling and optionally the media streams.
Interoperability	IP telephony signaling usually has to traverse a series of SIP servers between the caller and the called party. These servers are often hosted in different administrative domains. To ensure correct routing, the signaling has to provide interoperability.
Usability	The handling of IP phones must be similar to traditional end devices to ensure high usability. Additionally, new features such as service creation must be supported.

Relations Between Business Factors and Assets

The business factors privacy and accounting are in some cases contradictory. Users often want to keep their calls private, while billing information must be collected so that calls can be charged correctly. The requirement of confidentiality and interoperability has to be achieved in a way that both can be fulfilled. The signaling must be encrypted in so that it still protects the user's content but also allows the correct routing.

Identifying Security Needs

For IP telephony the standard protection is applicable. This set comprises confidentiality, integrity, availability, and accountability. Telephony is an integral part of today's

Table 14.4   Security needs

SECURITY NEEDS	EXAMPLE
Confidentiality	Protection of signaling information and media data against inadvertent or unauthorized disclosure.
Integrity	Protection of signaling information against inadvertent or unauthorized modification
Availability	Protect the available services against unauthorized users. Prevent attacks that make the service unavailable, such as denial-of-service (DoS) attacks.
Accountability	Attribution of responsibility for actions. Ensure the right charge for the delivered service.

business processes. It not only has technical requirements, but also needs the full range of protection. The individual security needs are shown in Table 14.4 with examples.

Determine Types of Security based on Business Factors

The next step is to determine the required security properties. The decision is based on the assets and business factors already identified. The summary of this process is shown in Table 14.5.

Table 14.5   Required security properties

ASSET TYPE	REQUIRED SECURITY PROPERTIES	BUSINESS FACTOR	DISCUSSION
Configuration data	Confidentiality Integrity Availability Accountability	Accounting	The configuration of the IP telephony end systems contains critical data about the servers and gateways to use. The server configuration data contains sensitive data, such as the registered endpoints and numbering plans.
Media data	Confidentiality Accountability	Interoperability	Transmitted voice traffic needs to be protected against eavesdropping.

Table 14.5 Required security properties (*continued*)

ASSET TYPE	REQUIRED SECURITY PROPERTIES	BUSINESS FACTOR	DISCUSSION
Billing information	Confidentiality Integrity Availability Accountability	Accounting	Data that is collected to enable billing needs to be in accordance with existing privacy legislation.
Signaling data	Confidentiality Integrity Availability Accountability	Interoperability	Intruders might inject malformed or false signaling information in the network. Sniffers can intercept the signaling to observe the communication behavior. However, signaling servers (for example SIP proxy servers) also need to inspect the signaling to ensure correct routing of the signaling messages.
User services	Integrity Availability	Usability	Techniques such as CPL allow users to create their own non standardized services. These should only be available for the authorized user.
End points	Integrity Availability Accountability	Usability	IP phones might be locked by a password protection scheme.
Server	Integrity Accountability	Interoperability	The servers along the signaling path need to route the signaling messages. Therefore, they need to have a trust relationship, if the signaling should be protected.
Gateways	Integrity Availability Accountability	Accounting	Gateways from the IP network to the PSTN produce cost be relaying the calls to the traditional telephone network.

Evaluation, Refinement

After identifying the assets and their security needs, the next refinement is to apply risk assessment: an ASSET VALUATION (103) that determines the importance of the assets to the company, a VULNERABILITY ASSESSMENT (125) to analyze possible vulnerabilities, and a THREAT ASSESSMENT (113) to determine the threats to the assets. Based on these, a RISK DETERMINATION (137) can be performed. Table 14.6 lists the results after these patterns have been applied.

Table 14.6 Risk assessment

ASSET TYPE	VALUATION	VULNERABILITIES	THREATS
Configuration data	Billing information, system set-up	Weak password, insecure transmission of data, for example passwords.	Sniffing, brute force attacks
Speech data	Sensitive content	Unprotected media streams.	Sniffing, eavesdropping
Billing information	Sensitive content	Unprotected transmission.	Sniffing
Signaling data	Sensitive content	Weak or no encryption, authentication or integrity check.	Sniffing, intruder
User services	Service	Implementation flaws.	Forged service, hijacking
End points	Service	Implementation flaws, no authentication or authorization.	Fraud, denial-of-service
Server	Important functional block	Implementation flaws, insecure configuration, no authentication or integrity checks.	Flooding, spoofing, forged messages, hijacking, denial-of-service
Gateways	Important functional block	Implementation flaws, insecure configuration, no authentication or integrity checks.	Flooding, hijacking, fraud, denial-of-service
Conferencing units	Functional block	Implementation flaws, insecure configuration, no authentication or integrity checks.	Flooding, hijacking, fraud, denial-of-service

14.6 Applying Individual Security Patterns

In this section we show how we matched different security patterns according to the protection needs of the different asset types. We also show how the use cases are resolved. The relationship of patterns to assets and protection needs is shown in Table 14.7 on page 498.

Table 14.7 Assets, needs and patterns

ASSET TYPE	PROTECTION NEEDED	PATTERN
End system		I&A REQUIREMENTS (192)
	Local access to phone	PASSWORD DESIGN AND USE (217)
		BIOMETRICS DESIGN ALTERNATIVES (229)
		HARDWARE TOKEN DESIGN ALTERNATIVES (66)
		ROLE-BASED ACCESS CONTROL (249)
	Remote access to phone	PASSWORD DESIGN AND USE (217)
		SECURE CHANNELS (434)
		ROLE-BASED ACCESS CONTROL (249)
Server	Remote access	PASSWORD DESIGN AND USE (217)
		SECURE CHANNELS (434)
		ROLE-BASED ACCESS CONTROL (249)
		SECURITY ACCOUNTING REQUIREMENTS (74)
	Routing	KNOWN PARTNERS (442)
		PACKET FILTER FIREWALL (405)
Signaling data	Transmission	CERTIFICATE AUTHORITY (82)
		SECURE CHANNELS (434)
		SECURE COMMUNICATION (80)
		PUBLIC KEY EXCHANGE (81)
		SESSION KEY EXCHANGE WITH PUBLIC KEYS (81)
Media data	Transmission	SECURE CHANNELS (434)
		SECURE COMMUNICATION (80)
		PUBLIC KEY EXCHANGE (81)
		SESSION KEY EXCHANGE WITH PUBLIC KEYS (81)

Placing Calls

Signaling information, both SIP messages and H.323 PDUs, are sent over the public Internet. A packet sniffer can be used to observe the signaling information. An attacker with access to the network and knowledge of the IP addresses of participants is able to inject malformed or harmful signaling information. The registration (and de-registration) and the session set-up procedure are particularly vulnerable, and therefore need to be protected. As shown in Table 14.5, signaling requires protection in the four categories confidentiality, integrity, availability, and accountability.

Configuration of the IP Telephony Server

The use of IP telephony components requires administrative restriction in many cases: only a small and trusted group should be allowed to operate the system. Moreover, communication partners often need to be aware that the other partner can be identified and trusted. The basic concept to fulfill these requirements is to provide identification and authentication. I&A REQUIREMENTS (192) guides the process of defining a set of functional and non-functional requirements for an identification and authentication process.

A generic way to protect IP telephony devices against unauthorized users is to query for a password. PASSWORD DESIGN AND USE (217) describes best practice for designing, creating and managing passwords.

Public key cryptography is used to realize identification and authentication schemes that require some sort of key-distribution mechanisms for public keys. Public Key Infrastructure (PKI) implements such a distribution mechanism. The relevant factors for PKIs are described in PKI DESIGN VARIABLES (66).

Access control is spread among the end devices and individual servers. This requires that all devices are kept consistent. A SINGLE ACCESS POINT (279) for the whole system would be preferable. The personal configuration of the phones, such as address books or ring tones, is still located at the phones, although critical settings are usually kept at a central location. The distribution of the settings to the phones must be provided securely. The log-in procedure is handle by a CHECK POINT (287) that provides a SECURITY SESSION (297) for an authorized user.

The access pattern, in combination with this authorization, allows ROLE-BASED ACCESS CONTROL (249): for example, a regular user can be distinguished from an administrator, user only having access to the appropriate settings of the telephony system.

Configuring End System

IP telephony end systems are telephone-like device ('hard' phones) or software programs ('soft' phones). These devices are usually configured by the administrator. However, user are allowed to personalize their phones. Personalization comprises settings such as personal phone books, ring tones, and short dials numbers. To protect hard phones against misuse, access control models should be implemented—see for example AUTHORIZATION (245) and REFERENCE MONITOR (256). Only authorized users should have access to the phone. To achieve this, users logging in should be identified and authenticated and I&A REQUIREMENTS (192) should be fulfilled. The majority of available phones provide local access using the keypad and remote access via Telnet or HTTP.

A generic way to protect IP telephony devices against unauthorized users is to query for a password. PASSWORD DESIGN AND USE (217) describes best practice for designing, creating and managing passwords. To protect remote access, SECURE CHANNELS (434) are required to prevent password sniffing.

Alternative protection schemes can be found in BIOMETRICS DESIGN ALTERNATIVES (229) and HARDWARE TOKEN DESIGN ALTERNATIVES (66). These techniques are especially valuable for end systems such as IP hard phones. A finger image scanner embedded in the case of the phone is a good example of an easy-to-use biometric system. A CRYPTOGRAPHIC SMART CARD (82) is typical of a hardware token-based protection scheme. Additionally, this kind of token offers the possibility of personalizing the IP phones with stored address books, short-dial numbers, and configuration settings.

IP phones generally have two different access modes, one for the user and one for the administrator. ROLE-BASED ACCESS CONTROL (249) is therefore needed. Both roles (user and administrator) also imply different levels of security requirements.

Registration

The registration process provides the information needed for the mapping from the symbolic addresses to the actual IP addresses of the users in the system. Additionally, the re-registration enables a keep-alive mechanism for the server. The registration server needs to know whether the user registering is they person they claim to be (KNOWN PARTNERS (442)). Additionally, the user wants to be sure that they are not using a fake registration server. There is thus a mutual interest in the true identity of both partners and the mechanism for authentication (I&A REQUIREMENTS (192)). An established method to prove identities is authentication by certificates. A CERTIFICATE AUTHORITY (82) issues the approved server certificates. SIP uses a mechanism to force authentication on any request by applying HTTP authentication [FHH+99].

Telephony messages might still be forged by an attacker. Cryptographic methods are required to ensure the integrity of the message. Public key techniques usually provide a signing mechanism. The signed message can be validated by the receiver. If the validation is successful, the integrity of the message is not violated.

14.7   Conclusion

IP telephony is an example of a complex business critical system. Security analysis of available IP telephony products shows a number of severe vulnerabilities. The interesting observation is that known errors and flaws of network applications and products have been repeated. These errors could have been avoided up front if existing knowledge about flaws in this area had been considered. Security patterns provide such knowledge in a unified form.

Use cases have been used to identify common processes in the domain of IP telephony. Starting from these use cases, the patterns described in this book have been applied in the proposed way. This procedure would allow a planner with knowledge of IP telephony and security to secure their systems. The use of security pattern allows the overall security of IP telephony set-ups to be increased. Additionally, patterns could be used during the design phase of IP telephony solutions to reduce possible flaws.

CHAPTER

15

Supplementary Concepts

*Jails and prisons are the complement of schools; so many less as you have
of the latter, so many more must you have of the former.*

Horace Mann

There are several concepts that complement security patterns. In this book we present selected approaches: in particular, we discuss security principles that are useful when implementing security patterns. We also discuss the concept of misuse cases, inverted use cases to illustrate functions it should *not* be possible to perform in a system.

This contribution is based on a submission to EuroPLoP by Aaldert Hofman and Ben Elsinga [HE03]. Andreas L. Opdahl and Guttorm Sindre have been invited to contribute to the misuse cases. We will collect further known supplementary concepts at the accompanying Web site http://www.securitypatterns.org, such as attack trees that can be used to model a concrete security threats landscape more precisely [Sch99], and UML security extensions [UMLSec] that can be used to integrate security requirements into a system specification.

15.1   Security Principles and Security Patterns

Organizations often lack a clear vision of how to approach the security challenge at the corporate and enterprise level, that is, based on business factors and actual context. To adjust the level of security to business strategy and image, we need to know how the organization perceives information security.

The issue is that a common language for expressing and dealing with security at a corporate level that is understood by all stakeholders is missing.

Multiple aspects cause a number of key miscommunications and misunderstandings about how to address information security:

- *It's only technology.* A common misunderstanding, for example by boards of directors or business managers, is that information security is only about firewalls, anti-virus software and cryptography. That's not true.

- *Diversity in stakeholders.* Business managers, IT professionals, auditors, vendors, and so on are very diverse. They all think about the risk the organization faces, but all within the context of their own professional roles. Miscommunication is a big risk.

- *Different professional languages.* Business managers, IT professionals, auditors, and so on all have their own professional languages. Usually, these languages are not the same, causing miscommunication and misunderstanding.

This section provides an introduction to security principles for expressing and dealing with security at a corporate level by providing a framework of terminology, including a method for selecting the most appropriate security principles to deal with security at a corporate level. In the following we introduce:

- A framework for security principles
- Methods to select security principles

This section is based on a paper that was first issued to EuroPLoP 2003 and was shepherded by Andy Longshaw. At EuroPLoP2003 the paper was discussed in a workshop and comments improved it considerably.

A security principle in this context is defined as a high-level model for expressing the way the organization thinks about security. Such a high-level model can suit the business model of the organization, is typically summarized by a short phrase that can be explained and understood by everyone (!) involved in the safety and security of the organization. Some common examples are 'Need to Know,' 'Perimeter Defence,' or 'Issue-Driven.'

When thinking about these common examples, you'll find that it's not easy to choose. Some principles might be opposites, others might strengthen each other. This is why we thought of a framework for positioning security principles, consisting of:

1. Mindset principles at a strategic level, for example 'What is your mindset about security?'

2. Architectural principles at a tactical level, for example 'How do you want to implement your defence?'

3. Execution principles at an operational level, for example 'How do you want to act?'

Mindset principles are used by the organization to formulate its security strategy. The context of architecture principles is defined by the mindset, and ultimately the context of the execution principles is highly dependant on the culture of the organization, combined with the mindset principles that the organization uses to formulate its security strategy. Because implementing a corporate or organization security strategy consistently requires a lot of change, this is where the human factor plays an important role.

Selecting the right principle(s) is not easy. Some principles overlap, some are opposites, some use the same words for different subjects, while some principles aim at different areas of information security.

We identified two methods for selecting the right combination of principles given a certain context. The first is based on a 'best and worst practice' approach. The second is based on an approach that gives organizations the ability to grow in security level based on their business requirements. Both methods are described in this section in more detail. A combination of these methods is even possible, although we did not look into that.

Analogous to patterns, there benefits and liabilities of using security principles. We identified the following benefits:

- Well-named principles are almost self-explanatory and could even replace existing policies and documents. At the least, they make it easier to 'live' the policies and to write more vital documents.

- Security principles provide a very powerful mechanism for expressing a security strategy and communicating this strategy to a broad audience.

- Security principles can be combined into scenarios, which makes it easier for the organization to make a roadmap and evaluate possible options beforehand.

- Mindset, architecture, and execution principles can be related to each other, enabling sharing of best practices and continuous improvement. This leads to sets of directly-related principles, enabling consistency over how to handle security.

We have also identified the following liabilities:

- Like all other security approaches, security principles are not a silver bullet. Apart from the right security principle, you still need practical experience, expertise, and hard labor to realize a solid solution. A security principle is an ingredient to success, not a guarantee of success.

- Because not all security principles are documented in full detail and related to lower-level security principles, for the time being creativity and expert information is needed to implement security principles at the working level.

Selecting Principles Based on Opposites

We start with a simple approach for selecting principles to improve the corporate security level.

1. Go through the principles and mark all of them that are used by the organization you're dealing with.

2. Walk through the tables for mindset principles and execution principles in the paragraphs that follow to see if you can find principles identified in step step 1 that are actually bad practices. Note that we could not identify any bad architecture principles, so only the architecture principles themselves are listed.

3. For all bad practices, consider selecting the opposite principle.

4. Prioritize selected principles and plan to implement them.

5. Obtain senior management commitment to execute the plan accordingly.

Note that it does not make sense to select and implement all the principles listed in the table during the first implementation. It is much better to start with the three most important mindset principles and the two most important execution principles. Note that changing people's mindset takes time. The simpler the message, the greater the chance of success.

Mindset Principles

We identified twenty-seven different mindset principles, listed in terms of best practices and bad practices. Although we know that the world is not simply black or white, we deliberately choose to present the principles as either good or bad to position them as clearly as possible. You can probably think of specific situations where good practices turned out bad, or where bad practices turned out to be good after all.

Architecture Principles

We identified ten architecture principles, but did not find any bad practices. We are still wondering why it is easy to identify bad practices for mindset and execution

Table 15.1   Mindset principles

BAD PRACTICE	GOOD PRACTICE
Security as a technical issue	Security as a business issue
Uncontrolled access	Need to protect Need to know
Risk unawareness, risk avoidance	Manage risk
Point solutions	End-to-end security, entity-to-entity security
Violate the law	Obey the law
Safety unawareness	Safety before security
Security by obscurity	Keep it open
Make it complex	Keep it simple
Trust your security	Fail securely
Trust your vendor	Security goals before means
Fortress mentality	Time-based security
Trust your employees	Trust nobody

Table 15.2   Architecture principles

GOOD PRACTICE
Security guard
Perimeter defence
Divide and conquer
The network as a battleground
Peace or war
Immune system
Layered security
Defence in depth
Watch the watchers
Enlist the users

principles, but not for architecture principles. Perhaps architecture principles have already been through an implicit selection process before they are described and published.

Execution Principles

We identified fourteen execution principles, listed in terms of good and bad practices:

Table 15.3 Execution principles

BAD PRACTICE	GOOD PRACTICE
Security at any price	Return on investment
Security as a desert	Security in every change
Ignore security patches	Proactive maintenance of security
Wait for the auditor	Mature through time
Top-down approach only	Issue-driven
Paralysis by analysis	Just do it together
Ignore security incidents	Respond on security incidents

Selecting Principles Based on Maturity Levels

A more advanced approach is to introduce categories of principles that can be applied as a group based on the maturity level of the organization. We identified the following maturity levels:

- IT-centric but ad-hoc
- IT centric and 'in control'
- Business-aligned and 'in control'
- Ecosystem-integrated and agile

The most practical approach here is to have a workshop with senior management to determine the level they want to implement within three years. The roadmap to the intended level is very important: if senior management wants to make more steps in the coming three years, make sure that you plan the arrival of the intermediate maturity levels as well.

Generally Good and Bad Security Principles

We consider these principles as generally good, despite the level of maturity. See Table 15.4 on page 509.

Likewise, we consider these principles to be generally bad, despite the level of maturity. See Table 15.5 on page 509.

Table 15.4 Generally good security principles

PRINCIPLE TYPE	PRINCIPLE NAME
Mindset	Obey the law
Mindset	Safety before security
Mindset	Keep it open
Mindset	Keep it simple
Mindset	Trust nobody
Architecture	Perimeter defence
Execution	Proactive maintenance of security
Execution	Just do it together
Execution	Respond to security incidents

Table 15.5 Generally bad security principles

PRINCIPLE TYPE	BAD PRACTICE NAME
Mindset	Risk avoidance
Mindset	Violate the law
Mindset	Safety unawareness
Mindset	Security by obscurity
Mindset	Make it complex

Table 15.5 Generally bad security principles (*continued*)

PRINCIPLE TYPE	BAD PRACTICE NAME
Mindset	Trust your security
Mindset	Trust your employees
Execution	Security at any price
Execution	Ignore security patches
Execution	Top-down approach only
Execution	Paralysis by analysis
Execution	Ignore security incidents

IT-centric ad-hoc (anti) Principles

At the IT-centric ad-hoc maturity level, security is viewed as a technical issue only and is solved on an ad-hoc basis without managed change processes or an overall security vision or plan. You will probably not be surprised that at this level a lot of bad practices are applied. Security principle bad practices applied at this level are:

Table 15.6 Bad IT-centric ad-hoc principles

PRINCIPLE TYPE	BAD PRACTICE NAME
Mindset	Security as a technical issue
Mindset	Uncontrolled access
Mindset	Risk unawareness
Mindset	Point solutions
Mindset	Trust your vendor
Mindset	Fortress mentality
Execution	Security as a desert
Execution	Wait for the auditor

IT Centric and 'in control' Principles

At an IT-centric and 'in control' maturity level, security is viewed as a technical issue, but formal change processes and a structured process are in place to manage security. Although mindset at this level is very technology-oriented, technical risks are managed. Security principles that are applied at this level are:

Table 15.7   IT-centric and 'in control' principles

PRINCIPLE TYPE	PRINCIPLE NAME
Mindset	Need to know
Mindset	Manage risk
Mindset	End-to-end security
Mindset	Time-based security
Architecture	Layered security
Architecture	Enlist the users
Execution	Security in every change
Execution	Mature through time
Execution	Issue-driven

Business-aligned and 'in control' Principles

At a business-aligned and 'in control' maturity level, security is viewed as a business issue. The level of security is of strategic importance for the organization and is broadly perceived in this way. There are formal change processes in place, and a security organization to manage security. Business requirements drive security requirements, not the other way around. Security principles applied at this level are:

Table 15.8   Business-aligned and 'in control' principles

PRINCIPLE TYPE	PRINCIPLE NAME
Mindset	Security as a business issue
Mindset	Need to protect
Mindset	Manage risk

Table 15.8 Business-aligned and 'in control' principles (*continued*)

PRINCIPLE TYPE	PRINCIPLE NAME
Mindset	End-to-end security
Mindset	Fail securely
Mindset	Security goals before means
Mindset	Time-based security
Architecture	Security guard
Architecture	Divide and conquer
Architecture	Layered security
Architecture	Defence in depth
Architecture	Watch the watchers
Architecture	Enlist the users
Execution	Return on investment
Execution	Security in every change
Execution	Mature through time
Execution	Issue-driven

Ecosystem-integrated and Agile Principles

At an ecosystem-integrated and agile maturity level, security is viewed as a business issue, but at the same time business is highly dependent on co-operation with business partners. A network of organizations therefore has to work together to provide added value to the customer. Continuity problems and leakage of confidential information within one organization will have a negative effect on all the organizations that profit from the value chain.

Because of the amount of electronic interaction of the target organization with a lot of other organizations, security needs to be agile as well. It must be easy to adopt and differentiate the security level based on the characteristics of the communication partners. Risks are eminent, but the target organizations have a lot of mechanisms in place to control security incidents of different sorts and severity in near real time.

Business requirements of the entire value chain drive security requirements. Being highly adaptive is just a means of survival in the turbulent business environments and networked economies we see today. Security principle practices applied at this level are:

Table 15.9   Ecosystem-integrated and agile principles

PRINCIPLE TYPE	PRINCIPLE NAME
Mindset	Security as a business issue
Mindset	Need to protect
Mindset	Manage risk
Mindset	Entity-to-entity security
Mindset	Fail securely
Mindset	Security goals before means
Mindset	Time-based security
Architecture	Security guard
Architecture	Divide and conquer
Architecture	The network as a battleground
Architecture	Peace or war
Architecture	Immune system
Architecture	Layered security
Architecture	Defence in depth
Architecture	Watch the watchers
Architecture	Enlist the users
Execution	Return on investment
Execution	Security in every change
Execution	Mature through time
Execution	Issue-driven

Introducing Mindset Principles

Embedding security in an organization can be done in many ways. Whether or not this is successful depends on non-technical aspects like the type of organization, the environment, regulations, the type of business, the maturity of the management functions and business processes, and the maturity of IT processes. Besides this, human and cultural aspects are very important as well.

This wide range of factors makes it sensible to document how you perceive security, in order to create a clear and uniform starting point for embedding security in the organization. Mindset principles can be used to build a corporate security strategy, building perception on security.

Security as a Technical Issue

In the mindset of general management, security is perceived as a purely technical issue. A technical problem needs to be resolved with technology: the IT department is the main source of action. Security is not on the agenda of the general management team and business requirements are weak. IT management owns the problem: the IT department knows everything about technical issues. The CIO, ICT/information manager is the problem owner and it should stay that way. Of course, they're the one to blame when incidents occur. People from the ICT department are aware of the problem, they think. If something goes wrong, the IT department gets the blame. The challenge is to achieve a sufficient level of protection by technical means, that is, to be pretty sure that nothing can go wrong. What needs to be protected and why is not an issue. Projects tend to be delayed because security is a bottleneck. Business people ask themselves why security hampers new business activities, or why security always seems to be the problem?

Security is a Business Issue

In the mindset of general management security is perceived as an enabler for new business and/or improved business processes. Business processes can easily cross boundaries of organizations towards customers, partners and citizens. Security is on the agenda of the management team. The team is committed to keep the level of security in balance with the actual level of threats to business processes. Security is an important subject in every business contact of the organization. For every new business initiative, a risk analysis is performed to make sure that risks are managed from the business perspective. Security isn't about risk avoidance—it's about risk management.

Uncontrolled Access

There are no formal procedures for authorization management. It is not clear who in the organization are authorizing people. There is a lot of trust within organizations that no-one will misuse their rights to look at or use information and applications other than is strictly needed to perform a specific role. The culture is open, nobody has a problem with the fact that the amount of information that is widely shared is very high. Efficiency and simplicity in doing the job is more important than doing it securely. Management is not committed to information security at all.

Need to Protect

The organization performs a corporate risk assessment to determine which information assets are very important for the organization or its stakeholders. This analysis will also supply information about why certain information assets are important. The security aspects that are determined are confidentiality, integrity, and availability. When the risk threshold set by the business owner is exceeded, the asset will be protected accordingly. The stance of this principle is that everything is permitted unless explicitly forbidden.

Need to Know

A person is only granted privilege to use a particular information asset if there is really a business need for it, for example the person genuinely needs the information to do their job. The rationale is that if people can access more informational assets than they need to fulfil their job, the risk of security incidents will increase. Authorization processes are strict, formal, and highly granular. Role-based access is used to lighten the security control and maintenance burden. The stance of this principle is that nothing is permitted unless explicitly granted.

Risk Unawareness

People in the organization are not aware that identifying risk and managing risk can be a valuable instrument for cost-effective security. The threats that are inherent to information systems and network infrastructures are not, or not fully, understood. If an incident really becomes a disaster, the organization is not prepared for it. Information security is not on the agenda of senior management. Computers never make errors and it will stay this way. Computer literacy is not very high: people are happy if they can get along with their computer, do their job with the computer, and that the thing does what it should do.

Manage Risk

Risk is the item that needs to be managed. The organization wants to be 'in control.' People and organizational units are appraised on how they are able to manage risk. If an organizational unit believes it is 'in control,' then the evidence for that needs to be delivered as well. Costs for security need to be balanced against the benefits. Risk is not something to be afraid of, as long as risk is identified, analyzed and managed. Incidents are carefully analyzed to make sure that risk models are accurate enough. Information assets are protected according to their value to the business of the organization.

Risk Avoidance

Risk is something to be afraid of. If something goes wrong, the major question is 'Who gets the blame?' People need to be near 100% sure that an initiative does not raise problems before a product or service will be released. 100% security doesn't exist. 100%-delta does—the discovery that your security is non-existent. The art of information security is to make this delta as close to the real need as possible, with a cost in proportion to the damage that would be caused to the business if no security measures were taken at all.

If the cost of near 100% risk avoidance is higher than the benefits, we simply delay the project, cancel it, or ask for a bigger budget. People who can convince others that there is still a security hole in the product are rewarded. If you think that things might work then you are in danger. Reviews are very formal, quality is far more important than time.

Point Solutions

If there is a security problem, the organization will buys a product to solve the problem. There is no complete overview of the overall security solution, for example ICT architecture. If a product does not fulfil the requirements, the organization buys a new product. There is a large variety of security products that overlap in functionality, there are some security vulnerabilities, and it is hard to integrate information systems because the security solutions are not interoperable. Security control and maintenance needs to be performed on a per-product basis. There is no corporate management framework with which security products can be managed centrally. Synergy is not the issue. The organization has a lot of budget holders who can buy the security product they like at any moment.

Entity-to-Entity Security

Instead of trust between machines (end-to-end security) there must be trust between the business actors themselves, such as the people behind the machines. Entity-to-entity security can build on end-to-end security, but it's more than that. Creating trust between people is a hard job, while losing trust is easy. Non-technical aspects play a role here: the type of business relationship, the way incidents are detected and handled, positive public relations, open communications, and management commitment to maintain the trust relationship.

End-to-End Security

The complete chain from initiating machine, through different network components, to the machine that serves the request, needs to be secure. All links of the chain need to be strong enough. Security attributes like confidentiality, integrity, availability and auditability are designed and implemented and must be delivered by the entire chain. Based on the end-to-end characteristics, the attributes of the intermediate components are derived. If multiple organizations are responsible for part of the infrastructure, the derived end-to-end characteristics will be part of the service level agreements and agreed security measures.

Violate the Law

Factors to promote compliance with existing legislation are missing for a variety of reasons. People are not familiar with existing legislation in most of its details, or don't give priority to it because it will not be enforced anyway. Computer legislation can be too complicated, or organizations are willing to pay the penalty if they are caught. The chance of being caught times the penalty is much lower than the business benefits of not obeying the law. The organization can also be under high pressure, there is no time, money or resources to obey the law. If the organization is caught it will not really hurt the corporate image. Everybody drives too fast with their cars, so why comply with computer legislation? The rationale of existing legislation is not understood or recognized.

Obey the Law

The organization makes sure that the laws of the countries within which the organization needs to comply are implemented. Not obeying the law would impose too much risk to the corporate image. The trust of stakeholders in the organization would vanish if laws were not obeyed. Every initiative or project is double checked against legislation. The organization has a strong legal department, and an internal auditing department to make sure that laws are implemented properly. External and specialized advice is requested as well.

Safety Unawareness

People are unaware that safety-critical information systems need a higher security level than security-critical systems. Networks and information systems are shared between them. If somebody is injured or dies because of an incident, everybody is amazed and wonders how this could ever happen, or just think that it was just bad luck.

Safety Before Security

The organization gives more priority to the security of life-critical systems than the security of non life-critical systems. Life-critical systems are subject to thorough security and statistical analysis, reviews and formal evaluation. Infrastructure of life-critical systems is preferably separated from non life-critical systems infrastructure, although there's pressure to combine them for the sake of cost reduction, minimization of control and maintenance, and user convenience.

Security by Obscurity

Can also be called: Leverage Unpredictability

The strength of the security solution is completely based on the fact that only a very few people know what the security solution is. There is no way for other people to review the security solution because it is hidden from them. The proof of the pudding is in the eating, so the real world will determine how strong the solution is.

Keep it Open

Everyone who is interested can learn the security solution, which is well understood and verified by a lot of people. Strength is determined by the secrecy of the key(s). The key length will be long enough to prevent brute force attacks, together with additional security measures to keep the key(s) secret. The problem is to keep the key secret.

Make it Complex

The security solution is more complex than necessary in the hope that an attacker will have more problems attacking a complex solution than a simple one.

Keep it Simple

Embrace simplicity. Keep things as simple as absolutely possible. Security is a chain: the weakest link breaks it. Simplicity means fewer links. Complexity is the enemy of security.

Trust Your Security

People think that the security solution is bullet-proof. Nobody considers that the security solution might fail. A failing security solution will result in business discontinuity in most of the cases. There is a larger emphasis on preventive security measures.

Detection, repression, correction, and evaluation are not developed very well. Multiple security defences are not applied. The first defence is perceived as being strong enough.

Fail Securely

Everything that can fail, will fail—the only question is when the security solution will fail. In the case of failure, the solution will still have a set of predefined security characteristics even when the primary security defence has failed. The solution will detect when primary protection fails and will transfer to the secondary security protection and/or risk avoidance scenario.

Trust Your Vendor

If the vendor of a security product claims the product is secure enough, then the organization will use the product. There is also no need to obtain security requirements or perform a risk analysis, because the vendor of the security solution can be trusted. The vendor is dominant and knows what is good for the organization. Security is a technical problem that can be solved by the right product from a trusted vendor. (Note that this solution can be found in day-to-day life too.)

Security Goals before Means

The organization sets clear business goals and derives its end-to-end security characteristics from them. Additional risk analysis will provide the input for a logical security solution. Security services that are required can still be correlated with business requirements easily. The organization looks for products that can be used to implement the logical security solution only if the solution is clear and well understood by business people. The security product is explicitly evaluated against well-understood security requirements. The logical security solution (for example architecture) is the stable factor through time.

Fortress Mentality

Security measures are mainly concentrated towards the boundaries of the organization. The outside world is the cause of all security incidents. All the internal employees can be trusted for 100%. There is no need to enhance the security level within the organization, because the security fence between it and the outside world will handle all possible attacks now and in the future. Interactivity with the outside world is minimized to avoid risk.

Time-Based Security

The organization is aware that security measures will fail, the only question is when. If an attacker (internal or external) has enough time and resources, they will break the first security defence. The only thing the organization can do is delay a successful attempt to break its security. This is why the organization applies detection mechanisms so that it knows when an attack starts. The time to detect and react to an attack should be shorter that the time the attacker needs for a successful attack.

Trust Your Employees

Employees might be screened before being employed, after which they will be trusted for life. There is no need to reduce risks that are related to internal employees. Employees are more loyal to the organization they work for than towards themselves. A lot of organizations have built their security on this principle. Note that this solution can also be found in day-to-day life. The writers or security principles do not want to suggest that this principle is the first option they thought of.

Trust Nobody

Nobody can be trusted. Loyal employees cannot be trusted if the reward for fraud is high and the chance of detection is low. The organization does not want to put their employees under temptation. 'Four eyes'—that is, two people—principles are applied for critical transactions. The internal security is as high as the security towards the outside world. There is a strong focus towards compliance, formal procedures, and internal control. Detection, response mechanisms, and disciplinary actions are applied to make fraud unattractive.

Introducing Architecture Principles

Selecting and setting a proper mindset is a good start, but you need more than that to implement security throughout your complete IT infrastructure. You need some guiding principles on whether or not to implement security controls, as well as how, where and when to implement them. Architecture principles help you to express how security should be embedded in your IT.

Security Guard

The security guard centrally screens requests for business services. The guard has the intelligence to detect malicious requests. If the guard authorizes the request, it can be trusted. The guard will implement the security policy, so the rest of the business logic can be simple and does not need to handle security exceptions.

Perimeter Defence

A special security zone is applied to protect the inside from the outside. The idea is that the bad guys are outside and the good guys are inside. A perimeter defence can consist of a number of components, depending on its design. Firewalls are used to control the traffic across the perimeter defence. If a perimeter defence is the main security protection, then it's like building a fortress, hard on the outside and soft on the inside.

Divide and Conquer

The corporate security problem is divided into a number of smaller ones by introducing the concept of security domains. A security domain can be based on a number of criteria such as platform, organization boundary, geographic location. Security domains can be nested, and every security domain has its own specific security policy and derived procedures. If a domain does not have its own security policy, the security policy of the next higher-level domain will be applied. Interactions between security domains are subject to both general and organization-specific procedures.

The Network as a Battleground

The network is viewed as a military arena. Military concepts are applied to protect the information assets, like 'defence in depth,' 'early warning,' 'deception' and 'stealth' techniques. Fighting back is also one of the options. A response team leader uses the network diagram the same way as generals use their maps of terrain during a campaign.

Peace or War

The security policy of the organization is not static, but stateful. If there peace the policy 'business as usual' is applied and enforced. In case of an emergency, the organization switches to a higher state of alert with a stricter security policy. Defending the organization has priority over a fast business response.

Immune System

The organization is protected in the same way that a human body protects itself against diseases. The protection system evolves as time progresses. Feedback, detection and (formal) evaluations are used to improve the protection system.

Layered Security

The security solution is build up by applying a number of layers of protection and/or abstraction. In this way the attacker has to break through a number of protection layers, and at the same time the layers themselves can be relatively modular and simple.

Defence in Depth

The security solution is build up by applying a number of layers of protection. It is essential to defence in depth that security mechanisms are protected by other security mechanisms. The defence in depth principle can be an extension of the time-based security principle.

Watch the Watchers

Audit your own processes regularly. Guard the guards and double-check security measures taken in the past for effectiveness and boldness. Watch the Watchers can be viewed as an extension to the 'trust nobody' mindset principle.

Enlist the Users

Security can't work if users aren't on your side. Social engineering attacks are often the most damaging and can only be defended against with user education. Security awareness training programs are therefore very important weapons on the security battleground. Users are asked to report security incidents and weaknesses immediately. The users are the (human) sensors of the protection system.

Introducing Execution Principles

After setting mindset and architecture perception, there's still an important issue left: day-to-day use of your IT requires guidance on how to handle security at execution time. Apart from this, execution principles are interesting, because they show what the transformation in security level will look like.

Security at any Price

Security is viewed as a binary concept: something is secure, or not secure at all. It might be that the impact of compromised security is simply too high, if the organization is non-commercial and there is no need for an economic justification. In the case of safety-critical systems it may be impossible or unethical to even calculate an economic justification.

Return on Investment

Every security solution requires economic justification. Risk analysis techniques are used to calculate the 'cost' of the solution versus its 'value.' The organization correlates the set of security measures with the business processes that are enabled. The cost and benefits of security measures are well understood.

Security as a Desert

Information assets and business processes are created based on the requirements for the functionality they need to fulfill. No attention is paid to security during the creation of change process for an information asset or business process. The organization has the perception that security can be bolted onto the solution if this really necessary. It's more like hiring more agents as soon as people feel that the situation has become unsafe.

Security in Every Change

The most effective moment to incorporate security is at the moment the asset is 'born.' It is like implanting the right DNA when a cell is created. It is easier and more cost-effective to change or create information assets the right way from the start than afterwards. Security is integrated into change procedures and project management methodologies. Risk analyses techniques are used to determine the right level of protection, aligned with business needs. Security requirements can even influence important design considerations.

Ignore Security Patches

Security patches issued by solution providers are installed too late, such as after a major virus or worm incident has happened, or not at all. Short-term business continuity is much more important than the actual security level. Patching security has no priority. Business managers are unaware that security patches should get priority over getting the job done.

Proactive Control and Maintenance

Special control and maintenance processes are in place to make sure that security patches issued by solution providers are installed as soon as possible. Security is viewed as an important aspect to ensure business continuity in the medium term.

Wait for the Auditor

The organization uses an auditing process to improve its security if needed. Security measures are implemented afterwards if they are implemented at all. There is no real attention to security during change processes.

Mature Through Time

The organization proactively seeks ways to improve its security in a fundamental way. Maturity models are used to identify the current level of security, and targets for future security levels are set and agreed. There is a formal planning, execution and reviewing process to make sure the new security level is reached. Security is seen as a subject with multiple comfort levels.

Top-Down Approach Only

Security is improved exactly according to the book. First a corporate security policy is drafted and signed off. Security baselines are written and enforced. Every information system is subject to a risk analysis. Security controls resulting from these risk analyses are incorporated into a security plan. The plan is executed and the security controls are implemented. In the end the auditor audits the results of the process.

Issue-Driven

The organization recognizes that securing everything is not feasible. Resources need to be used most effectively. Differences between 'as is' and 'to be' are seen as a security issue and prioritized and clustered based on risk-management techniques. The most important and/or the easiest issues to solve get highest priority.

Paralysis by Analysis

Thinking about security is much more important than really making things more secure. People spend so much time and money in analyzing threats and designing the security solution that there is no time or money to implement it. When control is finally realized and the 'Eureka!' effect is there, the world might have changed so that the solution is outdated or no longer needed. There is no real pressure on concrete results: security is only an intellectual challenge, like solving a puzzle.

Just do it Together

The organization follows top-down principles, but recognizes that this requires too much time and money. Awareness is an issue and security controls can't be implemented all at once. A more practical approach is taken. A security baseline is implemented and analysis is performed on critical information systems. Workshops are used to mobilize people, make them aware, and speed up the process. Twenty percent of the time results in eighty percent of security controls.

Ignore Security Incidents

Security incidents are not proactively detected, administered, and managed. Incidents are things people do not like to talk about or remember. Success is what counts. Incidents mean trouble that should be forgotten as quickly as possible.

Respond to Security Incidents

Security incidents are proactively detected, administered, and managed. Security incidents are an important feedback for the organization on how well it is protected. Security incidents are evaluated and are an opportunity for improvement.

15.2 Enhancing Security Patterns with Misuse Cases

Misuse cases visualize unwanted system behavior such as security violations alongside required system behavior in diagrams that are inspired by use cases. Together, use and misuse cases offer a way to represent patterns of security threats and requirements in a way that is meaningful to end users during problem analysis and requirements determination. This section explains the basic concepts of misuse cases in relation to use cases, and discusses how and why to use them to represent security patterns.

Basic Concepts

Misuse cases extend regular use case diagrams with two new node types [SO01]:

- Misuse cases represent unwanted system behavior, that is, behavior that causes harm to some stakeholder if it is allowed to complete. Misuse cases thus complement regular use cases [Jac92]. They are shown as filled ovals in diagrams.
- Misusers represent entities that either intentionally or inadvertently initiate misuse cases. Misusers thus complement regular actors [Jac92]. They are shown as filled stick men in diagrams.

In addition, there are two new relationship types between use and misuse cases [Alexander]:

- A *threaten* relationship from a misuse to a use case indicates that the misuse case exploits one or more vulnerabilities within the use case.
- A *mitigate* relationship from a use to a misuse case indicates that the use case prevents, thwarts, detects, or otherwise responds to the misuse case.

The regular relationship types *extend*, *include*, *generalize*, and *use* can also be used between misuse cases and between misuse cases and misusers [SO00]. Table 15.10 shows the available node and relationship types in misuse case diagrams.

Table 15.10 Node and relationship types in misuse-case diagrams

FROM/TO	ACTORS	USE CASES	MISUSERS	MISUSE CASES
Actors	generalize	use		
Use cases		generalize extend include		
Misusers			generalize	use
Misuse cases		threaten		generalize extend include

The figure on page 527 shows the 'Non-repudiation of origin' component of the Common Criteria for IT Security Evaluation [ISO15408] as a misuse case diagram. In this diagram, the topmost use case represents a regular functional requirement, that is, that the proposed system must be able to transmit information from an originator to a recipient. The transmission commits the originator to further action, for example providing payment later. The diagram also shows a misuse case that represents a security threat to the transmission function, that is, that the originator can later deny having provided the information, and thereby renege on their commitment.

Below the misuse case is another use case, which represents a corresponding security requirement, that is, that the system must be able to prove the identity of the originator of the transmitted information. In the figure, use cases thereby represent both regular functional requirements and security requirements, but they are shown with the same icons because they both represent required system behaviour. See figure on page 527.

Representing Security Patterns

Misuse case diagrams are useful for drawing attention to security issues during problem analysis and requirements determination, but they only describe security threats and requirements at a very high level. More detail must therefore be provided for misuse cases to properly represent security patterns:

- Firstly, misuse case diagrams must be embedded in a consistent standard pattern format that uses a combination of textual fields and diagrams. Misuse case diagrams fit nicely with the pattern idea, because triplets of use cases, threatened by misuse cases that are mitigated by security use cases, correspond, respectively, to

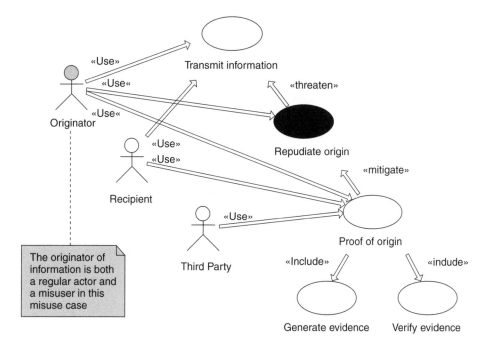

Misuse case diagram for 'non-repudiation of origin'

the context, problem, and solution parts of a security pattern when supplemented by additional, textual and other information.

■ Secondly, the details of each use and misuse case in a diagram must be described in a consistent standard format. For regular use cases several templates are available ([KG00], [Coc01], [Rum94]) that can also be used to represent security use cases and that have been adapted to represent misuse cases too [SO01]. Below we show a textual description of the misuse case 'Repudiate origin' from the figure on page 527. The most important part of a use or misuse case description is its basic and alternative paths. In principle, any notation for representing regular use-case paths can be adapted to represent misuse, by interpreting each path as a description of unwanted, as opposed to required, behavior.

Misuse Case Name: Repudiate origin

Summary: An originator transmits information through the system to a recipient, but later denies having provided the information.

Author: The Common Criteria Project Sponsoring Organizations

Date: 2003-10-22

Basic path:

1. The originator provides information to the recipient through the system, thereby committing to some further action (for example, paying for an ordered product, a reservation, or a requested transaction).
2. The system transmits the information.
3. The recipient receives the information and performs some action based upon it (for example, delivering a product or service, making a reservation, performing a transaction on behalf of the originator).
4. The originator denies having provided the information.

Alternative paths:

1. The following steps replace the steps in the basic path 1 to 3.

    1.1. The recipient requests information from the recipient.
    1.2. The originator provides the information to the recipient through the system.
    1.3. The system transmits the information.

2. Same as the basic path, but with multiple recipients.
3. Same as alternative path 2, but with multiple recipients.

Mitigation points:

1. In basic path step 2, when the system transmits the information, it also provides proof of origin to the recipient.
2. In basic path step 2, the system may also provide proof of origin to the originator, or to a third party.
3. The system provides proof of origin to the recipient, originator or third party as a new step business path 5.

4–6. Same as mitigation point 1–3, but for alternative path 1.

Extension points: None.

Triggers:

1. Always true (this can happen at any time).

Preconditions: None.

Assumptions:

1. The information provided by the originator is in some way committing for the originator.
2. The recipient wants the originator to fulfil the commitment.

Mitigation guarantee: If the originator denies having provided information, the recipient is able to obtain—or already possesses—evidence of the origin of the information, and this evidence can be verified by the system. Evidence and verification of origin can also be obtained by the originator or by third parties.

Related business rules: None.

Potential misuser profile: Technically unskilled—any person can claim that an impostor transmitted the information on their behalf.

Stakeholders and threats:

- Recipient, who may be harmed by the originator reneging on their commitment, for example by not receiving payment for a product or service delivered by the recipient to the originator.
- Third party, who may be harmed by the originator reneging on their commitment, for example by having guaranteed payment for a product or service delivered by the recipient to the originator.

Terminology and explanations: None.

Scope: Entire business and business environment.

Abstraction level: Misuser subgoal—the main misuser goal is to benefit from some requested action without having to fulfill their commitment.

Precision level: Focused.

Security Patterns at the Organizational and User Levels

A central idea behind misuse cases is that unwanted system behavior such as security violations is not just a design, implementation, operation, and maintenance problems, but an organization- and user-level issue that must be considered during problem analysis and requirements determination for several reasons:

- In some cases, security problems may be eliminated altogether by careful problem analysis and choice of architecture requirements. For example, instead of dealing with information confidentiality through a secure ICT infrastructure and during design and later phases, it may not be possible to store the information in an integrated manner and in a single place, instead relying on client-side software to collect and integrate the information from multiple, independent sources at use time. Such solutions can only be identified and selected in the early development phases.
- Even when security problems cannot be eliminated, they can often best be dealt with by organizational or physical countermeasures, or by a combination of organizational, physical, and technological means. Leaving security to be dealt with during design or later means that organizational, physical, or combined

countermeasures may not be identified at all, or may involve extensive redesign of the system.

Misuse cases are therefore a promising means of representing security patterns at the organization and user level, describing the types of misusers they involve, and the types of planned system functions they exploit, independently of design and later concerns. Such security patterns can be used for tool-supported reuse during problem analysis and requirements determination, for teaching, presenting and discussing security issues and solutions, and for browsing large collections of security-related information. Most of these security patterns are not yet identified or written, pointing to an important line of further work on security patterns and misuse cases.

Today most security patterns tend to focus on design, implementation, operation, and maintenance problems and—as in the sense of the Common Criteria—on security evaluation. The organization- and user-level visualizations provided by misuse cases are not always applicable to or helpful for patterns meant for design and later phases. For example, not all the patterns explicitly involve actors and misusers and, even when they do, the corresponding misuse case diagrams may be too simple too convey much information.

Nevertheless, misuse case diagrams can contribute to making design- and implementation-level patterns useful during requirements elicitation and specification. Specifically, misuse cases can drive work on organization- and user-oriented security requirements towards design and later phases in a systematic fashion. This ensures that design- and implementation-level security patterns are chosen only after security issues have been explicitly considered at the organization and user level. It also ensures that choices of security patterns can be traced back to organization- and user-level requirements. Traceable security decisions are an important prerequisite for appropriate change management and for systematic security management of operational systems in the face of changing threats: for example, when new vulnerabilities are identified in supporting software.

Further Reading

A more detailed introduction to misuse cases, along with further examples, is provided in [SO00], and practical example can be found in [Ale02]. A template for describing misuse cases in detail is presented in [SO01], and guidelines for using misuse cases in practice are given in [SO00]. Reuse of misuse and security use cases is discussed in [SFO03], and experience with representing security patterns from the OWASP project [OWASP] using misuse cases is reported in [Brei02].

CHAPTER
16

Closing Remarks

*When I examine myself and my methods of thought, I come to the
conclusion that the gift of fantasy has meant more to me than any talent for
abstract, positive thinking.*

Albert Einstein

More than ever, the trustworthiness of software systems is an important prerequisite
for the success of current and future business in the digital world. We see an ever-
increasing trend of new security vulnerabilities at different levels. It is alarming that
so many incidents can be traced back to well-known problems that have proven, well-
known solutions. Why does this happen? And is there a way out? We answer these
questions by commenting on quotes from the security specialist Bruce Schneier:

■ Complexity is the worst enemy of security
■ Security is all about trade-offs you take with respect to your always limited
  resources

531

- There's no other way to handle the complexity than by breaking it up into manageable pieces

Complexity is the Worst Enemy of Security

Security has become more problematic due to the increasing complexity of organizations and systems. This complexity is due at least in part to the increase in open exchange of information and the rate of change of technology and business processes. Software controls more and more areas of our life, leading to a fast-growing, complex landscape of applications and technical systems. Every new software version has new features, and the release cycle of software products is getting shorter and shorter. All of these factors are positive in many ways, but they also make security more difficult to achieve. However, we can achieve a measure of security by learning from past errors and making use of this knowledge to avoid at least the well-known issues.

Security is all About Trade-offs You take with Respect to Your Always Limited Resources

This makes security a perfect domain for representation by patterns. Security patterns allow you to make more conscious security decisions about the systems you build. Today security is often a problem, either when designing a system, or worse, after it is deployed. Few experts have the knowledge to integrate good security design into system development. On the other hand, the bulk of development teams lacks such security skills. In summary, security seems to be a 'black art' that only an exclusive circle of 'magicians' can perform well. The problem is made worse by the tendency to wait until specific security problems occur in system development instead of defining an organization strategy up front.

Design patterns came into life at OOPSLA more than a decade ago. They transfer knowledge about object-oriented design and software architecture and give it a common name. Patterns represent this knowledge based on experience and elaborate the consequential trade-offs an engineer faces when applying a pattern. Before design patterns, OO-design was a black art, just as security is now.

Since then, design patterns have shown themselves to be a perfect vehicle for transferring OOP expertise to mainstream technology. Security patterns try to repeat that success by making the knowledge and trade-offs of security practice accessible, just as design patterns did for OOP. Security patterns provide names and a common understanding to security techniques and show their value and their limitations honestly.

Our vision is that security patterns will leverage the design of secure systems, because they transfer knowledge of proven solutions that help to balance the competing forces.

There's No Other Way to Handle the Complexity than by Breaking it Up into Manageable Pieces

Security patterns provide a way to break up the domain of security problems into smaller pieces, and of making the complexity of applications, systems and the environment manageable. A set of security patterns is more accessible than traditional sources of security knowledge. Security patterns are small, clearly-structured nuggets of knowledge and provide explicit linkage to other security patterns:

- They explicitly state the problem—making them suitable for novices who don't know the solution, only the problem
- They specify the context—that is, assumptions and preconditions that describe the situation in which the problem occurs
- They show how a solution changes the context—that is, the application of a pattern has consequences the user should know about

Furthermore, individual patterns are integrated by a security taxonomy and a set of organization-level patterns that provide overall guidance and give coherence to the solutions. Security patterns are also valuable for experts, for example as a reference. In the course of adding and reviewing the bits and pieces of this book, we realized ourselves that even experts are not experts in every field of the security domain.

Use Them. Give Feedback. Contribute.

Security patterns are an evolving sub-discipline within the pattern community. This book is the first compilation of security patterns contributed by the pattern community. The scope of potential security patterns and the changing nature of security issues are such that we cannot address all security problems in a single book. The mining of new security patterns therefore will remain an important activity for the future. The main goal is to define the overall landscape of security patterns and to provide a significant start toward making solutions available.

We ask you to use the security patterns that are documented here. Use them to improve the security of your organization and to improve the design of your applications and systems. In doing so, we ask that you evaluate them and determine whether they could be improved. Although many people, both authors and reviewers, have contributed and tried hard to deliver high-quality patterns, there is always room for improvement. Give us feedback if you find blind spots, or if you feel that a particular detail is missing or could be made more specific.

When you use security patterns and get used to the benefits of applying patterns, you might identify your own patterns. Share them with others and integrate them. We recommend highly that you visit a pattern conference, in part to experience the spirit of patterns personally. During shepherding and writer's workshops, groups of experienced software engineers take a critical look at candidate patterns. This helps to ensure that both the structure and the content of patterns are useful for potential readers.

The End?

If you would like to give us feedback or submit a new pattern candidate, send us an e-mail to book@securitypatterns.org. Over time, accompanying material for the book, as well as errata, will be made available at our security patterns site, which can be accessed at the following URL:

    http://www.securitypatterns.org

References

[Abrams95]   M. Abrams, S. Jajodia, H. Podell, eds., 1995: *Information Security An Integrated Collection of Essays*, IEEE Computer Society Press, January 1995
              `http://www.acsac.org/secshelf/book001/book001.html`

[ACL]   JANET-CERT: *Cisco ACL Example*
              `http://www.ja.net/CERT/JANET-CERT/prevention/cisco/`
              `cisco_acls.html`

[ACM]   ACM: `http://www.acm.org`

[Ack03]   R. Ackermann: *Gateways and Components for Supplementary IP Telephony Services in Heterogeneous Environments*, PhD Thesis, July 2003

[AD01]   C. J. Alberts, A. J. Dorofee: *SEI, OCTAVE Criteria*, Version 2.0, CMU/SEI-2001-TR-016, December 2001
              `http://www.sei.cmu.edu/pub/documents/01.reports/pdf/`
              `01tr016.pdf`

[ADE+99]   M. Arango, A. Dugan, I. Elliott, C. Huitema, S. Pickett: *Media Gateway Control Protocol (MGCP)*, RFC 2705, Oct. 1999

[ADV]   Security Advisor: `http://securityadvisor.info`

[AfB1999]   Association for Biometrics (AfB) and International Computer Security Association (ICSA): *Glossary of Biometric Terms*, 1999
              `http://www.afb.org.uk/docs/glossary.htm`

[AIS+77]   C. Alexander, S. Ishikawa, M. Silverstein, M. Jacobson, I. Fiksdahl-King, S. Angel: *A Pattern Language: Towns - Buildings - Construction*, Oxford University Press, 1977

[Ale79]   C. Alexander: *The Timeless Way of Building*, Oxford University Press, 1979

[Ale02]   I. F. Alexander: *Initial Industrial Experience of Misuse Cases in Trade-Off Analysis*, in *Proceedings of IEEE Joint International Requirements Engineering Conference*, 9-13 September 2002, Essen, pp. 61–68
http://portal.acm.org/citation.cfm?id=731617

[Alert03] Unitel: *Alert Mailing List*
http://www.unitel.cx/services/alert.html

[Alexander] I. Alexander: *Misuse Cases: Use Cases with Hostile Intent*, IEEE Software, 2003, 20(1), pp. 58–66

[Amo01]   M. B. d'Amorim: *Proxy-to-Proxy, a Structural Pattern for Leveraging Security on Highly-Distributed Internet Applications*, in Proceedings of SugarLoafPLoP, 2001

[And01]   R. Anderson: *Security Engineering – A Guide to Building Dependable Distributed Systems*, John Wiley & Sons, 2001

[ANA+87]   C. Alexander, H. Neis, A. Anninou, I. King: *A New Theory of Urban Design*, Oxford University Press, 1987

[APM]   Appropriate Process Movement: *Risk to Pattern Table*, 2002
http://www.aptprocess.com/whitepapers/risk/RiskToPatternTable.htm

[Arg]   Argus Systems Group: *Trusted OS Security: Principles and Practice*
http://www.argus-systems.com/products/white_paper/pitbull

[ASA+75]   C. Alexander, M. Silverstein, S. Angel, S. Ishikawa, D. Abrams: *The Oregon Experiment*, Oxford University Press, 1975

[Ashbourn2000] J. Ashbourn: *The Distinction Between Authentication and Identification*, 2000
http://www.avanti.1to1.org/authenticate.html

[AW02]   I. Araujo, M. Weiss: *Linking Patterns and Non-Functional Requirements*, in Proceedings of PLoP, 2002

[ASR+01]   R. Ackermann, M. Schumacher, U. Roedig, R. Steinmetz: *Vulnerabilities and Security Limitations of Current IP Telephony Systems*, in *Proceedings of the Conference on Communications and Multimedia Security (CMS2001)*, Darmstadt, pp. 53–66, May 2001

[Bace01]   R. Bace, P. Mell: *Intrusion Detection Systems*, NIST Special Publication on Intrusion Detection Systems, November 2001
http://cs-www.ncsl.nist.gov/publications/nistpubs/800-31/sp800-31.pdf

[Bar99]   Y. Bartal, A. Mayer, K. Nissim, A. Wool: *FIRMATO: A Novel Firewall Management Toolkit*, in *Proceedings of the 20th IEEE Symposium on Security and Privacy*, pp. 17–31, Oakland, California, April 1999

[Bau97]   D. Baumer, D. Riehle, W. Siberski, M. Wolf: *Role Object*, Chapter 2 in *Pattern Languages of Program Design 4* (N. Harrison, B. Foote, and H. Rohnert, eds.), Also in Proceedings of PLoP, 1997
               `http://jerry.cs.uiuc.edu/~plop/plop97`

[Bec97]   K. Beck: *Smalltalk Best Practices*, Prentice-Hall, 1996

[Bro99]   F. L. Brown, J. DiVietri, G. Diaz de Villegas, E. B. Fernandez: *The Authenticator Pattern*, in Proceedings of PLoP, 1999
               `http://jerry.cs.uiuc.edu/~plop/plop99`

[BH04]   B. Blakley, C. Heath, et al: *Security Design Patterns*, Technical Guide, Open Group, 2004

[Bis03]   M. Bishop: *Computer Security: Art and Science*, Addison-Wesley, 2002

[BL73]   D. E. Bell, L. J. LaPadula: *Secure Computer Systems: Mathematical Foundations and Model*, Technical Report M74-244, The MITRE Corporation, Bedford, MA, USA, 1976

[Bor01]   J. Borchers: *A Pattern Approach To Interaction Design*, John Wiley & Sons, 2001

[Bra89]   R. Braden: *Requirements for Internet Hosts*, Communications, RFC 1122, October 1989

[BRD98]   A. M. Braga, C. M. F. Rubira, R. Dahab: *Tropyc: A Pattern Language for Cryptographic Software*, published in [PLoPD4], 1999

[BRJ98]   G. Booch, J. Rumbaugh, I. Jacobsen: *The Unified Modeling Language User Guide*, Addison-Wesley, 1998

[Brei02]   G. F. Breivik: *Sikkerhet som Troll av Eske* (Norwegian only), 2002
               `http://www.ub.uib.no/elpub/2002/h/704003/Hovedoppgave.pdf`

[BSI02]   Bundesamt für Sicherheit in der Informationstechnik: *IT Baseline Protection Manual*, Bundesanzeiger, 2002

[Bugtraq03]   SecurityFocus: *Bugtraq Mailing List*
               `http://www.securityfocus.com/archive/1`

[CA]   CERT-AU: *Australian Computer Emergency Response Team*, September 2003
               `http://www.auscert.org.au`

[Cam90]   N. A. Camillone, D. H. Steves, K. C. Witte: *AIX Operating System: a Trust-worthy Computing System*, in *IBM RISC S/6000 Technology*, SA23-2619, 1990

[CAS]   *Computers and Security*:
            http://www.compseconline.com/publications/prodcsec.htm

[CERTa]   CERT Coordination Center: http://www.cert.org/

[CERTb]   *US-CERT Vulnerability Note Field Descriptions*, Carnegie Mellon University, 2004
            http://www.kb.cert.org/vuls/html/fieldhelp

[Chi84]   R. E. Childs Jr., J. Crawford, D. L. House, R. N. Noyce: *A Processor Family for Personal Computers*, in *Proceedings of the IEEE*, Vol. 72, No. 3, March 1984, pp. 363–376

[Chu02]   A. Chuvakin: *Intrusion Detection Response*, April 2002
            http://www.linuxsecurity.com/feature_stories/ids-active-re-sponse.html

[CMU03]   Carnegie Melon University (CMU): *Systems Security Engineering Capability Maturity Model*, Model Description Document, Version 3.0, June 2003
            http://www.sse-cmm.org

[COBRA02]   *Computer Audit, Systems Audit and Information Security Audit Made Easy!*, 2002
            http://www.securitypolicy.co.uk/securityaudit/index.htm

[Coc01]   A. Cockburn: *Writing Effective Use Cases*, Addison-Wesley, 2000

[Coe03]   M. Coetzee, J. H. P. Eloff: *Virtual Enterprise Access Control Requirements*, in *Proceedings of the 2003 Annual Research Conference of the South African Institute of Computer Scientists and Information Technologists on Enablement Through Technology*, 2003, pp. 285–294

[Cop92]   J. O. Coplien: *Advanced C++ – Programming Styles and Idioms*, Addison-Wesley, 1991

[CPA]   D. Coderre: *Auditing: Computer-Assisted Techniques for Fraud Detection*, The CPA Journal, August 1999
            http://www.nysscpa.org/cpajournal/1999/0899/departments/D57899.htm

[CSI03]   Computer Security Institute: http://www.gocsi.com

[Cugini00] J. Cugini: *Web Usability Logging: Tools and Formats*, Information Technology Laboratory National Institute of Standards and Technology (NIST), 2000 http://www.itl.nist.gov/iaui/vvrg/cugini/webmet/paper-aug2000.html

[CVSS]   Common Vulnerability Scoring System, 2005
            http://www.first.org/cvss

[Cyb03]   CyberGuard Corporation: *Defense in Depth: Applying a Fortified Firewall Strategy*, white paper, January 2003

[DC]   DFN-CERT: *Zentrum für sichere Netzdienste*, September 2003
            http://www.cert.dfn.de

[DCD+02]   J. Duro, R. Crosslin, D. Dennie, P. Jung, C. Louden, D. Shepherd: *A Practical Approach to Integrating Information Security into Federal Enterprise Architectures*, IR229T1, Logistics Management Institute, McLean, VA, October 2002

[DeC02]   S. De Capitani di Vimercati, S. Paraboschi, P. Samarati: *Access Control: Principles and Solutions*, in *Software – Practice and Experience*, pp. 397–421, 2003

[Del04]   N. Delessy-Gassant, E.B.Fernandez, S. Rajput, M.M.Larrondo-Petrie: *Patterns for Application Firewalls*, in Proceedings of PLoP 2004

[DEVX]   Devx: http://www.devx.com

[DoJ02]   Department of Justice: *Overview of the Privacy Act of 1974*, May 2004 Edition, US DoJ, Washington, DC
            http://www.usdoj.gov/04foia/04_7_1.html

[Dys04]   P. Dyson, A. Longshaw: *Architecting Enterprise Solutions: Patterns for High-Capability Internet-Based Systems*, John Wiley & Sons, 2004

[EH02]   B. Elsinga, A. Hofman: *Controlled Access Patterns*, in Proceedings of EuroPLoP, 2002,
            http://hillside.net/patterns/EuroPLoP2002/papers.html

[Eps99]   J. Epstein: *Architecture and Concepts of the ARGuE Guard*, in *Proceedings of the 15th Annual Computer Security Applications Conference*, pp. 45–54, Phoenix, Arizona, December 1999

[Ess97]   W. Essmayr, G. Pernul, A. Min Tjoa: *Access Controls by Object-Oriented Concepts*, in *Proceedings of IFIP WG 11.3 Eleventh International Conference on Database Security*, August 1997

[EU95]   European Union: *Directive 95/46/EC of the European Parliament and of the Council of 24 October 1995 on the Protection of Individuals with Regard to the Processing of Personal Data and on the Free Movement of Such*

Data, Official Journal of the European Communities, No. L 281, 23rd November 1995, pp. 31–50

[EU02]   European Union: *Directive 2002/58/EC of the European Parliament and of the Council of 12 July 2002 Concerning the Processing of Personal Data and the Protection of Privacy in the Electronic Communications Sector (Directive on privacy and Electronic Communications)*, Official Journal of the European Communities, No. L 201, 31 July 2002, pp. 37–47

[Eve04]   M. Evered, S. Bögeholz: *A Case Study in Access Control Requirements for a Health Information System*, presented at Australasian Information Security Workshop 2004 (AISW 2004), Dunedin, New Zealand, 2004

[Evidian]   Evidian: *Product Description and White Papers*:
http://www.evidian.com

[Farshchi03]   J. Farshchi: *Wireless Intrusion Detection Systems*, November 5, 2003
http://www.securityfocus.com/infocus/1742

[FBK99]   D. F. Ferraiolo, J. F. Barkley, D. R. Kuhn: *A Role-Based Access Control model and Reference Implementation within a Corporate Intranet*, ACM Transactions on Information and System Security, Vol. 2, No. 1, Feb. 1999, pp. 34–64

[Fer00]   E. B. Fernandez: *Metadata and Authorization Patterns*, technical report, Florida Atlantic University, 2000
http://www.cse.fau.edu/~ed/MetadataPatterns.pdf

[Fer01]   E. B. Fernandez: *An Overview of Internet Security*, in *Proceedings of the World's Internet and Electronic Cities Conference (WIECC 2001)*, Kish Island, Iran, May 2001

[Fer02]   E. B. Fernandez: *Patterns for Operating Systems Access Control*, in Proceedings of PLoP, 2002
http://jerry.cs.uiuc.edu/~plop/plop2002/proceedings.html

[Fer03a]   E. B. Fernandez, J. C. Sinibaldi: *More Patterns for Operating System Access Control*, in Proceedings of EuroPLoP 2003, pp. 381–398
http://hillside.net/europlop/europlop2003/

[Fer03b]   E. B. Fernandez, R. Warrier: *Remote Authenticator/Authorizer*, in Proceedings of PLoP 2003, http://hillside.net/patterns/

[Fer03c]   E. B. Fernandez: *Layers and Non-Functional Patterns*, in Proceedings of ChiliPLoP 2003, Phoenix, AZ, March 10–15, 2003

[Fer04]   E. B. Fernandez: *A Methodology for Secure Software Design*, 2004 International Conference on Software Engineering Research and Practice (SERP'04), Las Vegas, NV, June 21–24, 2004

[Fer75]   E. B. Fernandez, R. C. Summers, T. Lang: *Definition and Evaluation of Access Rules in Data Management Systems*, in *Proceedings of the 1st International Conference on Very Large Databases*, Boston, 1975, pp. 268–285

[Fer93]   E. B. Fernandez, M. M. Larrondo-Petrie, E. Gudes: *A Method-Based Authorization Model for Object-Oriented Databases*, in *Proceedings of the OOPSLA 1993 Workshop on Security in Object-Oriented Systems*, pp. 70–79

[Fer94]   E. B. Fernandez, J. Wu, M. H. Fernandez: *User Group Structures in Object-Oriented Databases*, in *Proceedings of the 8th Annual IFIP W.G.11.3 Working Conference on Database Security*, Bad Salzdetfurth, Germany, August 1994

[FF99]   R. Flanders, E. B. Fernandez: *Data Filter Architecture Pattern*, in Proceedings of PLoP, 1999

[FHH+99]   J. Franks, P. Hallam-Baker, J. Hostetler. S. Lawrence. P. Leach, A. Luotonen, L. Stewart: *HTTP Authentication: Basic and Digest Access Authentication*, RFC 2617, June 1999

[FH97]   E. B. Fernandez, J.C. Hawkins: *Determining Role Rights from Use Cases*, in *Proceedings of the ACM Workshop on Role-Based Access Control*, pp. 121–125, 1997

[FIPS112]   National Institute of Standards and Technology (NIST): *Standard for Password Usage*, Federal Information Processing Standards Publication 112, Gaithersburg, MD, 1985

[Firesmith2003] D. Firesmith: *OPEN Process Framework (OPF) Authentication Requirements*, OPEN Process Framework Repository Organization, 2003
`http://www.donald-firesmith.com/index.html?Components/Work-Products/RequirementsSet/Requirements/AuthenticationRequirements.html~Contents`

[FLS+03c]   E. B. Fernandez, M. M. Larrondo-Petrie, N. Seliya, N. Delessy, A. Herzberg: *A Pattern Language for Firewalls*, in Proceedings of PLoP, 2003

[FOIA96]   U.S. Congress: *FOIA – The Freedom of Information Act*, 5 U.S.C. § 552, As Amended By Public Law No. 104-231, 110 Stat. 3048, U.S. Congress, Washington, DC, 1996

[Fow97]   M. Fowler: *Analysis Patterns*, Addison-Wesley Professional, 1996

[Fow03]   M. Fowler, *Patterns of Enterprise Application Architecture*, Addison-Wesley Professional, 2002

[FoYo98]   B. Foote, J. Yoder, D. Riehle, M. Tilman: *Metadata and Active Object Models*, in Proceedings of PLoP, 1998, technical report #wucs-98-25, Dept. of Computer Science, Washington University, September 1998

[FP01]   E. B. Fernandez, R. Pan: *A Pattern Language for Security Models*, in Proceedings of PLoP, 2001

[Fra99]   G. Frascadore: *Java Application Server Security using Capabilities*, Java Report, issue March/April 1999, pp. 31–42, March 1999

[Fra01]   M. Frantzen, F. Kerschbaum, E. E. Schultz, S. Fahmy: *A Framework for Understanding Vulnerabilities in Firewalls using a Dataflow Model of Firewall Internals*, Computers & Security, Vol. 20, No. 3, 2001, 263–270

[FS03]   E. B. Fernandez, J. C. Sinibaldi: *More Patterns for Operating Systems Access Control*, in Proceedings of EuroPLoP, 2003, `http://www.hillside.net/europlop/`

[FW03]   E. B. Fernandez, R. Warrier: *Remote Authenticator/Authorizer*, in Proceedings of PLoP, 2003

[FWF94]   E. B. Fernandez, J. Wu, M. H. Fernandez: *User Group Structures in Object-Oriented Databases*, in *Proceedings of the 8th Annual IFIP W.G.11.3 Working Conference on Database Security*, Bad Salzdetfurth, Germany, August 1994

[GASS04]   M. Görtz, R. Ackermann, J. Schmitt, R. Steinmetz: *Context-Aware Communication Services: A Framework for Building Enhanced IP Telephony Services*, in *Proceedings of 13th International Conference on Computer Communication and Networks (ICCCN 2004)*, Chicago, USA, October 2004

[Geodsoft2002a] GeodSoft Website Consulting: *Good and Bad Passwords How-To: An in Depth Analysis of Good, Bad, Strong and Weak Passwords, Password Cracking Techniques and How-To Reduce Password Vulnerabilities*, 2002 `http://geodsoft.com/howto/password/`

[Geodsoft2002b] GeodSoft Website Consulting: *Password Management*, 2002 `http://geodsoft.com/howto/password/password_admin.htm`

[Gindin01]   T. Gindin: *Requirements for Technical Non-Repudiation*, January 2001 `http://www.ietf.org/proceedings/00dec/slides/PKIX-1/`

[Giu99]   L. Giuri: *Role-Based Access Control on the Web using Java*, in *Proceedings of RBAC'99*, pp. 11–18, ACM 1999

[GoF95]   E. Gamma, R. Helm, R. Johnson, J. Vlissides: *Design Patterns – Elements of Reusable Object-Oriented Software*, Addison-Wesley Professional, 1995

[Gol99]   D. Gollmann: *Computer Security*, John Wiley & Sons, 1999

[Google]   Google Security Directory `http://directory.google.com/Top/Computers/Security/`

[Gra68]   R. M. Graham: *Protection in an Information Processing Utility*, in *Communications of the ACM*, Vol. 11, No. 5, May 1968, pp. 365–369

[Ham73]   K. J. Hammer Hodges: *A Fault-Tolerant Multiprocessor Design for Real-Time Control*, Computer Design, December 1973, pp. 75-81

[Har01]   J. M. Hart: *Win32 System Programming*, Second Edition, Addison-Wesley Professional, 1997

[Has02]   J. Hassell: *RADIUS – Securing Public Access to Private Resources*, O'Reilly, 2002

[Haf05]   M. Hafiz, R. E. Johnson: *The Security Architecture of qmail and Postfix*, `https://netfiles.uiuc.edu/mhafiz/www/ResearchandPublications/SecurityArchitectureofqmailAndPostfix.htm`, 2005

[HE03]   A. Hofman, B. Elsinga: *Security Paradigm Pattern Language*, in Proceedings of EuroPLoP 2003

[Hen01]   P. Henry: *An Examination of Firewall Architectures*, CyberGuard Corporation White Paper, April 2001, `http://www.cyberguard.com`

[Herr02]   D. S. Herrmann: *Security Engineering and Information Assurance*, Auerbach Publications, 2002

[HF99]   M. Heuser, E. B. Fernandez: *RPC Client: A Pattern for the Client-Side Implementation of a Pipelined Request/Response Protocol*, in Proceedings of PLoP, 1999

[HHR02]   D. Hybertson, J. Heaney, A. Reedy: *Conceptual Aspects of Security Patterns*, position paper for Security Focus Group, in Proceedings of EuroPLoP, Irsee, Germany, 2002

[HHR+02]   J. Heaney, D. Hybertson, A. Reedy, S. Chapin, T. Bollinger, D. Williams, M. Kirwan, Jr: *Information Assurance for Enterprise Engineering*, in Proceedings of PLoP, Monticello, Illinois, 8-12 September 2002

[HLF00]   V. Hays, M. Loutrel, E. B. Fernandez: *The Object Filter and Access Control Framework*, in Proceedings of PLoP, 2000

[HMR+98]   F. Huber, S. Molterer, A. Rausch, B. Schätz, M. Sihling, O. Slotosch: *Tool Supported Specification and Simulation of Distributed Systems*, in *International Symposium on Software Engineering for Parallel and Distributed Systems*, pp. 155–164, 1998

[HP]   Hewlett Packard Corporation: *Virtual Vault* `http://www.hp.com/security/products/virtualvault`

[Hur00]   M. Hurler: *Sec://House – A Data Warehouse for Software Vulnerabilities*, Master's thesis, Darmstadt University of Technology, 2000

[IBM]   IBM: *E-business patterns*
            `http://www-106.ibm.com/developerworks/patterns/index.html`

[IBM2]   IBM: *Extended Enterprise Business Pattern*, IBM Developer Works, February, 2004
            `http://www-106.ibm.com/developerworks/patterns/b2bi/index.html`

[IBM3]   M. Sachs et al: *Executable Trading-Partner Agreements in Electronic Commerce*, IBM T. J. Watson Research Center, January, 2000

[IDWG02]   Intrusion Detection Working Group: *Intrusion Detection Message Exchange Requirements*, Draft October 22, 2002
            `http://www.ietf.org/internet-drafts/draft-ietf-idwg-requirements-10.txt`

[IETF99]   IETF: *Internet Draft on Non-Repudiation Requirements*, September 1999

[ISG00]   The Internet Society, Network Working Group: *Internet Security Glossary*, Request for Comments (RFC) 2828, May 2000
            `http://www.faqs.org/rfcs/rfc2828.html`

[ISM]   InfoSecurity Magazine: `http://www.scmagazine.com`

[ISO/CC1999] International Organization for Standardization: *Common Criteria for Information Technology Security Evaluation*, Version 2.1, 1999, CCIMB-99-031, ISO/IEC JTC 1 adopted CC 2.0 with minor modifications in June 1999 as ISO/IEC 15408, Version 2.1, `http//:www.commoncriteria.org`

[ISO13335-1] International Organization for Standardization: *ISO/IEC TR 13335-1, Information Technology – Guidelines for the Management of IT Security – Part 1: Concepts and Models of IT Security*, 1996

[ISO13335-3] International Organization for Standardization: *Technical Report ISO-13335-3 Part 3: Techniques for the Management of IT Security*, American National Standards Institute, 2002

[ISO13335-4] International Organization for Standardization: *TR 13335-4:2000, Information Technology - Guidelines for the Management of IT Security - Part 4: Selection of Safeguards*, First Edition, 2000-03-01

[ISO13888]   International Organization for Standardization: *Information Technology – Security Techniques – Non-repudiation*
            ISO/IEC 13888-1:1997: *Non-Repudiation - Part 1: General.*

ISO/IEC 13888-2:1998: *Part 2: Mechanisms using Symmetric Techniques*

ISO/IEC 13888-3:1997: *Part 3: Mechanisms using Asymmetric Techniques*

[ISO15408] International Organization for Standardization: *Common Criteria for Information Technology Security Evaluation*, Version 2.1, 1999, CCIMB-99-031, ISO/IEC JTC 1 adopted CC 2.0 with minor modifications in June 1999 as ISO/IEC 15408, Version 2.1

[ISO17799] International Organization for Standardization: *Information Technology – Code of Practice for Information Security Management*, ISO/IEC 17799, 2000, re-released 2005

[ITD] IEEE: *IEEE Transactions on Dependable and Secure Computing*

[ITS] IEEE: *Computer Society Technical Committee on Security and Privacy*
http://www.ieee-security.org/

[ITU03] International Telecommunication Union: *H323: Packet-Based Multimedia Communication Systems*, November 2000

[Jac92] I. Jacobson et al: *Object-Oriented Software Engineering: A Use Case Driven Approach*, Addison-Wesley Professional, 1992

[Jaw00] J. Jaworski, P. J. Perrone: *Java Security Handbook*, SAMS, Indianapolis, 2000

[JBR99] I. Jacobson, G. Booch, J. Rumbaugh: *The Unified Software Development Process*, Addison-Wesley Professional, 1999

[KG00] D. Kulak, E. Guiney: *Use Cases: Requirements in Context*, Addison-Wesley Professional, 2003

[KBZ01] S. R. Kodituwakku, P. Bertok, L. Zhao: *A Pattern Language for Designing and Implementing Role-Based Access Control*, in *Proceedings of the 1st Australian Conference on Pattern Languages of Programming*, 2001

[KC97] N. L. Kerth, W. Cunningham: *Using Patterns to Improve our Architectural Vision*, IEEE Software, 14(1):53-59, January 1997

[KE02] D. M. Kienzle, M. C. Elder: *Final Technical Report: Security Patterns for Web Application Development*, DARPA Contract F30602-01-C-0164, 2002
http://www.modsecurity.org/archive/securitypatterns/
dmdj_final_report.pdf

[Kel97] M. Kelley: *Windows NT Network Security, A Manager's Guide*, Lawrence Livermore National Laboratory, 1997

[Kell03] A. Kelly: *Pattern: Encapsulate Context*, in Proceedings of EuroPLoP 2003
http://www.allankelly.net/patterns

[Kin01]   C. King et.al: *Security Architecture*, Osborne/McGraw Hill, 2001

[Kru00]   P. Kruchten: *The Rational Unified Process: An Introduction*, Third Edition, Addison-Wesley Professional, 2003

[Lar05]   C. Larman: *Applying UML and Patterns*, Third Edition, Prentice Hall PTR, 2004

[LDAP00]   The Internet Society, Network Working Group: *Access Control Requirements for LDAP - RFC 2820*, 2000
               http://www.faqs.org/rfcs/rfc2820.html

[Lea94]   D. Lea: *Design Patterns for Avionics Control Systems*, Draft Version 0.9.6. November 20, 1994
               http://g.oswego.edu/dl/acs/acs/acs.html

[Lea99]   D. Lea: *Concurrent Programming in Java*, in *Concurrent Programming in Java: Design Principles and Patterns*, Second Edition, Addison-Wesley, 1999

[Leh02]   S. Lehtonen, J. Pärssinen: *A Pattern Language for Cryptographic Key Management*, in Proceedings of EuroPLoP, Irsee, Germany, 2002
               http://hillside.net/patterns/EuroPLoP2002/papers/
               Lehtonen_Paerssinen.zip

[Liesen02]   D. Liesen: *Requirements for Enterprise-Wide Scaling Intrusion Detection Products: A Criteria Catalog for IT Executives*, IDS Users and Vendors, 2002, http://www.snort.org/docs/IDS_criteria.pdf

[LinuxPAM]   A. Morgan: *Linux-PAM*,
               http://www.kernel.org/pub/linux/libs/pam

[Losa97]   F. Losavio, A. Matteo: *Use Case and Multiagent Models for Object-Oriented Design of User Interfaces*, Journal of Object-Oriented Programming, Vol. 10, No. 2, May 1997, 30-40

[Liu2001]   S. Liu, M. Silverman: *A Practical Guide to Biometric Security Technology*, IT Professional, Jan–Feb 2001
               http://www.computer.org/itpro/homepage/jan_feb01/
               security3.htm

[Louridas00]   P. Louridas: *Some Guidelines for Nonrepudiation Protocols*, ACM Sig-Comm, October 2000
               http://www.acm.org/sigcomm/ccr/archive/2000/oct00/louri-
               das.pdf

[LP01]   S. Lehtonen, J. Parssinen: *A Pattern Language for Key Management*, in Proceedings of PLoP, 2001

http://jerry.cs.uiuc.edu/~plop/plop2001/
accepted_submissions/accepted-papers.html

[LS00] J. Lennox, H. Schulzrinne: *Call Processing Language Framework and Requirements*, RFC 2824, May 2000

[Mei03] J. D. Meier et al: *Improving Web Application Security: Threats and Countermeasures*, Microsoft, 2003

[MBS03] R. Leming: *Best Practice in Information System Management*, Mint Business Solutions, 2003
http://www.mintsolutions.co.uk/pages.asp?p=43

[MGS03] H. Mouratidis, P. Giorgini, M. Schumacher: *Security Patterns for Agent Systems*, in Proceedings of EuroPLoP, 2003
http://www.hillside.net/europlop/

[Mic00] Microsoft Corporation: *Windows 2000 Security Technical Reference*, Microsoft Press, 2000

[Mof88] J. D. Moffett, M. S. Sloman: *The Source of Authority for Commercial Access Control*, Computer, Vol. 21, No. 2, IEEE, pp. 59–69, February 1988

[MSDN] Microsoft Developer Network: http://msdn.microsoft.com/

[NG98] F. Das Neves, A. Garrido: *Bodyguard*, published in [PLoPD3], 1997

[NIST800-12] National Institute of Standards and Technology (NIST): *An Introduction to Computer Security: The NIST Handbook*, NIST Special Publication 800-12, Information Technology Laboratory, 25 August 2003
http://sbc.nist.gov/cyber-security-tips/800-12/800-12Word.html

[NIST800-30] G. Stoneburner, A. Goguen, A. Feringa: *Risk Management Guide for Information Technology Systems*, NIST Special Publication SP800-30, National Institute of Standards and Technology (NIST), 2001

[NIST800-33] G. Stoneburner: *Underlying Technical Models for Information Technology Security: Recommendations of the National Institute of Standards and Technology (USA)*, NIST Special Publication SP800-33, National Institute of Standards and Technology (NIST), December 2001

[NIST800-35] T. Grance et al: *Guide to Information Technology Security Services*, NIST Special Publication NIST SP800-35, National Institute of Standards and Technology (NIST), 2003

[NIST800-63] W. E. Burr, D. F. Dodson, W. T. Polk: *Electronic Authentication Guideline*, NIST Special Publication NIST SP800-63, National Institute of Standards and Technology (NIST), 2004

[NIST03]   National Institute of Standards and Technology (NIST): *Computer Security Resource Center*, `http://csrc.nist.gov`

[NIST2004]   National Institute of Standards and Technology (NIST): *Electronic Authentication Guideline*, NIST Special Publication 800-63, Version 1.0.1, September 2004
                `http://csrc.nist.gov/publications/nistpubs/800-63/SP800-63v6_3_3.pdf`

[Nou00]   N. A. Noureldien, I. M. Osman: *A Stateful Inspection Module Architecture*, in *Proceedings of TENCON 2000*, Vol. 2, pp. 259–265, Kuala Lumpur, Malaysia, September 2000

[NSA02]   National Security Agency (NSA): *Information Assurance Technical Framework (IATF)*, Release 3.1, Fort Meade, MD, September 2002,
                `http://www.iatf.net`

[NW01]   J. Noble, C. Weir: *Small Memory Software: Patterns for Systems with Limited Memory*, Addison-Wesley Professional, 2000

[Oak01]   S. Oaks, *Java Security*, Second Edition, O'Reilly, 2001

[OASIS]   OASIS Open 2005: *OASIS Standards and Other Approved Works*,
                `http://www.oasis-open.org/specs/index.php#wssv1.0`

[OASIS00]   Coverpages hosted by OASIS: *Trading Partner Agreement Markup Language (tpaML)*, September 2000,
                `http://xml.coverpages.org/tpa.html`

[OMB2003]   Office of Management and Budget: *E-Authentication Guidance for Federal Agencies*, Memorandum M-04-04, Washington, DC, USA, 16 December 2003
                `http://www.whitehouse.gov/omb/memoranda/fy04/m04-04.pdf`

[OWASP]   The Open Web Application Security Project (OWASP)
                `http://www.owasp.org/`

[Pel01]   T. R. Peltier: *Information Security Risk Analysis*, Auerbach Publications, 2001

[Pet01]   R. Peteanu: *Best Practices for Secure Development*, Vol. 4.03, October 2001
                `http://www.modsecurity.org/archive/best_prac_for_sec_dev4.pdf`
                `http://www.cgisecurity.com/lib/best_prac_for_sec_dev4.pdf`

[Pfl03]   C. P. Pfleeger: *Security in Computing*, Third Edition, Prentice-Hall, 2003

[Pip03]   Pipex: *Pipex Firewall Solutions*,
                `http://www.security.pipex.net/about.shtml`

[PLoPD1]   J. O. Coplien, D. C. Schmidt (eds.): *Pattern Languages of Program Design*, Addison-Wesley Professional, 1995 (a book publishing the reviewed Proceedings of PLoP, Monticello, Illinois, 1994)

[PLoPD2]   J. O. Coplien, N. Kerth, J. Vlissides (eds.): *Pattern Languages of Program Design 2*, Addison-Wesley Professional, 1996 (a book publishing the reviewed Proceedings of PLoP, Monticello, Illinois, 1995)

[PLoPD3]   R. C. Martin, D. Riehle, F. Buschmann (eds.): *Pattern Languages of Program Design 3*, Addison-Wesley Professional, 1997 (a book publishing selected papers from the Proceedings of PLoP, Monticello, Illinois, USA, 1996, the Proceedings of EuroPLoP, Irsee, Bavaria, Germany, 1996, and the Telecommunication Pattern Workshop at OOPSLA '96, San Jose, California, USA, 1996)

[PLoPD4]   N. Harrison, B. Foote, H. Rohnert (eds.): *Pattern Languages of Program Design 4*, Addison-Wesley Professional, 1999 (a book publishing selected papers from the Proceedings of PLoP, Monticello, Illinois, USA, 1997 and 1998, and the Proceedings of EuroPLoP, Irsee, Bavaria, Germany, 1997 and 1998)

[POSA1]   F. Buschmann, R. Meunier, H. Rohnert, P. Sommerlad, M. Stal: *Pattern-Oriented Software Architecture – A System of Patterns*, John Wiley & Sons, 1996

[POSA2]   D. C. Schmidt, M. Stal, H. Rohnert, F. Buschmann: *Pattern-Oriented Software Architecture – Patterns for Concurrent and Networked Objects*, John Wiley & Sons, 2000

[POSA3]   P. Jain, M. Kircher: *Pattern-Oriented Software Architecture – Patterns for Resource Management*, John Wiley & Sons, 2004

[POSA4]   F. Buschmann, K. Henney: *Pattern-Oriented Software Architecture – On Patterns and Pattern Languages*, John Wiley & Sons, to be published in 2005

[Pri04]   T. Priebe, E. B. Fernandez, J. I. Mehlau, G. Pernul: *A Pattern System for Access Control*, in *Proceedings of the 18th. Annual IFIP WG 11.3 Working Conference on Data and Applications Security*, Sitges, Spain, July 25–28, 2004

[Pry97]   N. Pryce: *Abstract Session: an Object Structural Pattern*, Chapter 7 in [PLoPD4] (N. Harrison, B. Foote, and H. Rohnert, eds.). Also in Proceedings of PLoP 1997
http://jerry.cs.uiuc.edu/~plop/plop97

[PWC01]   PriceWaterhouseCoopers: *Designing a Secure Framework for the Competitive Enterprise*, 2001

[Rau97]   L. Rau: *Inferno: One Hot OS*, Byte, June 1997, pp. 53–54
               http://www.byte.com/art/9706/sec4/art2.htm

[RC]   RUS-CERT: *DV-Sicherheit an der Universitat Stuttgart*, September 2003
               http://cert.uni-stuttgart.de/

[RFC2109]   D. Kristol, L. Montulli: *RFC 2109 – HTTP State Management Mechanism*,
               1997

[Riehle2002]   D. Riehle, W. Cunningham, J. Bergin, N. Kerth, S. Metsker, Anonymous
               Contributor: *Password Pattern Language*, 2003
               http://hillside.net/patterns/EuroPLoP2002/papers/Riehle.zip

[Ris00]   L. Rising: *The Pattern Almanac 2000*, Addison-Wesley, 2000

[Rom02]   S. Romanosky: *Enterprise Security Patterns*, in Proceedings of EuroPLoP,
               2002
               http://hillside.net/patterns/EuroPLoP2002/papers/Ro-
               manosky.zip

[RSC+02]   J. Rosenberg, H. Schulzrinne, G. Camarillo, A. Johnston, J. Peterson,
               R. Sparks, M. Handley, E. Schooler: *SIP: Session Initiation Protocol*, RFC
               3261, June 2002

[Rum94]   J. Rumbaugh: *Getting Started: Using Use Cases to Capture Requirements*,
               Journal of Object-Oriented Programming, pp. 8–23, 1994

[Rus02]   R. E. Rustad, Jr: *Guide to OpenBSD Packet Filtering Firewalls*, Kuro5hin
               article, November 2002
               http://www.kuro5hin.org/story/2002/11/23/14927/477

[Rus89]   V. F. Russo, R. H. Campbell: *Virtual Memory and Backing Storage Manage-
               ment in Multiprocessor Operating Systems using Object-Oriented Design
               Techniques*, in *Proceedings of the Conference on Object-Oriented Program-
               ming Systems*, Languages and Applications, 267-278, October 1989

[SAML]   OASIS: *Security Assertion Markup Language (SAML)*
               http://www.oasis-open.org/committees/security/

[Sal75]   J. H. Saltzer, M. D. Schroeder: *The Protection of Information in Computer
               Systems*, in *Proceedings of the IEEE*, 63(9):1278–1308, September 1975

[San96]   R. Sandhu et al: *Role-Based Access Control Models*, IEEE Computer, Vol. 29,
               No. 2, February 1996, pp. 38–47

[SANSa]   J. Bayne, SANS Institute: *An Overview of Threat and Risk Assessment*,
               Version 1.2f, 2002
               http://www.sans.org/rr/paper.php?id=76

[SANSb]   SANS Institute: `http://www.sans.org/rr`

[SANSc]   SANS Institute: *The SANS Security Policy Project*
                `http://www.sans.org/resources/policies/`

[SANSd]   SANS Institute: *SANS Information Security Reading Room*
                `http://www.sans.org/rr/`

[SANSe]   SANS Institute: *The CVA Process*,2004
                `http://www.sans.org/newsletters/cva/#process`

[SANSf]   SANS Institute, Track 4: *Hacker Techniques, Exploits and Incident Handling*,
                `http://www.sans.org/kansascity04/description.php?track=t4`

[SCF+96]   H. Schulzrinne, S. Casner, R. Frederick, V. Jackobson: *RTP: A Transport Protocol for Real-Time Applications*, RFC 1889, January 1996

[Sch99]   B. Schneier: *Attack Trees*, Dr. Dobb's Journal, December 1999
                See also
                `http://www.schneier.com/paper-attacktrees-ddj-ft.html`

[Sch01]   B. Schätz: *The ODL Operation Definition Language and the AutoFocus/ Quest Application Framework AQuA*, technical report TUM-I1101, Technische Universität München, 2001

[Sch03]   M. Schumacher: *Firewall Patterns*, in Proceedings of EuroPLoP, 2003
                `http://www.hillside.net/europlop/`

[Sch03b]   B. Schneier: *Beyond Fear*, Copernicus Books, 2003

[Sch]   M. Schumacher (ed.): *The Security Patterns page*
                `http://www.securitypatterns.org`

[Seffers2001]   G. I. Seffers: *How Biometrics Works*, Federal Computer Week, April 30, 2001
                `http://www.fcw.com/fcw/articles/2001/0430/pol-biobox-04-30-01.asp`

[SEI2004]   Software Engineering Institute: *e-Authentication Risk and Requirements Assessment: e-RA Tool Activity Guide*, Pittsburgh, PA, USA, May 2004
                `http://www.cio.gov/eauthentication/era.htm`

[SF02]   M. Schumacher, E. B. Fernandez: *Focus Group Report: Thinking about Security Patterns*, in Proceedings of EuroPLoP, 2002

[Sha02]   J. S. Shapiro, N. Hardy: *EROS: A Principle-Driven Operating System from the Ground Up*, IEEE Software, pp. 26–33, January/February 2002
                See also `http://www.eros-os.org`

[Sil03]   A. Silberschatz, P. Galvin, G. Gagne: *Operating System Concepts*, Sixth Edition, John Wiley & Sons, 2003

[SFO03]   G. Sindre, D. G. Firesmith, A. L. Opdahl: *A Reuse-Based Approach to Determining Security Requirements*, in *Proceedings 9th International Workshop on Requirements Engineering: Foundation for Software Quality (REFSQ'03)*, Klagenfurt/Velden, Austria, June 2003

[Smith2002]   R. E. Smith: *Authentication: From Passwords to Public Keys*, Addison-Wesley Professional, 2001

[SNL05]   C. Steel, R. Nagappan, R. Lai: *Core Security Patterns: Best Practices and Strategies for J2EE, Web Services and Identity Management*, Prentice Hall, to be published in 2005
               http://www.coresecuritypatterns.com/

[SO00]   G. Sindre, A. L. Opdahl: *Eliciting Security Requirements by Misuse Cases*, in *Proceedings of TOOLS Pacific 2000*, pp. 120–131, 2000

[SO01]   G. Sindre, A. L. Opdahl: *Templates for Misuse Case Description*, in *Proceedings of the 7th International Workshop on Requirements Engineering, Foundation for Software Quality (REFSQ'2001)*, Interlaken, Switzerland, June 2001

[Socks]   IETF: *SOCKS Protocol*, http://www.socks.permeo.com/

[Sof03]   Software Technologies, 2003
               http://www.sofaware.com/ (use Knowledge Base link)

[Sol]   Solsoft, Inc: http://www.solsoft.com

[Som98]   P. Sommerlad: *Manager*, in [PLoPD3], Addison-Wesley, 1997

[SoRu98]   P. Sommerlad, M. Rüedi: *Do-it-Yourself Reflection*, in Proceedings of EuroPLoP, 1998 (contains PROPERTY LIST and ANYTHING)

[SR01]   M. Schumacher, Utz Roedig: *Security Engineering with Patterns*, in Proceedings of PLoP, 2001

[SRM03]   M. Schumacher, U. Rödig, M-L. Moschgath: *Hacker Contest*, Xpert.press, Springer Verlag, 2003 (in German)

[Sum97]   R. C. Summers: *Secure Computing: Threats and Safeguards*, McGraw-Hill College, 1997

[Swan00]   D. Swanson: *Secure Strategies*, Information Security Magazine, October 2000

[Swi83]   D. C. Swinehart, L.C. Stewart, S.M. Ornstein: *Adding Voice to an Office Computer Network*, IEEE GlobeCom, November 1983

[Synlogic] Synlogic: http://www.synlogic.ch/en

[SZ92] J. F. Sowa, J. A. Zachman: *Extending and Formalizing the Framework for Information Systems Architecture*, IBM Systems Journal, 31(3), IBM Publication G321-5488, 1992

[Tilton2002] C. Tilton: *Understanding Biometric Technology and Its Implementation*, Tutorial M2, 18th Annual Computer Security Applications Conference, 9 December 2002, Las Vegas, USA

[Tivoli] IBM: *Enterprise Security Architecture using IBM Tivoli Security Solutions* http://www.redbooks.ibm.com/pubs/pdfs/redbooks/sg246014.pdf

[UMLSec] J. Jürjens: UMLsec homepage, http://www4.in.tum.de/~umlsec/

[Vicom] InterGate Firewalls from Vicomsoft, http://www.vicomsoft.com/

[Vim03] S. De Capitani di Vimercati, S. Paraboschi, P. Samarati: *Access Control: Principles and Solutions*, in *Software – Practice and Experience*, Vol. 33, No. 5, April 2003, pp. 397–421

[VSW02] M. Völter, A. Schmid, E. Wolff: *Server Component Patterns – Component Infrastructures Illustrated with EJB*, John Wiley & Sons, 2002

[Wheel99] A. Wheeler: *Payment Security and Internet References*, May 1999 http://www.garlic.com/~lynn

[Wel99] I. Welch: *Reflective Enforcement of the Clark-Wilson Integrity Model*, in *Proceedings of the 2nd Workshop in Distributed Object Security*, pp. 5–9, OOPSLA 1999, November 1999

[Woo79] C. Wood, E. B. Fernandez: *Authorization in a Decentralized Database System*, in *Proceedings of the 5th International Conference on Very Large Databases*, pp. 352–359, Rio de Janeiro, 1979

[Woolf96] B. Woolf: *The Null Object Pattern*, in [PLoPD3], Addison-Wesley, 1997

[WT03] J. Whittaker, H. H. Thompson: *How to Break Software Security*, Addison-Wesley, 2003

[WTS03] J. Wack, M. Tracy, M. Souppaya: *Guideline on Network Security Testing*, NIST Special Publication 800-42, National Institute of Standards and Technology (NIST), 2003

[Yahoo] Yahoo Security Directory http://dir.yahoo.com/Computers_and_Internet/ Security_and_Encryption/

[YB97] J. Yoder, J. Barcalow: *Architectural Patterns for Enabling Application Security*, in Proceedings of PLoP, 1997

[Zac87]   J. A. Zachman: *A Framework for Information Systems Architecture*, IBM Systems Journal, 26(3), IBM Publication G321-5298, 1987

[Zac99]   W. H. Zack: *Windows 2000 and Mainframe Integration*, MacMillan Publishing Company, 1999

[ZIFA]   ZIFA – Zachman Institute for Framework Advancement
`http://www.zifa.com/`

[Zie02]   R. Ziegler, C. Constantine: *Linux Firewalls: Packet Filtering*, News Riders, March 2002
`http://www.informit.com/articles/article.asp?p=26121&rl=1`

[Zwi00]   E. D. Zwicky, S. Cooper, B. Chapman: *Building Internet Firewalls*, O'Reilly, Second Edition, 2000

Index

ABSTRACT FACTORY, 331

ABSTRACT SESSION, 252

Access control, xii, 16, 24, 26, 30, 63, 243–264, 499

  based on data sensitivity, 253

  based on task, 249

  controlling access to features, 305, 313

  detecting imposters, 323

  determining requirements, 268

  enforcement, 256

  matching rights to role, 259

  of objects, 332

  of processes, 343, 346

  supporting state, 298

  to files, 350

  to memory, 339

  to objects, 335

Access Control Entries, 333

Access control list, 246, 333

Access control model patterns, 67

ACCESS CONTROL REQUIREMENTS, xxxi, 70, 163, 265, 266, 267–278

ACCESS CONTROL SERVICE, 63

Accountability, xii, 16, 20, 50, 74, 76, 495, 498

Accounting, 355–402

ACCOUNTING SERVICE, 63

Acknowledgements, xxxiii

ACM Transactions on Security, 27

ActivCard, 66

ACTOR REGISTRATION, 67

ACTOR REGISTRATION OR ENROLLMENT SERVICE, 63

AIX, 258, 344, 349

Alexander, Christopher, 11, 50, 283

ANYTHING, 300, 552

Apache Web server, 294, 440

APPLICATION SERVER ARCHITECTURE, 427, 442, 450

APPLICATION SERVERS, 452

APPLICATION-LEVEL FIREWALL, 404

Application-specific attack, 405

Appropriate Process Movement, 62

ARGuE, 409

Asset

  business, 90

  confidentiality, 131

  critical, 148

  integrity, 131, 149, 161, 170

  properties, 20

  valuation, 22, 104

ASSET VALUATION, 60, 103–112, 137, 138, 139, 140, 141, 142, 147, 496

ATM card, 66

Audit and accounting, xix, 24, 74, 76, 369, 494, 495

  patterns, 73

AUDIT DESIGN, 75

Audit log, 358, 372, 378

AUDIT REQUIREMENTS, 75, 368, 369–377, 378

AUDIT TRAILS & LOGGING DESIGN, 75

AUDIT TRAILS AND LOGGING REQUIREMENTS, 75, 76, 368, 377, 378–387, 395
Authentication
    See *Identification and authentication*
AUTHENTICATOR, 30, 71, 322, 323–327
Authorization, xii, 16, 17, 24, 50, 499, 514
    independent structure, 245
    need for flexibility, 245
AUTHORIZATION, 68, 244, 245–248, 250, 252, 342, 346, 347, 349, 350, 351, 354, 410, 499
AUTHORIZER, 327
Authors
    about, xxiii–xxxiii
    responsibilities, xxx
AUTOMATED I&A DESIGN ALTERNATIVES, 62, 64, 206, 207–216, 228, 229, 232, 238
Automated mechanisms, in security taxonomy, 25
Availability, of data, xii, 20, 50, 482, 495, 498, 515, 517
AVAILABLE AND PROTECTED SYSTEMS, 83

Barcalow, Jeffrey, xxx, xxxi, 266
Beck, Kent, 5, 11, 13
Bell-LaPadula security model, 254
Beraha, Lara, 425
Biba security model, 254
Biometrics, 32, 62, 65, 166, 168, 169, 207, 208, 209, 211, 214, 229–241, 327, 476, 500
    cost, 231
    error types, 231
    existing uses, 230
    false acceptance, 231
    false rejection, 231
    mechanisms in common, 229
    vulnerabilities, limitations, 230
BIOMETRICS DESIGN ALTERNATIVES, 62, 64, 211, 228, 229–241, 498, 500
Birrer, Andreas, 425
Black list filter, 462
Blocking malicious sites, 411
BODYGUARD, 30
Book
    about, xv
    conclusions, 531–534

guidelines for reader, xx
inception, xxx
intended audience, xvii
organization, 49–52
structure, xviii
Boundary protection, 24, 43, 281
Breach propagation, 174
British Standards Institute, 39
BS 7799, 39
Büchel, Bruno, 425
Buffer overflow attack, 116, 128, 411, 458
BUILDER, 334
Burton Group, 43
Buschmann, Frank, xi, xxiii, xxx, 88, 425
Business asset, 90
Business continuity, 149
    planning, 174
Business model, integration of security, 148, 162
Buzzi, Lukas, 425

Call Processing Language, 485
Case study, 481–501
Center for Environmental Structure, 11
CERT Coordination Center, 27, 43, 45, 135
CERT Knowledgebase, 130
CERT-AU, 44
CERTIFICATE AUTHORITY, 498, 500
CERTIFICATE REVOCATION, 82
Certificate Revocation List, 83
CHAIN OF RESPONSIBILITY, 292, 294, 295, 296
Challenge-response protocol, 67, 226, 476
Chaos Computer Club, 44
Chapin, Susan, xxiii, xxx, 88, 191, 266, 359
CHECK POINT, 30, 70, 258, 266, 278, 284, 286, 287–296, 297, 299, 300, 301, 304, 309, 311, 313, 315, 319, 478, 479, 499
Cisco, 171, 455
Clark-Wilson model, 30
COBRA security audit method, 376
COMMAND PROCESSOR, 309
Common Criteria, 40, 366, 526, 527, 530
COMMON PERSISTENT STORE, 426, 427
Common Vulnerability Scoring System, 135
Communication
    security, 434
    third-party vulnerability, 174

Communications of the ACM, 27
COMPOSITE, 251, 252, 344, 351, 354
Computer Incident Response Teams, 43
Computer Security Institute, 27
Computers and Security journal, 27
Conference, on security, 27
Confidentiality
    asset, 131
    data, xi, 16, 20, 32, 35, 50, 80, 90, 96, 488,
        494, 495, 498, 515, 517, 529
Configuration management, 25, 26, 40
CONTROLLED EXECUTION ENVIRONMENT, 30, 71, 73,
        322, 330, 346–349, 354
CONTROLLED OBJECT FACTORY, 30, 71, 72, 322,
        331–334
CONTROLLED OBJECT MONITOR, 30, 71, 72, 322,
        332, 335–338, 345, 346, 347
CONTROLLED PROCESS CREATOR, 71, 322,
        328–330, 345
CONTROLLED VIRTUAL ADDRESS SPACE, 73, 339–342,
        349, 354
Coplien, James O., 5
CORBA, 294
Cost
    access control trade-offs, 323
    of access control, 268
    of asset compromise, 104
    of biometric techniques, 231
    of security, 90, 149
CREDENTIAL PROPAGATION, 77
Critical asset, unauthorized access, 162
CRYPTOGRAPHIC KEY GENERATION, 80
Cryptographic key management patterns, 80
CRYPTOGRAPHIC SMART CARD, 82, 500
Cunningham, Ward, 11, 37

Data
    availability, xii, 20, 50, 482, 495, 498, 515,
        517
    confidentiality, xi, 16, 20, 35, 50, 80,
        90, 96, 488, 494, 495, 498, 515,
        517, 529
    ensuring security in transit, 435
    integrity, xii, 16, 17, 20, 32, 35, 50, 80, 81,
        495, 498, 515, 517
    protection from unauthorized access, 427

    protection of sensitive, 435
    unauthorized disclosure, 16, 21, 495
Data Encryption Standard, 225
Data packet, correlating, 417
Deception, 21, 521
DEDICATED WEB, 452
Delessy-Gassant, Nelly, xxiv, xxxi, 404
DEMILITARIZED ZONE, 79, 182, 183, 266, 409, 410,
        424, 426, 427, 429, 430, 434, 435, 439,
        449–456, 459, 467, 471, 475
Detection, 20, 23, 24, 33, 43, 75, 76, 148, 519,
        520, 521
Devx, 27
Dewar, Rick, xxxiii, 322
DFN-CERT, 43
DICTIONARY WORD, 227
Digital certificate, 437, 445, 447
Diligence, 23
Disaster recovery, 25, 108, 112, 133, 149,
        162, 174
Disruption, 21
DISTRIBUTED AUTHENTICATOR, 327
DNA, 229, 233, 523
DOMAIN, 349
Dyson, Paul, xxiv, xxxi, 424

Eclipse JDT, 317
Elder, Matthew C., 83
Elsinga, Ben, xxiv, xxx, xxxi, 503
e-mail worm, 115
Embedded data attack, 411
ENCAPSULATED CONTEXT, 304
Encryption, 26, 43, 80, 132, 176, 182, 211, 225,
        424, 426–433, 434–441
    parameters, 391
    public key, 81
Enforcement, of access control, 256
Enterprise
    architecture resources, 42
    business strategies, 17, 19
    communication with partners, 174
    framework, 53
    security, 47–58, 85–185
    security standards, 38
ENTERPRISE PARTNER COMMUNICATION, 61, 62, 88,
        173–185

Enterprise security
  patterns, 59
  root pattern, 89
ENTERPRISE SECURITY APPROACHES, 61, 87, 148–160,
    162, 163, 164
ENTERPRISE SECURITY SERVICES, 61, 87, 101, 160,
    161–172, 192, 193, 267, 268, 360
EROS, 344, 349
EuroPLoP, xxiii, xxiv, xxvi, xxx, 12, 13, 31, 32,
    424, 503, 504
Evidian Access Master, 462
Evidian PortalXpert, 478
EXECUTION DOMAIN, 73, 343–345, 347, 349
Execution, controlling domain, 343, 346

FACE RECOGNITION, 65, 240
FACTORY, 332
FACTORY METHOD, 331
Fernandez, Eduardo B., xxv, xxx, xxxi, 191,
    244, 266, 322, 404
FEW PANES, 11
FILE AUTHORIZATION, 71, 73, 350–354
File control block, 352
File, rights of access, 350
FINGER IMAGE, 65, 240
Firefox, 440
Firewall
  architecture patterns, 77
  Gauntlet, 409
  InterGate, 415, 420
  Linux, 409
  multi-homed, 455
  packet-filter, 405
  patterns, 403–421
  Pipex Security, 415, 420
  proxy, 411
  state table, 418
  stateful, 417
  stealth, 455
Force, xviii, 3, 6, 10, 32, 33, 34, 35, 36, 37, 39,
    41, 51
Foreword, xi
403, 404 errors, 460
Fowler, Martin, 5
FRONT DOOR, 80, 266, 304, 424, 442, 462, 463,
    470, 471, 472, 473–479

Frontdoor, 214, 425, 478
FTP password, 214
FULL ACCESS WITH ERRORS, 265, 266, 278,
    305–311, 312, 315, 316
Fullerton, Mei, xxv, 244

Gähler, Felix, 425
Gamma, Erich, 2, 12
Gang-of-Four, 2, 4, 12, 31
Gauntlet Firewall, 409
Google Security Directory, 27
Görtz, Manuel, xxv, xxx, xxxi
GPS, 208

H.323 protocol, 484, 489, 492, 498
Hacker groups, 44
Hafiz, Munawar, xxxiii, 266, 404
HAND GEOMETRY, 65, 241
Hardware token, 447
HARDWARE TOKEN DESIGN ALTERNATIVES, 66, 228,
    498, 500
Heaney, Jody, xxv, xxx, 88, 191, 266, 359
Heath, Craig R.P., xxxiii
Helm, Richard, 2, 12
Henney, Kevlin, 425
Herzberg, Angela, 404
Hillside Europe Group, xxix, xxxiii
Hillside Group, xxix, 13
Hofman, Aaldert, xxvi, xxx, xxxi, 88, 503
HTTPS protocol, 178, 183, 303, 437, 439,
    458, 477
Huber, Marcel, 425
Hybertson, Duane, xxvi, xxx, 88, 191, 266, 359

I&A DESIGN ALTERNATIVES, 64
I&A REQUIREMENTS, 62, 63, 163, 192–206, 207,
    212, 217, 229, 232, 234, 272, 325, 364,
    372, 382, 391, 399, 498, 499
IBM, 62, 77, 184, 251, 478
IBM S/38, 341, 345, 349
IBM S/6000, 341, 344, 345, 349
Identification
  See Identification and authentication
Identification and authentication, 24, 187–241
  design alternatives, 207
  patterns, 62

strategies, 208
supporting change, 288
IEEE Computer Society, xxix
IEEE Transactions on Dependable and Secure
    Computing, 27
INFILSEC Systems Security, 44
INFORMATION OBSCURITY, 78, 424, 426–433, 434
Informix, 255
InfoSecurity Magazine, 27
INTEGRATION REVERSE PROXY, 79, 304, 414, 424,
    427, 442, 462, 463, 465–472, 473, 475,
    478, 479
Integrity
    asset, 131, 149, 161, 170
    data, xii, 16, 17, 20, 35, 50, 80, 81, 495, 498,
        515, 517
    message, 500
    structural, 119
    transaction, 397, 399, 400
Intel Pentium, 341, 345
Intel X86, 345
INTERCEPTOR, 30, 258
InterGate Firewall, 415, 420
Internet Explorer, 440
Internet Security Systems, 44
Internet, secure applications, 423–479
INTRUSION DETECTION DESIGN, 76
Intrusion detection error, 389
INTRUSION DETECTION REQUIREMENTS, 75, 368,
    388–395, 454
IP telephony, xix
    applying security patterns, 497
    case study, 481–501
    components, 484
    fundamentals, 483
    how security patterns could help, 500
    overview, 482
    signaling and media streaming, 485
    use cases, 488
    vulnerabilities, 488
IP-level payload, 405
IPSec, 440
IRIS RECOGNITION, 65, 241
ISO13335, 39, 101
ISO13335-1, 39
ISO13335-3, 111, 121, 136, 146
ISO13335-4, 158, 170, 376, 385, 394, 400

ISO13888, 401
ISO15408, 40, 91, 92, 204, 364, 366, 376, 385,
    394, 400, 526
ISO17799, 39, 101, 111, 184, 376
IT Baseline Protection Manual, 41

J2EE, xxvii, 83, 251, 259, 262
J2EE SECURITY, 83
Java, 30, 251, 258, 338, 430, 431
    development environment, 317
    version 1.2 security, 338
Java Security Manager, 258
Java Virtual Machine, 344
Johnson, Ralph, xxxiii, 2, 12, 266

Kerberos, 431
Kerth, Norm, 37
Kienzle, Darrel M., 83
Kirwan, Malcolm, xxvii, xxx, 88, 191, 266, 359
KNOWN PARTNERS, 79, 424, 432, 437, 442–448,
    498, 500

Lai, Ray, 83
Larrondo-Petrie, Maria M., xxvii, xxxi, 404
LDAP, 182, 275, 292, 475
Lea, Doug, 50
Legislation
    compliance with, 174
    privacy, 90
Lehtonen, Sami, xxx, xxxiii, 80
Leonhardt, Ulf, 425
LIMITED ACCESS, 71, 265, 266, 278, 310,
    312–319
Linux, 289, 353
Linux Firewall, 409
LOAD BALANCED ELEMENTS, 439
LOG FOR AUDIT, 76
Longshaw, Andy, xxvii, xxxi, 404, 424, 504

Mac OS, 285
MAGNETIC CARD, 66
MAIN ENTRANCE, 283
Malicious activity, detection from audit
    trail, 378
Man in the middle attack, 129

Management support mechanisms, in security
    taxonomy, 25
MANAGER, 299, 300, 301
Marquardt, Klaus, 424
Memory, rights of access, 339
Message integrity, 500
Microsoft Developer Network, 27
Mindset, for security principles, 514
Mint Business Solutions, 99
Misuse case, enhancing patterns, 525
MITRE Corporation, 88, 158, 170, 191,
    204, 214, 266, 275, 366, 373, 384,
    394, 400
Model, access control, 243–264
Montorfano, Alessio, 425
Mozilla, 440
Multics, 341, 344, 345
Multi-homed firewall, 455
MULTILEVEL SECURITY, 68, 244, 253–255
MYSQL, 302

Nagappan, Ramesh, 83
National Institute of Standards and Technology
    See NIST
.NET, xxvii, 259, 262, 430, 431, 438, 440
Netscape, 440
Neumann, Peter N., xxxiii
Newsgroups, mailing lists, 45
NIST, 42, 123, 130
Non-repudiation, 24, 75, 76, 77, 526, 527
NON-REPUDIATION DESIGN, 76
NON-REPUDIATION REQUIREMENTS, 76, 368,
    396–402
NOUNS AND VERBS, 11
NULL OBJECT, 292, 296, 314

Object, rights of access, 332, 335
One-time password, 66, 207, 210, 212, 226,
    473, 474, 476
ONE-TIME PASSWORD TOKEN, 66
OOPSLA, 532
Opdahl, Andreas L., xxvii, xxxi, 503
Open Group, 83
Open Source Vulnerability Database, 130
OpenBSD Packet Filtering Firewall, 409
Opera, 440

Operating system, access control patterns, 71,
    321–354
Oracle, 251, 255, 262, 302
Organization of patterns, 49–52
OWASP project, 530

PACKET FILTER FIREWALL, 77, 247, 404, 405–410,
    411, 414, 416, 417, 419, 421, 457,
    458, 498
Packet, correlating, 417
Pan, Rouyi, 244
Pärsinnen, Juha, xxx, xxxiii, 80
Password
    bad practice, 221
    confidentiality, 218
    current thinking, 225
    design pattern, 217
    forces on procedures, 218
    good practice, 219–226
    pattern language, 227
    protection in operating systems, 429
PASSWORD DESIGN AND USE, 62, 64, 217–228, 327,
    498, 499
PASSWORD PROTECTION, 227
PASSWORD QUALITY, 227
Pattern
    access control, 243–264
    access control model, 67
    accounting, 355–402
    Alexander form, 11
    and security principles, 504
    applying to IP telephony, 497
    approach, 1–13
    asset valuation, 103
    assigning rights, 249
    assigning rights to roles, 259
    at a glance, 2
    audit and accounting, 73
    automated I&A alternatives, 207
    avionics, 50
    catalogs, 7
    characteristics of security patterns, 31
    conclusions, 531–534
    concurrent and networked systems, 5
    control of process creation, 328
    control of virtual address space, 339

controlling access to files, 350
controlling execution domain, 343
controlling object access, 335
controlling object access rights, 331
controlling system access, 279
controlling user interface access, 305, 312
cryptographic key management, 80
defining execution rights, 346
determining access control requirements, 267
determining audit requirements, 369
determining audit trail and logging, 378
determining identification and authentication
   requirements, 192
determining intrusion detection
   requirements, 388
determining non-repudiation
   requirements, 396
determining risk, 137
documenting, 9
enhancing with misuse cases, 525
enterprise security, 59, 89
firewall, 403–421
firewall architecture, 77
for categorizing sensitive information, 253
for enforcing access restrictions, 256
forces, xviii, 3, 6, 10, 32, 33, 34, 35, 36, 37,
   39, 41, 51
guiding third-party communication, 173
history of patterns, 11
history of security patterns, 30
human–computer interaction, 5
identification & authentication, 62
identification and authentication, 187–241
identification and authorization
   deployment, 287
information obscurity, 426
isolating Web servers, 449
Java security patterns, 30, 251, 258, 338
landscape, 59–83
mapping, 53
mapping to enterprise, 53
memory constraint, 5
mining security patterns, 37
not an island, 4
operating system access control, 71, 321–354
organization scheme, 49–52
organization, user level, 529

packet-filter firewall, 405
password design, 217
protecting server software, 457
proxy firewall, 411
resolving problems, 6
resource management, 5
risk management, 59
scope, 47–58
scope of patterns, 48
secure communication, 434
secure Internet applications, 78, 423–479
securing IP telephony, 493
security, 29–45
security accounting requirements, 360
selecting security approaches, 148
selecting security services, 161
selection of biometrics, 229
server components, 5
shepherding, 12
stateful firewall, 417
supplementary concepts, 503–530
system access control, 69, 265–319
system authorization, 245
systems, 7
target audience, 5
the pattern community, 12
threat assessment, 113
towards languages, 7
tracking security access, 297
tracking user session, 473
ubiquity, 4
unifying Web addresses, 465
validating Web users, 442
verifying subject, 323
vulnerability assessment, 125
Web access control, 473
Pattern form, 2, 9
Pattern language, 7
   example, 8
Pattern mining, 37
   Kloster Irsee brewery, xxxiii
Pattern-Oriented Software Architecture, book
   series, 9
Pfister, Markus, 425
Phrack, 44
PHYSICAL AND PROCEDURAL I&A, 64
Physical mechanisms, in security taxonomy, 25

Pipex Security Firewall, 415, 420
Pitbull, 255
PKI, 35, 66, 208, 209, 211, 214
    performance/security trade-off, 437
    session key exchange, 437
PKI Authenticator, 326
PKI Design Variables, 66, 228, 499
Planning, xix, 23, 52, 53, 57, 524
    business continuity, 174
PLoP conference series, 12, 32
Pluggable authentication module, 289, 291, 294
PortalXpert, 462
Prevention, 23, 33, 43, 76, 148, 149
PriceWaterhouseCoopers, 99
Privacy legislation, 90
Problem resolution with patterns, 6
Procedural mechanisms, in security
        taxonomy, 25
Process
    rights of access, 343, 346
    rights of process, 328
Property List, 300, 552
Protection
    from protocol-based attack, 458
    of public systems, 450
Protection Reverse Proxy, 79, 266, 286, 414,
        424, 427, 442, 450, 451, 457–464, 467,
        468, 469, 471, 473, 475, 478, 479
Protocol, protection of attack, 458
Proxy, 416
Proxy-Based Firewall, 77, 404, 411–416, 417,
        421, 467
Public Key Database, 81
Public Key Exchange, 81, 498
Public Key Infrastructure
    See PKI
Public Switched Telephone Network, 482

RADIUS, 326
Rational Rose, 261
Recovery from security violations, 90
Reedy, Ann, xxviii, xxx, 88, 191, 266, 359
Reference Monitor, 30, 67, 69, 71, 244, 248,
        256–264, 335, 336, 337, 340, 346, 347,
        349, 499
Registration services, 24, 63, 67, 487, 488, 490,
        492, 498, 500

Registration, device, 484
Remote Authenticator, 327
Resource Lifecycle Manager, 301
Resources, general security, 26
Response, 20, 23, 24, 26, 43, 76, 148, 520, 521
Retinal Scanning, 65, 241
RFID tag, xii, 66
Riehle, Dirk, 227
Right
    allocating for files, 350
    allocating to memory, 339
    allocating to objects, 332
    allocating to process, 335, 343, 346
    allocating to processes, 328
Risk
    assessment, 23, 87, 104, 114, 126, 138
    management, 22, 85–185
    management patterns, 59
    mitigation, 87
    software outsourcing, 175
    to assets, 114
Risk Determination, 61, 136, 137–147, 148,
        151, 497
Role, 252
Role Based Access Control, 179
Role Rights Definition, 67, 69, 244, 250,
        259–264
Role, classification, 249
Role-Based Access Control, xxxi, 30, 68, 179,
        244, 248, 249–252, 256, 259, 264, 291,
        292, 296, 315, 319, 354, 498, 499, 500
Romanosky, Sasha, xxviii, xxx, 88
RSS, 173, 182
RUS-CERT, 44

SAML, 326
SANS Institute, 27, 42, 101, 121, 135
Schneier, Bruce, 531
Schumacher, Markus, xxviii, xxx, xxxi, 88, 191,
        322, 359, 404
Scope of patterns, 48
Secure Assertion, 76
Secure Channel, 447
Secure Channels, 79, 80, 424, 430, 434–441,
        444, 447, 498, 500
Secure Communication, 80, 498

Secure Internet applications patterns, 78
Secure Sockets Layer, 303, 437, 438, 440, 470
SecurID, 66, 212
Securing IP telephony, 493
SECURING LOCAL NETWORKS, 227
SECURING WIDE AREA NETWORKS, 227
Security
    accounting, 356, 361
    and security patterns, 504
    approaches to, 23
    architecture principles, 520
    capture function, 357
    Clark-Wilson model, 30
    communication, 434
    conferences, 27
    cost, 149
    enhancing patterns with misuse cases, 525
    enterprise, 85–185
    enterprise standards, 38
    execution principles, 522
    foundations of, 15–28
    integration into business model, 148, 162
    mechanisms, 25
    mechanisms and implementations, 17
    mindset principles, 514
    operational, run-time resources, 43
    pattern landscape, 59–83
    policies, 19
    propagation of breach, 174
    property of asset, 149
    resources, 26
    response, 162
    review mechanism, 358
    selecting principles, 506–513
    services, 17, 24
    storage mechanism, 357
    strategy, 19
    strategy and policy, 17
    supplementary concepts, 503–530
    taxonomy, 17
    training, 25
    violation, 21
    Web standard, 326
    wireless, 394
SECURITY ACCOUNTING DESIGN, 74
SECURITY ACCOUNTING REQUIREMENTS, 163,
    360–368, 369, 388, 396, 498

Security Advisor, 27
Security approach
    detection, 20, 23, 24, 33, 43, 75, 76, 519,
        520, 521
    diligence, 23
    planning, xix, 23, 52, 53, 57, 524
    prevention, 23, 33, 43, 76
    response, 20, 23, 24, 26, 43, 76, 520, 521
Security companies, 44
Security incident, discovery, 162
SECURITY NEEDS IDENTIFICATION FOR ENTERPRISE AS-
    SETS, 60, 86, 89–102, 106, 113, 121, 148,
        151, 157, 164, 176, 182, 429, 493
Security pattern, 29–45
    characteristics, 31
    conclusions, 531–534
    history, 30
    in Java, 30, 251, 258, 338
    organization, user level, 529
    reasons for, 34
    sources, 37
Security policy, 24, 25, 40, 42, 90, 412, 520, 524
Security principles
    architecture principles, 506
    execution principles, 508
    mindset principles, 506
    selecting, 506–513
    selecting principles, 508
SECURITY SESSION, 70, 189, 266, 278, 284, 286,
    289, 290, 291, 292, 295, 296, 297–304,
        309, 311, 313, 315, 319, 477, 479, 499
Seliya, Naeem, xxviii, xxxi, 404
Sensitive data, protection, 427, 435
Session Initiation Protocol, 484, 498
Session key exchange, 437
SESSION KEY EXCHANGE WITH CERTIFICATES, 82
SESSION KEY EXCHANGE WITH PUBLIC KEYS, 81, 498
SESSION KEY EXCHANGE WITH SERVER-SIDE
    CERTIFICATE, 82
SESSION MANAGEMENT SERVICE, 62
SHORT MENUS, 11
SIGNATURE VERIFICATION, 65, 241
Sindre, Guttorm, xxix, xxxi, 503
SINGLE ACCESS POINT, 30, 70, 175, 176, 178, 265,
    266, 278, 279–286, 287, 288, 289, 291,
        296, 323, 324, 327, 410, 464, 479, 499
SINGLE SIGN ON, 327

Single sign-on, 188, 196, 208, 214, 304, 325, 424, 474, 478, 479
SINGLETONS, 304
Sinibaldi, John, 322
Smalltalk, 8
SMART CARD, 67
Smart card, 66, 82, 166
SOCKS protocol, 415
Software development, outsourcing risk, 175
Solaris, 258
Sommerlad, Peter, xxix, xxxi, 88, 191, 244, 266, 359, 424, 478
Sørensen, Kristian Elof, xxxiii
SPEAKER VERIFICATION, 66, 241
SQL injection attack, 128, 310
Stal, Michael, 424
STANDARD PANES, 11
State table, 418
STATEFUL FIREWALL, 78, 404, 410, 416, 417–421
STATEFUL PACKET FILTER FIREWALL, 420
STATEFUL PROXY-BASED FIREWALL, 420
Stealth firewall, 455
Steel, Chris, 83
STRATEGY, 289, 291, 293, 296
STRIDE, 123
Structural integrity, 119
SUN, 83
Supplementary concepts, 503–530
Swiss Software Engineering Network (SWEN), xxix
System
    access control patterns, 69, 265–319
    architecture resources, 42
    danger to integrity, 280
    protection of public systems, 450
    recovery, 24
Systems Security Engineering Capability Maturity, 99

Telekurs, 478
Telnet, 302, 490
Thomsen, Dan, xxxiii, 404
Threat
    assessment, 23
    identification, 114
    likelihood, 138

THREAT ASSESSMENT, 61, 105, 113–124, 125, 126, 133, 137, 138, 140, 141, 147, 497
Threat Modeling, 123
Time-division multiplexing, 482
Tivoli, 478
    Access Manager, 462
Trading Partner Agreement, 184
Transaction integrity, 397, 399, 400

UML security extensions, 503
Unauthorized disclosure, 16, 21, 495
Unified Modeling Language, 10, 91, 251, 282, 347
Unix, 285, 353
UNREGISTERED USERS I&A REQUIREMENTS, 67, 216, 228
USENET, 44, 45
USER AUTHENTICATION PASSWORDS, 227
Usurpation, 21, 22

Validation
    of business partners, 443
    of customers, 443
Veincheck/Vein tree, 233
VIRTUAL ADDRESS SPACE, 30
Virtual Private Network
    See VPN
Virtual Vault, 255, 330
Virus, blocking, 405
Vlissides, John, 2, 12
VPN, 35, 43, 179, 182, 440
Vulnerability
    assessment, 23, 126
    protecting against future, 458
    severity, 138
VULNERABILITY ASSESSMENT, 61, 105, 125–136, 137, 138, 139, 140, 141, 142, 147, 496

WEB APPLICATION SECURITY, 83
Web server
    hardening, 458
    patching, 458
    unifying URLs, 465
Web services, unifying sign-on, 473
WebSphere, 251
White list filter, 462